Weighted Down

The Complicated Life of Skip Spence

Cam Cobb

OMNIBUS PRESS

London / New York / Paris / Sydney / Copenhagen / Berlin / Madrid / Tokyo

Weighted Down

The Complicated Life
of Skip Spence

CONTENTS

Foreword

When I met Omar in 1987, I didn't know anything about Skip Spence or Moby Grape. It was only after learning about Omar's own musical talent and subsequent questions that he told me his dad, Skip, had played for Jefferson Airplane and Moby Grape. He didn't elaborate or give many details. Thankfully, my mom was able to fill me in as she knew exactly who Skip was. I was puzzled. Omar and I had been close friends for a couple of years, and it seemed like being the son of a famous musician would be something he would have talked about more.

After we were married, Omar finally shared some of his memories of Skip. The picture was painted with the imperfect scrawls of a young boy's perspective, but the sense of loss, confusion and abandonment were clear. Those conversations were rare, so I was surprised when one day he came home angry about an article that had been written, which detailed Skip's fall from stardom to mental illness. In response, Omar took up pen, paper and guitar to defend the father he didn't know, with a song called 'Strings of Life'. That process was the beginning of Omar's journey to reconsider what he thought he knew about his father.

Sometime in the early nineties, Omar was contacted by Skip's half-brother, Rich Young, who had just recently learned of the family connection. Rich had planned a reunion with Skip and invited Omar to go. Omar was torn between meeting the father he hadn't seen since he was 3 years old, and the feelings of resentment he carried for so long. I remember saying something to the effect that I was afraid that if he didn't go, he would regret it for the rest of his life. Despite his reluctance, Omar ended up going to the reunion, where his imperfect, childlike memories came face-to-face with the reality of Skip.

I was just an outsider at the reunion – the person in the background observing – but I saw something amazing that day. The connection was immediate, between father and sons and father and daughter. It was beautiful. It seemed, for Skip, that no time had passed. He recognised all four of his children, remembered their names and told them short stories about the past. For Omar, it was a process of coming full circle from resentment to understanding, to forgiveness and love. Now, so many years later, I cherish my observations of Omar's short relationship with his dad in those last few years before Skip's passing. This book paints a picture of Skip Spence – the incredible highs, the devastating lows, and the times when there was a bit of both. It's a story worth telling and one, I believe, worth reading

MYTH AND TRUE

He was almost the guitarist of Quicksilver Messenger Service. He could have been a Doobie Brother. He *was* the drummer of the Jefferson Airplane. And he most definitely co-founded Moby Grape back during that season of possibilities, the summer of '66.

At that point, Alexander 'Skip' Spence was a psychedelic poet of the Bay Area; an impish, happy-go-lucky rock star. Then, as the Summer of Love dawned, he'd storm on stage at the Monterey Pop Festival like a man on fire. Moby Grape's debut album had just been released and they were garnering critical praise.

But he didn't stay with his bandmates for long. By the next summer he was gone, locked up in New York City's Bellevue psychiatric hospital. The story goes that he'd tried to attack two of the band members with an axe.

According to popular legend, Skip Spence hopped on a motorcycle in December '68, after release from the prison ward at Bellevue, and rode all the way down to Nashville, Tennessee... in his pyjamas, no less. Arriving in Music City, he reputedly got off the motorbike, swept into Columbia Records' studio, and recorded his first and last solo album. Accompanied only by himself, with no other musicians.

With a new decade fast approaching, *Oar* came to vinyl in the

1

spring of '69, just months after Skip's own release from hospital. On its first pressing, it sold only 700 copies and was long believed to be Columbia's worst-selling album. But now, after decades of lingering in out-of-print banishment, *Oar* has classic status. You can even find it in a deluxe boxset version.

And that was it. Spence was done with rock'n'roll; done with the music business. From that moment, he'd only make fleeting cameo appearances at gigs and on other artists' albums.

In the 1970s/80s, he spent time in mental wards, halfway houses and jails, or lived on the street. After losing his children for decades, he was reconciled with them in the 1990s – only to become terminally ill.

Shortly before he passed away, Skip Spence made one last recording, for an *X-Files* tie-in album. It was reportedly rejected because it was too spooky… for *The X-Files*. Really?

• • •

Not all of this can be true, can it?

Well, some of it is and some of it isn't. Skip Spence's life was like his lyric, 'myth and true.' To untangle the myth from the truth, we'll need to trek through the narrative of his life, riding the turbulence along the way.

To get to a starting point, we need to travel back to post-war Canada, in the city of Windsor, province of Ontario, south of the Detroit River.

CHAPTER ONE

FROM WINDSOR TO OHIO

It was cloudy on that spring day, with the temperature climbing to an above-average 62F in the afternoon. On Thursday 18 April 1946, in Windsor, Ontario, for three cents you could pick up the evening edition of the *Windsor Star*.

A banner headline plastered near the top let everyone feel the chill of the Cold War: 'MORE RUSS[IAN] SPY ACTS TOLD', it read in big, bold letters. The story gave an update on the preliminary hearing for Israel Halperin, a Queen's University professor charged with committing acts of espionage for the Soviet Union. (Mathematician Halperin would be cleared at trial, but the age of anxiety was only just beginning.)

Under the smaller headline 'GANDHI TALKS WITH BRITISH' was a two-paragraph report on the father of modern India's seventy-minute conference with members of a UK cabinet mission. It marked the final days of the British Raj, as the vast nation moved towards independence. A short piece titled 'Crowds Jam Jerusalem' described the security measures undertaken in the Middle East's much-disputed holy city, in the hours leading up to Good Friday.

Then there were stories on starvation in South Africa, a steel shortage in the US, China's ongoing civil war and the debate over nationalising coal in Canada. Scattered throughout these pages were self-help articles on parenting, with such titles as 'Parents Worst Offenders Spoiling Child' and 'Make Unpleasant Only Things Child Shouldn't Do.'

On page thirty there were four fleeting birth announcements, with the final one reading: 'SPENCE – Mr. and Mrs. A.L. (Jack) Spence of 2237 Howard Ave., wish to announce the birth of a son on April 18th, 1946 at Hotel Dieu Hospital.'

It should have been 'Jock,' not 'Jack.' Nevertheless, arriving nine months after his father returned from fighting in Europe, Alexander Lee Spence came into the world at the dawn of the Baby Boom.

In the months leading up to his son's birth, Alexander Lett 'Jock' Spence worked as a salesman for Electrolux, peddling vacuum cleaners door to door. Once considered to be luxuries, these appliances were becoming regular items in homes across North America in the early days of post-war consumerism.

Gwenn Spence packed her travel bag in the hospital room, ready to leave with her husband and baby boy. At 5ft7, she stood nearly as tall as Jock as they exited the maternity ward. Brought home for the Easter weekend, little Alex Spence's first mile-and-a-half journey would have circuited east along Giles Boulevard then southward on Howard Avenue.

On the way, they would pass Spence's Market at 2279 Howard Avenue. Jock's uncle, James, had first opened his grocery store towards the end of the Great Depression. Just past Spence's Market was where Jock and Gwenn were living, the home of Jock's father and stepmother, Alexander Llewelyn (Alex) and Violet Rose (Vi) Spence.

With the arrival of a new baby, the semidetached home was getting crowded. Alex and Vi had their own young son, 5-year-old Paul Spence – Jock's half-brother. The younger couple had been living there since Jock returned from the war, but they were hunting for their own place to live. Before the winter, they would relocate to East Windsor.

Alex and his family, meanwhile, were also on the move. Applying

4

for 4-C resident visas in the US on 22 November, Alex, Vi and Paul received six-month permits a week later.

On Friday 2 December, Jock's father and his family moved out of Windsor, trekking due south. Driving through the D&C (Detroit-Canada) Tunnel, they were starting a journey that circuited all the way down to Phoenix, Arizona. The temperature in Windsor and Detroit that day would climb to 26F, while in Phoenix it reached 78F.

After settling into much warmer surroundings, Alex found a job in the hospitality industry – at first in room service, before going on to become transportation manager of the Paradise Inn, a swanky resort hotel at the base of Camelback Mountain. In short order, the family moved into a lot at Phoenix's Evergreen Trailer Park at 1928 East Thomas Road.

Meanwhile, Jock stayed on with Electrolux in Windsor, whilst playing the occasional gig as a semi-professional piano player and selling the publication rights to some of his own songs.

He had written his first song in 1930, when he was 15, living with his two brothers, two sisters, mother and stepfather in Brockville, Ontario. Throughout late 1936/early 1937, he regularly headed to Schenectady, New York, to perform live on WGY Radio.

By 1940 Jock settled in Windsor, renting a room on Victoria, an affluent avenue lined with massive Victorian- and Edwardian-style homes. His father and stepmother had lived a couple of miles to the south in the more modest Howard Avenue neighbourhood. Whilst working for Electrolux he performed on both sides of the Detroit River, opening the Palace Hotel in Windsor's east end in May 1941.

The following spring, in March 1942, he enlisted in the Royal Canadian Air Force (RCAF) in Hamilton, Ontario. After completing a five-month training program at Camp Borden, Jock got his wings on 30 April 1943.

As with so many pilots at the time, he was transferred to fight in the war in Europe. Whilst serving, he continued to both write and perform music. Some of his songs were even aired on the BBC, like 'Only Yours' and 'Too Much Illusion.'

Jock also covered ballads like Cole Porter's 'In The Still Of The Night' and 'Maybe', the latter made famous by Perry Como and Eddie Fisher. His own writing was in this same romantic style.

Returning to Canada in July 1945, Jock was discharged two months later, at age 30. Still gigging in Windsor and Detroit, he became a member of the Composers, Authors and Publishers Association of Canada, Limited (CAPAC) in January 1946. Over the next few years, he sold over a dozen songs to publishers in the US and UK.

On 12 June 1948, Gwenn gave birth to a daughter, Sherry, at Hotel Dieu Hospital. Three months after, on 16 September, Jock applied for a US residency visa. It was denied. A lingering 1934 conviction for fraud – back when he was 19 years old and struggling in the throes of the Depression – was cited as the reason. He decided to appeal, awaiting a verdict from the US Department of Justice's Immigration and Naturalization Service for ten months.

Meanwhile, the Spence family moved into a new home on Lena Avenue. Located on Windsor's western edge, the compact bungalow was in Old Sandwich Town, a part of the city that somehow missed out on the post-war boom.

Before the end of the year, Gwenn's 66-year-old retiree father, Arthur Henry Reed, moved in and the household grew to five. Born in Berlin, Ontario (renamed Kitchener during the First World War), Arthur had worked as a travelling salesman for decades – residing mostly in Toronto, the Canadian prairies, where Gwenn was born, and for a portion of the 1920s, Chicago, Illinois.

In January 1949 Jock took the plunge and started working full-time as a musician. He was contracted to play nightly at the popular Commodore Club on Chatham Street, in Windsor's downtown core. His daily trek was three miles and his working 'day' ran from nine in the evening until half past one in the morning.

• • •

One day in mid-June 1949, the temperature climbed to 87F in London, Canada. Although it was well above the city's average high for the month, a strong breeze provided steady relief.

With brown hair, brown eyes and a pencil-thin moustache, Jock Spence strolled along a well-kept geometric lawn. Standing 5ft8, weighing approximately 175lbs, he ascended a gentle hill on the campus grounds of the University of Western Ontario in his airman's uniform.

Standing atop the hill was a Gothic-style structure made of a combination of limestone and sandstone. At the midpoint of the building's front façade was a tower 130ft tall, built in honour of local servicemen killed in the First World War.

During the more recent conflict, Jock had flown with the Bluenose (434) Squadron of the RCAF, formed at RAF Tholthrope, England, in June 1943. Located about ten miles north of York, the air station served as the squad's home base for half a year.

Though he kept his medals and dog-tags in a small wooden box for the rest of his life, he spoke just as little of his combat experience as many other veterans. Yet tales of his wartime antics were passed down through the family.

Jock's first cousin, James, was stationed at RAF Mildenhall, Suffolk, with the 419 Tactical Fighter Training Squadron. According to family folklore, Jock sometimes flew a Handley Page Halifax heavy bomber south to visit his cousin. The two would sometimes fly to London for some much-needed R&R, dancing and socialising.

On 13 August, a team flew over the Italian Alps to Milan on Squadron 434's first bombing raid. In December, Bluenose Squadron moved 35 miles north to RAF Croft on the northern edge of Yorkshire. In two years, the squadron's 2,582 pilots would fly 198 missions with 484 aircrew operational casualties and eight additional casualties. The overall casualty rate was approximately one in 5.25.

Whilst in Europe, Jock flew over thirty missions to targets scattered across France and Germany. During these months he was either on a dangerous sortie or waiting for one to begin. In neatly printed handwriting, he kept a record of each. On 9 September 1944, he flew to Dortmund, Germany, in a Halifax bomber. Starting at 3:46 in the afternoon, the mission ran for over five hours and ended at 9:06 in the evening. He summed it up in a fifty-word entry in his log:

> 'Very concentrated, very large orange coloured fire, jettisoned 2 – 500lb bombs hung up, both port engines hit by flax, D.N.A. [distinguished networking agent], fuselage holes, mid under holed, mid VG [velocity vs. gravity loads = flight-operating strength of aircraft], injured left upper arm, engines hit by flax over target area, feathered port inner engine on account of oil pressure, effort looked good.'

In such no-nonsense terms, Jock Spence chronicled a string of perilous missions. Those sorties were now half a decade in the past and a world away from this quiet, late spring afternoon in London, Canada.

Still, on Tuesday 14 June 1949, sixty-five RCAF pilots received awards of valour at the university. Field Lieutenant Alexander Lett Spence was given a rare Distinguished Flying Cross. Of Canada's quarter-million pilots in the Second World War, including nearly 100,000 serving overseas, Jock was one of only 4,018 to receive the award.

A story in the *Windsor Star* reported on the ceremony that same day. In her column, Annie Oakley (not the sharpshooter of *Annie Get Your Gun* fame) quoted the official citation:

> *'[Flying Officer] Spence has completed a tour of operational duty during which he has attacked many heavily defended targets. On one occasion during attack on Aulnoye-Aymeries, [France] two engines of his aircraft were seriously damaged and the flight engineer was seriously injured. Despite these harassing circumstances, this officer*

8

pressed on and successfully completed his mission. He has at all times
displayed courage, devotion to duty, and a fine fighting spirit.[1]

Jock Spence's mission to Aulnoye-Aymeries started at 6:32 in
the early evening of 25 March 1944, ending over six hours later
at 11:40 p.m. Jock's log for that mission, which could so easily
have proved fatal, totals just 22 words:

'Bombing good, A/C [aircraft] hit over target don't know by what,
engineer wounded, starboard engine U/S [unserviceable], made
crash landing at Friston, crew safe.'

On the day of the awards, Jock had a whole entourage with him.
His mother and stepfather came all the way from Ottawa in the
east; his wife, son, two brothers (Bert and Tom) and cousin followed
him to the campus from Windsor. A photograph taken in front of
its arts building shows Jock standing proudly with Gwenn and their
3-year-old son, Alexander Lee ('Skip,' as the family always called
him), in front of them. (Sherry Elizabeth, their daughter, remained
back in Windsor, having just turned a year old a few days earlier.)

After the ceremony ended, the sixty-five pilots scattered back to
various towns and cities. Jock had to get back to Windsor quickly.
He was in his twenty-fifth week of entertaining at The Commodore
Club, just a few blocks from the Detroit River and directly across
the water from downtown Motor City.

Formerly The Windsor Club, the upscale lounge had become
popular among local businessmen. Filling both piano and vocal duties,
Jock took requests in The Marine Room nightly. The schedule was
hard work but steady, giving him a chance to make a living as a
professional musician. In time he became a steady draw, earning a
reputation for his vast repertoire of tunes. In the *Windsor Star* of
February 1949, Annie Oakley laid on the acclaim: 'Catalogued in
his cranium is an amazing number of songs hits, old and new. The
listener has only to joggle his memory with a title, and out it comes.'[2]

Less than two weeks after the awards ceremony, Jock's application for residency status in the US was approved. On 1 August, five days after her husband took the bus through the D&C Tunnel to Detroit, Gwenn crossed the border. For the next two months, the couple remained in Detroit as Jock finished his run at The Commodore. Playing his closing night on 25 September, he then headed down to Covington, Kentucky, for a run of shows in the Kentucky-Ohio border town. As reported in the *Windsor Star*, the musician – who, as a war hero, had become something of a local celebrity – began his journey south on 5 October.

But Gwenn's father soon took ill and they had to return. Arthur passed away at the Hotel Dieu Hospital – which, over the last three years, had seen the births of his grandchildren Skip and Sherry – in early November. He was buried a few blocks away in Windsor Grove Cemetery. On 23 November, Jock and Gwenn drove back across the Ambassador Bridge to Michigan with their two children. The Spence family would never again reside in Canada.

Initially, the Spences lived east of central downtown Detroit, renting a modest two-storey home on Springle Street – a few miles from the affluent city of Grosse Pointe Parke. Jock also had a cousin nearby: Gordon Spence, who lived in Detroit's west end with his wife and two sons. Like Jock he was a 4-C immigrant, having settled in the city in March. Following in the footsteps of Alex, Gordon worked as a customs officer.

For a time, Jock returned to work in sales, but the family didn't stay in Detroit for long. In May 1951, he sent a postcard to the *Windsor Star* from a gig in Salamanca, New York. 'Still usin' my fingers to good use,' the pianist wrote. By the time the newspaper received it, the Spence family had relocated to Ohio.

Two months later, Jock was performing 250 miles south at The Embassy Club in Knoxville, Tennessee. Over the next few years, he took all sorts of gigs in and around Ohio: short- and long-term engagements, some in restaurants, others in hotels. It meant the family was constantly on the move.

Through the late autumn and winter of 1951/52, the Spences lived a couple of hours east of Cincinnati in Portsmouth, a small city on the north bank of the Ohio River, directly across from Kentucky. Performing at The Trade Winds, a restaurant at Eighth and Chillicothe Street, Jock played nightly except for Saturdays. Billed as 'The Sensational Sentimentalist' in the *Portsmouth Times*, he later moved to The Coral Reef, a dinner club on Gallia Street. At both venues, performances started at nine or ten in the evening and ended at two in the morning.

But Portsmouth itself was struggling. After reaching 40,000 at the dawn of the Depression, the city's population would decline to about half that by the end of the century. Unable to find more gigs in the city, Jock started to look elsewhere. By the summer of 1952, he was playing nights at Stein's Hideaway on Poplar Street, Cincinnati, in the largely working-class Over-the-Rhine neighbour-hood.

The family also found time to trek back northeast to Flower Round Lake in Lanark County, Ontario, in the summer of 1952 or 1953. Jock drove the entire 750 miles. With highway speed limits hovering around 50mph, the trip would have taken at least 15 hours.

Skip and Sherry were both under 8 and had never travelled such a distance in a single journey. Switching from the bustle and industry of Cincinnati to the quiet greenery of the Lanark Highlands was a new experience for the kids, but for Jock it was a homecoming.

Lanark County blankets about 400 square miles of southeastern Ontario, circa thirty miles north of the line that runs from Kingston to Brockville, west of the Ottawa Valley, and just south of the city of Renfrew. It is covered with towering maple, hemlock, oak and beech trees, as well as wetlands and patches of the rocky Canadian Shield.

For thousands of years, the Anishinaabe and Iroquois lived on the land. In the first half of the 1800s, much of the area was settled by immigrants, predominantly from the Lanarkshire region of

11

Scotland. On arrival, they found themselves thrown into a rugged lifestyle where survival depended on the success of crops, wellbeing of farm animals, availability of firewood and sturdiness of winterised shelters. Among those early migrants were some of Jock Spence's ancestors, including the Deachman and Lett families who came to Ontario from Scotland and Ireland in the 1820s.

Over the decades, the land was logged, farmed, mined and settled. Sixty years later, in 1884, the Kingston and Pembroke Iron Mining Company completed a rail line that ran over a hundred miles up and down the county, from Kingston to Renfrew. Known as the K&P, the line wound through lumber and mining communities like Robertsville and Wilbur. Along the way, it passed by a quiet village named Flower Station, located at Flower Round Lake. It was still operating as a commercial rail line when Jock, Gwenn, Skip and Sherry made their way to Flower Station in the early 1950s.

Jock's mother, Effie Elizabeth Deachman, had been born in Flower Station on 19 May 1893, as the second of ten children. Her parents – Alexander Monroe 'Sandy' Deachman and Margaret Catherine Lett – lived their entire lives in Lanark County. When Effie turned 17, she started working as a mail clerk. Before she reached 20, she was living with her husband, Alex Spence, nearly 2,000 miles away in Saskatoon, Saskatchewan, by which point the couple had their first child, Vivian, born 10 December 1912. But the young couple returned to Lanark, where Jock was born on 29 December 1914 – the second of five siblings.

Alexander Llewellyn Spence had been born on 5 July 1890, to John and Mary Ann Spence in Fergus, Ontario, a largely Scottish town about 75 miles northwest of Toronto. He was their third son, but Alex never got to know his own father. Just one week after he was born, John Spence passed away of a glandular disease after suffering years of tuberculosis.

All at once, Mary was a widow with three young sons, John (who was 5), James (4) and Alex (only a week old). A year and a half after losing her husband, Mary Spence married William Crickmore, a local farmer who himself was a widower with three children of his own. In 1896, the two had a daughter together, named Myrtle, and just over a decade later the family moved to the newly established city of Saskatoon in the Canadian prairies. Until William's death, in 1930, the couple ran a farm toiling through much longer winters and colder temperatures than those of Southern Ontario.

Arriving in Saskatoon as a teenager, son Alex soon found a job as a fireman but later worked as a locomotive engineer. By the time he was 22, he was married to Effie.

By 1921 he and his family journeyed west again, living north of Saskatoon in Rosthern. But this was where the couple divorced. Effie would remarry and raise her five children with her new husband, Clarence Giffen, in Brockville, Ontario – just south of Lanark County.

Meanwhile, Alex Spence settled in Windsor, where by 1928 he became a customs officer. A few years later, at the age of 48, he remarried to Vivian Rose Saunders and had a son, Paul James Spence.

Though Jock would later join his father in Windsor, he spent his formative years in eastern Ontario. Raised by his mother and stepfather in Brockville, he spent many of his summers as a boy and teenager about seventy-five miles north, at Flower Round Lake. Today, it isn't much different than it was when Jock visited in the 1920s, or when his family travelled there three decades later.

Surrounded by a few cottages and lush greenery, Flower Round Lake has a perimeter of about three miles and a maximum depth of approximately 40ft. Effie and Clarence had a cottage with two cabins there, called Fairvale. Over the years, Effie (whom Skip and Sherry called 'Aunt Effie') and Clarence ('Uncle Bunky') rented out the lakeside cabins in the summertime.

If visiting Flower Round Lake was a kind of pilgrimage for Jock in the early 1950s, it was an adventure for Skip and Sherry. At one point, the children made their way down a path that ran from the cabins to the lake. They found a small rowboat at the water's edge and, after Skip talked his sister into testing it, pushed the boat into the water and climbed inside. The oars were heavy, but somehow Skip and Sherry managed to row themselves further and further out into the deeper waters. Sherry still recalls getting into a lot of trouble on that summer day, at the point when their parents found them.

But that wasn't the end of their adventures. Sherry remembers how Skip locked her in the outhouse and, not long after that, she got stung by a deerfly, which kept her off her feet for a few days. Knowing how deerfly bites can be serious, Gwenn quickly treated her daughter with a home remedy. Sherry recalls her tending to the swollen leg with bread soaked in evaporated milk.

At this time, there was no longer a refrigerator at the Flower Round Lake cottage. 'I know we had to eat our oatmeal with evaporated milk,' adds Sherry, 'which was totally gross!'

In taking his family to Fairvale, although they may not have realised it at the time, Jock Spence gave Skip and Sherry a view into their father's youth. Though he had settled hundreds of miles away from Lanark County, he had roots and family there. Years later, it would also be his final resting place. At his own request, Jock was buried just a few miles from Flower Round Lake, at Clyde Forks Cemetery, on 7 May 1965.

Skip Spence never returned to Flower Round Lake after visiting as a child. His family had to make the long journey back to Ohio, as his father needed to get back on the treadmill of performing gigs.

In the autumn of 1952, Jock was performing at the Barr Hotel a couple of hours north of Cincinnati, in Lima. Unlike Portsmouth, Lima was growing in the post-war boom, especially after the city's Tank Plant resumed its manufacturing output during the Korean War. But that gig didn't last long. By June of 1953, Jock was playing at The Tropics, a Tiki-themed supper club in Dayton, Ohio. Having recently reopened after a fire, the club featured a large piano bar stretching across the restaurant's Bamboo Room. Then, a couple of months later, he shifted to another Dayton venue.

Jock Spence dressed in a tuxedo for his gig on North Main Street, one of his last performances in the city. At number 210 stood an eighteen-storey structure, with a dark-brown-and-white brick and terra cotta façade. Constructed in 1929, at the last moment before the Great Depression, the structure was built in a Beaux-Arts style well matched by its Art Deco interior.

By 3 December 1953, Jock had been playing the cocktail lounge at the Dayton Biltmore Hotel every night for three months, except Sundays. His run had started shortly after the newly redecorated Kitty Hawk Lounge was unveiled.

The lounge would see visits from some legendary figures over the years, including Elvis Presley – who'd stay at the Dayton Biltmore on 27 May 1956, five months after making his first recordings for RCA Victor in Nashville – and John F. Kennedy, who'd give a speech at the Biltmore on 17 October 1960, twenty-two days before he won the presidential election. Nearly thirty years after Jock's run at the Biltmore, the building was designated a federal historic site.

Playing there was a highlight of his time as a gigging musician in Ohio, but change was in the air. Jock and Gwenn had been in the US for just over four years by the end of 1953. For much of that time, the family had been living in Ohio, where Jock was constantly on the move, finding long and short-term gigs across the state. To find some measure of stability, the family then trekked all the way to Phoenix, Arizona – adopted city of Jock's father, Alex.

For the next few years, a silver Airstream trailer at the Evergreen Trailer Park would be home to Gwenn, Skip and Sherry. Jock, meanwhile, found himself back on the road, working in sales and pursuing gigs in restaurants, clubs, hotels and resorts; occasionally sending letters and money home to his family.

CHAPTER TWO

PHOENIX

It sounded like a buzzsaw. The hum of the engine was deafening as the crop duster glided through the blue sky. Looking down, the boy could see most of the city and the river that flowed through it, from east to west.

From Salt River, the much narrower Grand Canal wound northward and then veered to the west. Just below the canal, where North Twentieth Street met with East Thomas Road, was the patch of land where the boy lived. But it was difficult to pinpoint it in the distance.

Evergreen Trailer Park looked like two horseshoes fitted together with a road running between them. At the park's entranceway was a large, open, green space. From up above, the trailers were like little dots on the ground. When the plane turned south they went out of view. After gliding south for a short while, the pilot turned the crop duster around and the buzzing sound of its engine changed.

Heading north again, the boy gazed into the less familiar distance. Looking to the northeast, he could see the larger buildings of the city's downtown core as well as hundreds of smaller homes in surrounding residential communities. They looked like tiny boxes from high above.

Extending out from the city were clear patches of land. Some of them ran all the way over to a line of mountains that towered along the eastern edge of the city limits. At the very bottom of the range the boy could see Camelback Mountain, which he'd encountered numerous times up close. Standing 1,300ft high, Camelback marked the southernmost peak of the Phoenix Mountains. Scattered around its base were a handful of resort hotels, which he could just make out from his vantage point. His grandfather worked in one of those hotels.

As the plane turned around, the buzzing sound of its engine changed, moderating its tone again as the crop duster gradually lowered its altitude. Soon, all the hotels around Camelback Mountain disappeared behind an assortment of other buildings.

As the plane descended almost to the ground, the boy's stomach lurched. After a few short moments it was all over. The crop duster came to a stop and the pilot, a man in his sixties, helped his young passengers out of the cockpit.

Skip had never flown before. Neither had his sister. In all their time living in Phoenix, the two had never seen the city from above. They thanked the pilot, whom the children knew as Mr. Shook. Mr. and Mrs. Shook lived just across the road from the Spence family at the trailer park. They were an older couple who did not have children of their own, but did have six Dachshunds that Skip and Sherry played with whenever they visited.

Gwenn and her children had moved into Evergreen when they first arrived in Phoenix, around 1953. They lived in an Airstream trailer owned by Jock's younger brother, Bert, while the lot itself was once the home of his father, Alex.

Around the trailer was a little, white-picket fence and near its entrance was a small garden with roses and sweet peas. The Airstream itself was of a fair size, with a dining space to the right of the entrance and a little kitchenette. At the other end, to the left of the entrance, was a small bedroom area. Just outside the main entranceway was a cabana that served as a living room.

At night, Skip slept out in the cabana while his mother and sister took the bedroom. Their pet cat – named Purr, because it purred so loudly – slept wherever it wanted. At a window directly at the head of the bed was a swamp cooler, where cockroaches could scurry in from time to time. 'But mostly they could be found in our outside bathroom, which had a sink, toilet, and shower,' Sherry Spence recalls.

When Gwenn sometimes took her children to visit her best friend, Dorothy Hose, Sherry would ask if she could take a bath. For the kids, getting to use a large washroom with a bath was a luxury.

The couple who managed the trailer park had a son of the same age as Sherry. But apart from him, the young Spences were the only schoolchildren at Evergreen. Most of the folks there were older than their mom and many were retired.

While the Spence children would visit with some of the older residents of the park, like the Shooks, over time Sherry and the managers' son became close friends. His mother was an Avon lady, making her a little glamorous in the eyes of the children. Six decades later, Sherry still recalls being crushed when she had to say goodbye to 'HD' (Harold Dean), the day that her family moved away from Evergreen Trailer Park.

Working at a local dress shop, Gwenn had to leave her kids on their own sometimes. Though they didn't have bicycles, they got up to all kinds of adventures and became the closest of siblings. Even getting to school was like setting out on a quest. They had to cross East Thomas Road, adjacent to the trailer park, which seemed so wide and busy; then they'd make their way across a large field and through a residential area.

One day they trekked all the way to the shopping centre where their mother worked. Somehow, the pair became separated as Sherry fell behind. As the Arizonan afternoon sun beat down on the streets below, she had to make her own way home. 'It was so hot out you could fry an egg on the sidewalk! And I wasn't wearing shoes,' she reminisces.

And of course, there other were mishaps along the way. Not least because Skip's sense of abandon and carefree nature were forged in his early years.

When the two were alone at the trailer one time, Sherry decided to make a mud cake. She carefully arranged some mud in a cakepan in the trailer's kitchenette and decided, as it was a birthday cake, that it needed candles. After placing a few in the cake, one of the kids lit them and managed to catch the curtains on fire. Somehow the fire got put out before the trailer burned down, but the two found themselves in big trouble with Gwenn.

Another time, when their mom arrived home, she was shocked by Skip walking up to her to excitedly show how he'd shaved his eyebrows off. As she was taking it all in, Sherry jumped out and announced, 'Me too!'

Then, while playing catch, Skip accidentally hit his sister in the head with the ball. With blood gushing from the wound both siblings became frightened, even a little frantic. In tears he brought his sister back to the trailer, before she was taken to a doctor to be stitched up.

Evergreen Trailer Park did not have a swimming pool, so Gwenn sometimes took the kids on a bus to a nearby public pool. Sometimes they went on their own, and it was whilst swimming that Skip recognised a teenager at poolside. He climbed out to approach a local celebrity on the rise.

The teen's parents had moved to Phoenix a few years earlier because of his asthma. But he'd sang country music at the Grand Ole Opry Roadshow with his brother and had been on local and national TV. Within a decade, Wayne Newton would have his first *Billboard* hit with 'Danke Schoen' – a Vegas-style tune Bobby Darin had given him.

Starstruck, Skip completely forgot about his sister as he chatted with the singer. Meanwhile, in panic mode, Sherry was frantically dog paddling to keep her head above water. Luckily, someone else came to her rescue.

Sherry recalls seeing very little of her own musician father during those years, but she does remember taking a trip to The Broadmoor, a palace-like hotel where Jock was performing. 'It was all full of swank,' she muses. The hotel was about 800 miles northeast of Phoenix, at the base of Cheyenne Mountain in Colorado Springs.

To make the long journey, the three Spences took a Greyhound bus. Sherry sat beside her mom while Skip sat alone in the seat behind them. As the bus got closer to Colorado Springs, Gwenn and Sherry started to talk about what they were going to eat. Skip, meanwhile, was getting queasy. When Sherry said she would love some pumpkin pie, it was too much for her older brother – who vomited out the window.

The resort's golf course was immaculate, like a well-kept park that kids couldn't play in. When the children stepped into the vast dining room, they were in awe. All the tables had white linen tablecloths and they ate lamb for the first time – which they didn't particularly enjoy.

Back in Phoenix, Alex Spence would drive to the Evergreen Trailer Park in his Lincoln Continental on occasion, to pick his family up for a visit. He now lived about four miles away, in Camelback East Village. Sometimes he took his grandkids to the hotel where he worked, about seven and a half miles from the trailer park. A 1950s postcard promoted the Paradise Inn Hotel as follows:

> 'Paradise Inn is the first large winter resort hotel built in the Phoenix area since the War. Located at the base of Camelback Mountain, its rooms and verandas overlook the city of Phoenix to the south and the broad expanse of Paradise Valley to the east.'

Camelback Mountain has always been a presence in Phoenix, even before the city formally existed. Long ago, the ancient Hohokam culture established a sacred site in a cave on the north side of the mountain. In 1879, President Hayes designated the mountain as a part of a vast reservation for the Maricopa tribes, but within a few months the decision was reversed. By the midpoint of the twentieth century, much of the mountain's surrounding area was privately owned.

Over the decades, lavish resort hotels had sprung up around the base of the mountain, including the Jokake Inn (opened in 1926), the Camelback Inn (1936) and the Paradise Inn (tail-end of World War Two). Bustling in the wintertime, they offered fine dining, horseback riding, golf and, for the adventurous, outings to the desert.

The Paradise Inn was popular with snowbirds and locals, who booked its main hall for large events and galas. Alex Spence had started working there in the late 1940s. Now he parked his Lincoln in the main lot and walked the kids over to the grand entranceway, with two large palm trees flanking the main doors. The well-groomed lawns were incongruous against the untidy green patches of the mountain that towered as a backdrop.

Alex led the children to the hotel lounge, where Skip would always order a Roy Rogers (cola mixed with grenadine syrup, garnished with a maraschino cherry) while Sherry would ask for a Shirley Temple (ginger ale, splash of grenadine and maraschino cherry). Getting to spend time with their grandad, who was always so warm and friendly, was nice enough – but drinking mocktails in the Babylonian-like surroundings of the Paradise was something else entirely.

In April 1956, around the time Skip turned 10 years old, he received another treat: his first acoustic guitar, bought by his mother. Enamoured with rock'n'roll, he started teaching himself how to play the instrument right away.

Back in January, Elvis had his first chart-topper on the *Billboard* Top 100 with 'Heartbreak Hotel'. The following month, Carl Perkins climbed all the way to number two with 'Blue Suede Shoes'. In March, Little Richard released a single that included 'Long Tall Sally' as the A-side (number thirteen) and 'Slippin' And Slidin'' as the B-side (number twenty-seven – back in the day, the dual sides of a 45 earned different chart positions by airplay and jukebox plays).

Two more landmarks were reached in the week of Skip's 10th birthday. On 14 April, Presley recorded 'I Want You, I Need You,

I Love You' in Nashville, Tennessee; two days after that, Chuck Berry cut 'Roll Over Beethoven' in Chicago, with Leonard and Phil Chess producing. Both songs were released the following month, with Elvis reaching number three and Berry climbing to number twenty-nine.

In June, as young Skip Spence was about to finish fourth grade, Little Richard released the classic 'Rip It Up' (number twenty-seven) backed with 'Ready Teddy' (number forty-four). All those songs burst onto the radio within six short months – from only four artists who were part of the rock'n'roll explosion.

With only a six-string guitar and maybe a few barre chords, there was so much to play, so many possibilities. Rock'n'roll was completely fresh. It was as though another Big Bang had gone off and suddenly there was an expanding universe.

Just as Skip was figuring out how to play the latest hits, a young boy an ocean away, named Paul McCartney, would trade in his trumpet for an acoustic guitar. There were so many other young, nascent musicians around the world caught up in the same moment. (Over the years Skip would also tutor himself on other instruments, including the Japanese koto).

As his son continued to teach himself the guitar, in early-to-mid-1957 Jock returned to Phoenix. He'd come to prepare his family for heading further west. At the summer end of the school year, the Spences packed their belongings and crammed everything they possibly could into their car. Whatever did not fit – including old toys and boxes of photographs – was put into storage, never to be retrieved.

The Spences said their goodbyes to friends and family. Sherry couldn't bear to part from her little friend HD. Purr, their pet cat, was left behind too.

She and Skip bade sad farewells to Grandad Alex and Aunt Vi. Though no one knew it, it was the last time they would all see each other. Then Jock, Gwenn, Skip and Sherry drove out of Phoenix in their cram-packed car. They were going to California.

CHAPTER THREE

GOING TO CALIFORNIA

Jock Spence took a right out of Evergreen Trailer Park. Sitting in the backseat, the kids looked out the rear window as they drove west and the entrance to the trailer park gradually disappeared. They must have wondered when, or perhaps if ever, they would return.

Because the car was so packed it was sluggish. Taking Thomas Road westward, the Spences passed the upscale Phoenix Country Club and the more affordable Encanto Park Golf Course, on their way to the edge of town.

Near the city limits Jock turned right onto Route 60, cutting northwest on a sharp angle. Interstate 10 didn't yet exist, so Route 60 was the best way to Northern California.

It veered northwest and then cut southward again at Wickenburg. With a heavy load, lower speed limits and a roundabout path, the trek out of Arizona took much longer than it would today, back in the summer of 1957. Back in the era when rock'n'roll was young.

Close to the California state border, the Spence family passed the southern edge of the Colorado River Reservation. It was established for the Mohave and Chemehuevi peoples in March 1865, as the American Civil War finally drew toward its end.

Continuing west on Route 60, the car lumbered through the Colorado Desert, cutting along the southern edge of Joshua Tree National Park. Passing Indio, the road transformed itself into Highway 99. It continued west, with Los Angeles to the south and Angeles National Forest to the north.

Curving northward, the family passed Bakersfield, Fresno, Merced and Modesto on their way to the Bay Area. They arrived in Oakland exhausted from their almost 800-mile journey.

The trek from Phoenix to Oakland was one of the longest in Skip's young life to that point. But then the Spences were about to embark on a new life, nearly two and a half thousand miles away from his birthplace. A full three thousand miles away from his dad's own hometown, all the way out in Lanark County.

Approaching Oakland from the southeast, Jock turned onto MacArthur Boulevard. Because the MacArthur Freeway had not yet been built, West MacArthur was still a part of Route 50 and marked the main entrance to Oakland for many out-of-towners.

The oft haphazard artery of twelve miles hadn't been a part of the city's original plans. Named after General Douglas MacArthur, who'd led the US Army through bloody Pacific battles, it comprises many streets fused together into a single boulevard in the spring of 1942.

Driving onto MacArthur from the south, you start at Joaquin Avenue, in San Leandro. Winding north and west, MacArthur leads through a mix of commercial and residential areas; remnants of segregation; traditionally wealthy neighbourhoods, others recently gentrified, some struggling to survive. Due to its stitched-together nature, MacArthur sometimes becomes a one-way street or is inter-sected by freeways.

Back in the 1950s, a stretch of the boulevard featured an array of motels for the weary traveller. Heading north, Jock and Gwenn considered which one they might choose.

The beleaguered family had reached some sort of terminus. It was nearly the edge of the North American continent, before it disappeared into the Pacific; that motel strip was like a whole new world. For a few months in the middle of 1957, it would also become a home to the family.

• • •

Shortly before the Spences arrived, Oakland had its hottest day on record, reaching 104F on 24 June 1957. The humid city was very different to the constant dry heat of Arizona.

Unlike Phoenix, Oakland also had the possibility of earthquakes. In March, the Bay Area had experienced a 5.7 magnitude tremor that became known as the 1957 San Francisco earthquake. With landslides, one dead and forty injured, it was a reminder that everyone was living on the unpredictable, sometimes unforgiving, Hayward Fault.

As they acclimatised to life in the Bay Area, Jock and Gwenn started scouting around for a place to settle more permanently. Finding something just south of Oakland, they moved the family into a house in the rapidly growing town of Hayward. Still, the kids were sad to leave another pussycat behind – a stray they found on MacArthur Boulevard and named (naturally) Mac.

Located in the East Bay, Hayward is south of San Leandro and across the bay from San Mateo. During the post-war boom, the town's population jumped from under 15,000 in 1950 to nearly 27,000 in 1960. At the time, Hayward's economy was dominated by food canning, salt production and manufacturing – particularly armaments and aviation materials.[3]

From late 1957 to late 1958, the Spences lived in Hayward. During this time, Skip finished sixth grade.

The furnished house the family was renting had a pond in the back with goldfish, which the kids fed oatmeal. Best of all, it had a living room where Jock could play an upright piano and Skip could practise on the guitar. After years living in the Airstream trailer in Phoenix and spending months in a motel on MacArthur Boulevard, the rented house in Hayward was a welcome luxury.

In early 1958, when young Skip was approaching his 12th birthday, on the other side of the globe his rocking idol, Little Richard, had a life-changing experience on tour in Australia. Seeing a red fireball burst across the sky one night in Sydney, he was shaken up enough to want to quit rock'n'roll and pursue a life in the service of God.

Learning of this and feeling deeply upset, a young Skip looked up Richard's number – listed as Richard Penniman – and impulsively gave the musician a call. Decades later, he told *LA Weekly*, 'He told me he'd seen the light, and didn't want to sing 'Tutti Frutti' anymore... I didn't care, I thought he should be playing rock and roll, not that religious stuff.'[4] Little did he know, but Little Richard would reappear in his life a decade and a half later.

Back then, music took on a bigger role at home. Skip started to dabble in songwriting at a young age. Sherry recalls her brother playing guitar on the couch, sketching out new tunes, as she tried to watch TV in the living room.

And of course, Jock was still playing songs all the time. Sometimes they were old standards he'd been performing in lounges or dining halls, on the radio, at nighteries, hotels or resorts for decades.

At other times he tinkered away, composing little ditties on the fly. One time, while she sat beside her dad on the piano bench, Jock made up a little song for his daughter: 'Beautiful, Beautiful Brown Eyes, I'll Never Love Blue Eyes Again.'

Sherry was just starting to collect her own 45s. Over the next few years she'd amass her own personal favourites including doo-wop numbers, early R&B songs by James Brown and hits by vocal group The Platters. Though mom Gwenn was not a musician herself, she did have a collection of jazz standards to add to the Spence family's musical soundtrack. It was the popular music of the day, echoed in some of her husband's own repertoire.

While they were living in Hayward, Jock took Skip and Sherry to watch Latino-tinged rock'n'rollers The Champs perform in a local theatre. The band was riding high in 1958, reaching the peak position on *Billboard* on 28 March with catchy instrumental 'Tequila.'

But life was not only about music. One time, while playing checkers with his daughter, Jock suddenly promised Sherry he'd get her a bicycle if she won. When she did, he picked up a used bike that cost about $15. Looking back, Sherry has a strong suspicion that her father lost on purpose.

After a year in Hayward, the Spences moved about twenty-five miles north to Walnut Creek. With a population still under 10,000 at the time, it was quieter than the bustle of Oakland, San Francisco and San José. For two years, the family lived in a house on a hill in the Tice neighbourhood, in a tiny cul-de-sac named Riders Court. During that time Skip attended junior high, finishing grades seven and eight.

When an aunt passed away in Canada, Gwenn came into what was a substantial inheritance then – about $5,000. With the extra money she bought her husband a strawberry-pearl Buick, as well as a whole new batch of furniture for the house.

In 1960, Jock drove the kids on the 30-mile trek to the Candlestick Park stadium. Though the San Francisco Giants didn't reach the playoffs in 1960, the local baseball champs had a good season. With a 79-75 win-loss record, they came in fifth place in the National League, finishing sixteen games back of the champion Pittsburgh Pirates. Sherry recalls watching Willie Mays, the Giants' acrobatic outfielder, who at 29 was already a perennial all-star.

During that second year in Walnut Creek, the family also received sad news from Phoenix. On 23 August 1960, just a month after turning 70, Alex Spence died of a probable coronary, possibly resulting from tuberculosis. (Alex's own father, John, had died during an outbreak of the same disease, seven decades earlier.)

If Skip and Sherry had been wondering when they'd return to the Paradise Inn for mocktails with Grandad Alex, those hopes were dashed. While Jock returned to Phoenix for his father's funeral, the rest of his family stayed in California. But Sherry still has a letter that Aunt Vi later wrote, urging Gwenn to bring the children for a visit.

It was around that time that the family picked up and moved again, relocating about fifty miles south to the bottom tip of the San Francisco Bay. It was while living in San José that Skip Spence moved into adulthood; not only would he come into his own as a young musician, he'd marry young and become a father.

• • •

For millennia, the Santa Clara Valley was home to the Native American Ohlone people. After being part of the Spanish Empire, and then the Mexican Republic, in 1848 it was absorbed into the United States of America.

Within that valley, about forty miles inland from the Pacific Ocean, is the city of San José. Home to one million, it's the tenth most populated city in America today. It's also at the centre of Silicon Valley – economically, culturally and politically. Back in the early 1960s the region was still primarily agricultural, known as the 'Valley of the Heart's Delight.' It was also one of the folk-music hubs of the West Coast.

When the Spence family arrived in San José, the city was much smaller than it is now. In 1960, it had a population of 200,000 and was only the fifty-seventh most populous city in the US.

At the dawn of the sixties, Mayor Anthony P. 'Dutch' Hamann was in the middle of his almost twenty-year reign and his industrial growth campaign for San José. Just five years earlier, the Ford Motor Company had opened its massive assembly plant on the outskirts; in a couple more years, it would start churning out a popular new model called the Mustang.

The move to San José marked the Spences' fourth shift in as many years. Initially, the family rooted itself in a long-stay motel called the Pepper Tree Inn.

At that point, they had a pet parakeet which used to perch on Jock's head and was able to say 'pretty boy' – which was what they named him. Then, someone accidently left the front door open one day. Sherry remembers watching in horror as the bird, already out of its cage, flew out the door and perched in a big tree for a few moments. Then it flew away to its freedom.

Skip had become enamoured with art at this time. He sometimes worked on drawings at his bedroom desk, designing pictures and colouring them in with Indian ink. One time he knocked over his bottle and spilled ink all over the floor, to his parents' mortification. It's the one time Sherry remembers her father losing his temper. 'My dad was furious,' she recalls. 'I'm sure it was related to saying goodbye to the deposit.'

Though the Spences continued to move around, sometimes from one apartment to another on the same street, they stayed put in the city of San José. By the time they were living in a complex on Kollmar Drive, Jock had found work as a sales manager for a Canadian company called National Display.

At one point, he had a kit with red and black paint and large sheets of white paper, designing ad signs for businesses around the city. To sell his sign-making services, he'd go out on the road from time to time. Sometimes he returned with a pittance and on a few occasions he came home with a jackpot. It was the nature of the game.

Gwenn, meanwhile, had started to work as a saleswoman at L. Hart and Son, a department store at South Market and West Santa Clara Streets in the downtown area. She also cleaned units after tenants in the apartment blocks moved out, to help pay the rent. 'My mom actually had to get assistance, welfare, for a time,' Sherry explains. 'It was so hard on her because she was a very proud person.'

But on another occasion, Jock returned from a trip absolutely flushed with cash. Sherry recalls the family venturing out to a grocery store and stocking up the shopping cart. While on that grocery run, the family bought perhaps more than they ever had before on a single trip. She still remembers how much in awe she'd been: it was the first time she'd seen her parents spend money on such luxuries as paper napkins.

Around that time, Sherry remembers Skip sitting outside the apartment with a cardboard peace sign one afternoon. He was protesting America's growing involvement in Vietnam, after President John F. Kennedy's authorising of MACV (Military Assistance Command Vietnam). It was a small, very personal act of political activism that coincided with his first steps into the folk-music scene.

An old black and white photograph captures this moment. It shows Skip wearing jeans and a white T-shirt, seated on a folded blanket with his legs crossed. With close-cropped hair he squints in the sunlight looking straight into the camera. With a cigarette in one hand and a pen in the other, he's writing in a notebook. It was the same way in which he'd draw, sketch and write out song lyrics in notebooks throughout his entire life.

In his first few years living in San José, the teenaged Skip attended Andrew Hill High School. It was here that he met guitarist Billy Dean Andrus, as well as several others who shared his love for music. Like Skip, Bill had been writing his own songs for a while. At the time, his family was living in a housing community behind the apartment complex on Kollmar.

It was a time that stepped up Skip's musical involvement. 'Where I remember him playing so much was in the living room of our apartment on Kollmar Drive in San José… This was annoying to me when I wanted to watch TV,' recalls Sherry.

High school wasn't only a musical journey for Skip; he also had regular buddies like Butch and Scott Nuessle, who lived in the same community. But, ever protective of his younger sister, Skip never let any of them date Sherry. That was out of the question.

He dropped out after finishing grade ten, when he was 16. Like nearly one-third of all Americans in the early 1960s, Skip Spence would not complete high school. Sometime in the late summer of

1962, he headed to Nevada. In a postcard to his sister, marked 15 September, Skip wrote in cursive writing:

Dear Sherry –
What say newt. How are all of your boyfriends there? As you know I ran into a little trouble up here but I'm O.K., Really. How is [name might be Doretha]? Say hi to her for me and ask her to write if she wants to. You write too damn it. It's cold up here. It's really sharp in Reno and Tahoe. I'm a about a quarter of a mile from the lake! Well hope school is alright there.
With soon love Skip.

Skip was up in Sparks, Nevada, near Reno, which gets much hotter than San José in the summertime and much colder in the winter: from 91F down to 24F. Reno also gets about 22 inches of snow every year.

Nearly a month later, he sent a second postcard to his sister, postmarked 9 October:

Dear Sherry,
How are you kid? How's school for you? I'm O.K. The weather here is 33° in the daytime. Brrrr. I'm going to bring some guys home for you. Tell Sue and Pat hi at school and your girlfriends, whoever I forgot to mention. I'll bring you back some poster from where I work. [undiscernible]... Write damn it.
Love Skip.

Three months later, he'd make a decision seemingly at odds with his opposition to violence. But perhaps in some way he wanted to be like his dad – who'd been both a war hero and a musician.

It had reached 54F in San José on Tuesday 22 January 1963. On that day, a 16-year-old Alexander Lee Spence enlisted in the US Naval Reserves. According to his military records, his birthday was 16 April 1945 – one year before his actual birthdate. But he was 17 years old on paper, at least.

31

His immediate future comprised a couple of months of basic training. While completing his training in San Diego, Skip wrote to his sister twice on United States Navy letterhead notepaper. The first letter was dated 24 March 1963:

Dear Sherry,

Hi – man you're lucky. Never have you ever had bad news like this is. Honest to god. I was talking in ranks today so they made me wash my hat in the can. Everybody was laughing. We get about 6 hours sleep at night and the rest of the time we can [undiscernible] of march, march, march and wait. How's your boyfriends and all that? Boy I sure miss you all. Tell Frank and Tony hi and to write if they want give them my address, O.K.? Tell mom that the stains washed out. And be sure and be good.

> *Love,*
> *Skip*
> *PS: Would you give Bill my address? I think I gave it wrong to him. Thanks.*

The second letter was postmarked two days before his 17th birthday, 16 April 1963. In the same cursive style as before, he wrote:

Happy Easter
Egg on you too –
Dear Sherry,
I'm sorry I couldn't write sooner but this stuff is pretty rushed. We go over the side next time. So it shouldn't be too bad after that. I'm anxious to hear those records again. I'll be playing them all the time probably. [Undiscernible] and anyone else I know. O.K. I've got to run pretty soon. So be good. And I'll bring you something back from Mexico. (We're only 13 miles away.)

> *Bye for now,*
> *Love,*
> *Skip*

After he completed his basic training, Skip returned to San José and found a job at the Del Monte pickle factory at the corner of Seventh and Jackson. He settled into a routine of weekend military drills and daywork during the week.

In that same month of April 1963, Skip met Patricia May Howard.[5]

'The first time I met Skip was at a party at Billy Dean's house,' she recalls. 'It was his birthday or something. I had never gone to any parties before. My mom wouldn't let me. But there was a thing going on between Skip and [Nancy] and he was on the outs with her.'

Nancy was an adopted child living with the Andrus family at the time, who became an early girlfriend of Skip. She would leave the family home to move up to Alaska.

'The party was in the den area, and we were all just sitting around talking, and Skip and Billy Dean came in through a window and they just started singing, 'If I Had a Hammer'.'

In 1962, 'If I Had A Hammer' was a hit for folk revivalists Peter, Paul and Mary. Its origins were surprisingly controversial. First performed by Pete Seeger at a 1949 legal fundraising for the US Communist Party, the McCarthy era would have viewed the song's hammer as paired with the sickle of the Soviet flag.

'They were just singing songs and after they sat down, Skip and I started talking,' continues Pat. 'He asked me for my phone number, and I wouldn't give it to him. Skip said, "Why not?" And I said, "I just don't give my number to anybody." He kept bugging me the whole time, but I wouldn't give it to him.

'After that party I didn't see Skip for a couple of weeks, but one day he drove by when I was walking outside. He had a blue Corvair, I think. He passed by in the car, and he then stopped and said, "Hi." He had his uniform on with the white pants and the collar. We were talking and he told me he was in the navy. He asked me for my number again, and then I gave it to him that time.'

Going out to parties and to watch movies at drive-ins, they did just what a young couple would do. But it got more and more serious.

Meeting Gwenn for the first time was a little nerve-wracking. 'I remember Skip's mom in the little kitchen in their apartment,' says Pat. 'She had red hair and she was holding a cigarette. Skip just said, "I'll be back in a few minutes." So, he leaves me there with his mom. Well, I was very quiet, and she was pretty cool to me.'

But she couldn't block the path of teenaged love. 'Skip gave me an engagement ring on my 16th birthday, which was in July,' Pat recalls. 'He had this little box, and he took the ring out and showed it to me and asked, "Would you marry me?" I said, "My mom's not going to accept this." I didn't show it to my mom then.'

But before the end of 1963, Pat was expecting their first child. The young couple moved into an apartment together at 1348 Danube Way, a mile away from his mother's flat on Eastwood Court and just under three miles from the Del Monte plant.

By this point Skip and Sherry's parents had suddenly separated, with Jock moving to Lincoln Avenue. Whilst shuffling between work at the factory from Monday through Friday and on training exercises with the Reserves on weekends, young Spence prepared for his fast-approaching wedding.

On 15 March 1964, the two married in a Catholic ceremony in San José, in tune with Pat's family background. Just 15 at the time, Sherry Spence went to the wedding with her friend Mimi, who would later marry her brother's close friend Scott.

Although Sherry had not had more than the odd sip of wine or beer up to that point, she somehow downed thirteen glasses of champagne at the Sunday reception. Feeling dizzy, she climbed into the back of a car that belonged to Pat's mom, Ida, and promptly went to sleep.

A while later, she was awakened when Ida, Pat's two younger brothers and younger sister jumped into the car in the early hours of the morning. 'We're going to go get some pancakes,' Ida cheerfully told her new in-law. Already feeling woozy, the suggestion nearly made Sherry throw up.

As for the newlyweds, with Pat's due date five months away the couple readied their apartment for the baby's arrival. Sherry became close friends with Pat. Whenever she visited their apartment around this time, she remembers her brother arriving home smelling like a pickle jar.

At some point in 1964, Skip grew tired of work at the pickle factory and left to work as a salesman at the Levitz Furniture Shop. Constantly on the go, he fell into a routine of daily work and preparations at home for the baby on weekdays, with regular naval exercises on weekends. On top of all those commitments, he somehow carved out time for writing and playing music – specifically the folk music he was then immersed in.

CHAPTER FOUR

SOUTH BAY FOLK

'There was a folk community in San José, there was one in Berkeley, and one in Palo Alto,' guitarist Geoff Levin recalls. 'The community in Palo Alto was centred around [Jerry] Garcia. I met Jerry through David Nelson, who was one of the founders of The New Riders of the Purple Sage.

'Garcia was primarily a banjo player at the time. He had different bluegrass bands, and to me the most notable was the Black Mountain Boys,' says Levin. As one of the fathers of improvisational electric guitar, Jerry Garcia demonstrates just how diverse the musical landscape would become.

'When I played with them, we had Scott Hambly on mandolin and then David Nelson came in on mandolin, and we had Sandy Rothman on guitar and vocals. I was the youngest member, just out of school. I was the kid. I was really a guitar player, but I picked up the bass pretty quickly,' says Levin.

At the time 18-year-old Geoff was with Jerry Garcia and Robert Hunter in the Black Mountain Boys, they played numerous shows at Top of the Tangent in Palo Alto. It wasn't, however, the primary scene venue.

'Down in the South Bay the whole community was centred around the Offstage.' Levin confirms. 'My own band, The Piney

Creek Ramblers, performed there. It opened in '63. Skip came a tiny bit later. I think I met Skip early in '64. It might have been at the Shelter. Skip was on the cusp of the almost overnight transition from folk music in the Bay Area to folk-rock and rock.'

At that time, the South Bay was firmly rooted in America's folk revival, which was still trucking as The Beatles were captivating the hearts of Americans youth. More political than rock'n'rollers, most folkies were also purist in their style – that is, until Dylan went electric.

With Billy Dean Andrus, Skip Spence had formed a roving folk duo (or sometimes a trio – according to a surviving photo that shows them with an unidentified female singer).[6] 'Billy Dean was like Skip's brother,' Pat Spence reflects. 'They were playing a lot of folk music back then, just as a duo.'

Not yet 18 when he got married, Spence was in that grey zone that occupies the space between youth and adulthood. As he stepped closer to fatherhood, music took form as both a career and a life destination.

Steeped in the regional music scene, he and Andrus pursued their own brand of folk, developing a flat-picking style on the guitar. As was not unusual for the era, their stage name was in a constant state of flux – ranging from such monikers as Michael and David Aarons or the Aaron Brothers to the Andrus Brothers or the Andrus Twins.

When Geoff Levin went on to form The Piney Creek Ramblers, he brought his younger brother, Robbie, into the band. Born in 1949, bassist Robbie Levin was one of the youngest folkies in the South Bay scene. As Robbie was finding his feet as a young musician, Skip Spence was both a friend and mentor.

While the folk-music revival gained momentum all over the USA in the early sixties, the West Coast nurtured multiple interwoven communities and venues – from places like The Troubadour and Ash Grove down in Los Angeles to Coffee and Confusion, the Coffee Gallery and the Cabale up in the Bay Area.

In between those points, a cluster of tightknit folk venues popped up in and around the South Bay. For a time, San José was home to small clubs that acted as beacons for budding folkies local or traveller, folk aficionados, or anyone looking for genial conversation accompanied by acoustic music.

One popular San José club, The Offstage Folk Music Theatre, was located at 970 South First Street. Jorma Kaukonen was a regular at the venue. 'Before the Offstage [name] came by it was the Folk Theater,' he explains. 'That was before Kantner and the guys took it over... around late '64.

'The Offstage was a little storefront,' he adds, 'and when I say little... I doubt that it seated more than fifty people on a crowded night. There was sort of a bay window in the front, and the stage was in the window area. So, when you were performing, your back was to the street with the window glass behind you when you were facing the audience. Behind the audience was a little counter with an espresso machine, and behind that was a unisex bathroom and then a tuning room the size of a large hotel closet.'

'It was pretty cozy,' Pete Grant recalls. 'The Offstage was really narrow, it was the size of a little mom and pop store. The stage was along the long wall with no more than five rows of seats before the aisle between the seats and the opposite wall.'

Though it was small, the Offstage was a virtual Grand Central Station of activity. In its time, the venue featured intimate performances by a variety of musicians on the verge of stardom, notoriety, or even tragedy – sometimes all three.

There was guitarist Paul Kantner, who came down from Palo Alto and sometimes managed the club. Kantner co-founded the Jefferson Airplane just a couple of years later. Then there was singer-songwriter David Crosby, who'd soon go on to co-found The Byrds and Crosby, Stills and Nash, before his solo career.

There was also David Freiberg, who, like Kantner, sometimes managed the Offstage – before forming Quicksilver Messenger Service and slogging through jailtime for the first of multiple marijuana busts. For a time, Kantner, Crosby and Freiberg all lived together in a communal house down in Venice, Southern California.

Of those days, Kantner would tell *JamBase*, 'When I left Santa Clara University, where Jorma [Kaukonen] went as well, there was a fledgling group of people who went to San José State College, which was a party school; it's where all the fuck-offs went. There was this great burgeoning beatnik community that I fell into accidentally, of people from David Freiberg and David Crosby to Sherry Snow, Jesse Fuller and Malvina Reynolds.'

Sherry Snow was one half of folk duo Blackburn & Snow, with Jeff Blackburn (who'd later show up in a reunion version of Moby Grape and bequeath Neil Young the line, 'It's better to burn out than it is to rust'). She'd also sing for a while with Dan Hicks, ex-frontman of The Charlatans.

Jesse Fuller was the one-man band who wrote 'San Francisco Bay Blue'; he didn't record his first album till he was 62 but had a huge influence on Dylan. Malvina Reynolds, folk musician and political activist, wrote 'Little Boxes', the 1962 song that satirised America's move to the suburbs. Her lullaby 'Morningtown Ride' and her protest song 'What Have They Done To The Rain' were hits for The Seekers and The Searchers in '64 and '65, respectively.

'We started a little folk nightclub in San José and would sell marijuana from under the bar,' recalled Kantner. 'We also started a little music store and Jorma gave guitar lessons. It was a nice little community of musicians that extended from San José into Palo Alto.'[7]

Kaukonen fills in the picture: 'If you were a folkie back then – regardless of whether you were sort of a bluesy guy like me or more a group finger-guy like Paul Kantner, and I'm not sure how to categorise Skip because he was always his own person anyway – there was a whole sense of community that was engendered among folkies of all stripes. I think it would be hard to replicate that today.'

Thinking back, Grant recalls one lazy Sunday especially well. 'There wasn't much going on one Sunday. So, I went around the block to smoke some pot and when I got back [to the Offstage] there was this guy playing a twelve-string guitar, and he was playing this hypnotic stuff that just blew me away. It was the first time I ever saw David Crosby.'

Other performers he recalls include Pat Simmons and Herb Pederson, later the respective guitarists/co-vocalists of The Doobie Brothers and The Desert Rose Band, along with Jerry Garcia and his later Grateful Dead bandmate, a young Ron McKernan, who performed at the club on occasion. (He came to be known as 'Pigpen' in his days with the Dead, before meeting his own untimely death in March 1973.)

There was also a young female singer from Texas who'd perform in duos, or sometimes a trio, with nimble guitarists Kaukonen and Steve Mann.[8] Janis Joplin was just a few years away from stardom and the heroin overdose that would take her life (in October 1970).

'Paul Foster ran the Offstage,' Grant explains. 'It was open every Friday and Saturday and then we had a hoot on Sundays. It was pretty much like an open mic. But you'd get together in various combinations, and you'd go next door to the laundromat and run down a couple of songs and then go back out on stage and play.'

Foster was an artist who designed and drew many of the Offstage's event posters and handbills. He was also chums with Jack Kerouac's Beat muse, Neal Cassady, and became one of Ken Kesey's Merry Pranksters.

Like so many others, Kaukonen holds fond memories of that era. 'The vibe was always friendly,' he muses. 'If you went to go to a hootenanny, or an open mic as it's called today, there could be a guy like Ale Ekstrom – who dressed like an eighteenth-century British seaman and played the concertina, I mean, he had everything but a parrot and a pegleg – or somebody like Stevie Schuster playing a jazz flute, or Rand Conger playing flamenco or classical, or somebody doing bluegrass.

'It could be anything! There wasn't that sense of artistic division, there was just that sense of community, that we all liked cool stuff that mainstream America wasn't into at the time.'

With Billy Dean, Skip played a variety of smaller venues in and around the South Bay, including the Brass Knocker in Saratoga and the Shelter, a coffeehouse and folk club located at 438 East William Street. It was about a mile northeast of the Offstage, just a few steps from the San José State University campus.

The Shelter took its name from the constant threat of atomic warfare amidst the nuclear arms race and never-ending Cold War. Once a pizza parlour, it was run by Paul Ziegler, who also gave lessons on blues, folk and classical guitar. He'd also go on to join Billy Dean Andrus' band, Weird Herald, and later play with Jefferson Airplane offshoot Hot Tuna.

'The Shelter was across the street from where we lived,' Pat Spence recalls. 'There was a bookstore next door. It was an open mic type thing. Skip used to play there when Aaron was a little baby, so I couldn't go and watch him.'

Pat had given birth to the couple's first son, Aaron Dean Spence, at the Alameda Naval Hospital on 8 August 1964. 'I named Aaron after Moses' brother in the Bible. And Dean was after Billy Dean's dad,' she confirms. 'Him and his wife were always open to having all the kids hanging out at their house. There would always be five or six couples there. And Pat Simmons [of The Doobie Brothers] was one of them.'

Skip was officially discharged from the Naval Reserves the following month. He had served four months and seventeen days of active duty out of service totalling one year, seven months and twenty-seven days. According to his discharge papers, he was 'Eligible for Reenlistment.' It would have to wait.

For now, the budding singer-songwriter would continue to toil at Levitz Furniture. It was a job and it paid the bills, after all. But it wasn't his passion.

Music was the dream to aspire to. Skip had seen his father pursue it as a career ever since he was a toddler in Windsor, Ontario. He'd grown up without much money, but his mom was hardworking and very caring. His family home was happy. His dad was gentle and loving, although he wasn't around much. So why not aspire to have fun and to do what you want to do?

Skip would strive to perform on stage just like Jock had. But in the late summer of '64, it was American folk music that captured his imagination. As a part of the South Bay folk scene, his infectious energy would impress all those around him.

While he may not have yet reached the age of majority, Skip already had the aura of a free spirit. Of course, while he was an exuberant, artistic soul, he was also a husband and father holding down a job.

'I think he kept that close to his vest,' multi-instrumentalist Pete Grant reflects. 'He didn't broadcast much about having a family or having a day job.'

'I think I met Skip at the Benner Music Company on Stevens Creek Road,' recollects veteran guitarist Jorma Kaukonen. 'That's where Paul [Kantner] and I and Pete Grant and a bunch of other guys taught [guitar]. My recollection of Skip back then wouldn't have been of him as a performer. He was a little younger than me, but he was also married and had kids.'

A September 1964 poster advertisement from the Shelter depicts a week in the club's short life, capturing a moment forever. Beside a drawing of the instrument at the bottom of the poster are the words, 'Guitar instruction by Paul Ziegler & Alex Spence.' On the left is a narrow column identifying the acts performing over the coming week, with Bill Andrus and Skip Spence listed as holding down the Monday night slot just weeks after the latter became a dad.[9] Effectively, he appeared twice on the poster, as tutor and performer.

'It was a bigger space than the Offstage,' Pete Grant reflects. 'The Shelter was just a big room. It must've been a restaurant at some time. From the stage there were glass windows to your right that went out to the street. The unique thing was that you could play folk and you could also play rock'n'roll at the Shelter.'

Hand-drawn posters from mid-1964 promised air-conditioning, coffee, tea, hot chocolate, hot and cold cider, lemonade and

Kool-Aid. 'We feature the finest coffee and entertainment in the Santa Clara Valley,' ads boasted.

More significantly, in late June it was announced: 'The Shelter proudly presents the amazing Jerry Kaukonen, One of the very finest guitarists anywhere. If you've heard Jerry before you won't miss this performance, if you haven't heard him, you won't dare miss it!' Already, by his mid-20s, he was a revered American roots musician.

Though its lifetime was brief, the Shelter became a major hub in the South Bay folk scene after the Offstage closed its doors. It hosted teenagers Spence and Andrus, just 18 and 17 in the late summer of 1964, as well as more experienced musicians like Kaukonen and Kantner – relative old-timers in their early 20s.

Throughout this period, Skip was a prolific songwriter. 'Before we formed our own short-lived band,' Pete Grant recollects, 'Skip and I would get together over at his place, and he would show me different parts of songs he was working on.' Laughing, he recalls skip's generosity and cavalier approach. 'There was one song he played, and I remember he said, "I'll give that to you."'

Like Grant, Geoff Levin was struck by Spence's natural songwriting ability. 'I understand this now,' he recalls, 'but I didn't understand it then. Skip was one of the first singer-songwriters. He was one of the first in the Bay Area, and pretty much in the country.'

'Before singer-songwriters, most people covered other people's material,' Grant acknowledges. 'They didn't write their own stuff. I mean, you had Dave Van Ronk, and Joan Baez, and Dylan. Dylan broke the mould big time. I think Dylan paved the way for people like Skip. Malvina Reynolds, who wrote 'Little Boxes', played the Offstage, but she was more seasoned.

'Mostly, people were performing folk standards. My first impression of Skip was being blown away by how he sounded incredible singing his own songs. I have a picture of Skip playing his acoustic guitar and me being blown away.'

'His enthusiasm was *always* infectious,' Grant reflects. 'Hanging out with Skip was so bubbly exciting. That was the norm.'

(In the summer of 1965, Pete Grant would briefly play in The Manes with Spence and Robbie Levin, gigging in Lake Tahoe. Later focusing on the dobro, he'd go on to collaborate with a great many artists over the years, including an impactful appearance on The Grateful Dead's *Aoxomoxoa*.)

Amid those happy days of writing songs and performing, tragedy struck. Just as Skip was ready to step into the world of rock'n'roll, he lost his father on Saturday 1 May 1965. Jock Spence, who was only 50 years old at the time, likely succumbed to a heart attack.

• • •

Sherry Spence cannot recall a time when her father ever yelled – apart from when Skip spilled Indian ink all over his bedroom floor. Jock may have said 'damn' once or twice, but apart from that he never swore. She doesn't recall him ever taking a drink either.

Jock Spence was both a gentle man and a talented musician. Listening to a recording of him at the piano, he does justice to old classics like 'Maybe', written by Allan Flynn and Frank Madden, 'In The Still Of The Night', by Cole Porter, 'Our Very Own', by Victor Young and Jack Elliott, and indeed his own ballad, 'I Might Never Have Been Lonely'. You can also hear the resemblance in his voice, in terms of pitch, to that of his son.

As music was Jock's sometime livelihood and always his passion, it was a constant backdrop to his son's early life. Sometimes Jock would play old standards, other times he made up little ditties on the spot. Just as he started writing songs in his mid-teens, so too did Skip. Music would *always* connect him to his departed father.

'Even though we moved around a lot,' Skip recalled in a one-page bio sheet put out by Columbia Records in 1967, 'there was always music in our home. As long as I can remember, my whole life has been music.'

Three days after Jock's passing, on Tuesday 4 May, a memorial was held in San José. The city was windy but warm that afternoon. The service was held at 2 p.m. at Willow Glen Mortuary on Lincoln Avenue, just down the road from Jock's apartment. Following that, his body was flown to Ottawa, Canada, where his mother, Effie Giffin, was living.

Making a final journey, Jock was then taken to Flower Station, in Lanark County. It was near the cottage he had gone to in the summers of his youth; the place he had last visited with his family over ten years earlier. On the warm, breezy Friday afternoon of 7 May 1965, a second memorial was held at Young's Funeral Home, officiated by Jock's uncle, Alexander Deachman.

With six nephews serving as pallbearers, Jock Spence was buried that same day at Clyde Forks Cemetery. But his son and daughter were unable to travel the nearly 3,000-mile journey to Lanark County for the ceremony.

Throughout his life, Skip Spence was deeply sensitive. While he was breezy and carefree on the outside, he felt things deeply. As he got older he carried with him, and often kept at bay, some deep regrets.

Sherry was then a month shy of her 17th birthday, while her brother had turned 19 just weeks before. Many years later, the siblings would learn a secret about their father. But in the here and now, in the spring of 1965, Skip was ready to dip into the world of rock'n'roll – and a variety of paths would soon appear before him.

CHAPTER FIVE

BEYOND THE SOUTH BAY

Sometime in late 1964 or early 1965, Skip Spence tried LSD for the first time. His trip-sitter was the older Levin brother, his friend and fellow musician.

'I was Skip's guide for his first acid trip,' Geoff Levin confirms. 'I had already taken acid, so I was then able to take someone else on an acid trip. I don't know if I want to take credit for being the first one to turn Skip on to something as strong as acid, but I did it.

'That particular time,' he recalls, 'I was excited that he trusted me enough for me to be his guide. We did it right around the college, San José State. There was a grassy area, I can't remember exactly where it was, but we hung there for a while, because he was tripping out.

'The acid was good. I think I was reading out of *The Tibetan Book Of The Dead*... It was a little bit of a "How To" going around for how you become a guide. You know, what you do when you help somebody who is going on their first acid trip.'

Geoff is likely referring to Timothy Leary's 1964 book, *The Psychedelic Experience: A Manual Based On The Tibetan Book Of The Dead*. When Skip was introduced to LSD it was still legal in California. The state would not criminalise it until 6 October 1966.

'So, I think we spent about three hours together. It was very serene. He got a lot out of it. For him, it was kind of a beatific experience. I think there was nothing negative. There were students all around us and we were just lying on the grass and chilling out. I don't think I saw him much after that. But that experience for him, I remember, was good.'

Many years later, speaking with Jill Wolfson for *The State* newspaper, Spence thought back to his trips on LSD. 'Acid was like heaven, a moment of God, inspiring, tragic. I must have taken it a hundred times, a thousand times,' he testified.[10]

'Shortly after that first acid trip,' Levin recalls, 'the transition for Spence occurred. Overnight, we all literally dropped folk music and got into rock.'

Change was in the air. Like so many folkies, Skip Spence's musical path changed when Bob Dylan famously went electric – first on side A of *Bringing It All Back Home*, released March 1965, and then, notoriously, at the Newport Folk Festival that July.

'Dylan was the final straw in making it okay to actually plug in. Prior to that we all looked down our noses to anyone who was electric,' Levin reminisces.

Dylan had given The Byrds permission to record and adapt 'Mr. Tambourine Man.' When it was in the can and slated for an April release, he went to check out the band at Hollywood club Ciro's on 26 March 1965. He ended up performing with them and they were all photographed sitting together outside. One of the photos was used on the back cover of The Byrds' debut album.

When 'Mr. Tambourine Man' was released as a single on 12 April, it quickly climbed to number one on both sides of the Atlantic. And then on 25 July, his second night at the Newport festival, Dylan played an all-electric set and all hell broke loose…

'One thing that I can remember that was a milestone was when Barbara Dane [folk, blues and jazz singer] got up on stage… just her and an electric guitar,' recalls Levin. At that point, our biases were kind of shifting because there was this big upheaval with Dylan getting up on stage with The Band,' in 1966, on his first all-electric tour.

'So, Dylan and Barbara were catalysts and symbols of what was going to happen in the Bay Area,' notes the folkie turned rock'n'roller. 'Within two weeks to a month, everyone was buying electric guitars and starting bands. And Skip was no different. Shortly after that I lost touch with Skip, because I think he moved up to San Francisco.'

For a brief time, 19-year-old Skip Spence was without a band. But further change was coming. It all started one day when he arrived home and told his wife he was tired of working at the furniture shop. He wanted to pursue music as a career.

Pat was expecting their second child at the time, but she too must have realised Skip's window for a career was closing. She agreed to temporarily move back in with her mom and the couple got rid of their apartment.

Spence headed northeast, to Tahoe. Early on, he struck up a friendship with Val Pease, a 17-year-old singer who'd just graduated from high school in nearby Placerville. Now he was working on a survey crew in town – a rural boy as familiar with country music as he was with folk.[11]

'I met Skip in South Shore Lake Tahoe in the summer of '65,' Val remembers. 'We met through the local music scene. I was singing occasionally at the American Legion Hall. There was a fellow there named Jim Burgett who would get me up to sing.'

So Spence and Pease formed a band, The Manes, with both on vocals and guitar. 'We played some Stones and stuff like that,' Val recalls. 'Skip was turning us onto some Byrds. We were doing a lot of cover tunes. It wasn't a real serious effort, but we were making noise,' he chuckles warmly.

'One member of the band was Jim Alexander [on bass] and I think our drummer was called Myron Bobson. Jim Burgett leased us his brand new, all-silver Mosrite guitars to use, and we played the Legion Hall one or two nights a week. We played for a short while, before Skip left for San Francisco.'

Thinking back, he adds, 'Skip was just a character; he was a funny guy. Him and another guy in the band, I think it was Jim Alexander, could put on perfect British accents. So, we'd go into local restaurants and Skip and Jim would slide into their limey accents and really get a lot of attention that way.' The Beatles' *A Hard Day's Night* movie had been a landmark; young guys like Skip could have fun playing up the mock-Brit bit for all it was worth.

That summer, Spence briefly rotated The Manes' lineup to suit everyone's schedules. For a very short time, he recruited some friends from San José to step in and join him for a couple of gigs. As bassist Robbie Levin recalls, 'The rock thing didn't really start until '65. Until then, everybody was doing acoustic stuff and it was that folk bluegrass background.' It was also the period of transition that led from folk to folk rock to the 1960s rock scene.

Acoustic instrumentalist Pete Grant, who was also in The Manes for a short time, recalls of Skip, 'You would just totally get caught up in his energy for everything. Before long we had a band which lasted for a short while. I guess Skip knew this guy who was a drummer on the south shore of Lake Tahoe and we put together a band with Skip and me and Robbie Levin [on bass] and the drummer.'

Pete also refers to a band member he can't remember the name of – likely Val Pease. The different band members cited by Val himself suggest that The Manes, a temporary band, had a fluctuating lineup whenever Skip trekked to Tahoe in the summer of 1965.

'We were really winging it, doing Beatles and Byrds songs,' recalls Pete. 'But we did well, considering how poorly prepared we were. We just played a couple of shows. One, I believe, was at an American Legion Hall. It was a weekend summer dance. The place was right on the highway. It was just a big old room. We called ourselves

The Manes because of our hair. Skip especially had quite a mane at that point.' Chuckling he adds, 'I'm sure that music was the third thing that people came out for when we performed.' When the audience was there to drink and to flirt, the band were way down the list.

'I can't remember how The Manes got started,' Levin admits. 'All I remember is driving to Tahoe with Skip in a convertible. It's a couple of hours to go from San José to Tahoe. But I'd never driven in a convertible before and driving in an open convertible for two hours just trashed me!' Laughing, he adds, 'And I was sitting in the back seat too!

'When we got to Tahoe, I remember we got to this house where we were sleeping that night, and I was so wiped out I just crashed. It was crazy. And ever since that trip, and I guess I was 15 or 16 at the time, I have never liked convertibles.'

Pete Grant has a more dramatic recollection from The Manes' brief existence. 'We almost got knifed,' he recalls. '…We went to see another band. It was at a time when we really looked the part with our Beatles haircuts and everything. Anyway, the band we went to see was a really good cover band. They were performing at some high school. And when we were leaving after the show, we were right next to a cop one minute and the next minute I felt this stab in my back. I turned around and a Mexican kid said to me, "Don't you ever come back here."'

The rough areas of SF and Oakland were really rough at this time. Taking a wrong turn could lead to a potentially dangerous neighbourhood situation.

Grant momentarily pauses. 'I don't know if Skip got the same treatment as me, but we never did go back to that school.'

As for The Manes' music, Levin recalls, 'it was rock'n'roll, Rolling Stones stuff… It was an interesting transition to go from all acoustic instruments to all electric instruments. The real big influence was The Beatles and The Rolling Stones, and Skip just loved the Stones. He was a Beatles fan, but he *really* loved that driving rock'n'roll of the Stones. I remember in Tahoe we opened with 'Satisfaction', but I think we also did 'King Bee' and some other stuff off the first two Stones albums.'

After a string of summertime rehearsals and gigs, The Manes called it a day.

For Robbie Levin, those times left a deep imprint, 'When you're young and you have a mentor in your life who makes such an impression on you – well, I had my older brother... but Skip was the first musician who came along and just saw me as an equal. And that was special. It has a real special place in my memories.'

In the autumn of 1965, as Spence was on the verge of joining the Jefferson Airplane, older brother Geoff would put together a new band and brought Robbie into the mix. In early 1968, People! released a cover of The Zombies' 'I Love You'. Selling over a million copies, the psychedelic pop single reached number fourteen on *Billboard* and became an international hit.

By that point, the Levin brothers had lost touch with their old friend. Still, though they only knew Spence for a short time, their special bond grew out of the South Bay folk scene.

Of those days, Robbie Levin recalls, 'You know, when I was around Skip, he smoked a little grass, but I didn't think he was into anything else at all. I didn't think he was into any hard stuff. Later on, I heard stories about what had happened to him and I was kind of crushed. I always wanted to go find him and try to help him, but it never happened.'

Once again, Skip found himself between bands. Partnering up once more with high-school friend Billy Dean Andrus, he returned for a while to folk.

• • •

A photograph in the Wednesday 18 August 1965 issue of *The Fremont Times* shows 'Bill Andrus and Alex Andrus' sharing the stage. Though Skip has a mop-top, the two 'brothers' are dressed formally in dark pants, Billy in a dark dress jacket and Skip in a button-down white shirt. They're holding acoustic guitars, standing huddled around stage microphones.

But Billy Dean would ultimately take his own separate path, joining the army and then going AWOL. He'd re-emerge on the music scene in 1967, forming Weird Herald with Paul Ziegler who used to run the Shelter.

(With two talented songwriters at the helm, Weird Herald would release a hauntingly beautiful folk song as a single – 'Saratoga James', b/w 'Only Yesterday' – and cut a solid, though sadly still unreleased, album between late 1968-69.)

It was likely that *The Fremont Times* photo led to a new opportunity for Skip. 'We were looking for someone to add to [The Topsiders],' guitarist Jim Sawyers remembers.[12] 'Someone who could write and sing well.'

Formed in Fremont in 1964, the four original Topsiders all went to Washington High School.[13] By the time the spring of '65 rolled around, the band's lineup included Jim on lead guitar, David Tolby on second guitar, Tom Antone on bass and Ken 'Toad' Matthews on drums.[14]

Continuing the narrative, Sawyers adds: 'We saw an article in one of the newspapers about [Skip] and drove to San José one night to hear him playing at... the Shelter.' Invited into the band that same night, the folkie was intrigued. Like many acoustic musicians around that time, Spence was keen to make the shift from pure folk into something like folk rock – or maybe even straight rock'n'roll.

'We had a couple of rehearsals,' Sawyers recalls, 'and he mentioned changing the name and offered the possibility of us using the name The Other Side, with the caveat that another group in San Francisco might want to use it, and that he might actually need to go play with them if they wanted him.' That 'other band' ended up calling themselves the Jefferson Airplane. Skip would hook up with them in early September, after playing just one show with The Other Side. It was 'in Fremont at some teen club,' Sawyers recalls.

'We were sad and disappointed to see Skip go,' he says, 'but happy for him he made it to the big time with Jorma and Jack who were pals of his from the Shelter.' As Spence parted company with The Other Side, he also drifted away from some of his folk buddies, including Robbie and Geoff Levin and Pete Grant.

Still, Geoff remembers his friend's youthful verve with great fondness. 'There was so much heart and so much potential,' he muses. 'Skip was really ahead of his time in a way. You can hear that in *Oar*, the album he later recorded... It's one of those things where you can't predict the path someone's going to take. I mean, if he hadn't gotten messed up with drugs it could've been different,' he says, with palpable regret.

'That picture I have epitomises Skip. He had a childlike quality. And there was a joy in his smile. I don't know if he could deal with the fact that he was so talented, and he was so likeable to so many people.'

CHAPTER SIX

THE JEFFERSON AIRPLANE

In the spring and summer of 1965, at the time Skip Spence was playing with The Other Side, The Manes and Billy Dean Andrus, there was another new group taking form in San Francisco.

At its centre was Ohio-born, San Francisco-raised Marty Balin. By 23 he had put out a couple of singles on the small label Challenge Records. Though both failed to chart on release in 1962, Balin was steadfast. He went on to form a folk quartet, The Town Criers, in the spring of 1963.

Regularly performing at The Drinking Gourd, a well-known club on Union Street, the band moved through the popular venues of the Bay Area folk circuit: Coffee and Confusion, the Hungry i, the Coffee Gallery and Barney Gould's Gold Rush.

When The Town Criers dissolved in the summer of '64, Balin left music for a time and worked in lithography to save up to study sculpture in Europe. Yet by the summer of '65, he was preparing to open a new venue backed by a small cadre of investors he'd rustled up.

Located at 3138 Fillmore Street, The Matrix would push folk into a new terrain. In itself, it was a larger space where alcoholic drinks were served alongside cups of espresso; where a dancefloor was adjacent to cocktail tables; and a bigger stage played host to traditional acoustic folk musicians, as well as those who wanted to plug in.

As Jorma Kaukonen explains, 'All these clubs that have relevance in the historical context were so humble at the time... The Matrix was a lot larger; I imagine it held maybe 150 people. It was on Fillmore Street in a neighbourhood that used to be called Cow Hollow... I think it was a block off Lombard Street.

'It was an actual club with a liquor license, which was a big deal because none of the coffee shops in the South Bay had beer and wine licenses,' he recalls. 'To us it was a pretty upscale club. If you think about the first gigs we did back then, we wore suit coats and starched shirts and stuff like that. It's really funny when you think about it. I mean, when people think about us looking like hippies but at that point the hippie hadn't really emerged yet.'

As the club was coming together, Balin put together a new folk group to serve as house band. He gathered guitarist Paul Kantner and singer Signe Toly, both of whom he knew from The Drinking Gourd, guitarist Kaukonen, whom Kantner highly recommended, and Jerry Peloquin to fill the drum stool, who Balin had met through his girlfriend. Filling out the group was Bob Harvey on bass, who at 27 was several years older than everyone else.

In a sign of wackier times to come, the nascent band took their name from Kaukonen's friend's pet dog: Blind Thomas Jefferson Airplane, in a partial nod to blues pioneer Blind Lemon Jefferson. Truncating the dog's name, the band dubbed itself the Jefferson Airplane and, on Friday 13 August 1965, played its live debut at The Matrix. But just a few weeks later, Peloquin was on his way out and Balin was searching for a replacement.

One day in early September, Skip Spence was playing his acoustic guitar in a Sausalito park when he crossed paths with a trio of musicians on their way to rehearsal. Guitarists John Cipollina and Jimmy Murray, along with bassist David Freiberg, would soon become three-fifths of Quicksilver Messenger Service.

Spence likely knew Freiberg from his time at the Shelter. The musicians got to chatting and the trio invited Skip to rehearse with them at The Matrix – which had opened just a few weeks earlier, south of the Wharf District.

Like the Shelter, The Matrix was once a pizza parlour but was now bridging the gap between folk and rock music. It was a step away from the coffeehouses, just as the old ballrooms and roller rinks started to metamorphose into what became the rock-ballroom circuit.

The entranceway to The Matrix was at the back, where a small bar stood. At the opposite end of the room, the small stage was the only part that was well lit. In all, the entire space measured about fifty by eighty feet.

This was where Spence, Cipollina, Murray and Freiberg ran through a few numbers, with Casey Sonnabend joining in on congas and percussion. In the early Quicksilver style, it was likely a kind of rugged, bluesy take on folk. As the budding quintet performed, Spence's sheer exuberance caught Marty Balin's attention.

Jerry Peloquin was playing his last gig as drummer with the Airplane in early September; with upcoming gigs already booked, a replacement was needed quickly. Skip's stage presence and overall *joie de vivre* as a guitarist was too intoxicating to ignore, but Marty decided to try to convince him to switch to drums.

As he later told rock journalist Jeff Tamarkin, 'Skippy was this beautiful kid, all gold and shining, like a little Buddha. I always go by people's vibrations, my first intuition. I just saw him and said, "Hey, man, you're my drummer." And he said, "No, I'm a guitar player."… I handed him some sticks and said, "Go home and practise and I'll call you in a week." He said, "Well, I'll give it a try." And he was great. His hands would bleed he would give so much. The girls would hang around the back of the stage just to get a look at him.'[15]

Recounting the events over a decade and a half later, Skip said, 'Marty told me they had enough guitarists but that I could play drums. I taught myself. I listened to records and just did what the others did. I learned drums because I wanted to get in a band. I wanted to be famous.'[16]

Like Balin, Signe Toly was struck by Spence's energy. Speaking with Tamarkin, she'd recall, 'All he wanted to do was be a part of that band. He didn't know how to play drums; he played from his heart. If you listen to every album he's on, that boy's just beating his heart out.'[17]

Kaukonen fills in the story. 'The Airplane rehearsed relentlessly. We rehearsed eight or nine hours a day. It's all we did. So, there was some hanging out [with old friends from the South Bay], but not as much as what happened earlier.

'Skip by that time was a well-known San José denizen, he was such a talented guy,' he acknowledges. 'When we were putting the Airplane together, most of the people came from the South Bay – like myself and Paul – and had moved to San Francisco, and Skip had already moved up there also… Marty had run into Skip playing someplace and he just liked the way Skip looked. Skip looked like a rock'n'roll star. I have no idea whether Skip had played drums before in his life, but he was such a talented guy. If you listen to the work that he does on [*Jefferson Airplane*] *Takes Off*, it's the work of a professional drummer.'

Jerry Peloquin played his last show with the group at The Matrix on Wednesday September 8 1965. When the Airplane returned to the club, on Thursday 16 September, a 16-year-old – Barry Lewis of garage band/Byrds fans The Hedds – was temporarily filling in on drums. The following night, both Lewis and Spence performed, with Spence taking the final set.

Lewis fills in some details about this fleeting time: 'I had just come back from Hawaii, I believe it was August or early September of 1965. I received a telephone call [perhaps from Matthew Katz, then manager of the Airplane] asking if I could play a gig with a new band at The Matrix.[18]

'I was eight or ten years younger than the other band members – I was 16 at the time – and I knew this would be a temporary

57

situation for me as they were much more "beat" than I was, and more mature. I remember Paul telling me that they would be bigger than The Byrds which I thought was impossible. How could anyone be bigger than The Byrds?'

In the late summer of '65, no one could tell just how big the Jefferson Airplane might become. 'I remember Matthew Katz being there,' Barry Lewis adds. 'He had this topcoat with a cape over the shoulders and a white Jaguar parked outside. He definitely had a presence and I took notice of him. I later played drums for one of his bands, Indian Puddin' and Pipe.'

Katz's name elicits strong reactions among those familiar with the stories of Jefferson Airplane, Moby Grape, It's a Beautiful Day and Lee Michaels. By the time he arrived in San Francisco from Massachusetts, Katz was in his late 30s. Born in 1929, the impresario had already lived a chockful of lifetimes by the mid-sixties.

Rock scribe Joel Selvin runs through a litany of Matthew Katz's past experiences in his rollercoaster saga *Summer Of Love*. According to him, Katz trained as a Jesuit priest, studied ballet, worked as a US Air Force chaplain and slogged in entertainment management. Adding to the list, Jeff Tamarkin claimed he also worked in vaudeville, manufacturing and as a folk singer-guitarist himself. Before scooping up the Jefferson Airplane, Katz managed DJ and budding author Fred Goerner, as well as several folk acts including The Countrymen.

Dressing flamboyantly, Katz sometimes wore a cape and sported a trimmed goatee beard. He would become a polarising figure in the Bay Area scene. On the upside, he energetically pursued a variety of marketing strategies to promote new bands under his wing. For the Airplane, he had thousands of little pins and bumper stickers made, proclaiming, 'Jefferson Airplane Loves You' – a phrase apparently coined by guitarist Kantner.

Katz arranged for young women to walk around at shows, distributing pins and bumper stickers to concertgoers, and took out ads to make the same proclamation in the entertainment pages of the *San Francisco Examiner*. When answering the phone in his office, staff reputedly chimed, 'Jefferson Airplane Loves You,' rather than simply saying, 'Hello.'

Katz even had airplanes towing banners that proudly displayed the catchphrase for all the Bay Area to see. These strategies helped create a buzz in those early days.

But there was a downside. The mercurial – or, some would argue, volatile – Matthew Katz got entangled in conflicts and vendettas with major players on the music scene, including powerhouse promoter Bill Graham. Over time, various musicians in Katz's stable would come to feel he was too opaque in his decision making and bookkeeping.

(This is what happened with some members of the Airplane in the spring and summer of '66, after Skip Spence left. Eventually, he lost his hold of the group and was fired by the end of the summer. Over the next twenty-one years, Katz would joust in court with various members of the Jefferson Airplane over ownership of the band's name and distribution of its royalties.)

Yet in the late summer of 1965, such considerations were not even clouds on the horizon. Katz still commanded the trust, and perhaps even awe, of his young protégés, including a 19-year-old Skip.

At the point he joined, about a month after their live debut, the Airplane was still very much a folk act. As Barry Lewis recalls, 'Jefferson Airplane was not much into rock as yet. They played amplified but had acoustic guitars with pickups, the bass player played an upright bass, much more folk than rock. I remember Signe being very nice and she had a good voice and the band itself had a good sound.'

Yet as impressed as he was, Barry knew he was only filling in temporarily. 'On Saturday night I showed up to play and Marty told me they had found a drummer. I think I played a set or two and then he finished the night; I think it was Skip but I didn't know him at the time – although I did get to know him later on when I was playing drums with [Mill Valley band] Butch Engle and the Styx. Skip liked Butch and would come around gigs to say hello.'

Lewis' recollections place Spence's live debut with the Airplane on Friday 17 September 1965. (If Marty Balin's timeline is accurate, it's likely he was recruited the week before.) Skip's life was about to change forever within a few whirlwind weeks.

The day after his first gig with the Jefferson Airplane, he and his bandmates attended singer Signe Toly's wedding. She was marrying Jerry Anderson, who, like her, was from Portland and was also working as lighting technician at The Matrix. Though Signe herself would not partake of LSD, her bridegroom tripped out at the wedding and so did Skip Spence.

Popular myth tells us Signe's wedding was the first time Skip dropped acid, but Geoff Levin has informed us otherwise. Nevertheless, the Airplane's original singer had sharp memories of how he was that night, which she shared with Jeff Tamarkin nearly four decades later. Signe still vividly recalls Spence spending most of the night 'in a corner, babbling incoherently, off in his own world,' she recounted.[19]

Just days after the wedding, the band were whisked down to Los Angeles for a series of auditions Katz had arranged. It was a busy trip that brought them briefly into the Hollywood orbit.

As bassist Bob Harvey recalls, '[Katz] arranged for us to make a demo at Columbia Records. We were also taken to Capitol Records and introduced to Voyle Gilmore, producer of The Kingston Trio. Voyle took us to lunch at the Brown Derby where we raised a few eyebrows.'[20] But the famous Los Angeles eatery was just a prelude. 'The afternoon got bizarre when we made a trip to Phil Spector's house,' he adds.

By 1965, Spector was already a legendary producer-songwriter, via the Wall of Sound he created at Gold Star Recording Studios, near the corner of Santa Monica and Vine in LA. Spector had created hits for a stable of artists including The Ronettes, The Crystals, Darlene Love and The Righteous Brothers: 'There's No Other (Like My Baby)', 'He's A Rebel', 'Da Doo Ron Ron', 'Then He Kissed Me', 'Be My Baby', 'You've Lost That Lovin' Feelin''. But the 25-year-old producer wasn't just famous for his pop genius – his eccentricity made him infamous.

As Harvey recalls, 'His bodyguards kept us standing in the hall for close to an hour. We were watched by two armed guards until Spector finally came downstairs and went into his study. We were told to set up and play in the hallway while Spector stayed in the study with the door ajar.'

Reaching a saner juncture of his narrative, the bassist adds, 'For me, the highlight of the day was a visit to a soundstage where they were shooting a sequence for *Big Valley*. We stood in the wings among the actors and stagehands watching Barbara Stanwyck do a scene. Some of the actors made insulting and derogatory comments about our long hair and general appearance.'

But the TV show's guest star was more courteous. 'Charles Bronson, who was waiting for his scene, was standing between Skip and myself as we watched the scene being shot. When the insulting remarks were thrown our way, Bronson turned to me and said, "Don't take offence, they're so far down the food chain, they're hurting for people to pay attention to them. They put you down to boost their own egos."

'At that moment I became a lifelong Charles Bronson fan – no matter the film, I always watched him slinging revenge and mayhem, and smiled to myself, feeling that I knew the man to be basically a gentle and thoughtful person whom I have always held in high esteem,' attests Harvey.

After visiting *The Big Valley*'s set, the band trekked back to the Palms, a secluded hotel-lodge in the Hollywood Hills. Too excited to sleep, Bob and Skip ended up writing a song together, partly inspired by their day's experience.

As Harvey explains, 'That night back at the room that Skip and I were sharing, I wrote in my journal, describing the exciting things we had done that day, but with special focus on the scene on the set of *Big Valley*.

'Skip asked what I was writing about… I shared with him my thoughts about Charles Bronson and told him how the phrase "hurting for people" had struck in my head. I read Skip the lines I had jotted down: "Hurting for people, got no time to hate…"'

'Skip went to Paul Kantner's room and borrowed his six-string and we worked out a melody. I kept adding lines and Skip had input to the lyrics. It's my best recollection that the melody and chord changes were mostly Skip's with me making a few suggestions. We spent that first night getting high and writing… 'Hurting For People."[21]

Scooting back to San Francisco, the Airplane jumped into a quick run of gigs, starting with the Coffee Gallery on Wednesday 22 September.

'The Coffee Gallery was on Grant Avenue,' Jorma recollects. 'One of the things that was so cool was that back then many of us moved to San Francisco because it was a cheap place to live. But if you know anything about San Francisco, nothing could be further from the truth today.

'The vibe of places like the Coffee Gallery was tied up with pre-hippie stuff,' he reminisces. 'It was more beatnik stuff. For those of us who had read Kerouac and were trying to break out of that post-Eisenhower mould, that vibe was important. I was introduced to the Coffee Gallery by Tom Hobson. He sort of held court there.'

Hobson was a singer-guitarist buddy of Jorma, who he'd later record his acclaimed *Quah* album with. (It was produced by Jack Casady of the Airplane/Hot Tuna.)

'They had all sorts of performers there. Janis [Joplin] played there, sometimes I played with her. I'm sure Skip would've played there too. Everybody played the Coffee Gallery.'

The night after the Coffee Gallery, the Airplane shared the bill at The Matrix with country-blues master Lightnin' Hopkins. Born in 1912, Hopkins met Blind Lemon Jefferson when he was just 8 and later went on to accompany the Texan blues legend. By 1965, Hopkins had been recording for decades and had become a legend in his own right. For Spence, sharing the bill with him was an honour. The blues had an authenticity for folkies like Skip, a similarly vivid on-the-road aspect in the stories it told.

A few days later, on Monday 27 September, an article on the Jefferson Airplane appeared in a daily paper. Writing for the *San Mateo Times*, Barbara Bladen introduced readers to the new band: 'Jefferson Airplane. Say it again. Jefferson Airplane. It's fun to repeat but what is it? It's a they and they are a wild new singing group who will appear at the Circle Star Theatre tonight [in San Carlos].'[22]

She went on to report on the group's early days, praising its manager along the way: 'Under the careful guidance and excellent business management of Matthew Katz, the young musicians have been making a big noise on the music scene by word of mouth alone. They've played a few clubs in San Francisco, have auditioned for several big recording companies and will return from sessions in Los Angeles today for the Peninsula engagement.'[23]

After a couple of weeks likely eaten up by rehearsing and writing, the band opened for comedian Larry Hankin at The Matrix on Friday 15 October. The following night, they played San Francisco's Longshoremen's Hall. Billed as *A Tribute To Dr. Strange*, the evening featured a handful of local acts, including The Charlatans. (As Marvel Comics' occult hero, Dr. Strange had become a cult figure to many hippies.)

'If you read about the history of San Francisco in the sixties,' Kaukonen reflects, 'The Charlatans really started the scene off in a lot of ways. They were established as a band before the Jefferson Airplane came together, and what an eclectic group of characters they were! But they really had their own sort of a scene together.

'So, they brought a lot of ambience to any gig that they did. Ritchie [Olsen]'s wife owned a second-hand store on Divisadero Street and everybody bought clothes there,' he elaborates. 'The band's whole scene was bound up in this odd, sort of extra-terrestrial family. So, to do a gig with The Charlatans at that point in time was very exciting.'

Dressed in clothing from the late 1800s, the rough-and-tumble group looked like a cross between Victorian dandies and a band of gunslingers from the Wild West. Ritchie Olsen was one of five founding members, and one of only two who stayed to record the band's only LP. (Sadly, it doesn't really showcase the energy they had back when they epitomised the scene in San Francisco.)

Also featuring vocalist/drummer Dan Hicks, The Charlatans played a lengthy stint at the Red Dog Saloon in Virginia City in the summer of 1965. The poster promoting the band's residency is now known as 'The Seed': its unique design helped catapult music posters from mere information providers into a whole new, far more elaborate, psychedelic style. Famously, before playing their first show at the Red Dog, the members of the band dropped acid – a moment some have referred to as the birth of acid rock.

In a 2014 interview with Jeff Clark, Bob Harvey looked back on that memorable show at the Longshoreman's Hall. 'The Great Society with Grace Slick was our opening band. That night is when she and Paul Kantner got together... The poster [for the show] was the very first psychedelic poster. I coloured it on acid. It was black and white, it was just an eight-by-ten black and white flyer. I spent twelve hours on that sucker, on acid,' he reminisces.[24]

That early Jefferson Airplane lineup wouldn't survive the month. Of his last few weeks with the band, Harvey told Clark, 'Matthew Katz, our manager, he paid for the demo to be made at Columbia. He still owns that demo. And he paid Jack Casady for my playing on it! He paid Jack Casady a thousand dollars and he wasn't on it... But Jack's a fine bass player.'[25]

With Jack Casady replacing Bob Harvey in late October, the

Airplane was in its third iteration in just over a month. The lineup would stabilise, remaining the same for about seven months.

It was around this time that Val Pease visited Skip in San Francisco. 'I went down for one of his first tapings with the Jefferson Airplane. It was in the Channel 5 studio. After it was finished Skip said, "We're gonna go over to Haight Street." Well, I'd never heard of Haight Street at that point. There was no such thing as Haight-Ashbury yet. It was there but it wasn't *known* yet.

'So, we went over to a jam session and it was quite an experience for me, being a hillbilly kid from Placerville, California. I was kind of out of my league. I think I was the only one drinking beer there, and they passed a joint to me and I turned it down. Casady was there and I think he was new to the band.'

Thinking back, Pease reflects, 'I didn't know Skip was a drummer, but he was a very talented guy. He could play anything, I think. I never saw him again after that day.'

On Saturday 30 October, the Airplane played its first gig with Casady on bass. 'The Harmon Gymnasium was a gym,' Jorma Kaukonen recalls. 'In those early years, when you played a college or a university and you played in a gym, it wasn't set up for doing concerts, like they might do at a gym today. The PA would've been the same PA that the announcer used to announce sports scores.'

Chuckling, he continues. 'So, it was less than a sonic experience. But we always loved that gig because also at that time there were so many [anti-war] demonstrations going on and Berkeley was really ground zero for that.'

The band had to get rehearsing to find a new equilibrium, with a recording contract within grasp. Skip must have felt the excitement and nervousness as much as anyone. In just a few months he'd shifted from The Topsiders – to The Manes – to performing as half of a duo – to a short-lived rehearsal band – to two different versions of the Jefferson Airplane. To boot, he'd also switched from guitar and vocals to drums.

In terms of his musical life, change was the only constant at that point in time. Amidst all the upheaval, with Pat just a few months away from having their second child, he remained the same capricious free spirit.

'I remember when Skip joined the Airplane,' Pete Grant recalls. 'I used to go up to the city to visit them. A number of them were staying at the same flat not far from the Castro [a neighbourhood in Eureka Valley]. One time their manager gave them each something like $100 or $120 to pay for food, and Skip went out and bought a leather jacket.'

Laughing, Grant adds, 'It was stylish. And it probably lasted much longer.'

CHAPTER SEVEN

THE AIRPLANE TAKES OFF

It was cool and cloudy in the Bay Area throughout the morning of Friday 10 December 1965. If you picked up a copy of the *San Francisco Examiner*, you would have seen numerous headlines on the Vietnam war: 'WAR OF SURVIVAL, [Secretary Of State Dean] RUSK SAYS HERE'; 'MARINES GO ASHORE, TRAP AND ROUT CONG'; 'VIET WAR AIM IS PEACE – RUSK'; 'LBJ PLAN FOR FAST BOMBERS.' At the centre of the front page was a short article titled, 'THE WAR'S TOLL.'

Though the war was a hot topic, another fight – over the freedom of expression – was being waged in the Bay Area. And in a peripheral way, Skip Spence was involved. He would become a part of music history that night.

Spence was in San Francisco that day. Pat was just three weeks away from giving birth. The Jefferson Airplane was scheduled to start recording its first album in Hollywood in less than a week, and set to take part in a new kind of event that evening. Instead of performing at The Matrix, the Airplane was earmarked to join a cavalcade of local and visiting acts at a benefit show at 1805 Geary Boulevard, about a mile directly south of the band's home turf.

A short blurb in the *Examiner* promoted the concert, on page 32: 'The San Francisco Mime Troupe, presenting a concert as their second Appeal Party for continued artistic freedom in the parks, tonight at 9 at Fillmore Auditorium.'

Situated in Lower Pacific Heights, the 1,315-seat venue stood on the southwest corner of Fillmore and Geary. Initially named the Majestic Hall and Academy of Dancing, the building was constructed over fifty years earlier, in 1912.

Over the decades, it had served as a dancehall and roller-skating rink before an entrepreneur took it over in 1954. Dubbing his purchase The Fillmore Auditorium, Charles Sullivan started booking bands for the roomy space.

On this cool December night in 1965, the Airplane and a whole slew of performers – under the guidance of a headstrong theatre-company manager – thrust the venue into entirely new territory. It was an event that would change the course of popular music, and it had been coming for a while.

• • •

It all started a few months earlier, around the time Skip disbanded the short-lived Manes and for a while was without a band. In late July 1965, theatre company the San Francisco Mime Troupe was an active component of the Free Speech Movement and an outspoken supporter of the Civil Rights Movement. It now planned to stage Hermetic mystic Giordano Bruno's *Il Candelaio* in Lafayette Park. Set for Saturday 7 August, the show was to be the latest instalment in the troupe's boundary-pushing series of *commedia dell'arte.*

Displeased with its recent track record, local officials saw things differently. In the following week, the Recreation and Park Commission would deem the performance 'unfit' for a city park, branding the troupe's adaptation as 'lewd and obscene.' This being a resetting of a play that dated from sixteenth-century Europe.

As the performance approached, tensions rose, and on Wednesday 4 August the city took swift action. Writing for the *Examiner* the following day, Harry Johanesen summed it up: 'The Recreation and Park Commission yesterday cancelled the San Francisco Mime Troupe's permit to stage performances in the city parks after denouncing the group's most recent show as indecent, obscene and offensive to both children and adults. The troupe's supporters immediately accused the commission of censorship.'[26]

Set on a collision course with city officials, the players ignored the order and pushed ahead with rehearsals, gearing up for their Saturday performance. Facing a certain showdown with authorities, actor-director Ron Davis addressed a thousand-plus crowd of supporters, curious onlookers and police that Saturday: 'Ladies and Gentlemen, *Il Troupe di Mimo di* San Francisco Presents for your enjoyment this afternoon... AN ARREST!'

Art was not just imitating life; the two were intertwined. Reporting for the *Examiner* the next day, Michael Fallon gleefully described the melee that followed: 'Actor Ron Davis, masked and clad in Italian Renaissance regalia, took a spectacular leap in Lafayette Park yesterday and landed in the arms of two police officers.'[27] Along with a few excited spectators, Davis was arrested.

As this drama was unfolding in Pacific Heights, Skip Spence was without a band but just a few weeks from crossing paths with his three future Airplane bandmates at The Matrix. From August to November, as Ron Davis awaited his trial, the Airplane landed in Los Angeles to record some demos. Bassist Jack Casady played his first gig with the band on Saturday 30 October, at Harmon Gymnasium at UC Berkeley. At that point, Davis' court date was just two days away.

During his 1 November trial, Judge Fitzgerald Ames soberly instructed jurors, 'the only factual issue for you to decide is whether Ronald Davis did in truth in fact maintain any performance in Lafayette Park on 7 August without first having obtained a permit to do so.' After deliberating for forty-five minutes, Davis was found guilty. On hearing his verdict, the director protested, 'I object. I don't think the issue of free speech was ever considered here.'[28]

With the performer facing the possibility of six months in jail and a $500 fine, Bill Graham, the troupe's plucky business manager, quickly put together an event to help raise funds for his appeal. Dubbed *The Benefit For San Francisco Mime Troupe – Appeal Party I*, the show was held the following Saturday at Calliope Warehouse, the theatre company's loft studio in the South of Market District. A handbill advertising the show proclaimed: 'The trial settled nothing. The Mime Troupe is determined to fight until the parks are returned to their only "owners," the people of San Francisco.'

Sharing the bill with the Airplane at the event was an array of local and faraway talent, including Beat poet Lawrence Ferlinghetti; San Francisco improv comedy group The Committee; two acts from New York: anarchic jugband The Fugs and folk multi-instrumentalist Sandy Bull; and The John Handy Quintet, a saxophone-led modern jazz group.

'That was the first time we met Bill Graham,' Jorma Kaukonen explains. 'At that time, you'd just go to a gig and we were so thrilled just to have a place to play.'

In only its second show with Casady, the Airplane had clearly moved beyond its acoustic roots. By this point, the band was pushing into the electric-folk territory of The Byrds. At least three numbers in the set were captured on tape that night; Graham would play those songs, probably the earliest live recordings of the Airplane, whilst guesting on a radio show a couple of years later.

The band was energetic and polished, weaving through a four-minute rendition of Balin's 'It's No Secret,' a nearly five-minute cover of John D. Loudermilk's 'Tobacco Road' (which, though only five years old, was well on its way to becoming a blues classic), and a Balin-Kantner original (and soon-to-be-B-side), 'Runnin' Round This World.' This was a group ready for the studio.

Following that 6 November benefit, the Airplane hunkered down to write and rehearse. In just under six weeks, they were set to record their first album at RCA Studios in Hollywood.

Bill Graham, meanwhile, masterminded another, bigger, fund-raising event. Which brings us to the show at The Fillmore Auditorium on the night of Friday 10 December 1965...

A few days before the event, the *San Francisco Examiner* donated ad space to support the concert, titled *SF Mime Troupe Appeal II – For Continued Freedom In The Parks.* Starting at 10 p.m., a hodgepodge of acts played throughout the night and into the morning, finally wrapping up at dawn. Performing alongside the Jefferson Airplane were The John Handy Quintet (again), the Gentlemen's Band, the Mystery Trend, The Great Society and others.

The show was a resounding success, much more so than antic-ipated, leading Graham to envision a career in music promotion. The following year, he'd leave his role as business manager of the SF Mime Troupe and take up promotion full time, with The Fillmore Auditorium serving as his marquee.

America's ballrooms were a perfect fit for the events that rock shows were becoming. Walls of amplifiers lined the stage and soni-cally blanketed the audience. Colourful light shows accompanied music that took listeners to new places. It was a world away from spaces like bowling alleys, makeshift bandstands or high-school gyms – which did not instantly disappear as music venues, but gradually faded over time.

Playing drums with the Airplane that night, Skip Spence was present at that first rock show at the Fillmore. It was the birth of a new age in popular music, the ground zero of the rock ballroom.

Less than a week after the benefit, the Airplane journeyed down to LA and started recording its first album at RCA Victor's Music Center of the World, at 6363 Sunset Boulevard. Entering RCA on Thursday 16 December, Skip just missed crossing paths with one of his favourite bands: only eight days before, The Rolling Stones had finished recording '19th Nervous Breakdown', having worked on their *Aftermath* album from 3-8 December.

As Kaukonen muses, 'Being such a huge Stones fan, just to be able to be in that same zone, it was very exciting to us at the time.

71

We sort of inherited Dave Hassinger, the engineer [who had been working with the Stones, among many others]. At that time, we were such novices in terms of the music business.'

Still, once in the studio, the Airplane quickly got down to business. In just three days, from 16-18 December, with manager Matthew Katz and his friend Tommy Oliver as producers, the group cut no less than fourteen tracks. Yet nearly all those cuts were set aside.

In fact, only 'It's No Secret,' Balin's early signature piece and the band's first single, would appear on *Jefferson Airplane Takes Off*. Six others – 'Chauffeur Blues', 'Tobacco Road', 'Let's Get Together', 'Let Me In' and 'Run Around', the censored version of 'Runnin' Round This World' with the 'trip' reference removed – were all reworked when the musicians returned to the studio in February, and again in March.

Six other cuts were either set aside or reworked completely. But they offer unique glimpses into the possibilities the band was pursuing at the time. Casady opens 'The Other Side Of This Life' with a powerful bassline on which Kaukonen layers energetic runs, as Kantner punctuates it all with his own rhythmic accents. Spence would later expand on this sort of guitar interplay with his next band, Moby Grape.

The Airplane revisited a Dylan track it had been working on for a while, 'Lay Down Your Weary Tune.' (The Byrds had just released their own version of the song on the *Turn! Turn! Turn!* album, on 6 December.) 'In The Midnight Hour' was also recorded in those whirlwind sessions. Written earlier that year by Wilson Pickett and Booker T. & the M.G.'s guitarist Steve Cropper, the soul song was already acquiring classic status.

Sherry Spence recalls her brother taking the spotlight in live shows with a drum solo during 'In The Midnight Hour.' She'd always hoped the Airplane would put the song on an album, but it wasn't to be.

Also recorded during those December sessions was 'Embryonic Journey,' a Kaukonen number the band rerecorded for its second album. 'High Flyin' Bird' takes sad snapshots of tragedy as the avian title creature flies high above the world. At two and a half minutes, the song is like a compact folk ballad.

(While the Airplane left this evocative early recording on the shelf, the band performed the song at the Monterey Pop Festival a year and a half later, in June 1967, and finally released it on the 1974 compilation *Early Flight*.)

According to Kaukonen, it was a steep learning curve for the band. 'From the LA standard,' he explains, 'we were rank amateurs in terms of working in a studio, when we started out. But Skip always had a lot of great ideas. He was just such an interesting guy. I'm a singer but I don't sing harmony, and Skip had all that stuff going on within him. He was a great lead singer and he also understood harmony, so he was very productive working in the studio with guys like Paul and Marty who were all about the harmonies. In retrospect, aside from Skip's personal idiosyncrasies, he had the potential to be one of the more professional guys in the band.'

Heading back to San Francisco as Christmas approached, Spence and his bandmates had a quiet couple of weeks save for a 29 December show at The Matrix. It was during this time, on Sunday 2 January 1966, that his wife Pat gave birth to Adam Paul Spence, the couple's second son.

Adam, like Aaron, is a biblical name. Paul was his given middle name in honour of Kantner, Spence's close friend in the Airplane. But his father didn't have much time to spend with the family. The band had a whole slew of shows and recording dates already pencilled into its calendar.

Six days later, on Saturday 8 January, the Airplane played a gig in a landmark venue. Located at the corner of Polk and Turk, California Hall is a couple of blocks north of San Francisco City Hall, just east of the Fillmore District. Built in 1912, it was funded by the city's German Association to serve its fellow immigrant German community, at that time centred on Polk Strasse (now Polk Street).

On that evening in early 1966, the Airplane shared the bill with hard-rockin' folk legends The Charlatans. (Spence would return to the hall with the Airplane three months later and again in the autumn, with Moby Grape.)

After the California Hall show, the Airplane returned to The Matrix for three nights, on 9, 11 and 12 January. Midway through the month the band trekked north, all the way to Vancouver for its first shows outside the United States.

On the weekend of 14-16 January, they played the old Kitsilano Theatre (then the Russian Theatre), sharing the bill with local folk-rock outfit the Tom Northcott Trio. But a 7 January *Vancouver Sun* article warned readers: 'No drinking will be allowed on the premises and a tough scrutiny will be maintained at the door to keep out rowdies and liquor-packing enthusiasts.'[29]

Jefferson Airplane played the mix of folk, blues, soul and rock'n'roll they'd been laying down in the studio, plus such songs as 'Baby What You Want Me To Do', 'Bringing Me Down', 'I'll Feel a Whole Lot Better', 'And I Like It' and 'Go To Her.'

Although everyone was travelling on a very low budget, Kaukonen has fond memories of the trip. 'When Skip and Signe were in the band we went up to Vancouver, BC, and did some shows there,' he recalls. 'We were up there for a little while. In those days we only had enough money for Signe and our manager to get a hotel room and the rest of us couch-surfed. I can't remember the names of the people we stayed with, God bless them, but Skip and I were at *somebody's* house.

'I think the Tom Northcott Trio was on the show. They were very professional. With the exception of Jack, when he got into the band, none of us – including Skip – had been, "professional rock musicians,"' he happily concedes. 'We were folkies, and the Tom Northcott Trio was slick, and they had a bunch of great songs. I wonder whatever happened to Tom.[30] When I think about that trip, I just remember how welcoming the music and art scene was up in Vancouver.'

February was another busy month. Over the first weekend, the band joined in on a string of shows at the Fillmore, billed as *Sights And Sounds Of The Trips Festival!* Organised by Bill Graham, they followed on the heels of a similar event the previous month. As the *Examiner* announced: 'TRIPS FESTIVAL, the big blowout two weekends ago, is going to be repeated today in a similar affair at 9 p.m. at The Fillmore Auditorium, with the Jefferson Airplane performing. Once again, lighting and sound effects will be employed during this bizarre dance-concert.'[31]

The original *Trips Festival* brought together rock bands, film-makers, experimental and political theatre groups, dance companies and light-show artists. Held from 21-23 January 1966, the event was put together by a conglomeration of countercultural figures including Stewart Brand, publisher of the *Whole Earth Catalogue*, Ramón Sender, co-founder of the San Francisco Tape Music Center, Ken Kesey and the Merry Pranksters.

By this point, *One Flew Over The Cuckoo's Nest* author Kesey had already organised several 'Acid Tests' where participants imbibed the still-legal LSD – the first of which was held two months earlier, on 27 November 1965. While the February follow-up event at the Fillmore was not as elaborate as its predecessor, it was Graham's first commercial show.

With the Filmore, going to a concert became something totally different. It was immersive, with higher quality sound, a colourful light show and a great view of the band on a full stage. (And of course hallucinogens were a part of this for many concertgoers.)

A couple of days later, the Airplane started a five-night stint at The Matrix (from 8-13 February). On 16 and 19 February, they headed back for more sessions at RCA, quickly laying down two tracks.

Then the musicians made the jaunt back to San Francisco for a Family Dog Presentation set up by promoter Chet Helms. Dubbed *A Tribal Stomp*, the show was held at the Fillmore on Saturday 19 February. Sharing the bill with the Airplane that night was a newly formed group called Big Brother and the Holding Company – five months away from Janis Joplin becoming their lead vocalist.

The handbill for the show was designed by Chet Helms, in collaboration with Wes Wilson. One of Wilson's earliest works, it features his classic lettering style – integrated into the art itself, blending into the image in the picture – along with a First Nations theme. (Over the next few months, Wilson would design the first ten Family Dog posters, as well as forty-five of the first fifty posters used by Bill Graham. The beautiful vibrancy of their designs were part of the whole music-light show-LSD trip experience.)

Two days after the show, the band got back to work on the album. During six days in the studio, the Airplane cut a total of seven songs: 'Runnin' Round This World' (version two), 'And I Like It', 'Bringing Me Down', 'Chauffeur Blues' (version two), 'Tobacco Road' (version two), 'Let's Get Together' (version two) and 'Don't Slip Away'. Cut on Monday 28 February, 'Don't Slip Away' was the first song by Skip Spence (in this case co-written with Marty Balin) to be recorded.[32]

To Kaukonen, Spence and Balin complemented one another as songwriters. 'But Skip straddled a lot of different universes. A lot of stuff that Skip did could've been like Flying Burrito Brothers stuff, or country rock, had he gone that way – but he could just do anything that he really wanted to do. I think he and Marty made a good team because Skip made it very *au courant*.'

Six of the seven songs recorded that February appeared on the band's debut, while 'Runnin' Round This World' would serve as B-side of the band's first single, 'It's No Secret'. But one line on the B-side – 'The nights I've spent with you have been fantastic trips' – caused RCA execs anxiety. Worried about its possible drug reference, the label would pull the whole song from *Jefferson Airplane Takes Off* before the LP's August release.

When the February sessions ended, the Airplane trekked back to the Bay Area for more shows. On the weekend of 4-5 March they played the Fillmore, sharing the bill with the up-and-coming

Quicksilver Messenger Service. Six months earlier, just before he was recruited into the Airplane, Skip had rehearsed with an early version of Quicksilver. Had things unfolded differently, he might have found himself in the band.

'Quicksilver is another one of those interesting bands,' Kaukonen reflects. 'They just had that energy and even though some of the guys in the band, like [bassist David] Freiberg, had come up as folkies, [lead guitarist] John Cipollina was always his own artist as a rock musician. I can see how Skip could've wound up being in that band in a parallel universe. They just had so much talent anyway and nobody sounded like them.'

Back in Hollywood, the Airplane returned to the studio to wrap up work on the album. Arriving at RCA on the Ides of March, the band once again missed The Rolling Stones by just a few days. Over four studio days (15, 16, 18 and 21 March), they cut 'Come Up The Years', 'Let Me In' (version two), 'Run Around' and 'Blues From An Airplane'.

Co-written by Spence and Balin, 'Blues For An Airplane' is simultaneously gritty and dreamy – with Spence's pounding on the drums matching Casady's rumbling bass, as Balin and Anderson glide over the rhythm with their gentle harmonies.

'Marty and Skip brought us the song when it was done so I wasn't a part of the creative process,' Kaukonen recalls. 'One of the things I do remember about Skip is that he was always an inviting person. He wasn't a songwriter who said, "Well, I need to write this song by myself." He played very well with others. And I think that had Skip not been involved in the writing of that it would've been very different.

'You know, 'Blues From An Airplane' is a very interesting little song, it's a very atypical folk-rocker, or whatever you want to call it. I think that there's no question that that uniqueness is Skip's footprint – because Marty, may he rest in peace, was a little more traditional in the way he structured songs. But Skip could go in a lot of different directions.'

77

What Jorma says is very true. Skip Spence's songwriting, his words, his music, would veer off in many directions, yet still somehow hold together. Not just across his entire output, but also within individual songs (as with, for example, 'Omaha').

While 'Blues From An Airplane' was eventually sequenced as the lead-off on *Jefferson Airplane Takes Off*, 'Runnin' Round This World' met a different fate. With RCA apprehensive about its lyric, the Airplane had to edit the track in the summertime. Summing up the absurdity, pioneer rock critic Ralph Gleason metaphorically mocked in late July, 'RCA Victor has pushed the Jefferson Airplane into redoing a lyric and wants them to cut their hair.'[33]

Thinking back, Jorma can't recall the band setting many songs aside. 'Many artists go into the studio with a surplus of songs. I wasn't writing in those days, but I remember that the songs that were brought to our rehearsals came as finished beings. Each one was like a completed universe.

'You know, nature abhors a vacuum, and as soon as that vacuum was filled we were done recording.'

CHAPTER EIGHT

AWOL

When recording wrapped on the first day of spring, the Airplane still had no time to rest. As March unfolded, they played the University of Santa Clara, the Athletic Field at UC Santa Cruz and the Civic Auditorium in San José.

The San José gig fell on the last Saturday of the month. It was likely during this jaunt to the South Bay, as the band was trekking around Skip's old stomping grounds, that he reconnected with his friend Robbie Levin.

'I can't remember what the circumstances were,' says Robbie, 'but it was my first time seeing Skip in a while. He was with the Airplane at that time. And he had this jacket on. It was a beautiful leather jacket with these airplane wings on it. It sticks in my mind because I could never afford to buy a jacket like that. It was from a famous clothing store in San Francisco that we used to go to, all the rock musicians used to buy their clothes there.

'I complimented him on that jacket, and he just took it off and gave it to me. We were about the same height and build, just a couple of tall, skinny, rock musicians.'

With the release of *Jefferson Airplane Takes Off* still a few months away, the band continued to gig throughout the spring. Over the first weekend of April, they played the Fillmore with Quicksilver

Messenger Service and The Hedds, both of which included some of Skip's musician friends. Running from two to six in the afternoon on 3 April, the last of three concerts marked the first Sunday afternoon rock show at The Fillmore Auditorium.

Catching up with old friends may have reminded Spence of his days performing as a frontman. In a couple of weeks he'd turn 20. Perhaps it underlined how much he still wanted to lead a band. He'd never really intended to be a drummer, after all. He'd penned a few songs with Marty Balin, but he was still stuck behind a drum kit.

'You know, he never did talk about [playing the guitar],' demurs Jorma Kaukonen. 'I know he did some playing on *Surrealistic Pillow* [the Airplane's second LP], but when he was in the band, I don't think he ever mentioned playing the guitar – not to me, anyway. I mean, he never *didn't* play the guitar because he always had it with him, but he assumed the role of being our drummer until he disappeared. Otherwise, he would've stayed our drummer and we wouldn't've gotten Spencer [Dryden].'

Perhaps Skip Spence started to consider his options that spring. While he was in a band with steady gigs and an LP coming out, he was surrounded by guitarists and songwriters. Jefferson Airplane had no need for *another* guitarist. The random musical reunion that weekend may have prompted him to consider just who he could be, to seriously think about going out on his own.

Four days later, the Airplane returned to the Fillmore for a show that combined rock music, literature and politics. Sharing the bill that night were two well-known poetic voices: Lawrence Ferlinghetti, San Francisco Beat poet and publisher, and Andrei Voznesensky, one of the Soviet Union's 'Children of the '60s'. Ferlinghetti was a romantic anarchist who realised, nonetheless, that social democracy was a more realistic aim. Voznesensky had become an international celebrity, due to his spoken-word performances and Soviet leader Nikita Khrushchev's vehement denunciation of him a few years earlier.[34] What both shared was an anti-establishment stance in their respective societies.

The following night, the band shared the bill with Quicksilver Messenger Service again, this time at California Hall. Over the rest of the month, the Airplane played shows at Veterans Memorial Hall in Santa Rosa, Harmon Gymnasium at UC Berkeley and The Fillmore Auditorium. (Also on the bill at that last show was blues legend Ligntnin' Hopkins.)

In a short article published on 15 April, *KRLA Beat* asked Skip to describe the music of Jefferson Airplane and he simply replied, 'We all play our own thing. We play our own thing together and it turns out to be one thing.'[35] Still, his days in the band were numbered.

At the end of April or beginning of May, we approach the point when Skip Spence parted ways with the Jefferson Airplane. What exactly happened between them remains cloaked in legend. As far as received wisdom goes, Skip went off to Mexico for an extended holiday without telling his bandmates. This was the general narrative given by Marty Balin in interviews.

According to Selvin's visceral history, *Summer Of Love*, Spence crossed paths with Martha Wax and a couple of her friends while hanging out at the Russian River one weekend.[36] Somehow, the idea of trekking to Mexico transformed into a plan and he apparently agreed to join them on the spur of the moment.

Martha was the 16-year-old daughter of Sausalito city councilor (and later mayor) Melvin S. Wax. It was her who had apparently first personally introduced Skip to the Airplane in September 1965, as she was in the park that day.

In short order, the group drove to Mexico in a van for some R&R. Apparently, Martha had known Skip for a while... and whether he went along with her and another young couple, or a small group, depends on who's telling the story.[37]

According to Balin's version, Spence then missed a show (although it might have been a rehearsal – or possibly a handful of rehearsals) and was promptly fired from the band. As he told Tamarkin in 1993, 'During the drug days he just got too drugged. Too many pretty women. He just went off one day. We went to a gig and somebody said, "Hey, Skippy went to Mexico." I said, "No, we got a gig tonight." But I found out he had gone to Mexico, drugged out, so we stopped his bank account.'[38]

In more recent years, bassist Jack Casady matter-of-factly explained: 'Skip was really multi-talented, with a good energy about him. He wanted to write songs and play guitar. But the Airplane had enough of those people already.'[39]

A slightly different story was hinted at in an *Oakland Tribune* article published in November 1967. When journalist Peggy King asked why he left the Airplane, Spence answered, 'I wanted to get back to guitar.' At which point his Moby Grape bandmate, bassist Bob Mosley, added, 'And wasn't Marty always giving you this... you know, thing?' To which Skip replied, 'Yeah, yeah.'[40] Friction had been present, even if he wasn't keen on talking about it.

So what really happened? Perhaps the true story was a mish-mash of all of this. Maybe he did go on a random holiday which irked his bandmates. Perhaps he was also tired of playing the drums, wanting to get back to the guitar and become a frontman again. Maybe Spence locked horns with Balin after he went AWOL. Of course, it's also possible he trekked down to Mexico knowing full well the trip would precipitate his exit from the band...

Whatever went down when Skip was fired, he apparently agreed to stay on until a replacement could be found. In the meantime, the band carried on.

Over the first weekend of May 1966, the Airplane returned to the Fillmore. The following Saturday, they played at an event titled *UCSC Spring Thing* at Coconut Grove in Santa Cruz.

Next, in a total break from the counterculture, they played a poolside charity fundraiser called *Peninsula Volunteers 'Step 'N Time' Gala*, held at the Cabana Hotel in Palo Alto on Sunday 22 May. As recounted a few days later in the *San Mateo Times*, a 'two-hour delay began with a missing microphone. Once found, the Jefferson Airplane, a rock'n'roll sextet, played for the guests who crowded around the pool in the late afternoon sun.'[41]

A high-school student who attended the event, David Biasotti, later described (to rock writer Bruno Ceriotti) how the Airplane opened with instrumentals. Skip chucked his drumsticks into a crowd of approximately 600 and announced he was leaving the band at the end of the show.

Just five days after that poolside performance, on Saturday 27 May, Signe Anderson, as she now was, gave birth to a daughter she'd name Lilith. Not only was Skip leaving the band, but so was Signe – though her departure was on behalf of her family and would take months to unfold.

Over the next week, the Airplane played the Civic Auditorium in Santa Cruz, followed by a six-night run at its Matrix home base. It's unlikely that Signe performed at any of those shows, with full duties taken by her co-vocalists Marty Balin and Paul Kantner.

Sharing the bill during that run of shows was The Great Society, who had a tight, powerful, pop-folk sound. Much of their power was generated by the heavy-hitting vocals of future Airplane singer Grace Slick.

At this time, Katz and Balin were at loggerheads. Questions about finances, such as advance monies from RCA and various expenses, as well as scheduling decisions, were the subject of ongoing dispute.

Amidst persistent confusion and growing suspicion, Katz's relationship with the Airplane sailed straight into choppy water. Mistrust reared its ugly head more and more.

Throughout this tense time, Katz arranged for Spence's replacement, Spencer Dryden, to audition and then fly up to San Francisco. The night after the last show at The Matrix, on Monday 6 June, the Airplane played at a private event for the Republican Alliance at the Sheraton Palace Hotel in San Francisco. It was Dryden's first performance with the band, but other members were infuriated by Katz aligning them with the Republican Party.

Speaking with *Hit Parader* a year and a half later, Dryden offered his thoughts on Spence's exit. 'Skip Spence was the drummer with the Airplane for about the first nine months of the group's existence,' he explained to the teen readership. 'He was formerly a rhythm guitar player and songwriter and he liked to sing. He'd had some drums in high school… Skip was developing beautifully, but he just wasn't happy being back at the drums. He wanted to be up front singing and playing a guitar. He eventually left. He's with Moby Grape now, singing, playing guitar and having a ball. It's a very good group.'[42]

'Well, my recollection is that one day Skip was there and the next day he was gone. According to rumour, he went off to Mexico with,' Kaukonen pauses, 'well, he *did* go to Mexico, and he did it with no advanced warning. And we had gigs.

'So, Matthew Katz, who was our manager at the time, brought Spencer [Dryden] up. I don't recall any overlap between Skip leaving and Spencer joining the band. In retrospect, we finished the record and we were planning on doing some gigs, and Skip was gone. Just like that.'

He'd briefly shone during his time in the Airplane. As Joel Selvin notes, 'Skip was bright and lively, and he cut a real character – and that was at a time when there were some *real* characters around… to stand out among people like Kantner and Jorma Kaukonen and Marty Balin, you know that's a lot of personality in one room!'

In June 1966, Spence was just over 20 years old. Over the previous twelve months he'd briefly played in The Other Side, formed and disbanded The Manes, performed as a folk duo with Billy Dean Andrus, rehearsed with a group that became Quicksilver Messenger Service and for nine months played in – and recorded the debut album with – the original Jefferson Airplane.

During that whirlwind year, his second son, Adam, was also born. As the baby approached six months of age, older brother Aaron neared his 2nd birthday. The release date of *Jefferson Airplane Takes Off* also fast approached, but their father found himself on his own again.

The summer of '66 was a time of uncertainty. It was also the beginning of an entirely new chapter of his life.

CHAPTER NINE

WHAT'S BIG AND PURPLE AND LIVES IN THE OCEAN?

Some call the summer of '66 the *real* Summer of Love. Hundreds of bands were scattered around the Bay Area, still rehearsing and finalising their lineups. Many were jamming, diving into a style of music that came to be known as psychedelic. Some were living together; nearly everyone was intermingling, venturing out to each other's shows, blending folk and blues and jazz and pop and soul, or whatever else they could summon up. Genres were suddenly becoming less distinct, as lines were blurred and styles were fused. Songs were also getting longer and longer.

Nearly everyone in the Bay Area was still unsigned in the summer of 1966: The Charlatans, The Grateful Dead, Quicksilver Messenger Service, Big Brother and the Holding Company, Sly and the Stoners (later Sly and the Family Stone), Sopwith Camel...

But Skip Spence's previous band, the Jefferson Airplane, was due to release its debut on RCA in mid-August. The dream of inking a contract with a major record label was now a viable possibility for the ever-growing cadre of Bay Area bands.

At the venues, Chet Helms' Family Dog Productions was just a few months old and still getting off the ground at The Avalon Ballroom. Bill Graham was still sorting out his license to regularly host rock shows at the Fillmore. Light shows at concerts had been around for a short while, but were still a relatively new idea. The whole notion of the ballroom rock show as a multimedia, multi-sensory, immersive experience was still taking form.

It was during this summer that Moby Grape came to be. When Spence exited the Airplane, he and manager Matthew Katz hatched a plan for a new band. As a naturally flamboyant showman, no longer would he be anchored at the back of the stage, hidden behind a drum kit.

Looking to the South Bay, Skip's first step was to approach an old friend from his folk days, young bassist Robbie Levin. Although Robbie was excited at the possibility of collaborating with his mentor again, he had numerous commitments to consider – not least playing bass in his older brother's group.

'Skip asked me to join his band,' he explains. 'But when he was starting to put together Moby Grape, I was already with People! I would've been 17 then. I remember that I wouldn't've been able to finish my senior year of high school. He hadn't found [bassist Bob] Mosley yet.'

Levin continues, 'I would see [Skip] afterwards, but he was playing and I was playing. We were both busy.' Pausing for a moment, he adds, 'I always feel a sort of loss that I never got to do that gig with him.'

So, Spence started to look beyond the Bay Area. In the early summer, when Katz was searching for Skip's replacement in the Airplane, he'd heard about a Los Angeles-based drummer named Bob Newkirk. Hopeful, Spence flew down to LA to check out the musician and his current band.

• • •

By the time Newkirk heard from Katz, the drummer had been gigging mostly around Southern California for about a year. The previous summer, he had joined up with guitarists Peter Lewis and

Ron Morgan, and bassist Tony Bellamy, to form a folk-rock outfit called Peter and the Wolves. Frontman Lewis was the son of Oscar-winning actress Loretta Young.

Formed in the summer of '65, Peter and the Wolves played early gigs at the Golden Embers in August. It was a San Bernardino club that featured go-go dancers in its Surf A-Go-Go Room and exotic dancers in its cocktail lounge.

Trekking east to Palm Springs the following month, the young band performed at a back-to-school dance party at the Desert Inn Hotel. Toiling throughout the autumn and winter, the band landed a residency at Gazzarri's on Sunset Strip in early 1966.

Unimpressed with the venue, Lewis later told music journalist Jud Cost it was 'definitely the uncoolest club on the Strip. It was mostly people there with sharkskin suits and their hair slicked back, and you knew if you had long hair you had to be cool or they'd kick your ass. It was a different kind of place. A lot of places Peter and the Wolves played were owned by these sub-mobsters, local enforcers. It was hard to get your money.'[43]

When the residency at Gazzarri's finished, the quartet trekked up to the Bay Area in April to play a weeklong run at Frenchy's. Located on Mission Boulevard in Hayward, Frenchy's was the only rock venue between Berkeley and San José.

By that point, Ron Morgan had left the group to join The Electric Prunes and Terry Furlong had stepped in on guitar. The following month, they played a short run at The Casbah in Van Nuys – but before those shows, Bob Newkirk exited the group to join The Joel Scott Hill Trio, a San Diego band that had local chart success with a garage-rock rendition of The Coasters' 'I'm A Hog For You'. 'That's sort of what broke up Peter and the Wolves,' Lewis told Cost. 'I hadn't been really satisfied with it anyway, because I was starting to write songs but nobody else was.'[44]

Born in Naples, Texas, in 1939, Joel Scott Hill had been active in the California music scene for years. He had a minor instrumental hit, the Duane Eddy-esque 'Caterpillar Crawl,' with The Strangers in 1959.

Following that, the group changed its name to Joel Scott Hill and the Strangers, then downsized to The Joel Scott Hill Trio in the spring of 1965. During that year, Hill's band featured future Turtle Johnny Barbata on drums, Lee Michaels on guitar and future Moby Grape bassist Bob Mosley.

Although Kent Dunbar stepped in to replace Newkirk on drums, he soon left Peter and the Wolves to join up with the future Love guitarist's Nooney Rickett 4. With the proverbial writing on the wall, Peter Lewis quietly folded his band.

In a short while, he found himself invited to join what remained of The Joel Scott Hill Trio – a trio now reduced to a duo. As Lewis later recalled, 'Finally the drummer [Newkirk] called me and told me that Joel wanted to play with me to get this folk-rock thing going. So they came over, but we didn't have a bass player. And Joel said, "I know this really great bass player, Bob Mosley, but he's nuts." And I said, "Well, shit man, nuts is happening."'[45]

San Diego-born Bob Mosley had formed The Misfits in 1962, with Eddy Dunn and Earl Steely on guitar and Ron Armstrong on drums. Quickly becoming the go-to opener for visiting acts in San Diego, The Misfits supported such names as Roy Orbison, Bobby Freeman and Bobby Day. In 1964, the band released a pair of singles, including 'This Little Piggy' b/w 'Lost Love' on Imperial Records, but neither charted. After opening for The Rolling Stones towards the end of the year, Steely got married and left the band. Rather than replacing him, they called it a day.[46]

At that point Mosley joined up with Hill. Through the spring, summer and early fall of 1965, the trio played residencies at The Action Club, LA, and the Whisky A Go Go, Sunnyvale. Later that autumn, they started a residency at the Tiger-A-Go-Go Club, at San Francisco Airport's Hilton Inn. Throughout the run of shows, he was gaining a reputation as a powerful, soulful singer/bassist.

Then one night in early 1966, two musicians arrived at the Tiger to check out his performance.

'I played in Joel Scott Hill's band up and down the Bay Area for about a year in '65,' Bob Mosley explains. 'We were playing at the Tiger-A-Go-Go at the airport in San Francisco when two guys showed up to watch the show. It was Don Stevenson and Jerry Miller. They had a jazz/R&B band called The Frantics and they asked me to join their band, and I said yes.'

By the time Seattle expats Stevenson and Miller tracked him down in early 1966, The Frantics had been shuffling around the Bay Area for over half a year as an R&B trio with a B3 Hammond organ. Somewhat of an institution, they had been a solid Northwest Coast outfit since the mid-fifties.

Miller joined the group in '64. Then, in July '65, as the band was trekking south to start a residency on Broadway in San Francisco, Nebraska-born drummer John Keliohor was seriously injured in a car accident.

Looking to the Seattle music scene, Don Stevenson was quickly recruited to fill in. Keliohor, meanwhile, once he'd recovered from a ruptured spleen, joined The Daily Flash, a band Stevenson had previously been poised to join.

In 1966 gigs began to dry up and The Frantics considered changing their style. Early in the year, sax player Bob Hosko left and suddenly the group was down to three. Ready to shift from pure R&B to a more psychedelic pop sound, Stevenson, Miller and keyboardist Chuck Schoning started to look for a bassist for the new lineup – which led them to the Tiger-A-Go-Go...

In the springtime, The Frantics headed into San Mateo to record a single for Action Records. The A-side was an R&B/pop melding called 'Human Monkey,' with a powerful vocal by Mosley, while the B-side was a ballad Miller and Stevenson co-wrote titled 'Someday.' As fans of The Beatles and The Byrds, co-vocalists Don and Jerry were very much into harmonies – but in Bob they'd found a potential frontman.

From Tuesday 17 May to Thursday 7 July, the band played a residency at the Drag'on A' Go Go. 'It had a stage that was elevated about fifty inches off the ground. It had a theatre curtain you could pull around the stage. It had a dancefloor and tables all around the dancefloor,' Stevenson remembers.

'We did something like ten sets a night there,' Miller recalls. 'It was in the days when we all had the same suits. And we did everybody's tunes. We did The Righteous Brothers and The Beatles. We did The Rolling Stones. It was like a nightclub. It might've held about 300.'

'One time,' Stevenson, adds, 'this guy was just irritating the hell out of Mosley and threatening him. The stage was elevated so Mosley just took his bass and bashed the guy in the head with it. The people in the club were on Mosley's side and just threw that guy out of the club.'

'The band fell apart when that gig ended,' Bob himself explains. 'I went back to San Diego. I played a couple of shows with The Vejtables around that time, and not long after that Joel asked me to join a band he was starting in LA.'

As the summer of '66 unfolded, Stevenson, Miller and Schoning hung on to rehearse as Luminous Marsh Gas. The band's psychedelic name was apparently a nod to author and counterculture icon Ken Kesey, LSD's Pied Piper.[47]

'We used to rehearse in San Mateo,' Jerry Miller recollects. 'It was a house that me and Don rented for 199 bucks. It had a swimming pool and about thirteen rooms.'

Instead of joining Luminous Marsh Gas in July, Mosley played a few gigs with Bay Area band The Vejtables and then headed with them to Hollister, California, to perform. Around that same time, Joel Scott Hill invited him down to LA to join the band he was starting up with drummer Bob Newkirk and guitarist Peter Lewis.

As Lewis later told Craig Morrison, 'So he [Joel Scott Hill] called Bob and I went out to pick him up at the airport. I remember Bob sitting at the bar with a goatee, completely unhip for those days, with his hair combed back and cut real short, kind of a military guy, with white Bermuda shorts, a tennis shirt and sneakers, drinking beer with his bass leaning up against the bar... I had to take him someplace, so we got into my car, driving back to Hollywood, and he hadn't said anything to me. Halfway to Hollywood, he says, "I can sing anything up to high C and sing like a motherfucker. What can you do?"[48]

Though the group had neither a manager nor any shows lined up, the four musicians already had their minds on recording. Rehearsing in earnest, the band booked a few hours of studio time to cut a demo. 'We recorded a song called 'Fall On You',' Mosley recalls. It was an original written by Lewis.

At that point, Katz called Newkirk and arranged to fly down to LA to check out the band. Suitably impressed, the manager offered to fly the four musicians up to San Francisco to rehearse with Skip Spence. Feeling uncertain, Joel Scott Hill decided to stay behind in LA.

Recalling the band's next step, Lewis later told Jud Cost, 'So Bob and I went with the drummer [Bob Newkirk], and Joel didn't go. When we got there we met Skippy because he'd just left the Airplane to go with Matthew. And we played together and started halfway looking around for another guitar player... For some reason Skippy and Bob didn't like the drummer, Bob Newkirk from Peter and the Wolves.'[49]

As Mosley recalls, 'I called up Ron Armstrong, who was the drummer in The Misfits, and asked him to come up to the Bay Area. He was in San Diego at the time, and he was in a band and didn't want to leave.'

With some regret, Ron Armstrong later noted, 'In 1967, back in San Diego, Bob Mosley called me from San José, California, and asked if I would like to drive up and play drums for a really cool band that he and some of his new friends from Seattle were forming... At the time I was making a good living in San Diego selling swimming pools plus doing drumming gigs. I also was about to get married, plus was nervous about leaving San Diego with no gigs set up there, thus no income, so I passed. Oops, missed that party,' he joked with a little wistful regret.[50]

'Jerry and I drove up to San Francisco,' recalls Don Stevenson. 'We had a meeting with Matthew Katz. He was the person who called it all together. We were invited up for an audition. We weren't really sure what it was for, but we knew Mosley from The Frantics. We'd played together earlier that year. So, Mosley called Jerry. I think Mosley had also known Peter from before. But I didn't know Skip.'

The audition-cum-rehearsal was set to be held at Katz's second-floor office, at 1725 Washington Street, San Francisco, just under a mile north of California Hall.

'Me and Don were living together with our wives and kids,' Jerry Miller explains. 'And Bob called up and said, "I got this guy, Peter Lewis. He's a good player. And there's Skip Spence's who's also good. But we need another guitarist and we need a drummer."

'So, we went up to meet Matthew [Katz] at his office... Skippy was there and I thought he was just a crazy guy back then. I didn't realise how much of a genius he was until later on. We had a rehearsal right at Matthew's office that day. When the five of us started playing it was like magic.'

Stevenson chimes in. 'When I first got there, Skip was sitting on the drums and just kind of messing around. So, we had to have a conversation about what we would do and we all decided that we would play our favourite rock'n'roll songs. Then Skip got off the drums, thank goodness... and got on the guitar, and we started playing old rock'n'roll songs. It was stuff that we all knew, like Jerry Lee Lewis songs and Little Richard songs. Then we played a Ricky Nelson song. I can't recall everything we played, but it was stuff that we all liked. And it clicked. I mean, it not only clicked – it was amazing!

'The interesting thing is that it was three guitars and a bass,' Stevenson thinks back. 'It was pretty amazing that right from the very moment we started somehow it all fit together. Mosley was a killer; he was powerful and pushing. It would've been a bit soft and folky if we didn't have Mosley. But with everyone together, it was folky, but it was also a bit of jazz and rhythm and blues and country and funky.'

'We knew we had something at that first rehearsal,' Mosley reflects.

As Lewis told Craig Morrison, 'We knew we had it. When we jammed together we thought, "We can kick anybody's ass now."'[51]

'Skip was absolutely energetic right from the beginning,' Miller muses. 'When we first played together up at Matthew's office, it was so unusual. I think we all knew right there that it had the possibility of being something. It was like we were all hit by a lightning bolt.'

Drummer Don Stevenson had that same sense of excitement from the get-go. 'When they [Lewis, Mosley and Spence] asked us, "What do you guys think?" at the end of the rehearsal, we [Miller and Stevenson] said, "We're going to head down the peninsula and we'll see what happens. You can let us know what you think and we'll get back to you."'

After pausing for a moment, he adds, 'But when Jerry and I were driving home, we were almost having a breakdown in the car we were so thrilled!'

Moby Grape was being born.

CHAPTER TEN

CORTE MADERA AND THE ARK

'We lived in a two-storey house in Corte Madera,' Pat Spence recalls. 'It was split, and two college students lived upstairs. We had two bedrooms and a kitchen and a living room. Aaron got out one night. He was about 3. I ran outside onto the street, and I ran to the cleaners that was by a strip of stores. I went to see if anyone saw him there and they said, "No, we haven't seen him."

'But then I got to the train tracks, and I saw this little figure. So, I ran down there and I kept calling his name. A train came by not too long after I got him.'

If you were heading north on Highway 101 and you passed through San José, San Mateo and San Francisco, then crossed over the Golden Gate Bridge, you'd find yourself in Marin County. Continuing northward, you'd drive through the greenery of the Golden Gate National Recreation Area, as well as Sausalito, Marin City and Mill Valley. About ten miles north of the bridge, you'd arrive at the town of Corte Madera.

If you exited onto Tamalpais Drive and headed west, you'd reach a fork in the road after about a mile. Veering to the right, you'd merge onto Redwood Avenue, a quiet treelined street with homes built in the early 1900s. If you parked your car on that avenue and went for a stroll (and if it was the late summer of 1966), you

94

might see a gray Porsche parked on the street. You might also see a two-tone gray Oldsmobile Rocket 88. Passing by a little white house on the north side of the avenue, you might also hear music emanating from an open window.

That house with a pitched roof was built in 1910, six years before Corte Madera was incorporated into a town. With three bathrooms and two bedrooms, it totals almost 1,800 square feet. It has a driveway on its right side, which leads into a garage, and to the left of the driveway is a long staircase that climbs up to the front entrance. Immediately above the garage is a large set of windows that look out from a living room. The sun pours in through those windows on bright days, covering the room in light.

Over several afternoons in that late summer of '66, five musicians sat in the house with acoustic guitars, practising songs that they knew, sharing snatches of new songs they were writing and swapping ideas. With five chairs arranged into a circle, the musicians chatted, harmonised, laughed, smoked and became a band.

'We started rehearsing at Skippy's place,' Don Stevenson recalls. 'The room we played in was really bright. It almost had a whole wall of glass. I didn't set up my drums there. I was just playing percussion on whatever and adding harmonies.'

'That's where we were introduced to [the song] 'Omaha',' Jerry Miller puts in. 'He didn't have a name for it back then, and then he just came up with 'Omaha' – but it doesn't really relate to the song.' Pausing for a moment, the guitarist adds, 'We were upstairs, and Skip had his babies there. It was the place he rented in Corte Madera. It was a pretty good size.'

Skip had been living at the house for most of the time during his almost ten months in the Jefferson Airplane. During that time, he'd travelled and toured with the band for less than a week in September '65, maybe a week that December, less than a week in mid-January '66, maybe two weeks that February and likely one week in March. He may have only been away from home for touring or recording sessions for about five weeks – though he'd still found time to take off to Mexico with a young woman.

'Don recalls, 'Skip would always be smoking. You know, some guys cut their guitar strings right down to the nub. Well, Jerry never did that. He'd always twirl them around into big circles. Skippy would cut them down, so they'd just be an inch or two long and then he'd stick his cigarette on the end of one of his guitar strings.'

'Skippy's brand was Lucky Strike,' Jerry adds.

During those early weeks, either Spence or Bob Mosley came up with the idea of naming the group after a popular joke that referenced Herman Melville's classic novel of the search for the great white whale: *Moby Dick*. The joke went, 'What's big and purple and lives in the sea? Moby Grape!'

'We got together at Skip's a few times,' Mosley says. 'I remember it was pretty hectic with his little kids there.'

'Skip had two kids at the time, and they were running around while we were rehearsing. It's hard to believe they're all grown up now,' Stevenson adds of Aaron and Adam – two men now well into maturity.

Shortly before the rehearsals got started, on Saturday 8 August, Spence's first son, Aaron, celebrated his 2nd birthday. The following Saturday, his former band would release their first LP on RCA Victor. Sales of *Jefferson Airplane Takes Off*, the first album to feature him as a performer and songwriter, were initially slow and it took a few weeks to appear in the *Billboard* Top 200. In the late summer too, the Airplane would fire their manager, Matthew Katz.

But Katz had a new band, Moby Grape, that was continuing to take form.

'We didn't go [to Skip's place] a lot,' Jerry Miller reflects. 'We also played acoustically at everybody's places. Sometimes we'd just haul out the acoustic guitars and practise the harmonies.'

Another early song they worked on was a ballad called 'Someday' – the B-side of the single The Frantics had recorded in San Mateo, back when the band was playing at the Drag'on A' Go Go. With Mosley taking lead vocals, 'Someday' featured intermittent harmonies by Stevenson and Miller, who co-wrote the song.

They knew they had a kernel of something, so they pitched the song to the rest of the Grape. Spence was hooked, helping his bandmates rework the lyrics and melody into something quite different.

'The version we did in The Frantics is almost unrecognisable next to the final version,' Don Stevenson observes of the far more soulful track later released in June 1967. 'But the idea was there. Skip was added as a co-writer. I think it was because he might've put the bridge in and then got Mosley to sing the bridge.'

With new songs taking shape at rehearsals, Moby Grape had the makings of a setlist. Soon, Matthew Katz called a business meeting.

Barely a few weeks old, the Grape met with him on Tuesday 8 September 1966. Along with his bandmates, 20-year-old Skip Spence signed a personal management contract. According to court documents from 2006, Katz was hired for a five-year period to render services as an advisor to Moby Grape.[52]

Yet the agreement didn't exactly forge a mutual bond between the young musicians and their manager. While he was set to receive 20 per cent of gross monies taken in by the band, it read, 'This agreement shall not be construed to create a partnership between us. It is specifically understood that you [Matthew Katz] are acting hereunder as an independent contractor.'[53]

As an early step, he arranged a residency for the Grape at a unique club in a houseboat community in Sausalito. 'After rehearsing at Skip's, we went to The Ark,' Don explains. 'It was a restaurant that had gone out of business. I don't know if Matthew owned it or rented it, but it didn't really have a stage when we first went there.'

Drydocked in Sausalito, just north of the Golden Gate Bridge, The Ark was an old sidewheel ferryboat that served as a restaurant and club in the early-to-mid-sixties. It floated whenever high tides flooded the mudflats at Gate Six of Waldo Point Harbor.

Before its days as an eatery, The Ark had an entirely different history, as ferryboat *The Charles Van Damme*.[54] In the late summer of 1966, Katz was part of a consortium seeking to redefine it as a cozy, out-of-the-way rock club. Along the way, it would become Moby Grape's basecamp.

Thinking about those early days, Bob Mosley recalls, 'There was a guy called Jim Lendersmith who used to be one of our roadies. I remember he was doing some work at The Ark to get it set up before we started playing there.' Lendersmith had lived with Miller and Stevenson when they rented an old Victorian house on Ralston Street in Belmont, before moving to San Mateo.

'Jim was blond and looked like a surfer. He drove a red Jaguar,' Don Stevenson adds. 'He was a carpenter, so we recommended him to Matthew, to help with the pre-construction work at The Ark.

'There used to be a saying for Esso gas that went, "There's a tiger in your tank." And there was a station in the Bay Area that had an actual tiger in a huge cage. Jim showed no fear, and he could go right up to that tiger and pet it. The big cat loved him. He was like an animal savant,' Don chuckles.

In the months to come, Skip Spence would spin right off the stage that Jim Lendersmith was building for the new venue. But Moby Grape was not the first group to play the newly refurbished club.

On Tuesday 27 September, The West Coast Pop Art Experimental Band started a nearly weeklong run with supporting act Light Voyage. When the LA band ended its residency at The Ark, on 1 October, Moby Grape got ready to hit the stage.

As the Grape was gearing up to play its first shows, Spence's previous band, the Jefferson Airplane, was weathering major transitions. After they'd fired Katz in August, Signe Anderson left the group to raise a family. Reviewing a Winterland performance in late September, the *San Francisco Examiner* offered a glance into the band's future: 'Perhaps the imminent departure of their girl vocalist Signe Anderson (whose participation last night was sporadic) has left them upset. Indications are that she will be replaced by Gracie Slick [of The Great Society].'[55]

Perhaps motivated by his loss of the Airplane, Katz set up another meeting with the Grape, on Monday 10 October 1966. On that day, Skip and his bandmates signed an addendum to their personal management agreement, a portion of which read:

> 'It is understood and agreed that the name "MOBY GRAPE" is the property of Matthew Katz. The undersigned has no ownership right, title, or interest in and to the name "MOBY GRAPE" and he is entitled to utilise the same, only pursuant to the license and consent of Matthew Katz which may be revoked and cancelled at any time...'[56]

Speaking decades later, Peter Lewis recalled how Spence was compelled to sign the contract addendum: 'We were going to sign for Elektra [Records] but were already signed up to Katz for the Moby Grape name. Elektra said we could change it if we wanted. But Katz went to Skippy and said: "We don't want these guys to throw you out like the Airplane did, right? Well, you're gonna have to get them to sign the name over to me because I can protect us." So Skippy did that.'[57]

The disputable validity and enforceability of the addendum would haunt everyone throughout four long decades of injunctions, cancelled shows and litigation.

The following night, the Grape started a run of shows at The Ark with former Joel Scott Hill keyboardist Lee Michaels and Light Voyage supporting. As Miller recalls, 'Lee had a trio at the time. They played mostly blues and rockin' blues.' From 11-23 October, the Grape played nightly at The Ark, except Mondays, sharing the stage from 8:30 p.m. to 2 a.m., or sometimes much longer into the morning.

The first news story on Moby Grape appeared in the Show Biz section of the *Examiner* on Friday 14 October 1966. The short piece announced: 'Peter Lewis, 21, turned down a ready-made movie career. The tall, handsome member of a new rock'n'roll group (Moby Grape) now at the Ark in Sausalito is the son of Loretta Young and director Tom Lewis.' The guitarist explained, 'Mother and I were pals until I let my hair grow long... but heck, I'm enjoying this. I can let myself go. My brother and sister are in movies but I'd hate to spend all day having a director tell me what to do.'[58]

In the early fall, Lewis, Mosley, Miller and Stevenson migrated to Marin County. Spence, meanwhile, stayed in his home on Redwood Avenue. 'We all got little places around Mill Valley after a little while,' Miller explains. 'Don was on [Lower] Alcatraz [Place in Mill Valley]. Bob was near me. I can't remember where Peter was. Skippy stayed up in Corte Madera.'

The Grape all drove to their rehearsals and shows in Marin County and San Francisco. 'I had a Rocket 88 [Oldsmobile] at the time,' Miller recalls. 'It was two-tone grey, just beautiful. Bob had a grey Porsche. It was a beautiful little car. He drove it so bad,' he adds, chuckling. 'He'd take off in high gear. That poor old Porsche!'

'I lived pretty close to The Ark,' Mosley recalls. 'Most of the time I just drove. One night after a show I remember walking home with Jim Mazzeo [lighting tech for The West Coast Pop Experimental Band]. We ended up passing through a biker party and had peanut-butter sandwiches.'

In short order, the band established a routine at the nightclub-ferryboat. 'When we got to The Ark, we'd rehearse in the daytime, in the late afternoon,' Stevenson explains. 'We played after hours there, so we'd be done at around three o'clock in the morning. At that point, we'd go over to the freezer and get all this terrible food and heat it up and then we'd eat and go home and crash. Then we'd get up and come back and do it all again.'

Just as the musicians had worked up songs acoustically in Corte Madera, they started with the same approach at The Ark. As Stevenson recalls, 'Most of our rehearsals didn't have drums until we wanted to [add them]. When we were at Skippy's and even when we were at The Ark, it was like a circle, singing and playing and offering different ideas. Our first rehearsals at The Ark were done as acoustic sets. Then, when we'd think we had it really good, we'd turn on the PA system and go to the stage. It was ready with all the equipment.'

After hitting the stage and plugging in, the musicians kept working their songs, fine-tuning arrangements and harmonies. Even during some of their shows.

'The Ark was great,' Miller reminisces, 'because we rehearsed there and we also performed there. One time we were playing 'Fall On You' and it didn't come out so right. So, we said, "You don't mind if we do it again, do you? We got it wrong." "No, we don't mind," they said. So, we went over it again. We must've done it three or four times and the people loved it. They could watch us develop.'

While Moby Grape quickly formed into a tight unit on stage, the five members of the band didn't see much of each other beyond their musical collaboration. 'We didn't socialise too much outside of rehearsing and playing gigs,' Stevenson recollects. 'If I did go out to do something, like check out some band, it would usually be with Jerry.'

But on stage, Skip Spence brought a vibrant intensity to his performances. It was the same charisma that had charmed Marty Balin the previous year and, earlier, impressed folks in the South Bay. Collectively, the band embodied pop, rock, psychedelia, blues, soul and folk. Don, Jerry, Bob and Peter had learned their craft performing at some very rough venues over the years, to which Skip added the more rarefied airs of the folk circuit.

'Skip was a ball of energy on stage, and he was like that off stage too,' Stevenson muses. 'It was hard for him to contain the energy that he had inside of him. He was really dynamic.'

As October unfolded and Moby Grape attracted a growing fanbase at The Ark, they mingled and jammed with a whole slew of local and visiting musicians. Having played with the Airplane for nearly ten months and being such a radiant personality, Spence was a known quantity. Some musicians arrived at The Ark looking for him.

As Lewis recalls, 'The word got out really fast – because Skippy was in the band – that we were really good, and Jerry Garcia and Big Brother [and the Holding Company] came around to see us. And that's the place I first met Neil Young and Stephen Stills. They'd met Skip when he was in the Airplane, and the guy at The Ark pointed me out as being in the band. So I spent the afternoon trading songs with those guys.'[59]

'We were friendly with the Buffalo Springfield,' Stevenson explains. 'Bruce Palmer was from Canada, like Skip. He was also kind of ethereal, a spiritual kind of guy. He was a great bass player, and I know him and Skip got along really well. We kind of gravitated toward those guys because we were playing with them for a while.'

In his vital retrospective interview, Lewis recalled, 'The first time I met Neil and Stephen, they came up to The Ark... They came over and said, "We're looking for Skip Spence 'cause we met him in LA and he's a friend of ours and we came up to see him." I said, "He'll be here tonight, 'cause I'm in the same band and we're going to play here." We spent the afternoon trading songs.'[60]

Like the Grape, Buffalo Springfield didn't have a single frontman. Both bands had great harmonies and multiple vocalists. Most of the songs on Buffalo Springfield's debut album would be sung by Richie Furay and Steve Stills, with some by Richie, Steve and Neil together. Neither the Grape nor Springfield had developed as a unit, but comprised musicians who came fully formed.

But Buffalo Springfield was never as eclectic as Moby Grape in terms of songwriting and performance style. In the Grape, everyone was a songwriter from the get-go.

'All sorts of people came out to The Ark,' Miller adds. 'Neil Young and the Buffalo Springfield, The [Grateful] Dead, Big Brother and Janis [Joplin], Ramblin' Jack [Elliott], John Cipollina and Quicksilver [Messenger Service]. Sons of Champlin were also there. It was full of these kinds of people. It was cool because it was a place to perform and rehearse.'

'Some of my happiest memories of those days,' Lewis later mused, 'were sitting around Mosley's apartment in Mill Valley with Stephen and Neil and Richie, smokin' dope and playing each other our songs.'[61]

'Matthew [Katz] was deathly afraid of getting doused. He was kind of strange in some ways,' Miller chuckles about the manager's fear of his drink being spiked. 'I can understand where he was kind of upset [after losing the Airplane], but he did a lot of things I didn't like, he did a lot of things the band didn't like. But he got us in the door at the beginning, I have to give him credit for that.'

In a matter of weeks, it'd become clear that Moby Grape was ready for the new rock ballrooms.

CHAPTER ELEVEN

THE BALLROOM BIDDING WAR

San Francisco was ground zero for the rock ballroom. It had started with Bill Graham's benefit for the San Francisco Mime Troupe at The Fillmore Auditorium, where Skip Spence had played with the Jefferson Airplane on that December 1965 night. As 1966 unfolded, Graham dived further into music promotion and got a license to host regular shows.

Meanwhile, Texan Chet Helms, later deemed by the *New York Times* to be 'the Father of the Summer of Love,' took over The Avalon Ballroom with his own Family Dog Productions. The Avalon was a dancehall located at 1268 Sutter Street, just a few blocks east of the Fillmore. Rapidly becoming the hottest venues in town, the Fillmore and the Avalon were coveted gigs among local and visiting performers.

Yet there was a snag. Bill Graham and Matthew Katz were locked in a dispute over who owned a piece of the Airplane. As of the summertime, Katz was out and Graham was on his way in.

For Moby Grape, it put the Fillmore out of reach. Consequently, just as Katz had arranged for the Airplane to play California Hall back in January and April, he booked the venue for the Grape on consecutive Fridays in the autumn of '66. Sharing the bill on that first date, 28 October, were three opening acts: Lee Michaels, West

Coast Branch, a band from Inglewood, and a little-known group from Seattle called American Dream. But rustling up an audience wasn't easy.

There was competition all over town that night. At the Fillmore, just a mile west of California Hall, Captain Beefheart and his Magic Band were headlining with The Chocolate Watchband, a popular garage-rock group from Los Altos, opening. Meanwhile, Quicksilver Messenger Service was at the Avalon, two miles west, with Sons of Champlin supporting. Local act Wildflower was playing The Matrix.

Those who did show up for Moby Grape's San Francisco debut were few, with the audience dwarfed by the vast hall. Disappointed but not defeated, the band rehearsed for its return the following week.

On Friday 4 November, Lee Michaels and American Dream returned to support the Grape, along with The New Tweedy Brothers from Portland. Michaels was an eclectic performer. Like Harry Nilsson, he was very comfortable on piano or guitar, but while Nilsson veered toward a Brian Wilson/Paul McCartney style, Michaels was more of a rocker. (Lee Michaels was also managed by Matthew Katz – and it ended just like many of Katz's other management interactions.)

Again, there was serious competition across town. Quicksilver Messenger Service was opening for Muddy Waters at the Fillmore, while The Grateful Dead was supported by The Oxford Circle at the Avalon. Big Brother and the Holding Company, meanwhile, took the stage at The Matrix.

In an unfortunate recurrence, the turnout at California Hall was disappointing. But, booked to play the Avalon the following week, the band remained hopeful.

'Chet [Helms] was more of a hippie type of deal,' Jerry Miller reflects. 'He was great, but he was more *let it flow* – and you could do anything you wanted. At the Fillmore, you'd play two times a night. And Bill [Graham] ran it really tight.'

For those first shows at the Avalon, Moby Grape opened for innovative Austin band The 13th Floor Elevators. It was just a few weeks after *The Psychedelic Sounds Of The 13th Floor Elevators* had been released by International Artists. Purportedly one of the first times the word 'psychedelic' was used in reference to music, the LP has become an icon of the era.

Like Skip Spence, the Elevators' bandleader, Roky Erickson, was a psychedelic pioneer whose flame burned brightly. Both also subsequently spent decades struggling with mental illness. Similarities aside, according to Paul Drummond's history of The 13th Floor Elevators, *Eye Mind*, the weekend when their path crossed with the Grape, in the autumn of 1966, was less than idyllic.

Arriving in the Bay Area about a week before those shows at the Avalon, various members of the Elevators caught the Grape performing at The Ark. One of the Texans' quirkier aspects was their use of an electrified jug as a wind instrument (making them a true jugband). Thinking back years later, jug player Tommy Hall's wife, Clementine, told Drummond: 'We went to hear the Grape at The Ark, and [lead guitarist] Stacy [Sutherland] stood there worshiping these guys. Then one of the band members got on the mike and said, "We've heard that The 13th Floor Elevators are in the audience, and we're not going to play anymore because we don't want them to steal any of our material." Stacy was in tears.'[62]

According to Clementinc Hall, when the two bands shared the bill at the Avalon, one member of Moby Grape tried to sabotage the sound system during the Elevators' performance. Whatever actually happened at The Ark and the Avalon on those nights, both bands were on the path to creating landmark albums.

Moby Grape's self-titled debut would immediately precede the summer of '67, while the Elevators' *Easter Everywhere* came out that following autumn. And then, in the late spring and autumn of '68, respectively, both Spence and Erickson would be institutionalised...

Two weeks after the Grape's 1966 debut at the Avalon, the band played its first gigs at The Fillmore Auditorium. 'So I made the deal for us to play the Fillmore,' Peter Lewis explained years later, 'because they wouldn't deal with Matthew.'[63]

'Matthew and Bill did not get along too good,' Jerry Miller laughs.

Over the last weekend in November 1966, the Grape opened at the bottom of a bill. Above them was The James Cotton Blues Band, led by the harmonica player who had been in both Muddy Waters' and Howlin' Wolf's bands, and recorded for Sam Phillips at Sun Records. Closing out each show was Spence's old band, Jefferson Airplane.

At about 9 p.m. on Friday 25 November, Bill Graham stepped onto the stage and walked over to the microphone. 'In the first of hopefully many, many appearances at the Fillmore', he announced, 'a great bunch of juvenile delinquents, Moby Grape'. A live recording from the evening features tight performances of two songs by Spence ('Rounder' and 'Indifference'), two by Lewis ('Stop' and 'Fall On You'), one by Mosley ('Bitter Wind'), one by Miller ('Miller's Blues') and two co-written by Miller and Stevenson ('Changes' and 'Ain't No Use').

The band also played an extended number it had developed collaboratively, called 'Dark Magic.' Running at nearly twenty minutes, it was their longest song and marked a shift to the long-form psychedelic jam.

Don Stevenson has fond memories of it. ''Dark Magic' was a fun song to play because it was a drone,' he explains, 'but it has a punctuation that is very energetic. The whole thing is a drone and that allowed the musicians to improvise and create this feeling of 'Dark Magic'. Skippy has a sense of foreboding with the feel of that song.'

Over time, four of those songs appeared on the band's debut and two others on their second album. All but 'Miller's Blues' and 'Dark Magic' ran between two-to-four minutes. Developing tightly arranged songs with complex three-, four- and sometimes five-part harmonies was Moby Grape's modus operandi, setting it apart from the other Bay Area bands.

Airplane guitarist Jorma Kaukonen was astounded by the Grape that weekend. 'With guys like Jerry Miller in the band, I mean, they exuded a level of musicianship that was mindboggling on some levels,' he recalls. '*And* they had all these great singers and song-writers!'

Throughout November 1966, the Jefferson Airplane recorded its second album, the classic *Surrealistic Pillow*. Skip sat in on some of the sessions, collaborating with old bandmates as well as the Airplane's newest members, Grace Slick and Spencer Dryden. Kaukonen recalls him playing guitar on parts of the album but can't remember which tracks – though Spence's own folky song, 'My Best Friend,' was the lead-off single.

The next weekend, 2-3 December, Moby Grape played the Fillmore once again, this time following Lee Michaels and opening for LA band Love. Love's impactful second album, *Da Capo*, had appeared in record stores a few weeks earlier.

Over the next couple of weeks, the Grape played at The Matrix from Tuesdays to Thursdays. Sharing the bill during that second run was acoustic guitarist Steve Mann – who, like Spence, had migrated north from the South Bay folk scene.

'I jammed with him a few times,' Miller recalls. 'He was really good. He got a bit out there later on, but I love his stuff. As a matter of fact, I still do some Steve Mann tunes in my shows. He was good friends with Mac Rebennack, Dr. John, who also sadly is no longer with us. I'm not sure if Skippy knew Steve from the South Bay. But Skippy had a whole different circle of friends he hung out with from down there. I don't know too much about that,' he muses.

For Spence, returning to The Matrix was a homecoming of sorts. It was also a time when, according to Lewis, things could have turned out very differently.

'At one point when Matthew [Katz] was out of the picture and we were playing The Matrix, Paul Rothchild – before he signed The Doors – came backstage and told us, "We want you on Elektra

Records. I'll give you anything you want,"' Peter recalls. 'They offered us 50 per cent of the stock in the company. And that's the only label where we could have made it. But that started this feeding frenzy, all these labels after us.'[64]

Perhaps recollection of events is bound to be a little fuzzy, after so long. While Moby Grape was certainly being pursued by Rothchild circa December 1966-January 1967, Jim Morrison and his compadres signed with Jac Holzman's Elektra back on 18 August, completing recording of their self-titled debut before the Grape's first gig at The Ark.

On Friday 23 December, the Grape played in a nine-band cavalcade at the Santa Venetia Armory back in Marin County. Billed as *Band Bash!*, it ran from 8 p.m. to 1 a.m.; supporting acts included Sons of Champlin, Morning Glory, Freedom Highway, The Beatables, The Nite Riders, Baltimore Steam Packet, Axons and Tiny Hearing Aid Co. As headliners, Moby Grape likely hit the stage last, probably around midnight.

A few hours before that, the Grape put on another performance at The Avalon Ballroom. Along with visiting act The Steve Miller Blues Band, playing their first Bay Area show, they opened for The Grateful Dead. The following night, Christmas Eve, all three bands were back at the Avalon for another nine o'clock show.

After spending Christmas with their families, the Grape reconvened the next day for an event at The Ark. Titled *Grope For Peace*, the concert featured a variety of acts, including Big Brother and the Holding Company and The Charlatans.

Three nights later, on Thursday 29 December, they returned to the Armory for another show with the Dead and fellow local act Morning Glory. For the last two nights of the year, Moby Grape played the Avalon with Lee Michaels and Country Joe and the Fish.

A recording from that weekend preserves strong performances of songs that would appear on the band's first two albums: 'Hey Grandma', 'Changes', 'Sitting By The Window', 'Rounder', 'Omaha', 'Bitter Wind', 'Murder In My Heart For The Judge'. Also in the set was 'Stormy Monday/Sweet Little Angel', a slow blues medley, melding two classics. While the first was written by T-Bone Walker and famously covered by Bobby 'Blue' Bland, the second was a blues standard made famous by Robert Nighthawk in the early 1950s and then by BB King later in the decade. Sung powerfully by Bob Mosley, the song had been in Stevenson and Miller's setlists for years.

The band's last show of 1966 was one of the few Pat Spence attended. 'I remember Skip took me to that New Year's Eve show at the Avalon,' she recalls. 'He just couldn't concentrate; he couldn't have me out there in the audience.' A laid back and jovial imp though he may have been (most of the time), it seems Skip could get quite jealous, or distracted, or likely both, whenever his wife was at a show.

But as showtime fast approached, it was another band member who caused concern. Mosley had slipped out of the dressing room. Stevenson and Miller bolted out the door to look for their missing bandmate.

Spence, meanwhile, wasn't worried. He was calm, seeming to have a sixth sense that everything was going to work out. His response to a band crisis could range from full-on tantrum to a kind of serenity.

His sartorial sense was also singular. 'I remember Skip was wearing some sort of old military outfit with plumes and feathers,' Stevenson says of that New Year's Eve show. 'He was tuning his guitar in the dressing room and just grinning from ear to ear. And Jerry and I went out and found Bob in a bar and then we came back to the show.'

'When we got back home that night,' Pat recalls, 'there was a bunch of people crashed all over our house. The band's road manager at the time, Jimmy, brought all of these people over and they partied at our house.'

Playing at the Avalon had closed 1966 on a high. At the dawn of the year, Skip's second son, Adam, had been born and he'd been a member of the up-and-coming Jefferson Airplane.

After getting ousted a few months later, he found his footing with Moby Grape, now one of the hottest acts in town. After rehearsals at his home up in Corte Madera and shows at The Ark, the Grape had conquered the ballrooms of San Francisco. All they needed was a recording contract. It was time for the ballroom bidding war.

• • •

In early January, Matthew Katz and Moby Grape started going back and forth with Elektra and Atlantic Records, negotiating for that essential contract. Katz had been on the outs with various members of the Grape since November, when they first played the Fillmore. By this point he was back in the picture and by mid-January Columbia was also pursuing the band, making it a three-horse race.

On Friday 13 January 1967, Moby Grape played two shows: one at the Avalon, with The Charlatans and Sparrow, and another at Santa Venetia Armory, alongside Big Brother and the Holding Company and Morning Glory. The following night, they returned to the Avalon. In town to scout Sparrow (later Steppenwolf) was an A&R executive from Columbia. Catching one of the shows at the Avalon, David Rubinson was blown away by the Grape's performance.

Speaking retrospectively, Rubinson recalled, 'I came out to San Francisco in December 1966, a month before the *Human Be-In* [held on 14 January 1967]. The best band out here then was Moby Grape. Bar *none*... Steve Miller, Sons of Champlin, and Moby Grape were *staggering* bands. Because they completely had their own stuff.'[65]

'I liked Rubinson right off,' Miller says. 'I thought he was pretty cool and had good ideas, and I respected Columbia. We also got together with Ahmet [Ertegun] over at Atlantic. And I loved Paul Rothchild [at Elektra]. He was so cool. He pretty much offered us *carte blanche*. We could be completely free with him.' Pausing, the guitarist adds in hindsight, 'But I don't know if that would've been the best thing for us. A little more discipline was probably what we needed.'

Mosley remembers recording a demo for Elektra around that time: 'We had Paul Rothchild at Elektra interested. He recorded 'Bitter Wind' with us, and he liked it. Atlantic was also interested: Ahmet Ertegun was there, and he had the Buffalo Springfield.'

While Jerry Miller and Don Stevenson don't recall recording audition demos for Elektra or Atlantic, they do remember playing for them at shows, as well as privately.

'We just played live for Ahmet, and we played live for David and all the Columbia people,' Miller explains. 'We invited them to the gigs, and also to where we were staying [down in LA], and we'd do some acoustic stuff for them.' On Wednesday 25 January, the band went into Columbia's LA studio to record a couple of audition demos: 'Looper', written by Lewis, and 'Indifference', by Spence.

After the offer from Elektra, Atlantic was quick to bite. With a second deal on the table, Moby Grape, or Katz, or possibly both, at least reputedly agreed to sign with Atlantic.

Elektra had offered Moby Grape the services of producer Paul Rothchild and artistic freedom. (Plus, according to Peter Lewis, 50 per cent of company stock.) Atlantic offered money in hand, while co-founder Ahmet Ertegun was ready to work alongside the band as producer. Columbia offered even more money, along with producer and newfound devotee David Rubinson. Elektra had The Doors; Atlantic had a slew of R&B and soul icons; while Columbia had Dylan and The Byrds.

Stevenson recalls the days when the Grape was being courted by a triumvirate: 'It's weird, I don't remember meeting [Columbia Records President] Clive Davis at that time. I think we just dealt with David Rubinson. I do remember we met Ahmet Ertegun. Who would've done the producing if we signed with Atlantic? Maybe it would've been Ahmet.[66]

112

'He was very hip,' Don acknowledges. 'He was laidback, and he just presented himself as a kind, logical businessman. When he mentioned the artists on his label, we were all impressed. He asked us if we'd like to be a part of that stable. That's how he talked.

'To me, it felt like we were number two with Paul Rothchild [at Elektra],' he demurs. 'It kind of felt like we'd be the go-to if everything fell through with The Doors. David [Rubinson] made us feel really special. He loved our music and was into it from the first time he heard it. He just had all kinds of great ideas and suggestions, and he was so enthusiastic. He told us, "You won't be able to walk down the streets of Mill Valley without people knowing who you are." And that really fit into where my head was at back then.'

According to biographer Robert Greenfield, the Grape agreed to sign with Atlantic. In his book on Ertegun, he writes: 'After Moby Grape had told Ahmet they would sign with Atlantic because he had promised to work closely with them on their album, one of the members of the group called to tell him that because [Columbia's Clive] Davis had offered them twice as much money, the band had signed with him instead. They had however inserted a clause into their contract that would permit Ahmet to come into the studio and work with them as much as he liked.'[67]

Ertegun never took the musicians up on that offer. In his own memoir, Davis described Moby Grape as 'another hip Columbia signing at the time, brought in by the talented A&R man David Rubinson.'[68] Several decades later, speaking with *Billboard* magazine, Ertegun said dismissively, 'the only thing I remember competing directly with Clive over was Moby Grape, and he got Moby Grape. Didn't mean anything.'[69]

Of course, at the time it meant a lot. As 1967 got underway, Moby Grape was bursting with possibility as a band.

Four days after recording their audition demos for Columbia down in LA, the musicians were back in San Francisco to play the Avalon. Titled *Mantra Rock Dance – Krishna Consciousness Comes*

West: SF Krishna Temple Benefit, the fundraiser for adherents of Eastern spirituality featured an array of local talent including The Grateful Dead and Big Brother. But the Grape was *the* act to catch in the Bay Area at that moment in time. Fans were lining up to see them and key rock critics on both the West and East Coasts were starting to take notice.

In the first week of February, *Crawdaddy!* declared: 'The most exciting and most sought after (by record companies) new group is San Francisco's Moby Grape. The Grape have an enormous impact on an audience. Three guitars, a very talented bass, and a drummer (all of whom sing well), they come on like a flash flood. Guitarist Skip Spence – who used to be drummer for Jefferson Airplane – radiates joy in all directions, turning on the group, turning on the audience, turning the whole performance into an event, a celebration. The Grape's music is excellent and is likely to get better – the group is only a few months old, and when they *really* get together, they'll be frightening.'[70]

Reporting for *The Village Voice* that same month, critic Richard Goldstein painted a picture of the signing frenzy in the Bay Area: 'Hip San Francisco is being carved into bits of business territory. The Jefferson Airplane belong to RCA. The Sopwith Camel did so well for Kama Sutra the label has invested in a second local group, The Charlatans. The Grateful Dead have signed with Warner Brothers in an extraordinary deal which gives them complete control over material and production. Moby Grape is tinkering with Columbia and Elektra.'[71]

On Tuesday 7 February 1967, the five members of Moby Grape signed a deal with Columbia Records. The bidding war had come to an end. Yet amid the excitement, the band's on-again-off-again relationship with their manager persisted, along with the desire of some members to sever the relationship entirely.

As Mosley says matter-of-factly, 'We went with Columbia because they said they'd get rid of Matthew Katz.' But a split wasn't immediately on the cards. For the time being, the management contract from September, along with the following month's addendum, bound the musicians to him.

As Lewis recalled, 'So they [the record companies] started calling Matthew instead of us, and that's how he got back in the game. We loved The Byrds, and that's why we went with Columbia, the worst place for us. You can sink or swim, and it doesn't matter to them.'[72]

Of course, Moby Grape did have an advocate at Columbia. As David Rubinson later stated, 'I put my job on the line for them. There was no such thing as rock and roll in 1967 at CBS. The Byrds and Paul Revere and the Raiders – that was it. When I brought the Grape in, they signed for five grand. I took them away from Elektra and Atlantic, who had money in the bank in escrow. I flew execs from CBS out here at my expense. I believed in them very, very, very much.'[73]

The press conference announcing the band's signing became an afternoon of enthusiasm and apprehension. Signing with Columbia was both a destination and a starting line. It was the moment all expectation jumped into hyperdrive. Word on the street was that Moby Grape would become nothing less than a blockbuster, and the press conference announced all this to the record industry. For the band, it was like crossing the Rubicon. The Grape could only move forward now, with superstardom as the only place they were headed.

At first all the attention had been exciting. In short order, there were long lines outside venues like the Fillmore and the Avalon, bringing with them a cartload of excitement and expectation. Then word got out on where the band members were living. Fans started showing up at the front door wanting an autograph; or a brief personal exchange; or something else.

For Bob Mosley, the attention was getting to be too much. The bassist recalls the day of the signing as being hectic. 'It was pretty crowded,' he says. 'There was a lot of focus on us, and we weren't prepared for it at all. I didn't like that too much.'

As Mosley points out, fame was exciting and draining all at once, and that was no different for Skip Spence. Stepping on stage every night, he reached for a level of pure showmanship: yelping, bouncing around, giggling, interacting with bandmates and fans with electricity and positivity.

For Skip, performing night after night was a matter of joyful self-expression. But as the weeks flew by, playing to growing expectations also created a pressure cooker.

With a recording contract in hand, it would soon be time for the band to enter the studio. But first they had a whirlwind month of gigs to get through.

CHAPTER TWELVE

WELCOME TO COLUMBIA

As one of the hottest acts around, Moby Grape was in demand for any musical event in the Bay Area. On Sunday 12 February 1967, the Grape performed at a benefit for the Council of Civic Unity at The Fillmore Auditorium. The Council had been around for twenty-one years by this point and had just elected a new president, Sausalito's mayor, Mel Wax (dad to Martha – see Chapter Eight). Working to combat racial and religious discrimination, the organisation set a $60,000 fundraising goal for its campaign focused on housing and work opportunities for minorities.

Also on the bill that night were some old friends and acquaintances of Skip Spence, including The Grateful Dead – whose Jerry Garcia he'd met in the South Bay days – and Sly Stone, whose *New York's Eve Freakout* show he'd recently caught at Redwood City. It was the first time the band had played the Fillmore since the shows with Love and Lee Michaels in early December. Just a few months earlier, the venue had seemed out of reach due to the Katz-Graham feud.[74] But the Grape was just too talented and popular for the fiery promoter to resist.

Jerry Miller has fond memories of hanging out at the Fillmore. 'We'd all get together in the green room. Sometimes we'd stay real late up there and chat and have a smoke,' he recalls. 'It was upstairs.

There was a balcony up there and we could sit and watch the bands. I remember watching Stevie Winwood and Traffic one time. We had our own little spot up there where we could chat during the breaks.'[75]

One of Aaron's first memories is of going to his dad's show as a toddler. 'I remember one time they played at the Fillmore and I was with my mom,' he recalls. 'She was on the left side of the stage and he was exiting on the right side of the stage, so she made me run across the stage with this crowd of people. My dad was wearing a long white shirt and I remember tugging on it, and he turned around and picked me up and walked me back across the stage. He stopped at the mic and he said, "This is my little son, Aaron Spence," and the crowd cheered.'

On Valentine's Day, Moby Grape played a show at The Ark with Big Brother and the Holding Company. With recording contract in hand, they were the conquering heroes returning to Waldo Point Harbor. Over the next weekend, 17-19 February, the Grape played three consecutive nights at the ferryboat nitespot, plus a Saturday show at Sausalito Auditorium with The Loading Zone.

'We'd go over to The Ark after shows just to jam,' Miller reminisces. 'Sometimes Jefferson Airplane would show up, Big Brother, Buffalo Springfield, Sons of Champlin, Lee Michaels, Ramblin' Jack, we'd all end up there after the gigs just to jam. I remember one time we were jamming with Sons of Champlin, and everything was working really good that night, we had their jaws open. But almost every night was wonderful there.'

Over the last weekend of February, the Grape shared the bill with The Charlatans at an event called *Neptune's Notion*. Also playing that night was one of the earliest architects of heavy metal, San Diego band Iron Butterfly.

Not every date was a triumph, though. Next, the Grape was booked to play the Fillmore on the afternoon of Sunday 26 February, with The Steve Miller Blues Band and blues legend BB King headlining. But somehow, the band managed to miss the gig.

'I don't think we played that show,' Miller explains. 'I believe we got there too late to play and we were just ashamed. We got the start time screwed up… It was real bad because I just love BB King. We got to play with him later on though [at the Fillmore East in June 1971] and he was great, a real gentleman.'

Though they were yet to tour outside the Bay Area, they still got up to some hijinks on the road. 'Peter had one of them classic hippie buses,' Miller remembers. 'We used to jump it, like in that car chase in *Bullitt*. We'd fly up and down those hills with Peter's wagon pretty good. But you're not supposed to do that, because when a Volkswagen bus goes off the ground its wheels go in.'

Chuckling, he adds, 'One time when we were out on the road, his cousin BJ went and put eyelashes on the headlights and wrote stuff, like "Love", on the side and turned it into a total hippie bus. Peter didn't care much for that.'

On Friday 3 March, the Grape played an event that ran from 7 p.m. to 7 a.m. called *First Annual Love Circus*. Presented by The Love Conspiracy Commune, the show was held at The Winterland Arena, at the corner of Post and Steiner Streets. It was their first time playing the venue, which Bill Graham had started using the previous fall. With a capacity of 5,400, Winterland was his go-to space whenever the 1,300-seat Fillmore, just a five-minute walk away, wasn't big enough.

'It was much bigger than the Fillmore,' Miller remembers. 'That's where they had all those winter shows, ice skating and all that, almost like an Olympic deal.'

The poster advertising the event promised that body and face painting would be available, inviting concertgoers to bring bells, incense, food, beads, flowers and costumes. While the *First Annual Love Circus* featured such acts as Love, The Grateful Dead and The Loading Zone, not everyone was happy with it.

Members of the Diggers – a San Francisco group of anti-capitalist activists and performers – saw the event as a commercialised rip-off of their own *Invisible Circus*. Heralded as 'San Francisco's digger underground answer to both the *Trips Festival* and the *Human Be-In*,' it had taken placed a week earlier. The Diggers picketed the show, and the Dead reputedly refused to perform until members of the activist group were allowed inside.

Two nights later, Moby Grape took part in the *Benefit For Newstage And Straight Theatre* at The Avalon Ballroom, alongside Big Brother, Country Joe and the Fish, Sparrow and the Dead. The Straight Theatre was formerly the Haight Theatre, an old movie house renovated and repurposed as a concert venue in the heady Haight-Ashbury days of 1966-69. Also performing was San Francisco Beat poet Michael McClure, at what was advertised as a costume party in the *San Francisco Examiner.*

Then the five musicians flew down to LA, entering the studio on Saturday 11 March to begin work on their first album.

Alone in Marin County, the Moby Grape wives got together at The Ark. 'When the guys went on tour or down to cut an album we were on our own, sometimes for weeks. When we wanted to have a break and get away from the kids, we went to The Ark because the band practised and played there all the time and we thought we'd be safe there,' explains Pat, Skip's wife at the time.

'The first time we all got babysitters; [third son] Omar wasn't born yet, but my mom came and helped with Adam and Aaron. She practically delivered Adam, she used to call him "Stuffed Pigeon." We made a day of it, there were four of us that first time.

'I had two Brandy Alexanders at The Ark,' Pat continues. 'This guy came up to me. He was a Hells Angel. He started talking to me and after a while he said, "Do you want to go to my place?" And I go, "No. I have my children at home." He said, "I have a snake in my house. Do you like snakes?" And I go, "Not really." And he goes, "They're really fun. I feed them rats. I put a rat in my house and it runs all around." I was with all the girls, so I was okay. We just wanted to get out of the house and dance.'

Down in LA, over the next two days the Grape recorded four songs with Rubinson producing, including Mosley's soulful 'Come

In The Morning', Lewis' charging 'Fall On You' and a new ballad by Miller and Stevenson called '8:05'. Over the years '8:05' would become a classic, covered by a variety of artists including Robert Plant, as well as Randy Bachman and Burton Cummings.

The band also recorded Spence's energetic 'Rounder' that day – but minus the vocals. 'I don't know why we didn't put vocals on that one,' Miller muses. 'That's one of the first songs we ever did. We first played 'Rounder' at Skippy's house in Corte Madera. It was right around the time he introduced us to 'Omaha'.'

''Rounder' is a funky little tune,' Stevenson puts in. 'I'm surprised that folk music was Skippy's main background. To me, his songs were well written and well thought out, and they had a lot of potential to put some good beats in there. He was just a great songwriter. I don't see the folk side in his songs – I mean, his music was pretty much cosmic.'

After just two jampacked studio days, Moby Grape flew back north for more shows in the Bay Area. On the weekend of 24-25 March, they returned to The Winterland Arena for a show with The Charlatans and The Chambers Brothers.

Set to open for The Byrds the following weekend, the quintet rehearsed non-stop over the next few days, desperately wanting to be on top form. While Mosley and Spence both looked up to the folk-rock pioneers, they'd been nothing short of a game-changer for Stevenson, Miller and Lewis.

'We all had a kind of reverence for The Byrds and we were all excited to play with them. With all that rehearsing, we were preparing ourselves to at least belong on the same stage as those guys. We wanted to represent ourselves, so they'd dig us,' Don Stevenson explains. 'Listening to The Byrds had a real impact on me. It personally changed my direction in music.'

On Friday 31 March and Saturday 1 April, the Grape and Andrew Staples opened for The Byrds at Winterland. While Moby Grape brought their intricate rock-pop stylings, Staples (actually a band name) veered towards a baroque psychedelic sound. The next day, all three acts moved to the Fillmore for a Sunday afternoon show. 'There wasn't a pair of jeans on the stage for those shows,' Jerry Miller reflects, showing the same degree of reverence toward The Byrds over half a century later.

But at that moment, disaster struck. Over the weekend, people posing as stage movers strolled into the venue and made off with the band's equipment. It included Stevenson's brand new Gretsch drum kit, Miller's beloved Gibson L5 guitar, named 'Beulah', and Spence's Gibson ES-335. He'd switched to the guitar of choice for such players as Chuck Berry and BB King only a few months before.

'Skippy was playing a red Martin when I first met him,' Miller recalls. 'Then he got a [Gibson] 335. We used to go to Satterley and Chapin over on Ellis Street whenever we got instruments or had something repaired. That was the best music store in the world! They had beautiful guitars there. They had D'Angelico, [Gibson] Super 400s... old stuff – they had millions of dollars' worth of guitars! Skippy's 335 was all white, and that's the one that got stolen with the band's equipment that weekend.'

'We were just all freaked out when it happened,' Stevenson adds, visibly fuming over a half-century later.

Everyone quickly borrowed or bought replacements to get through the weekend shows with The Byrds. A photograph, likely taken at the Saturday night or Sunday afternoon show, would be used for the back cover of Moby Grape's first album, showing Miller with his temporary Gibson 175 and Stevenson with his set of replacement Rogers drums.

Around this time, photographer Jim Marshall – whose dozens of iconic shots helped define the era – led the band around Marin County on a search for the perfect photographic image. He had been charged with the cover photo for the Grape's forthcoming LP.

Miller fondly recalls, 'It was just a beautiful day up in Marin, and we ended up in Fairfax posing in front of the Junktique store.'

'Skip had his hair all done nice,' Stevenson puts in. 'It was a long day and I got pretty annoyed, but Skip was just cool. He was light-hearted the whole time. For that photo that went on the album we just organised ourselves and formed our own sort of pod. We went into the [Junktique] store beforehand and got all those props, just from whatever was there. It gave us a sort of 1800s look.'

Holding his right hand over a washboard in the photograph, Stevenson prominently gave the finger in the shot used on the album cover. 'We started early in the morning. We were with Jim Marshall, and it was a long day,' he explains. Chuckling, Mosley adds, 'Don got upset about it, so he flipped [Marshall] off.'

On Wednesday 12 April, Moby Grape played a further benefit for the San Francisco Mime Troupe at the Fillmore alongside the usual Bay Area suspects, including the Airplane, the Dead, Quicksilver Messenger Service, The Loading Zone and Andrew Staples. On Saturday, they performed at a peace rally at Kezar Stadium, part of the *Week Of The Angry Arts*, sharing the bill with Country Joe and the Fish, Quicksilver, Big Brother, The Steve Miller Blues Band and Seattle-born folkie Judy Collins. Three days later, Skip Spence turned 21.

With each gig, the Grape's following was getting bigger and bigger – and a sizeable portion of that fanbase was made up of young musicians. One then aspiring drummer describes how he was floored when he first caught the band:

'I saw The Beatles and the Stones on their first American tours and when I saw the Grape, I thought they were better than both of them. The first time I saw them was at the Avalon. They were playing with Lee Michaels. And I thought, "These guys are incredible!" They became my favourite band.' Ten years later, 'Fuzzy John' Oxendine would play with a more jazz-focused version of Moby Grape.

But as April 1967 rolled along, the band flew back down to LA, returning to the Hollywood Hawaiian. With a handful of tracks in the can, it was time to finish the album. On Saturday 22 April, they cut four new songs, including the charged show-opener 'Hey Grandma', the fast-paced 'Changes', Lewis' pensive ballad 'Sitting By The Window' and Mosley's existential rocker 'Lazy Me'.

Skip Spence had been harmonising on Don Stevenson's 'Hey Grandma' powerfully for months by that point. As Stevenson recalls, 'We were just rehearsing, and Jerry and I were bringing the song in, and Skippy just started singing right away. And he put all that energy into it.' That same night, Moby Grape played Freedom Hall in the college town of Davis with Buffalo Springfield.

The next day, they cut another five more songs: including Mosley's hard-hitting 'Mr. Blues,' at once an homage to the blues and an in-your-face stand against depression, Miller and Stevenson's playful ballad 'Naked, If I Want To' and the romping country-rocker 'Ain't No Use.'

The other two recorded that day, 'Omaha' and 'Indifference', were written by Skip Spence. 'Because of the drum track, 'Omaha' had some pretty interesting drum fills,' Stevenson recalls. 'I remember Skip talking to David [Rubinstein] about the beginning of the track, how the guitars should come in one at a time. And he also talked to David about getting that sort of panoramic sound that goes from speaker to speaker at the very beginning.'

"'Indifference' was a shuffle,' Miller notes. 'I used to play a couple of [blues guitarist] Freddie King licks in there. It was fun to play. And 'Omaha' was just an ass-kicker. We usually used that at the end of our shows.'

Mosley admits, 'I don't remember recording 'Omaha', but I do remember Skip's other song, "Indifference." It was a pretty tricky song to record. We finished that album in about two weeks. We pretty much had all the songs when we went into the studio. David Rubinson was a lot of fun. He seemed to know what he was doing.'

Two days later, on Tuesday 25 April, the band finished recording 'Someday', the final track for the album. Miller and Stevenson had originally written and recorded the ballad with The Frantics in the summer of 1966, but the version the Grape recorded in the spring-time, co-written with Spence, was almost entirely different.

'When Skip and I sang 'Someday' together we decided we wanted it to be one voice. We wanted to make it so that listeners couldn't distinguish if it was him or me,' Stevenson warmly recalls of that final album session. 'It was supposed to be one unified form and you wouldn't be able to tell that it was two people. We wanted it to be just us. So, we practised breathing together and cutting off the notes at the right points. Skip and I did a lot of work on that. He was very creative in the studio.'

Miller arrived late that day. 'When I got in, [Don and Skip] had already put on those beautiful background voices. It was real nice. I originally wrote that song on the bass guitar. Then Don came and helped as he always did, and then Skippy added on those real high parts, and that just made the song beautiful.'

Like the debut album it originated from, 'Someday' has endured for over half a century. In more recent years, Grape fan Chrissie Hynde acclaimed: 'It's one of my top three albums of all time... Years later I realised that I'd lifted something for The Pretenders. I was listening back to 'Someday' and thought: "Wow! That's where I got 'Talk Of The Town'."'[76]

With recording sessions wrapped up and the album's release date just six weeks away, Spence and Lewis flew to New York with Rubinson to mix and sequence the LP. As Mosley recalls, 'Peter and Skip had the choice of what to put on the mix. They went to New York for the mixing after we finished recording the album. Don, Jerry and I weren't involved in that.'

Speaking with *LA Weekly*, the producer recalled, '[Engineer] Fred Catero and I mixed the record in New York, and Peter and Skip insisted on remixing, pushing up all the faders at once, which is why the record is so dense-sounding.'[77]

As the 6 June release date approached, Columbia Records confirmed its massive promotional campaign for *Moby Grape*. Elaborate press kits were designed and packaged, and a release schedule for the album's singles was finalised.

Writing in the 7 May issue of the *San Francisco Examiner*, famed critic Ralph Gleason reported the Grape had signed with Columbia and the label was 'preparing a big campaign for them.'[78] By then, the album's release was just four weeks away. Given some of the antics that would unfold in the following month, the publicity campaign would be almost overshadowed.

With the LP mixed and sequenced, Spence and Lewis flew back to the West Coast for a weekend of shows at The Winterland Arena. According to Tim Dellara, who knew Stevenson and Miller from The Frantics and would later become Moby Grape's road manager, it was around this time that he 'first met Skip at a rehearsal. It was just after the band finished recording its first album. They were practising at the heliport, which was right by The Ark. It was actually the first time I met Peter, Bob and Skip.

'Skip was just this happy, crazy guy,' reflects Dellara. 'He could get pissed at times, but most of the time he was just really happy – and that's not to say he wasn't really focused on the music.'

On Friday and Saturday 19-20 May, the Grape played the Winterland's *Rock Revolution*, sharing the bill with a variety of acts including Love and PJ Proby. By the time they stepped off the stage after their Saturday night show, the band were seventeen days away from release of their debut LP.

With the Avalon booked for the release party, Columbia was busy arranging to fly record executives and the music press into San Francisco for the show. Although it was commonplace to host such events in LA and New York, the record label wanted to capitalise on the growing interest in SF.

Before the release party, on the first weekend of June, Moby Grape was set to perform at the *KFRC Fantasy Fair And Magic Mountain Festival* at Mount Tamalpais State Park, Marin County. Billed as a benefit for Hunter's Point Child Care Center, the event was to be held at the Cushing Memorial Amphitheatre, a 4,000-seat, open-air venue.

In addition to Moby Grape, the lineup promised The Grass Roots, Sparrow, The 13th Floor Elevators, Sons of Champlin, Jefferson Airplane, Smokey Robinson and The Byrds. A short piece in the

San Francisco Examiner offered a handful of enticing details, promising 'a 40-foot-tall Buddha blowing incense and bubbles.'

It had now been a full year since Skip Spence parted ways with the Airplane; two years since his father had passed away. Already married for three years, his wife was expecting their third child in mid-October.

For all of that time, his life had been lived in high gear. As far as music was concerned, the free-spirited Spence seemed to just bounce from one success to another. But all of that would begin to change in the summer of 1967; the so-called Summer of Love.

CHAPTER THIRTEEN

FALSE STARTS

Los Angeles was breezy on the first day of June 1967. The temperature climbed to 65F in the afternoon. For ten cents you could buy a copy of the *Los Angeles Times*, which offered such ominous headlines as: 'ARABS MASS FORCE TO COMBAT ISRAEL'; 'JOHNSON MEETS WITH ADVISORS AS GLOOM OVER MIDEAST MOUNTS'; 'MONSOON SEASON'S DARK SKIES PORTEND GRIM VIETNAM OUTLOOK'; 'US BOMBERS AGAIN HIT HAIPHONG AREA, SMASH OIL DEPOTS'.

But all was not doom and gloom. If you flipped to Section V of the paper, you would read about an upcoming music festival set to unfold about 300 miles to the north. Of the event, Art Seidenbaum wrote: 'Monterey is girding power structures – official and electrical – for a mid-month festival of plug-in pop music that promises to lure 100,000 – how do you count 'em – 100,000 young people to one peninsula. Meanwhile in Los Angeles, the sponsors of this first international non-profit pop hurrah are trying to hold headquarters together.'[79]

That HQ was located at 8428 Sunset Boulevard. It looked like an empty lot, but there was 'a small refurbished building whose white-painted pop-postered walls shelter the spirit and mechanism of the [Monterey] festival, an art department, a publicity office and constantly inhabited conference rooms.'[80] About twenty feet above

128

was a vast billboard, proclaiming the name and date of the upcoming event: *Monterey Pop Festival...* 16-18 June.

The billboard also offered a full bill of acts set to perform at the event: The Mamas & the Papas, Simon & Garfunkel, The Beach Boys (who would later cancel), The Byrds, Ravi Shankar, Buffalo Springfield, Otis Redding, Jefferson Airplane – and, of course, Moby Grape.

The Grape wasn't currently in LA, but nearly 400 miles to the north. At home in Marin County, the musicians were gearing up for the *KFRC Fantasy Fair And Magic Mountain Music Festival.* But with continued heavy rains and the kick-off to the festival getting closer, organisers had to make a decision. In conversation with the State of California Department of Parks, with just a day to go, they decided to err on the side of caution and postpone the event.

Although it was delayed by only a week, Moby Grape was unable to take the rain check. After their album-release party, scheduled for Tuesday 6 June at The Avalon Ballroom, the musicians were set to fly east for a quick string of shows and promotions in New York City, before returning for Monterey at the midpoint of the month.

With the Marin County festival postponed, the band spent the first weekend of June just waiting. The release of their album was a handful of days away. It was marked to be a triumph, a sure-fire hit. After all, they'd been one of the hottest acts in the Bay Area virtually since their inception. For months they'd been receiving white-hot buzz, via word of mouth or such publications as *The Village Voice* and *Crawdaddy!*. Expectations among the folks at Columbia Records, producer Rubinson, manager Katz and so many of the band's loyal fanbase were high.

And why not? Moby Grape was a killer live act with original songs that boasted great variety; complex arrangements; impeccable harmonies; an infectious groove.

On Tuesday afternoon a contingent of hired hands flitted about, making the last touch-ups at the Avalon. Tables were set up;

decorations were on display; plates of food and drinks at the ready. When the doors opened in the early evening, an invited cavalcade of press, A&R executives and musicians strolled through the entranceway. They were struck by a scene that screamed of extravagance.

There were lavish press kits in boxes (precursors to the deluxe boxed set); Moby Grape wine bottles, balloons and other decorations. The *Oakland Tribune* reported that Columbia 'gave out scads of free invitations to hippies in the Haight-Ashbury, all of whom showed up to lend colour. Everyone was dancing and they dropped 30,000 baby orchid blooms on the floor, which became slippery and people began falling down.'[81]

To Tom Lewis, Peter's TV producer father who was in town for the event, all that PR may have seemed a little over the top. To Bob Dylan, who'd recently re-signed with Columbia and was hanging out in the band's dressing room, it might also have seemed a bit too much.[82]

Hitting the stage, the Grape ran through airtight performances of 'Ain't No Use', 'Rounder', 'Looper', 'Bitter Wind', 'Changes', 'Indifference', and 'Someday'. At one point, Janis Joplin stepped onto the stage to join in.[83] They played with authority and energy, impressing those new to the band and charming their many followers. For Katz, Rubinson and the suits at Columbia, it was a phenomenal night. Once again, Moby Grape had proven it was one of the best live acts in America.

It must have seemed at that moment as if nothing could go wrong. The band had the world at their feet. But after months of success, their luck was about to run out...

With the night winding down, the audience of 1,500 gradually left the Avalon. As they'd done many times before, various members of the Grape made their way across the Golden Gate Bridge for an afterhours jam at The Ark. On that night they had a small entourage in tow, including three 17-year-old, co-ed, high-school students from San Mateo who, according to later testimony, wanted to write an article for their school newspaper.[84]

The Ark was bustling with activity, so three members of the Grape headed out with the girl students to find a place to chat. Driving in two cars, they ended up at a fire trail above Marin City.

Shortly after the cars arrived, deputies Richard Russell and Frederick W. Garrison approached, carrying flashlights.[85] Skip Spence was present, shirtless and bare-chested. When Jerry Miller gave the deputies permission to look through the ashtray of the car he was borrowing, they found what they described as 'marijuana' – but likely only amounted to roach ends. At 2 a.m., Miller was arrested for possession (a felony) and all three musicians were accused of contributing to the delinquency of a minor (a misdemeanour).

Feeling tired, Bob Mosley had driven his Porsche back to his Mill Valley apartment earlier in the evening. Early in the morning, his sleep was interrupted by the telephone. 'Peter's wife, Diane, called me early in the morning,' the bassist explains. 'It was about two-thirty or three o'clock. She asked me to go with her and bail Pete and them out of jail because they got busted. I told her, "No, wait until the morning and call his dad." So, Pete's dad went over.'

After posting bail on Wednesday 7 June, an exhausted Spence, Miller and Lewis met up with Mosley and Stevenson to catch a plane out of town. Moby Grape was booked for a television appearance and a weekend of shows at a popular Manhattan club, Steve Paul's The Scene.

'I don't remember having a band meeting after the arrests,' Stevenson explains, 'but we did talk about it. It was probably when we were flying out to New York. Jerry and Peter thought it was kind of a tempest in a teapot.'

Joining the band on its trek eastward was newly deputised road manager Tim Dellara. 'I think I only went to one gig before Monterey,' Dellara recalls. 'That was in New York, at The Scene. The band played a TV show, with The Chambers Brothers and The Staple Singers. The first hotel Matthew put us up in was the Henry Hudson. And we got there and said, "Holy crap!" It was cheap!'

The following morning, Thursday 8 June, the story of the arrests cropped up in daily papers across America – whether in longer versions or a condensed UPI iteration. A piece in San Rafael's *Daily Independent Journal* reported: 'Three of the five members of Moby Grape, a rock'n'roll combo, were charged yesterday in Marin Municipal Court with leading a trio of "flower children" girls astray.'[86] Miller, the article reported, was also facing a charge of marijuana possession. To make matters worse, the unnamed writer went on to publish the home addresses of all three bandmates – who already had fans showing up at their door sometimes.

With the fiasco of the arrests making the press and a court appearance set for the following week, the Grape played The Scene from Friday 9 June to Sunday 11 June. Sharing the bill were the eccentrically loveable Tiny Tim and Toronto blues act John Lee and the Checkmates.

'The Steve Paul Scene was downstairs and it had a stage that was sort of a semicircle,' Stevenson remembers. 'It had a reputation for having top-flight entertainment... Janis Joplin was there one time. I remember having a conversation with her. She was telling me about her family, and how much she missed her family, and how being on the road was getting her down. You know, Janis could be really rough and tough, but she was also really vulnerable.'

When the Grape was performing in Manhattan, Skip also befriended a more typically mid-sixties girl vocal group from New York, named The Cake. Fixtures at the ultrahip Ondine Discotheque and Steve Paul's The Scene, the trio was discovered in early '67, signed to Decca and flown to California to record at Gold Star that June.

For a brief time, they stood on the verge of being the next big thing. Visitors to their sessions included Cher, Jimi Hendrix and Eric Burdon. But, after releasing a debut single, 'Baby That's Me,' in September, The Cake would miss out on the hit parade. Still, they drew endorsements from *American Bandstand* presenter Dick Clark and DJ Wolfman Jack. Teenaged lead singer Eleanor

Barooshian also drew the admiration of Skip Spence, with whom, it was rumoured, she had a fling.

While the New York trip went well, scornful comments about Columbia's massive marketing campaign started to seep into press reports on the band. The *Honolulu Star-Bulletin* offered a downbeat prediction: 'Moby Grape, a new San Francisco group, believes in producing by the bunch. Columbia Records has just released FIVE new singles and an album... Radio station program directors across the country are scratching heads over which single, if any, to program. Normally an artist released only one record at a time and the only decision faced by stations is which side to play. Maybe one side of the singles will catch on, but it won't be easy.'[87]

Pioneer rock critic Robert Christgau wrote in *Esquire*: 'I will be disheartened if one of the five singles recently released by Moby Grape – 'Omaha' and 'Changes' are the best – does not become an enormous hit.'[88] Unfortunately, 'Omaha' would soon drop off the chart and the Grape's chance of a Summer of Love hit faded away.

Back in California, Miller, Spence and Lewis appeared in a Marin County courtroom on Thursday 15 June. The three pleaded innocent to the charges they faced, with a jury trial booked for 14 August. Miller also pleaded innocent to the additional felony charge for possession; as it was a borrowed car and there were other revellers at the fire trail, the roach ends could arguably have been left by anyone. His preliminary hearing was scheduled for 30 June.

Once again, the home addresses of Spence, Lewis and Miller appeared in print. One unnamed reporter stereotypically described Miller as a 'longhaired and bearded member of Moby Grape.'[89]

The following day, the *Philadelphia Daily News* reported the band would be joining The Mamas & the Papas on their upcoming tour of the northeast, but echoed the *Star-Bulletin*'s scepticism about Columbia's elaborate promotional campaign.[90] Still, amid all the hype and bad press about the arrests, positive reviews of the Grape's debut kept popping up.

On Thursday 15 June, *The Tampa Tribune* noted: 'The Grape's disc contains a fine collection of hard rock interlaced with soft ballads.'[91] A few days later, *The Boston Globe* offered praise: 'Columbia has a strong new entry in the rock sweepstakes with the debut of Moby Grape.'[92] Then there was *The Honolulu Advertiser*: 'Moby Grape, that hot quintet, is finally beginning to happen. And why not? They're the epitome of modern pop-rock.'[93] In Montreal, *The Gazette* simply wrote: 'They can't miss.'[94]

One lonely negative review did appear in the *Los Angeles Times*. Acknowledging Columbia's massive marketing scheme, Pete Johnson added: 'But the album... is disappointing. Many of the songs sound harsh: voices are near the cracking point and instruments are competing for volume rather than blending.'[95]

Still, over the next few months, years, even decades, praise for *Moby Grape* would be near-unanimous. In his ever-perceptive prose, *Crawdaddy!* editor Paul Williams noted in the June 1967 issue: 'Moby Grape is one of those beautifully inextricable groups with four guitarists (including bass), five vocalists, five songwriters, and about twelve distinct personalities (Skip Spence alone accounts for five of them). The Grape is unusual for an SF group in that it does not have an overall, easily-identifiable personality. It is without question schizophrenic – which is nothing bad, because the group is extremely tight and they simply shift personality from song to song. Their music is always unified.'[96]

On Friday 16 June, Moby Grape played The Hullabaloo Club in LA. Originally built as a dinner theatre during Hollywood's Golden Age, the venue held about 1,200. Back in the early 1940s, $1,000 would get you a club membership with a lifetime cover charge and reserved seat. In 1967, a few dollars would get you a seat for the night to catch the Grape and Sons of Adam.

'There were go-go dancers when we were there,' Stevenson chuckles. 'They had girls dancing in cages and we were playing on a rotating stage.'

It was at that show that Rolling Stones road manager Michael Gruber first saw the Grape perform. 'There's thousands of kids sitting there... quiet,' he whispers. 'And I say, "What's goin' on?" And [the manager] comes on stage, and all he says is, "Moby Grape." He walks off the stage and they go on, and the kids go bananas. I say, "Who's this?" I'm captivated by it. I'm hypnotised.'

While the Grape was playing The Hullabaloo Club that night, the Monterey Pop Festival was getting underway a few hundred miles to the north. 'All the girls drove down to Monterey. I was pregnant with Omar at the time,' Pat Spence recalls. Laughing, she adds, 'We drove down and the guys flew down.'

At that time, band members were expected to keep their marriages quiet to portray an image of being single and available. 'We got to the motel and checked into our room,' Pat recollects. 'Skip went to a show, I think it was to see Janis Joplin perform. The next day we went for breakfast and Skip introduced me as his friend instead of his wife to another musician. This guy started talking to me and I started talking to him, and Skip got pushed out of shape by that. He didn't like it at all.'

'We flew down to Monterey,' Dellara chuckles, 'which seemed ridiculous at the time! I don't remember what hotel we were staying at, but Matthew got into it with Lou Adler [who was producing the *Monterey Pop* documentary film], saying he wanted something like a million dollars for them to film the Grape, and Peter and Skip *really* got upset about that.'

The next afternoon, everyone was backstage at the festival. 'I remember we were in the tent that they had for artists and there was a security guy there, and Clive Davis was trying to get in, and they weren't going to let him in,' Dellara recalls. Chuckling, he adds, 'I remember walking over there and big shot me said, "He's okay." And they let him in.'

135

'There were all kinds of people at the motel we were staying at, from different kinds of bands, and our wives were there, and Matthew was there,' Stevenson recalls. 'It was teeming with performers.

'I think it was Pat who made some hash brownies, and Matthew ended up having some,' he adds, laughing. 'He almost lost it when he found out what was in those brownies.'

'Monterey has to be my favourite memory of playing live with Moby Grape,' Mosley says. 'Me and Pete took acid the day we played Monterey and we were stoned out of our minds at night, after the gig. Later on, we went and saw Otis Redding [on Saturday] and Jimi Hendrix [on Sunday], and all those people. I walked right up to Brian Jones of The Rolling Stones. He was dressed in an English silk outfit.'

The two chatted about microphone set-ups for acoustic recordings. Bassist Bob remembered Jones' advice when recording his folk ballad 'Bitter Wind'.

Prior to their performance, the Grape spent Saturday afternoon wondering exactly when they were going on. Weeks earlier, the fivesome had been pencilled in to play Sunday, the festival's closing day. With cancellations, new additions and an ever-changing schedule, the band got shuffled to the Saturday evening lineup – but they didn't know exactly *when.*

'I have to take the blame for us going on first,' Miller confesses. 'No one wanted to go first – no one – and I just said, "What the hell, we'll go on." When we played, people were still setting up chairs and getting settled. It was just starting to get dark out, but then when it got dark the place just livened up real nice.'

Before the Grape opened the evening show, comedian Tommy Smothers stepped onto the stage to warm up the crowd: 'The first group tonight is kind of like in a more difficult position than other groups, because everyone's getting settled and someone has to start the show… It's a difficult position and let's have a warm hand… really, let's make it extra warm… for Columbia recording artists Moby Grape!'

Cheers, whistles and applause accompanied audience members meandering to their seats. Then the Grape stepped onto the stage. With Spence stomping his foot in time, the fivesome dove into electrifying performances of 'Hey Grandma', 'Indifference', 'Mr. Blues', 'Sitting By The Window' and 'Omaha'.

While documentarian director DA Pennebaker's crewmembers were capturing the Grape's powerful opener, Stevenson's vocal mic hadn't yet been hooked up, so Spence took the lead vocal on his own. But we can't be certain of whether any songs beyond 'Hey Grandma' were caught on film. As Katz was unable to come to an agreement with the filmmakers, the band's stunning set was banished from the classic 1968 film *Monterey Pop*.[97]

Spence was livid when he found out, exploding at his manager. As Miller remembers, 'Skippy didn't hold it back! You *knew* he was pissed when he was pissed.'

What made everything all the more frustrating was that the Grape had put on such a great show. Their soaring harmonies, lively guitar interplay, soulful introspection and bursting energy were, at least in in part, reflected in *Newsweek*'s review: 'San Francisco's Moby Grape led off the concert overshadowed by the rumour, fed by the ambiguous statements of the festival management, that The Beatles would appear for the record arena of 8,500. The Grape had a driving excitement and some very nice playing with the four guitars.'[98]

Writing for *The Village Voice*, Richard Goldstein observed, 'Moby Grape opened the last [Saturday] concert in fine form, although Skip Spence could be seen backstage beforehand, laughing at his fingers and making faces at the crowd.'[99]

The performance was a triumph. After exiting the stage amid a rapture of applause, the Grape could now mingle. 'After we finished, we got to kick back and enjoy everybody else,' Miller remembers. 'There were so many pipes and joints coming back and forth from all directions it got the head all spinning.'

Speaking with *Melody Maker* after the festival, Pete Townshend said: 'I was surprised by the San Francisco groups – they were fantastic. Moby Grape was very good indeed.'[100]

'I remember on the last day I was hanging out with Hendrix and some people backstage,' Stevenson recalls. 'We were just smoking a little binky and chatting about the concert and what was going on in general. He was excited about how important Monterey was turning out to be.'

• • •

When Monterey wrapped, Moby Grape returned home to Marin County with their families. They had to prepare for a quick string of shows with The Mamas & the Papas, followed by more promotion and another performance in Detroit.

On Friday 23 June, the Grape and The Blues Magoos opened for the chart-topping harmony quartet, plus Scott McKenzie, at the Convention Hall in Philadelphia. Decades later, Lewis recalled: 'By the time [The Mamas & the Papas] came on, people were filing out. The next day at breakfast, Mama Cass came up to us and said: "You guys are a bunch of punks. You should be grateful to tour with the biggest band in America." We survived one more date, then The Mamas & Papas kicked us off the tour.'[101]

The next day, the tour shifted to Cleveland for a show at the Public Auditorium, with the sunshine-poppy Buckinghams replacing The Blues Magoos' pop-rock. 'When I think of that little tour, I think of The Buckinghams,' Stevenson laughs. 'They did a terrible job on a great Johnny "Guitar" Watson song ['Mercy, Mercy, Mercy' – a top-five hit] – and that just turned me right off.'

For the Grape, Saturday 24 June turned out to be one of those days: bad press, late arrival and near punch-ups. Before the band even arrived in the Buckeye State, an Ohio paper ran a story on their album cover – which featured Stevenson's middle finger displayed over an old washboard. Local journalist Tom Campbell tsked: 'the cover of that album has become a real subject of

138

controversy. Across the country, radio stations (who were the first to see it) are registering strong objections to the featured picture. They feel it is in bad taste.'[102] It was not a good start to the day.

Arriving in town around noon, the Grape headed over to a local TV station with manager Katz, to do some promo work and rehearse for the evening show. As the start time of the concert neared and the band members were nowhere to be seen, The Buckinghams and The Mamas & the Papas camps got more and more apprehensive.

When it turned 8:30 p.m. and the show was set to begin, Moby Grape still had not arrived. The Buckinghams hit the stage, having agreed to play an extended set. When the Grape did finally show up, all hell broke loose.

According to Jerry Miller, 'We were late for some reason, I don't know what the reason was... Then we were gonna duke [The Buckinghams] down 'cause they pissed us off. We were rascals anyway. It was just us being punkish.'

'In my memory,' Dellara reflects, 'the reason we were late was because Matthew didn't want [the Grape] to go on first. And being late forced The Buckinghams to go on first. That's how I remember it.'

As far as Katz was concerned, the band was scheduled to perform after The Buckinghams and before The Mamas & the Papas.[103] According to *Billboard*, 'Moby Grape arrived twenty minutes after the 8.30 starting time... The Buckinghams, scheduled second, went on in their place, playing extra songs. Buckinghams' road manager Peter Shelton complained after two of the Grapes, Bob Mosley and Skippy Spence shouted to the audience from backstage during the Buckinghams sets.'[104]

After forty minutes of offstage pranks, simmering conflict and an unscheduled intermission, the Grape stepped on stage. But the whole fiasco nearly prevented them from performing at all. The Mamas & the Papas' tour manager, Louis B. Robin, later scoffed, 'Other than the obligation to the audience there was no reason to put them on.'[105]

'We were all ticked off,' Don Stevenson says. 'I just remember us dropping trow and giving them a bare ass as they were performing. It was really crude of us now that I think about it, but it seemed appropriate at the time.' Pausing for a moment, he adds, 'The Buckinghams were not happy with us and we were not happy with them. There were words spoken after the show.'

Nor did Moby Grape win any friends among The Mamas & the Papas. As Dellara recollects, 'The band played really well and I remember being backstage, and then Mama Cass came over and got into an argument with somebody – something was going on with her.'

'Coming on after us wasn't working too good,' Miller recalls. 'We were on fire at those shows, and The Mamas & Papas following us just didn't work. I remember Mama Cass kind of snapping at us one time, saying, "Who do you think you are?"'

Perhaps unsurprisingly, the Grape missed the last show of the tour, at Pittsburgh's Civic Auditorium. 'I think The Mamas & Papas decided they didn't want the Grape at the next show,' Dellara says. 'And the band took it to mean, and said, "Well, we played the shit out of them." [The Mamas & the Papas] didn't want a band playing before them that was better than them.'

With Pittsburgh off limits, Moby Grape rolled into Detroit for a TV appearance and evening concert (both arranged by Columbia's Detroit A&R executive, Russ Yerge). After appearing on *Robin Seymour's Swingin' Time* on CKLW-TV that Monday afternoon, they headed over to the swanky Upper Deck of the Roostertail Club for a show. It was opened especially for the Grape that night, with the public and a contingent of local DJs admitted free.[106]

Playing with typical verve, Skip Spence repeated something he'd done numerous times before at The Ark. As Stevenson recalls, 'Skippy spun right off the stage in Detroit. It was inadvertent. He wasn't paying attention and he just flew right off. But he landed on his feet and he kept right on playing – and jumped back on the stage without missing a beat. Skippy was a great showman and his energy was just spontaneous.'

On stage, he performed like a man possessed. The scant existing footage of the band playing live shows the level of energy he brought to each performance. Something that may well have exhausted him.

A few days after the appearance, the *Detroit Free Press* wrote: 'Moby Grape proved Monday night at the Upper Deck that all the advanced promotion wasn't wrong. They are really good. Guitarist Skip Spence told me they hope to help other good San Francisco groups happen if the Grape make it to the top.'[107]

While in Detroit, the band also received some much-needed good news from Marin County: Miller's felony charge had been dropped, so the guitarist no longer had to high-tail it back to the courtroom for a 30 June hearing. It was a welcome relief, but only a partial victory. The 14 August trial for Spence, Miller and Lewis was still on the docket.

Returning to California as the month wound down, Skip must have known all was not well. June 1967 had been a month of peaks and valleys; a time of outbursts of brilliance, punctured by moments of disappointment and deep frustration.

It was a strange time for the band. Until that month, everything had seemed to be going right. The debut release should have been a triumph. Instead, it could even be characterised as a minor disaster.

Columbia Records had spared no expense on local and national promotion: a lavish release party; pricey press kits; gobbling up print and radio ad space; follow-up events in New York and Detroit.

But beyond that, none of the five singles Columbia released at once had charted by the end of June. All that over-the-top promotion smelled like a gimmick. Indeed, it *was* a gimmick, which made the Grape look like sell-outs to some.

In the middle of June, Columbia had plastered advertisements all over *Billboard*, announcing the Grape's arrival, alongside a single article that documented the record company's marketing frenzy.[108] But, with three members of the band arrested the morning after the album's release party, amid negative headlines, Moby Grape became a coterie of ne'er-do-wells in the eyes of many.

Despite all that noise, Spence's creativity didn't go unnoticed. Rock scribe Paul Williams noted: 'Skip Spence's two songs make it clear that he's the most talented – though not the most prolific – songwriter of the group. 'Omaha' to my tastes the toughest cut on the album, is one of the finest recorded examples of the wall-of-sound approach in rock... 'Indifference' is another screamer, a well-constructed, brilliantly-executed shuffle number, to be sung on the street, loud, early in the morning, or listened to in the afternoon with your fist pounding the table.'[109]

But anything positive remained bittersweet. As the summer unfolded and their legal case hung over them, the tensions between the members of Moby Grape and manager Matthew Katz also got worse. As court documents reveal:

> Katz accompanied the band on its tour through the East, which had been arranged by Columbia. He undertook the responsibility of making all of the band's travel arrangements. Scheduling mix-ups and mistakes resulted in Moby Grape's continual failure to meet the schedule previously established by Columbia Records. The group arrived late for many engagements, while missing other engagements completely. This created ill will within the broadcast industry towards Moby Grape, and the band felt that Katz was responsible... By the time the musicians returned home to California after the tour, they had stopped talking to Katz.[110]

As June turned to July and the Summer of Love got underway, Skip and his bandmates stumbled forward.

CHAPTER FOURTEEN

PUTTIN' OUT THE KATZ

Four weeks after *Moby Grape* first appeared in stores, the LP made its debut on the *Billboard* chart at number 144. The next week it climbed sixteen spots to number 128. On 8 July, 'Omaha' debuted at number ninety-eight on *Billboard*'s Hot 100 singles chart. It was, at least, a start.

On Wednesday 12 July, Moby Grape played the Oakland Auditorium. After a day off, they played two nights at Centennial Coliseum in Reno, Nevada, sharing the bill with Melvin Q. Watchpocket, another Katz-managed act.

'I liked those guys,' Jerry Miller muses. 'They were pretty good. They were doing some John Prine [country-folk songs]... They might've come into The Ark sometimes, but I don't know if they were all together at that point.'

In the middle of July, *Moby Grape* jumped fifty-seven places, reaching number seventy-one on *Billboard*. 'Omaha,' meanwhile, climbed ten spots on the singles chart to number eighty-eight.

Meanwhile, the composer of 'Omaha' had been speaking with journalist Bob Fiallo, who was writing a piece on the album. 'My life is me,' said Skip Spence, equating it with his art. 'I've always been responsible for myself; I enjoy what I'm doing whenever I'm doing it, and I like doing a little of everything, as long as

143

I'm constantly creating. My real goal in life is to perform at my optimum.'[111]

Around this time, the Grape swept into Milwaukee to play a Catholic church hall. It was an era when a band that played the Fillmore one week could be playing a high-school dance the next. Describing the gig in his *Summer Of Love*, author Joel Selvin paints a chaotic picture: 'Mosley got a shock from the school's faulty microphone and threw it on the stage in anger. Spence, not to be left out, threw his down too. One of the school fathers, fearing the band would destroy the equipment, turned off the power. In the resulting fracas, Spence smashed his guitar on the stage, threw it into the audience, dropped his pants and mooned a nun. The police were summoned, only to arrive as Katz and the band were pulling away.'[112]

While the Grape was scheduled to perform at Steve Paul's club in New York on Monday 17 July, there's no record of that concert occurring. But just a few days later, on 20 July, they played a free show at the bandshell in Golden Gate Park. The *San Francisco Examiner* was sponsoring Thursday afternoon performances and, on that day, the Grape played alongside Melvin Q. Watchpocket.

As 'Omaha' stalled in the singles chart, on Saturday 22 July, and the album climbed another thirteen spots to number fifty-eight, the Grape trekked to Santa Monica for a concert with The Yardbirds, psych-pop band Strawberry Alarm Clock, Captain Beefheart and his Magic Band and The West Coast Pop Art Experimental Band. Although they were hampered by technical problems with the sound system, the *Los Angeles Times* reported, 'The Yardbirds and the Moby Grape received the most fervent applause.'[113]

'The Civic Auditorium was in the round,' Bob Mosley recalls of the venue then home to the Oscars. 'The Yardbirds played a great show that night,' he says of the Brit blues-pop band that would spawn Led Zeppelin.

'The Yardbirds were one of those bands that we went out and watched,' Stevenson adds. 'We didn't always watch the bands we were playing with, but sometimes we made sure we did. Captain Beefheart was playing that night, too, and he was also great.'

Jerry Miller has fond memories of the Civic Auditorium. 'That's a beautiful place to play,' he muses. 'I can play that one in my head over and over again. The sound in there was great and the people were great. The Yardbirds were wonderful and the Strawberry Alarm Clock were friends too. Everybody hung out together. We all were over at Peter Tork's [of The Monkees] house in LA, and nobody knew where anybody was. We'd end up being up at somebody's house and we might end up being there for a week, with everybody getting tuned up.'

By mid week, Moby Grape were in Washington, playing Gold Creek Park in Woodinville and then Eagles Auditorium in Seattle. 'I remember playing the Eagles, because I used to go there all the time and watch bands,' Stevenson reflects. 'They used to have some big shows there. I remember watching Little Richard, and Hank Ballard and the Midnighters, and LaVern Baker. After being at that place so many times it felt really cool to be playing there.'

Shortly after the Seattle show, on Friday 4 August, attorney Terence Hallinan appeared on behalf of Spence, Miller and Lewis as the musicians' upcoming jury trial was postponed from 14 August to 21 September. According to Hallinan, the band was up in Montreal on that day.

With their album standing at a respectable number twenty-nine on *Billboard*, the Grape started a string of shows on the West Coast. They began at the Fillmore, sharing the bill with The Electric Flag on 8-9 August. The American roots-fusion band's guitarist, Michael Bloomfield, later observed, 'I didn't like the San Francisco bands. I thought they were amateurish,' but made a notable exception. 'Moby Grape was slick, guys who had paid their dues in the clubs for a long time.'[114]

It wasn't yet two months since The Electric Flag had debuted at Monterey. It can't have been anticipated that former Dylan guitarist Bloomfield would record with the Grape just five months later.

After a Thursday show at the Avalon, with heavy cover-versions specialists Vanilla Fudge and Melvin Q. Watchpocket, the Grape trekked up to Portland for a Friday performance at the Masonic Temple, sharing the marquee with LA psych-poppers and Columbia labelmates The Peanut Butter Conspiracy. The next night, they were back in the Bay Area to play the Avalon again with the Fudge.

Following that burst of shows, Moby Grape flew down to LA. Columbia had booked studio time and rented a place in Malibu for the band to stay. Their label wanted a new album, pronto.

'The place [in Malibu] was just a dried-out shell,' Bob recalls. 'It had some furniture, but not much. There were bunk beds and we were all living there together.'

Travelling with the band was road manager Tim Dellara. 'It was a nice place,' he deadpans. 'You had sand in everything all the time. You had sand in your bed. I mean, you walked out the back door and it was all sand.'

'We were right on the beach in Malibu, so it was great to be there,' Don puts in. 'Mosley tried to teach us how to surf one day.' Chuckling, he adds, 'Well, he *tried*. It was an experiment. There are some photos of it on the *Wow* album.'

In this same milieu, Katz arranged for the band to both record a song for and appear in a movie, called *The Sweet Ride*, for a total of $5,000. The production would feature actors Tony Franciosa, Michael Sarrazin, Jacqueline Bisset and Bob Denver. With a touch of biker and surfer exploitation, the sordid story, told in flashbacks, takes place in and around a Malibu beach house. It involves a middle-aged tennis bum (Franciosa), a beatnik draft dodger (Denver), a surfer (Sarrazin), the leader of a biker gang and an abused young wannabe starlet (Bisset).

Tasked with cutting a song to supplement the eponymous theme tune (performed by Dusty Springfield), the Grape returned to the studio in the middle of the month. 'We wrote ['Sweet Ride (Never Again)'] in a sort of refuge area,' Stevenson recalls. 'It was almost like they were ordering a pound and a half of music. We were told, "There's a movie called *The Sweet Ride* and we want a song about it."

'So, we went outside the studio and sat in a spot where the stairs were, and I remember Peter and I and Jerry sitting there writing the song together. I think we recorded it the same day we wrote it. It was almost like a parody, with a Jimi Hendrix kind of sound. We thought it was humorous.'

Jerry Miller remembers the song's composition somewhat differently: 'I think Don and Bob were mostly responsible for that melody,' he says. 'And I came up with something else that went with it, modulating. It fit in. So, I think it got started off with Don and Bob – and Skippy had dosed me with some acid, so my head was spinning.

'He just handed it to me and said, "This is some powerful shit." And it sure was. I remember watching the sun on the beach and I just about went crazy. I was in control and then not in control. I had to rest a little after that.' Laughing, Miller adds, 'I don't think I've recovered yet.'

Not long after that session, Moby Grape spent a day filming on a set dressed to look like a bustling club on the Sunset Strip, called The Tarantula. *The Sweet Ride* was filmed throughout the late summer of '67 and would appear in theatres the following June.

• • •

Although it wasn't an instant bestseller, *Moby Grape* reached number twenty-five on *Billboard*, 19 August. It was something to celebrate. That same day, the Grape was in Santa Barbara, playing the Earl Warren Showgrounds along with psych-punk band Captain Speed, rapidly evolving folk/jazz-rock singer Tim Buckley and The Jimi Hendrix Experience.

'It always cracked me up that Hendrix opened for us,' Don muses. 'And it was another one of those times where we made sure we went out to catch the show. I mean, *it was Hendrix*.'

There was apparently a tussle over who should open the show. In his memoir, the late Experience drummer Mitch Mitchell recalls: 'The only time that the who-follows-who bit affected us was just a few weeks after Monterey at the Earl Warren Showgrounds... with Moby Grape, fine band... [but] they insisted, or at least one of them did, that they were topping the bill and going to close the show. We said fine and went straight for the jugular – wasn't a lot left for them in the gig by the time we'd finished.'[115]

But Hendrix wasn't fazed. A day before the gig, the guitarist sat down with the *Los Angeles Free Press* in a Sunset Strip motel for an interview. When asked about US acts he liked, Moby Grape was one of the first he namechecked;[116] chatting not long after with LA journalist Pete Johnson about West Coast acts, the Grape was the only one singled out for praise.[117] Months later, in Philadelphia for a gig at The Electric Factory, reporters for *Discoscene* asked why Jimi was wearing a Moby Grape button on his Navajo hat. 'Somebody put it on, and I never took it off,' he replied.[118]

'When I watched Jimi Hendrix in Santa Barbara,' Dellara muses, 'and by that time I'd seen Skippy play quite a few times, I realised that Skippy used his hands the same way Hendrix did.

'He would slide his hand up the neck of the guitar and do a flourish. There was stuff like that that I'd seen Skippy do a bunch of times and then I saw Hendrix do them.' Laughing, Tim adds, 'And then I didn't know who copied who. But there was certainly a connection – something going on there.'

'After the show with Hendrix,' Mosley recalls, 'me and Pete drove in my Porsche back to LA and we took a downer, a red. I blacked out on the road, and we had to go and get a room.'

In late August, the Grape played a quick succession of shows at the popular Whisky A Go Go on Sunset Strip. 'It was a bit crazy there, but it was a nice place to play,' Dellara recalls. 'It was loud and the crowd was good. People loved them.'

As Ringo Starr seemed to. He was seen sporting a 'Moby Grape Now' pin as he travelled to Wales, for a meditation seminar held by the Maharishi Mahesh Yogi, on 25 August.

Perhaps the drummer had perused *Melody Maker*, where UK journalist Nick Jones had recently praised the 'Hey Grandma' / 'Omaha' single: 'Nice new, now sound… a double-sider, of which 'Omaha' is probably the most distinctive and commercial… This Grape sound though is more slapping, energetic off-beats, typically hard, forceful music. Despite the lack of subtlety they're no slouches and the guitarist is a powerful nucleus to that driving sound. Either side is a hit record.'[119] Unfortunately, Jones' prediction was off as neither song charted in the UK.

By the end of August, Moby Grape had collaborated on four songs at their Malibu beach hideaway. On the final Monday of the month, they recorded a version of Mosley's folk ballad 'Bitter Wind,' which they'd been performing since the previous fall. Two days later, they got to work on Lewis' pensive ballad 'He'; on the last day of the month, they recorded 'The Place And The Time,' a new song by Miller and Stevenson.

'I didn't think 'Bitter Wind' was one of Bob's best songs at the time,' admits Stevenson. 'But as the years have gone by, I've grown to appreciate the lyrics. And Bob goes all Roy Orbison on it too. He really lets it go in the bridge!

'I thought 'He' was great,' Don adds. Peter always left a lot of space in his songs, so there was a lot of room to play, or *not play*, and a lot of room to figure out harmonies.

'The song Jerry and I wrote, 'The Place And The Time,' was almost like a puzzle where the pieces didn't quite fit… but they *looked* like they were going to. There was an unusual structure to the song. It wasn't your typical pattern,' he recalls.

While Spence didn't have any new songs to offer at this point, three of his would end up on the band's next album. But for now, the Grape put it on hold and headed out of town for more shows. Although it's been written that their record label abruptly called off the summer sessions due to lack of progress, Bob Mosley remembers things differently.

'Columbia only had the place for a couple of weeks. I don't remember anyone telling us we weren't recording quick enough. I don't remember any of that,' he demurs.

Leaving Malibu behind, the band trekked to Lake Tahoe for a pair of shows at the Kings Beach Bowl. On Saturday 2 September, Moby Grape shared the bill with local band The Creators and Inmates; the next afternoon, both bands returned for a Sunday performance.

'The sheriff had that place, I think,' Miller recalls of the venue. 'And his kid was in the band, and he was a fan of Moby Grape. So, they got us to play there so the kid could open for us.'

John Riordan, who played with The Creators and Inmates, recalls the Grape showing up stoned and over an hour late. Still, he fondly remembers standing in front of the stage, bantering with Skip between some of the songs.

That same weekend, *Moby Grape* reached number twenty-four, its peak position on *Billboard*. It would linger on the chart for another seventeen weeks, making its last appearance on 30 December. To boost sales, Columbia arranged for KFRC radio in San Francisco to host a poetry contest, with the winner contributing lyrics to the band's next album.

On Labor Day, *The Steve Paul Scene* TV special was syndicated nationally at 8 p.m. Moby Grape performed alongside such names as Aretha Franklin, The Chambers Brothers, The Blues Project and The Staple Singers. Taped months earlier, the Grape gave airtight performances of 'Hey Grandma' and 'Sitting By The Window.'[120] Skip Spence was completely dynamic on stage, like a bolt of electricity.

'Looking back,' Dellara reflects, 'Skip was the sparkplug that held it all together, kind of inexplicably. It wasn't like he was trying to hold them together, and I don't mean that it was falling apart. But he was *the thing* that held it together – his energy and his passion.'

On Saturday 16 September, a little-known band called The Castiles covered 'Omaha' at the opening night of The Left Foot, an over-13/under-18s club in Freehold, New Jersey. The band played the song again when it returned a couple of weeks later. Writing of his first trek to California, the singer and lead guitarist reflects: 'The morning came, the truck was loaded, the station wagon prepared; I was twenty-one and we were going west. West... dream time. West... California. That's where the music was. The Haight, San Francisco, Jefferson Airplane, the Dead, and Moby Grape, one of Steve's and my all-time favourite groups.'[121]

The 'Steve' he refers to is fellow guitarist Steve Van Zandt, and the singer himself is Bruce Springsteen. He'd perform 'Omaha' with the E Street Band decades later, after Skip Spence's passing...

There was also a group in the UK's West Midlands covering the Grape around this time. 'The Band of Joy, my first band with [drummer John] Bonham,' Robert Plant recalled years later, 'that's where it all started for me. We latched onto Moby Grape.'[122]

On the mid-month weekend of September 1967, the band was set to play the Continental Ballroom in Santa Clara, with New Delhi River Band and Om sharing the bill. Yet some advertisements also listed them playing a show that same Saturday at the Sacramento Memorial Auditorium, with The Turtles, Captain Beefheart and Sopwith Camel. Ads announced that the concert was 'intended to ameliorate teen-agers' sorrow at the resumption of school.'[123] It may have been one of those rare dates when the Grape played two shows – assuming Matthew Katz hadn't double-booked.

Four days later, the trial of Spence, Lewis and Miller was postponed once more. This time it was pushed back from 21 September to 16 November.[124]

The Grape, meanwhile, was booked for a string of shows for the northeast coast over the next few weeks. Then, on the last day of September, *Billboard* announced: 'Michael Heyworth of Point Richmond, Calif. is the winner of the KFRC "Sound of San

Francisco" songwriting contest. His tune will be in the next album by the Moby Grape, who judged the contest.'[125]

Meanwhile, the musicians' conflicts with Katz had come to a head. They'd decided it was time for a permanent change. The on-again-off-again relationship had been turbulent for a long time, locked into a treadmill of quickdraw bookings and cancellations, fluctuating recording itineraries, scheduling mix-ups, and a sense of confusion over expenses, income and decision making. The musicians were ready to move on.

In September 1967, the members of Moby Grape, through their legal counsel, formally notified Katz they were 'rescinding their agreements with him because of alleged violations of the Labor Code.'[126]

As the musicians tried to disentangle themselves, they decided to lay low for a while. With a run of performances already booked for the northeast coast, Moby Grape cancelled a run of upcoming shows at The Action House, Long Island, The Village Theatre, Manhattan, The Trauma, Philadelphia, and The Grande Ballroom, Detroit, citing a band member's illness as the cause.[127]

'I don't think anyone was really sick,' Don Stevenson notes. 'But there was a lot of tumultuous stuff going on at the time. People weren't happy with management and didn't want to tour until it got resolved.'

As the band was figuring out what to do next, Pat Spence gave birth to she and her husband's third son. They named him Orion Omar Kahn Spence – but when a hospital nurse kept referring to the newborn as 'Onion,' the couple decided to call him by his second name, Omar. At just 21 years old, Skip Spence had three children and had been married for three and a half years.

A few weeks later, on the last Saturday of October, he and his bandmates played a music and art festival at McNears Beach in Marin County. It was followed, on the first weekend of November, by two nights in Concord, at Bill Quarry's Concord Coliseum.

In between those two shows, the *Oakland Tribune* put together a lengthy piece on the band. 'Skip lends a sense of insanity to Moby Grape,' it acclaimed. 'His professed favourite things include "counsellors, surprises, miracles, faith, the colour green…" And he wears lots of green stuff – what looks remarkably like wolfbane around his neck, lei fashion.'[128]

Portraying him as a kind of bandleader, the *Tribune* added: 'The Grape agrees that it was Skip's writing, singing talent and guitar that "made the Grape sound".'[129] Looking to the future, the musicians indicated they were heading to New York on 5 November to record their next album, 'about twelve new songs, all our own material, of course.'[130]

When Spence, Miller and Lewis' trial was pushed back again, this time into the New Year, Columbia booked the band to stay in Manhattan all the way to 24 November. With a sense of optimism, the musicians stepped into a new phase of their career, thousands of miles to the east of their homes.

Little did they know, however, that it would be the beginning of the end.

CHAPTER FIFTEEN

YOU CAN DO ANYTHING

New York City was cool and breezy on Sunday 5 November 1967, only reaching 45F. The musicians arrived that day and checked into their hotel, ready to resume work on their second LP. Optimistically, the aim was to finish it over the next couple of weeks.

They woke up to another cold day on Monday. It had been over two months since they'd last set foot inside a recording studio. On that autumnal day in Manhattan, Moby Grape demoed seven songs: three by Lewis ('Looper', 'What's To Choose' and 'Stop'), two by Mosley ('Loosely Remembered' and 'Bitter Wind') and a pair by Spence ('You Can Do Anything' and 'Skip's Song' – later retitled 'Seeing').

It marked one of the last times they'd record as a 'live band' in the studio. From that point on, the fivesome mainly worked in makeshift configurations, laying bed tracks and adding parts separately, layer by layer. Still, none of that day's recordings and only one of the songs would find a place on the album.

'Looper' is a song about mistrust. The Grape had first demoed it ten months earlier, at their January 1967 audition for Columbia. Left off of *Moby Grape*, the song lingered on the band's setlist but was shelved once again. Another Lewis song, 'Stop,' is a folky flower-power number calling 'For love and understanding people to appear.' A third and final Lewis number recorded that Monday, 'What's To Choose,' is a languid snapshot of someone struggling with a relationship decision. Although the Grape would have a second crack at the song in February 1968, it would be shelved again. While Lewis offered four songs for consideration, only 'He' ended up on *Wow/Grape Jam.*

Of all the demos recorded, the one that perhaps best captured Moby Grape's trademark guitar crosstalk and vocal interplay was Mosley's soulful 'Loosely Remembered.' It was fast-paced and bursting with energy – but still, the band never returned to the song.

The two Spence songs demoed that day also, inexplicably, never made it onto the next album. 'You Can Do Anything' is an infectious romp, espousing the guitarist's freewheeling, free-spirited approach to relationships and to life itself.

'That was a weird one,' Bob Mosley chuckles about the quirky lyric, scat singing and hippie vibe.

'Skippy was always pretty funny,' Tim Dellara says of the split between Spence as a conversationalist and a songwriter, 'he could be funny when he was being really serious. He could get really serious about creation, and the world, and the senses, and perspective, and stuff like that. But even when he did that, he was funny.'

'I can remember recording that song,' Don Stevenson adds. 'It's catchy. I don't know why we didn't go back to it.'

But Spence had something else up his sleeve. He also offered up a song that eventually became a signature piece for the Grape, a compact epic at just under four minutes. 'Seeing' would end up as the closing, crowning track of the Grape's third album, *Moby Grape '69*, and possibly the high watermark of the band's output.

It is a reflection on truth and perception; a call to look behind the masks that people wear; to reach for deeper understanding. It's a penetrating piece that pushes the band, and its audience, into uncomfortable territory. While the Grape would record a second take of the song in January, they'd only finish it when desperately trying to jumpstart their third album in the spring of '68.

For Stevenson, it remains a powerful work. 'We did 'Seeing' a number of times,' he confirms. 'It was scary. It was good, but it was scary. When you're doing theatre or when you're doing music, you can move somebody to be scared. You can ask someone to be true, so true, it's uncomfortably true. And 'Seeing' was uncomfortably true. It's kind of dark and mysterious... and spiritual.'

'Seeing' has a lyric about looking through someone's exterior mask into their deeper identity, their soul. In the middle of the song, the singer cries out, 'Save me!' over and over again, as though the visions have become overwhelming.

'It has all of that creative genius that Skip possessed,' Don muses. 'And later on, it blossomed into a different thing. By the time Skip got to *Oar*, he was really disturbed. He went from being a sensitive, fun, magic man to being sensitive but off the rails. 'Seeing' could've been done on *Oar*. Skip could've done another version of it for that album. It's a great song and an amazing song to play.'

Skip had been taking acid for a couple of years by the point that he wrote 'Seeing,' so it's possible that the song's perspective came out of those experiences. In recent years, Peter Lewis said in a lengthy radio interview that 'Seeing' is like a precognition of what would happen to his bandmate.

Recording so many demos in one day, Moby Grape seemed to be on a fast track to finishing the album. But things didn't turn out that way. Shelving everything so far, the band recorded three new tracks over the next two weeks. The following Wednesday and Friday, they revisited 'Bitter Wind.' What had started as a thoughtful folk ballad, and a mainstay of their setlist, was transformed into an overblown production. All the studio effects layered onto the song took it a world away from Mosley's original vision, marking one of the Grape's biggest missteps.

In between those sessions, on Thursday 9 November, Moby Grape played two sets at The Village Theatre on Second Avenue, near East Second Street. The venue had a capacity of over 2,500 and was built in the mid-twenties, initially seeing life as The Commodore Theater. (In March 1968, Bill Graham would transform the venue into the legendary Fillmore East.)

In mid-November, the Grape recorded 'Can't Be So Bad,' a soulful Miller-Stevenson number with a horn section like a bullet train. From 17-19 November, they played the Café Au Go Go in Greenwich Village. 'The place was packed with press and Moby Grape fans,' recalls keyboard player Al Kooper – a founder member of Blood, Sweat & Tears, who made their debut at those shows.[131] The next day, on Monday 20 November, the band wrapped their November sessions with 'Murder In My Heart For The Judge.' A Miller-Stevenson number with Mosley on lead vocals, it stands among their best tracks.

When girl group The Cake arrived in a studio to tape an appearance on the nationally syndicated *Woody Woodbury Show* in December, 17-year-old singer Eleanor Barooshian was sporting a pair of red satin trousers and a T-shirt her friend Skip Spence recently gave her, prominently featuring the American flag. Ordered to change out of the shirt, the singer refused and cameras shot around her during the performance.

Speaking with Chris Campion years later, Eleanor recalled, 'That's when I started rebelling against [our manager] Charlie. It was the first T-shirt I owned, and Skip Spence was the second guy I had a snog with!'[132]

During that Manhattan sojourn, Moby Grape finalised a management contract with Michael Gruber, ex-road manager for The Rolling Stones. To the musicians, Gruber represented a way to get back on track.

The trial was still lingering; exclusion from the *Monterey Pop* film was a disappointment; the summer gigs and sessions were haphazard. None of the five singles got much airplay and the LP was slowly sinking down the *Billboard* chart.

But with new management and album sessions underway, they were ready to move forward. All those complications with Matthew

Katz were in the past, while a string of December gigs and more sessions earmarked for the New Year represented a path forward.

• • •

If the band was ready to forget about their ex-manager, Katz had certainly not forgotten Moby Grape. Since he was fired in September, he'd been managing a stable of acts, starting up his own record label and even his own ballroom.

In late September 1967, he'd sat down with Walterene Jackson of the *Examiner* to chat about the Bay Area music scene. At one point, Katz told the journalist he was managing four rock groups at the time – *including Moby Grape.*

When their conversation turned to the eclectic San Francisco sound itself, Katz waxed poetic. 'Trying to describe the Sound is like trying to describe air. It's nearly impossible,' he claimed.[133] But he then elaborated, 'The Sound is made up of folk music, rock and roll, Negro blues of the 1940s, jazz, gospel, country and western music, and it comes out of people's heads and minds.'[134]

To Katz, the Bay Area music scene was ripe for exploitation. 'The sound is spreading fast now,' he evangelised. 'All the kids who were here from Illinois and Missouri this summer and heard the San Francisco bands will be waiting for them to record now and they'll help spread the Sound.'[135]

The impresario believed that if the San Francisco sound could be harnessed, then the whole thing would explode. And he clearly envisioned himself as a key figure in the movement.

Shortly after the interview appeared, Katz announced the launch of his own record label – called, naturally, San Francisco Sound. That same autumn, he trekked up to the Pacific Northwest and set up his own ballroom, which he billed as a kind of outpost for the label. Located at 1214 East Pike, Katz's new venue was just a few blocks north of Seattle University. Formerly known as The Encore

Ballroom, he rechristened it The San Francisco Sound and promptly booked an array of acts for weekend shows.

By capitalising on the phrase, Katz was billing himself as the herald of the Bay Area vibe. But the same old problems would persist: bassist Skip Bowe, who performed at Katz's ballroom numerous times with his band Games, was one artist still expressing frustration about issues with payment decades later.[136]

An early poster for The San Francisco Sound popped up around Seattle in early November, announcing shows scheduled for the weekend of 17-18 November featuring West Coast Natural Gas Company, Tripsichord Music Box and Five Pound Smile, the first two bands being managed by Katz.

But if you looked close to the bottom of the poster, you would have noticed a line that read: 'Coming Soon... Moby Grape.' Yet the Columbia recording act had no intention of performing at Katz's venue. In fact the band wasn't even aware of it.

Designed by Wallace Studios, the poster gave the first indication of the ex-manager's knock-off act, which many have dubbed 'Fake Grape.' From that moment, Katz was set on a collision course that would see the musicians and their ex-manager jostle for ownership of the band's name (and its royalties) for decades to come.

• • •

Oblivious to what was unfolding up in Seattle, the Grape returned to The Village Theatre on 23-24 November. From there, they flew to Salt Lake City for a show on Saturday the 25th. With a capacity of over 4,000, The Terrace was one of the biggest and oldest ballrooms in America. Sharing the bill was Country Joe and the Fish and a relatively new LA band, Spirit.

According to *Student Life*, 'Spirit received a five-minute standing ovation and out-performed the Fish and Moby Grape who were billed above them.'[137] But the Grape didn't have time to brood, with a whole slew of shows booked for the next few weeks.

In late November, another poster popped up around Seattle, promoting a 1-2 December weekend at Katz's San Francisco Sound featuring It's a Beautiful Day and Tripsichord Music Box. Once again, an enticing little statement at the bottom of the poster promised the curious: 'Moby Grape is coming.'

Over that first weekend of December, the real Moby Grape played the Ambassador Theater in Washington, DC. 'We stayed in Georgetown somewhere,' Dellara recalls. 'I remember that because we had a truck that wouldn't fit into the garage in the basement, and I didn't realise that until we crashed into the basement.'

By midweek, the fivesome trekked 150 miles northeast, playing two nights at The Trauma in Philadelphia, on 6-7 December, without Peter Lewis. The Grape's third guitarist missed the shows and left them to perform as a fourpiece at the time. He was taking a break around this time while he dealt with a marital crisis and reconciled with his movie-star mom. Lewis was also reputed to be dissatisfied with the direction of the band.

Manny Rubin, the owner of the venue, was quoted as saying, 'This will be the highest priced act ever to appear at a club seating 110 people,'[138] with the same report noting that 'Moby Grape reportedly commands as high as $3,500 for a one-night performance.'[139]

Flying nearly 600 miles northwest, they played a two-night stand at Detroit's Grande Ballroom over the second weekend of December, sharing the bill with MC5, the leftist, protopunk band from Lincoln Park, Michigan.

'Tim Dellara was our road manager,' Stevenson reminisces. 'I think [roadie] Bobby Moore was with us too. And Bobby would room with Tim. So, Jerry and I would room together. Maybe Tim would room with Skip sometimes – especially if Bobby wasn't there. Peter would room with Bob sometimes. They were like Jerry and I.' Laughing, he adds, 'We had factions.'

A week later, Moby Grape was over 2,000 miles to the southwest, in LA, performing two nights at the 6,300-seat Shrine Auditorium.

According to the *Los Angeles Times*, the Saturday audience was unimpressed: 'As the Moby Grape, Country Joe and the Fish, the Blue Cheer, and the United States of America sent their electronic swells pulsing through the cavernous halls, the unmoved audience sat lumpishly on the floor.'[140] The reviewer tsked about the Grape: 'Its unrelenting shrillness is meant to give it a larger than life, three-dimensional impact, but the quintet lacks subtlety.'[141]

Moving over to the Sunset Strip, Moby Grape held court at the more intimate Whisky A Go Go for six nights, sharing the bill with Sweetwater, Big Brother and Iron Butterfly. Then, fatigued, everyone flew home the day before Christmas. In the forty-nine days between 5 November and Christmas Eve, the Grape had trekked about 11,000 miles, logged six days in the studio, recorded nine original songs and played nineteen dates.

Out on the road, Jerry Miller and Don Stevenson had a pre-existing tight bond. Bill Mosley and Peter Lewis had forged their own connection. Skip Spence was, in this sense, left on his own. He also faced different pressures as a musician. He hadn't come up through the same School of Hard Knocks as Stevenson, Mosley and Miller, learning his chops on the circuit. And while he wasn't a weak player by any means, he didn't have Miller's or Mosley's virtuosity.

But on the fretboard, Spence was a true innovator as well a master rhythm guitarist. He was also the showman in the band, as Tim Dellara puts it, 'the sparkplug.' The hyper-energetic one who attracted the eyes of the audience, exuding flamboyance and pure energy on stage.

Putting that level of energy into each performance night after night, electrifying the whole venue, may also have served to exhaust him. Energy can replenish itself when everything is going well, but it's more challenging when you're navigating choppy waters.

As Christmas rolled around, members of the band stayed with their families in Marin County for a much-needed break. Pat recalls that the Christmas of 1967 was likely the year when her husband got a royalty check for around $900, from his work with the Jefferson Airplane.

Still living in Corte Madera, at this time they had Mexican neighbors who were struggling. Caught up in the seasonal spirit, Skip's generosity got out of hand. He signed over the entire check to the young family, 'so they could have a nice Christmas and we did without,' says Pat.

She was not best pleased with her husband, to put it mildly, but Spence wasn't fazed.

CHAPTER SIXTEEN

FUNKY MOTORCYCLE FOXTROT

That second album remained elusive. The band had started recording it with David Rubinson in August, while staying at the Malibu beach house, before making their way to New York for more sessions in November. Set to return to Manhattan in mid-January 1968, for round three, first they had a few shows to play, a TV appearance to tape – and a jury trial to get though.

Around the time Adam Spence turned 2 years old, Moby Grape appeared nationally on *The Mike Douglas Show*.[142] The Grape opened with a lively version of 'Omaha' then followed with a gentle rendition of '8:05.'

By this point, Skip had taken to wearing a feather-boa guitar-strap on stage. 'Skippy was totally hip,' Tim Dellara muses. 'Skippy was the hippie. Nothing he would do would ever shock me. If Skippy wore something, he owned it. It fit him.'

A glance through photographs of his performances over the years confirms it. He didn't hesitate to experiment with different styles: suit, plumes, black leather, through to the classic white T-shirt/ jeans James Dean look. His life was his art.

After that pitstop to shoot the TV show in Philadelphia, the fivesome flew to Boston to play two nights (5-6 January) in what had been an abandoned parking garage. The Psychedelic Supermarket was only a few months old by the time the Grape arrived. Without any windows and desperately in need of repair, the venue held somewhere between 200-300 on good nights during its 1967-69 run.

After the Saturday night show in Boston, Moby Grape dashed back to California. The trial of Alexander Lee Spence, Jerry Miller and Peter Charles Lewis was finally about to begin.

Alongside defence attorney Terence Hallinan, the three defendants entered Marin County Superior Court on Thursday 11 January. Reporting on the event for the *San Rafael Daily Journal*, Stephen Cook wrote: 'Long-haired and modly dressed, the Moby Grape went into court yesterday and today to tell a tale of woe brought on by fame, fortune and tight pants.'[143]

Over the next two days, evidence was provided by the two arresting officers, members of the band and three teenaged girls. In answer to why the girls were out in the middle of the night with the three musicians, one of the high-school students answered, 'It was a journalistic exercise.'[144] As to why Spence wasn't wearing a shirt, 'the night of music making had made him uncomfortably hot,' according to Hallinan.[145]

Arriving back in court on Friday morning, Lewis felt apprehensive. As he later admitted, 'On the last day I took my toothbrush because I thought we were going to jail.'[146]

On Friday, the second day of trial, the jury of nine women and three men went into deliberation. After ninety minutes, they returned with a verdict. After they declared the three musicians not guilty, 'The rock'n'rollers smiled and bobbed their heads in thanks to the jury, while the three seventeen-year-old San Mateo County girls they had reportedly led astray gushed tears.'[147] Additionally, the jury 'returned a separate verdict for Miller, clearing him of violating a county ordinance by driving a car on a fire trail without permission.'[148]

This part of the Moby Grape story, at least, had a happy ending. Spence, Miller and Lewis weren't going to jail after all. Instead, they were off to New York to finish the album.

A poster from the time indicates the Grape was scheduled to trek to Madison, Wyoming, for two nights at The Factory, 12-13 January, with local band Buffum Tool Co. opening. But did Spence and his bandmates really play on the night of their acquittal? Don Stevenson says no. He has no recollection of ever playing in Wyoming. Frank Pytko of Buffum Tool Co. remembers filling in for the Grape that night, 'when they just didn't show up for some reason. Sorry, no refunds.'[149] As the gig had clashed with the rescheduled trial date, it seems that someone had forgot to cancel.

The day after the acquittal, *Billboard* reported on a new advertising campaign for Columbia Records in New York. Releasing fourteen new albums to fuel a sales drive, the company unveiled a 'dimensional structure featuring an assemblage of gear, cut-out names of various Columbia artists, album cover reproductions, and miscellaneous "pop art" objects.'[150]

(It would be followed by a bargain-priced sampler album, the first of its kind: *The Rock Machine Turns You On*. On the cover was a drawing of the eponymous Rock Machine by Milton Glaser – who later designed the 'I Heart New York' and DC Comics logos. The sampler offered a smorgasbord of new cuts from Dylan, The Byrds, Leonard Cohen, Simon & Garfunkel, Taj Mahal, The Electric Flag, Roy Harper, Blood, Sweat & Tears, The Zombies, Spirit and, of course, Moby Grape. Their contribution to the album was the driving 'Can't Be So Bad.'[151] Quickly becoming a hot-ticket item, the LP went on to sell about 140,000 units.[152])

On Sunday 14 January, the Grape arrived in New Jersey for a benefit show. Taking the stage at 2 p.m., they performed at South Plainfield High School for the Under 21 Club TAP program supporting the local March of Dimes – a charity in aid of the health of mothers and babies.[153] Perhaps the irony of Moby Grape playing a high-school benefit – two days after being acquitted of charges of contributing to the delinquency of minors – shouldn't be overstated.

Back in Manhattan, the Grape returned to the studio for the first time in nearly two months, on Monday 15 January. That first day they had another stab at 'Seeing,' originally demoed back in early November. The next day they recorded 'Never,' a powerful, slow blues number by Mosley. (The obvious melodical and lyrical similarities of Led Zeppelin's 'Since I've Been Loving You' have been much remarked upon. The Brit band would cut their own slow blues for *Led Zeppelin III* two and a half years later.)

At the end of the week, the Grape travelled to Philadelphia for a run at The Trauma, 19-20 January. Returning to Manhattan on Sunday, they recorded in a flurry but rarely as a fivesome. On Monday 22 January, the band cut a few versions of Jerry's blistering workout 'Miller's Blues,' as well as Mosley's soulful power-ballad 'Three-Four.' Two nights later, they were back again to record one of two new Skip Spence songs he'd been cutting rough demos of, playing acoustic guitar and drums himself. Over the next couple of weeks, the Grape cut versions of both 'Motorcycle Irene' and 'Just Like Gene Autry; A Foxtrot.'

Both are true novelties. 'Motorcycle Irene' is a jaunty folk-rock pastiche of biker songs, featuring a wild, sound effects-laden climax calling back to The Shangri-Las' 1964 hit, 'Leader Of The Pack.' Tim Dellara recalls Spence playing it to the band in a hotel room a few days earlier. 'I remember thinking to myself, "That's a really great song." And then I remember seeing reviews of it later on criticising it, and I was thinking, "What's not to like about that song?"'

'It's just an amazing song,' says Stevenson. 'But I have to say that I like the demo version better than the album version. It's truer. It doesn't have all those sound effects put in.'

For Mosley, 'Motorcycle Irene' stands out. 'I just like the words to that one,' he muses. 'Me and Skip learned 'Motorcycle Irene' in the Taft Hotel, in his room. I played bass and he played guitar and taught me the song. Then, we went into the studio the next day and recorded it.'

That same night, Moby Grape, minus Lewis, recorded some extended jams. Spence participated in two on piano, 'Boysenberry Jam' and 'Grape Jam #2'. At one point that evening, Electric Flag guitarist Mike Bloomfield stepped into the studio and played piano on 'Marmalade'.

'Mike Bloomfield came in and told me I sounded like Bobby "Blue" Bland on a couple of my cuts,' Mosley puts in. 'And he played piano and we just jammed. I don't know whose idea it was to do the album (*Grape Jam*, included as an add-on to the *Wow* LP), but Peter didn't play on it at all. He was in the West Coast.'

'All those jam sessions were done at night,' Dellara recalls. It was at a point when Lewis was already taking a break from the band. 'I think Peter may have gone home, or upstate, around that time,' Tim demurs. 'I think his family had a place upstate and they came and picked him up a couple of times with a sea plane in the East River I believe.'

The next night, Thursday 25 January, the Grape cut another pair of songs. 'Rose Coloured Eyes' was a poetic ballad by Mosley, while another novelty number by Spence spoofed the honky-tonk tradition. "Funky-Tunk' was kind of a country song,' Mosley recalls. 'That sped-up voice was my voice on that one.'

'I remember 'Funky-Tunk' was pretty cool because first off, when it breaks off from the part with the helium voice, it just breaks into one of the greatest country shuffles you ever heard,' Stevenson reflects. 'Seriously! It's really in the pocket.'

Chuckling, he continues, 'And at the end of it we go, "Do the Funky-Tunk, do the..." We had all these little sayings and I remember Skip was just going off. I mean, he must've had about twenty of them. So, he was going, "Do the birddog, do the haul-a-log, do the big frog, do the San Francisco fog..." Skippy was just going on and we were adding in too. I remember that was one part of those sessions we were really having fun, just laughing.'

Jerry Miller's happiest memory of working with Spence is on 'Funky-Tunk'. 'We laughed so hard, we almost pissed ourselves! We made that duck sound, you know?' he chuckles, then breaks into the song: 'Oh my dove, where are you goin'?'

When the weekend rolled around, the Grape trekked to Long

Island for two nights at The Action House, finally making up for that show they cancelled back in September. Located at 50 Austin Boulevard, it was the island's top venue at the time, with Vanilla Fudge as house band.

Back in the studio on Monday 29 January, Miller, Mosley and Stevenson recorded another jam session. By that point they'd gotten all the way up to 'Grape Jam #9'. Sitting in on piano was Joey Scott – arranger extraordinaire for Columbia, whose collaborations ranged from such names as Frank Sinatra and Gene Pitney to Frankie Valli and The Chambers Brothers.

The air in New York was damp and chilly as Skip climbed out of his taxi at the entrance to the Columbia recording studio, 207 East Thirtieth Street. On the slate for recording that day was his country-ballroom pastiche, 'Just Like Gene Autry; A Foxtrot.'

'Skip got Arthur Godfrey to come in and play ukulele on the song. It was kind of a production number,' Mosley recalls. Stevenson adds, 'Skippy was just full of little surprises. With 'Just Like Gene Autry', he just happened to see Arthur down the hall and he ended up involving him in the song. It was completely spontaneous.'

Somehow, the 21-year-old musician charmed Arthur Godfrey into playing on the track, as well recording an over-the-top introduction. By the late sixties, Godfrey was a radio and television legend – his variety show, *Godfrey's Talent Scouts*, had featured such diverse talents as Lenny Bruce, Tony Bennett, Patsy Cline and Pat Boone.

Collaborating with Spence tickled Godfrey, as it did everyone else in the studio – and his lead-off to the song was so unexpected that it left the musicians and producer Rubinson almost in tears of laughter in the control room. Spence orchestrated a song that was at once a throwaway gag and a sincere homage to his own talented father. It evoked Jock Spence's Cole Porter-inspired performances, rather than Gene Autry, the 'Singing Cowboy' of the title.

Delivered in a velvety smooth vocal, Spence wound his way through a lyric at once faux-melodramatic and convolutedly philosophical, crooning: 'You can only be to me what I used to be / Since I've been me lately, I find you hard to see.'

So, how did he come to write the wacky 'Foxtrot' after penning a harrowing classic like 'Seeing'? Somehow, between leaving New York in November and returning in January, Spence took a turn with his writing and stepped down the path of novelty and humour.

According to producer Rubinson, it was a lark – but an intentional one. As he'd later tell *BAM*: 'everybody was taking all this shit too seriously. There were people who had put bands together, basically, to give everybody a good time, and here were these records being torn to pieces and microscopically investigated by so-called music critics... so we wanted some humour. In looking back, I wish I'd done more of that.'[154]

'The Gene Autry song seemed like an attempt to do something completely different,' Dellara says. 'I thought it was cool, something completely different from what the band had done before.'

Yet desperation could also permeate the air. With Peter Lewis taking intermittent breaks, the band was often reduced to a quartet – sometimes even a trio or duo.

The Grape was always a combination of conflicting forces. Skip Spence personified this with his darkest, most desperate song. An apocalyptic opus, 'Seeing' returns to the original meaning of the word 'apocalypse': a revelation, seeing through dreams and deceit, boring through our personal walls to see things as they truly are.

'Save me,' Spence evokes voices crying out to the gods repeatedly, 'Save me...' It's a world away from that jolly callback to the past in 'Foxtrot,' where he croons, 'Living with you really is living life so freely.'

That oscillation was all over the roadmap of Skip's life and art. Introspection stood side by side with silliness. Joy with sadness. Genius walked hand in hand with folly.

Spence was like the trickster gods of myth, or the wise fool paradox from literature. He noticed things others missed. He gazed upon what others could not, or would not, see. He juxtaposed words and meanings in unexpected ways. Things came together brilliantly for fleeting moments, before they fell apart. Ultimately, he would look too deeply into his own darkness.

But on a chilly Wednesday at the end of January 1968, Skip was still in command of his life. He had a handle on his career and his family. As the day progressed, a final version of 'Just Like Gene Autry; A Foxtrot' was recorded by Moby Grape.

The laughs didn't last long though. The next day, Steve Katz and Al Kooper – then of Blood, Sweat & Tears – dropped into the studio for a visit. The atmosphere was about as tense as it could get.

'When we got off the elevator,' Steve Katz explained, 'something didn't feel right. Each member of the band was in a different place, a different corner of the studio and not talking to each other. I told Al that it might be best under the circumstances to leave... I had to leave before the jam started. The vibe was just too uncomfortable.'[155]

That night Kooper remained to play with Mosley and Miller, along with Rubinson sitting in on drums. The makeshift quartet recorded several jams, including 'Bag's Groove,' which would sit in the can for nearly four decades. But no matter how tense the mood had seemed on 1 February, it didn't stop Kooper coming back four days later.

In fact, over the past few weeks the mood at the Taft Hotel had been one of playful mayhem. At one point Skip raced around squirting people with a water pistol, Miller recalls. Then, perhaps in late January or early February, he pulled a prank that ended up being the proverbial last straw.

'I think we were at the Taft, which was the hotel that all the airlines used,' Dellara recalls. 'So, the lobby was always full of pilots and stewardesses and stuff like that. One time, Skippy thought it would be funny to ride the elevator down to the lobby in the nude and, when the doors opened, he just smiled and held out his arms. It stands out in my memory and that prank kind of captures Skippy for me.

'We got kicked out of the Taft after that,' Tim continues. 'Skippy's prank wasn't the only reason, because we'd been running up and down the halls, having fights with water guns. And they were pretty annoyed with us. So, I went to a hotel across the street and told them that we'd just landed and needed a hotel room.' Laughing, he adds, 'So we had a bellman from the Taft walk our luggage over to this other place.'

On Saturday 3 February, the band stepped back into Columbia Studios for another take of Lewis' pensive 'What's To Choose.' Two days later they dove wholeheartedly into studio wizardry, re-recording 'The Place And The Time'. As with 'Bitter Wind', this second, lesser version would end up on the album.

While David Rubinson has been pegged as the architect of Moby Grape's dalliance with studio effects, the producer later distanced himself from the process. 'As for me ruining 'Bitter Wind',' he'd contradict, 'Mosley heard a tape put up in error by a CBS engineer, was knocked out by it, and insisted a piece of tape go in backwards. We had a giant disagreement about this – I hated it. The other guys were there when that happened in LA, where *Wow* was also done. It was during their overblown *Sgt. Pepper* period.'[156]

That Monday, 5 February, Miller, Stevenson and Mosley recorded 'Black Currant Jam,' another extended studio improvisation with Kooper sitting in on piano. While Lewis didn't sit in on any of the jam sessions, Spence had dropped out after the first night, 24 January.

'Peter and Skippy weren't into jamming too much,' Miller explains. 'I was. I figured I'd always played with an organ trio, with a B3, drums and guitar – and I made a pretty good living at it. I'd never played with a band with two guitars until I went down to Texas and played with Bobby Fuller. Then when I heard The Byrds for the first time, I thought, "Yeah, that's cool, I can play with all the guitars!"'

Thinking back, Stevenson has regrets about the *Grape Jam* disc. 'Peter wasn't on the jam album,' he reflects. 'It was a terrible thing… First off, we didn't know they were recording all that stuff. But it was just a bunch of jams. There was no structure to any of it. We were just going off and a lot of it was just awful. I think Columbia put it on there so they could have a double album.'

With only a couple of sessions left, the Grape trekked to Waterville, Maine, on Friday 9 February, to take part in Colby College's Winter Carnival Weekend.[157] The next morning they turned around and made the 400-mile trek back to Manhattan, for two nights at The Anderson Theatre with Brit symphonic-rock band Procol Harum. With hundreds of miles ahead of them, travelling in two cars, everyone was getting nervous as they drove through a snowstorm.

Recalling that anxious trip, Miller recalls, 'I remember we were just putting along because it was all ice with snow on top of that. We were coming down through Boston and stuff. And it was so slick we had to go really slow. Then here comes Skippy at the wheel, going something like 100mph past us.' Laughing, he adds, 'And I think to myself, "Man, I'm glad I'm not riding with him."'[158] As was so often the case, Spence was having fun and taking some risks along the way.

With an audience of about 3,500 at the Anderson, a new rock venue, according to the *New York Times*, Moby Grape had 'been in better form, but still engendered considerable interest. A solid phalanx of four electric guitars and drums sets up quite a wall of sound, and the Grape's four voices at shriek volume are additional excitement-builders.'[159]

Two days later, on Tuesday 13 February, they returned to the studio and cut the final two tracks for the album. One was an electrified version of 'Naked, If I Want To'; the second was another dalliance into studio sound-collage, 'The Lake.'

After the sessions wrapped, music critic Ralph J. Gleason reported: 'Moby Grape has recorded a twin LP for Columbia with long jam session tracks with a host of guest performers including guitarist Mike Bloomfield and organist Al Kooper.'[160]

After recording *Moby Grape* at breakneck speed, the band had a hard time finishing their second album, *Wow*. Mosley wishes they'd been given more time to write before Columbia sent them back to the studio. With sessions spanning two weeks in LA (August 1967), two weeks in New York (in November) and a final month back in Manhattan (January-February 1968), Moby Grape was rarely recording as a quintet anymore. Instead, there were multiple versions of the band.

One version continued to write and record the kind of catchy pop, rock, folk, country and blues songs that appeared on the *Wow* disc. They most often followed a tight format of complex instrumentation and harmonies.

In terms of production, a few of these songs also fit into the Grape's second version, embracing studio and sonic effects. The third version of Moby Grape had existed ever since 1966, when the fivesome started experimenting with longform improvisation.

Whilst recording their debut in LA in the spring of '67, various members of the band had jammed with musicians such as Dr. John. But until 1968, the Grape had never put this sort of material on record.

All that changed in New York, but it wasn't just the band that was pulling apart. During the *Wow/Grape Jam* sessions, Skip Spence himself became a musical hybrid of serious songwriter and madcap. There was a sharp difference between his two sides and the crack was getting wider.

With the double album in the can, Dellara recalls that Moby Grape played a pair of clubs in Greenwich Village around this time – likely The Bitter End and Electric Circus. After a show at Tempo Dance City, Brooklyn,[161] on 17 February, the band flew westward for a weekend of shows in uptown Chicago on 23-24 February. Working as a foursome, the Grape played two sets a night at The Cheetah Club. It didn't go well.

Writing for the *Chicago Tribune*, Robb Baker described an evening that oscillated between surly and lacklustre. 'Ever since seeing Moby Grape's second set the first night they played Cheetah recently, I've been kind of down on the west coast group that, with their first album, had become one of my favourites. Admittedly, they had just gotten off a plane that night and it was late and one of them was sick and unable to perform – but they were still lifeless, rude to the audience... and not nearly so good as their album which was being played on the stereo in the downstairs entranceway.'[162]

Flying back to California, the musicians reunited with their families and took some time off while Rubinson mixed and sequenced the new LP. With the double set to be released on 3 April, they were scheduled to play shows at the Fillmore, Winterland, and in the Pacific Northwest.

Around this time, the bandmates also found homes in Boulder Creek, away from the bustle of the Bay Area. 'My brother had lived out there,' Dellara recalls, 'and I had suggested that we should maybe move there. It was out in the middle of nowhere, up in the mountains, maybe about twenty miles up from Santa Cruz. So, I remember one time Don and Jerry and I went out looking for places there. And eventually everyone got places... except maybe for Mosley. But when we moved in some of the locals got kind of outraged and called us something like the "undesirable hippie element."'

'I had money from [Columbia Broadcasting System], I remember I put down $5,000 for five houses so they could live near each other and write,' road manager Gruber remembers, with a home for Dellara being part of the deal.

For Moby Grape, moving to Boulder Creek offered affordable homes, respite from the hustle and bustle of SF Bay and, hopefully, a chance to get close again. To find the connection the band had in the early days. It was also a time when their families could find peace.

Throughout it all, Skip Spence stayed light-hearted. 'My dad was always laughing,' Aaron remembers. 'One time I was outside and there were all these ants, and some got in my diaper and my mom had to wash me up... my dad was just laughing as all that was happening.'

Soon, everyone in the band's circle got settled into new homes. 'Skippy's house was across the street from mine,' Dellara recalls. 'It was down a couple of houses, on Creek Drive. Most of the places there were built as summer cabins. It was originally a cabin community. So, they had the fake look of a log cabin with a living room and a bathroom and a couple bedrooms.'

But just as the bandmates were preparing for a new phase in their lives, something truly strange was about to happen.

CHAPTER SEVENTEEN

THE IDES OF MARCH

On Friday 15 March 1968, the fourth anniversary of his wedding to Pat, Skip Spence headed over a hundred miles east. Merced is a small city known as the Gateway to Yosemite. At 8:30 p.m., the doors of its American Legion Hall opened; about thirty minutes later, garage rockers The Flamin' Groovies took the stage to play their set.

At around 10:30 or 11 p.m., Moby Grape stepped onto the stage and played until one in the morning. It was a disaster. As concert-goer Michael Kennedy noted, 'Definitely the worst gig by the best band I have ever seen live.'[163] Rick Jackson, hired to work at the venue, recalled, 'I was... backstage at the teardown and Mosley had his head against the wall in a position that suggested if you touch him you would get cold cocked.'[164]

Playing a bad gig was not in and of itself wildly shocking. While the Grape was a stellar act live when on its game, it could (and did) have off nights. What was much stranger was what was happening 900 miles north, up in Seattle.

On Friday and Saturday 15-16 March, a band calling itself Moby Grape performed in Matthew Katz's club, The San Francisco Sound, at 1214 East Pike. Sharing the bill that night was Indian Puddin' 'n' Pipe, an act Katz was managing, which up to recently had been called West Coast Natural Gas Company. Even by this point, they were already at loggerheads with him over finances and ownership of the band name.

It wasn't about to get any less complicated.

The poster for that 15 March show may have said it was Moby Grape, as Katz was ready to assert he owned the name lock, stock and barrel. But in fact it was another act he was managing at the time, formerly Tripsichord Music Box.[165]

After playing those shows, Katz's version ('the Fake Grape,' in Moby Grape lore) trekked to Sun Valley to play at a soiree for international skiers in town for a competition. Reporting on the show, held Tuesday 19 March, for the *Reno Gazette-Journal*, Dick Dorworth wrote: 'A Pacific Heights lady from the upper spheres of finance and society gave a party where Moby Grape provided sound, Cutty Sark added lubricant, and a wide range of cultures, attitudes and backgrounds merged to provide character. Those uninitiated to hard rock sound found the 30 by 60 ft dancing room a bit too small for Moby Grape's amplifications. But the Germans solved the problem, stole the show, and gusted the mind by dancing like crazy with white cotton sticking from their ears.'[166]

Just a couple of weeks later, the ski-party band was revealed to be 'the "new" Moby Grape (same name, different set of madmen).'[167]

Even before it was revealed, a whole cartload of trouble was already trundling down the track.

The day after the ski party, in the *San Francisco Examiner*, Jack Rosenbaum relayed the following scoop in his 'Our Man On The Town' column: 'here's a switch: The hot SF rock group Moby Grape breaks up over internal friction after this weekend's engagement at the Fillmore. But look for it to rise again – same name, new faces. Their manager owns "Moby Grape" and isn't about to drop it.' The fight for the name of the band was now made public.

Meanwhile, members of the real Moby Grape were practising in their new surroundings at Boulder Creek. 'The band did most of its rehearsing at a place in Ben Lomond,' Tim Dellara recalls. 'There was a guy who had a place to rehearse, at the Town and Country Inn [on Highway 9]. It used to be a lodge and a dance place...'

On the other side of the USA, producer David Rubinson was publicising Moby Grape's soon-to-be-released second album. Speaking at a press conference held in Columbia's New York offices, the producer announced: 'We're putting out two albums. One has the regular twelve tunes on it. The other is the jam album. It's people who just fell by and grooved in the studio. Mike Bloomfield is in it. Al Kooper is in it.'[168]

What he didn't mention was that, with Lewis' total absence and Spence's minimal involvement, the bonus disc wasn't really a band effort. The label's heavy discounting of the 'double album' harked back to the gimmicks that overshadowed the band's brilliant debut, ten months earlier.

With *Wow/Grape Jam* due to be released in a matter of days, the Grape-Katz conflict was heating up. Back on the West Coast, the authentic Moby Grape was set to play the Fillmore on Thursday 21 March, followed by two nights at Winterland. At that point, despite what Matthew Katz had asserted in the *Examiner*, the band had no intention of breaking up.

On 23 March, *Billboard* reported on Katz's recent dealings with booking agency Ashley Famous. According to the article, he was now managing eight acts – though, interestingly, Moby Grape wasn't included on the list.[169]

Reviewing the band's 21 March Fillmore show, the *Examiner* sat down with Skip to talk about the band's situation: 'Moby Grape roared back into The Fillmore Auditorium last night and vehemently denied that their rock quintet is breaking up,' the report announced. 'Spokesman Skip Spence said, "We're still a group and still together; the other Moby Grape is the imposter." With that, Spence tosses the dispute of how many Moby Grapes there are back into the hands of the original group's former manager Matthew Katz, who claims rights to the Moby Grape name and has formed M.G. No. 2 to support his contention.'[170]

The *Examiner* went on to add: 'But the original band, at the Fillmore, by any other name would still be Moby Grape musically. Their first set last night was spirited and rowdy, full of the free rolling rhythm and rousing chaos that propelled them to fame last year.'[171]

'I can't recall how we first heard about Katz's own Moby Grape band,' Dellara says. 'It might have been from our booking agent.' Pausing for a moment, he adds, 'Jerry and I did go and watch Katz's band. I think it was in Santa Monica. We just went in and looked, and I think Matthew was there. We were amazed to see these guys who looked like they were dressed up to look like the guys in the band. And the whole presentation of the songs, at least the ones we saw, was in the Grape's style.'

The next weekend, Friday and Saturday 29-30 March, one of the two Moby Grapes played at The Cheetah Club in Los Angeles. That same Saturday, the other Moby Grape appeared on stage in Lewiston, Idaho. But which one was which? Speaking to *The Spokesman-Review* in Idaho, 'Tim Dellara, road manager for the group, said this is the original "Moby Grape" and not the newly-formed group calling itself the same name.'[172]

'We got there,' Dellara remembers. 'And they said we'll have some guys meet you to drive you into town because the Lewiston grade was very dangerous in those days. It still is. We had a driver and Skippy drove another car with a couple of the guys in it. And I remember Skippy flying by us going eighty or ninety miles an hour down that ridiculous downgrade.'

After the Saturday night show, Dellara recalls, 'We were the first long-hairs anybody'd ever seen in that town. And some groupies showed up at the motel in the night. Well, in the morning, the manager woke me up saying, "The police have called and they're on their way. You have to stay and wait for them."

'I looked out my window and I saw a young lady running down the street and a police car pulled her over. So, the police came to the motel and took us down to the station and I had to talk to the sheriff... or the chief.'

From our vantage point in time, it's hard to say exactly what happened. But this was Idaho in the 1960s. Parents would have been livid about their daughters hanging out with a bunch of scruffy ne'er-do-wells. Or maybe it was really the motel manager who called the cops, rather than the other way around, after hearing from the night manager about what was going down.

Tim continues: '[The sheriff] said, "The first thing we do when we take people in here is give them a haircut. So, all you guys are going to get haircuts." And I said, "This is their livelihood, this is their career. Their hair is part of it. Can we work this out?"

'We talked for a long time and eventually he went, "We have people who are willing to press charges. But I don't want to deal with this. You guys get out of town and don't come back." As I recall, the guys were all sitting on the floor against the jail cells. And they were a bunch of wiseasses. I went, "Shut up. Don't say anything. Stay shut up. Get up and let's go." And we left. I haven't been back since,' notes Tim ruefully.

Meanwhile, when Katz's Grape played The Cheetah Club it got panned. Pete Johnson's piece on the fiasco appeared in the *LA Times* on April Fool's Day: 'If you saw the Moby Grape at the Cheetah this weekend, you did not see the Moby Grape. The San Francisco group, due to release a double album in the next few weeks, fragmented just before Cheetah booked them. Their ex-manager offered the club a group he called the Moby Grape, and his offer was accepted. Meanwhile, the real Moby Grape got back together. Three members of the real Grape stopped in Friday to hiss the artificial Grape.'[173]

'I went to a club they [Fake Grape] were playing at one time. It was at some out-of-the-way place. I was just on my own that time,' Bob Mosley confirms.

To Dellara, it was a needling experience. 'Everybody was already annoyed with Matthew,' he emphasises. 'I'm not sure if we were surprised that it was happening, but we were certainly amazed that he was getting away with this. And we were getting feedback from people who were pissed about it – people who had hired Katz's band and didn't get what they'd expected. We thought it would just fall apart by itself.'

'It was unbelievable,' Don Stevenson muses, still bewildered by the situation. 'We were touring when all that happened. Someone came up to us and said, "How can you be here because Moby Grape is performing somewhere else tonight?" And we said, "What do you mean?" And they said, "Well, there's another Moby Grape." So, we were playing as Moby Grape and working our asses off, and the next thing we knew there was another band saying *they* were Moby Grape.'

Years later, Katz spoke with *LA Weekly* about the situation, asserting, 'That band was the Moby Grape, they were playing the Moby Grape's songs and their parts, and if I say a band is the Moby Grape, then they are the Moby Grape... Who cares who the members are? I own the name, it's mine!'[174]

On Wednesday 3 April, *Wow/Grape Jam* came out – minus all the hoopla that accompanied the release of *Moby Grape* ten months earlier. But even though the hype was over, the band's new double album quickly garnered a wave of attention.

On the upside, many reviews were favourable. Unaware of the album's protracted development, the *Green Bay Press-Gazette* said: 'One gets the feeling the Grape fully enjoys recording. Their robust, irreverent music and arrangements contain all manner of unpredictable twists, turns, jokes and production gimmickry.'[175] The *Tampa Bay Times* review was glowing: 'Best album yet by the Moby Grape is Columbia's *Wow!*'[176] Similarly positive, the *El Paso Times* cheered: 'Most listeners expect Moby Grape's *Wow* to be a sizzling, shattering hard rock album, but Moby Grape surprises everyone in mixing thought-provoking lyrics with a soft-hard rock music combo.'[177]

But reviews were mixed. The *Honolulu Star-Bulletin* reported that the album featured 'some better than average songs, interesting arrangements, but no unified group sound and no particular musical point of view. And then following in the footsteps of earlier gimmickists, sports one cut which must be played at 78rpm and features an introduction and ukulele by Arthur Godfrey.'[178]

Writing for the *Los Angeles Times*, Pete Johnson said, 'The second LP from the Moby Grape... has a much better sound than its predecessor. A number of performances, however, are marred by several songs unworthy of inclusion and some childish hokery on the *Wow* half of the record, including unnecessary sound effects in 'Motorcycle Irene' and a New Vaudeville Band/Mothers of Invention gimmick number called 'Just Like Gene Autry; a Foxtrot'.'[179] For some reviewers, having to change the record to the speed of an old 78 was one bonkers gimmick too many.

Aside from the dailies, noted rock critic Robert Christgau wrote in *Esquire*: 'The only follow-up record that makes it completely is Moby Grape's *Wow*. The group's first record, overpromoted and underproduced, was dismissed as a hype by people who should have been listening. Hopefully this one, which includes a free disc of improvisations called *Grape Jam*, will make up for it. The Grape can jam but on records tries to maintain a tight sound.'[180]

But in the spring of 1968, attention wasn't solely focused on the band's new album. Dave Donnelly of the *Honolulu Star-Bulletin* observed: 'But now another group, clandestinely calling themselves "Moby Grape" has surfaced in Seattle. One Moby Grape we'll believe, but two? Perhaps lawsuits are the only way to settle the pilfering of an established name.'[181] Little did anyone know at the time, but the Grape was soon to enter into the longest court case in music history – reaching into the next century.

Back in April '68, Katz's Grape made their way down to the Grand Canyon state. According to the *Arizona Republic*: 'Many people walked away from last weekend's Moby Grape concert with not only a song in their hearts, but an ache in their pocketbooks... The Moby Grape on stage definitely weren't the same group of recording fame.'[182]

As news of the Fake Grape spread like wildfire, the genuine article toured California. They kicked things off by playing a benefit at Winterland on the day of the album's release, organised to support striking DJs at KMPC-FM, alongside The Grateful Dead, Jefferson Airplane and Sweetwater. After playing the Selland Arena in Fresno on 6 April, the Grape spent a weekend at The Carousel, 12-13 April, a new artist-run venue in the Bay Area (which would be taken over by Bill Graham in the summertime). Five days later, Skip Spence would turn 22.

On Monday 22 April, Bob Mosley recorded a demo of his new ballad, 'It's A Beautiful Day Today,' alone on acoustic guitar. It marked the beginning of the Grape's work on what would be their first post-Spence album.

Two days later, Mosley went back into the studio and added a powerful vocal track to the chorus of 'Seeing'. It was five months since the band had first demoed Skip's powerfully compact piece. ''Seeing' was a different kind of song to play,' Bob remembers. 'It was a little spacey. I didn't think it was a hit song, but I thought it was pretty good.'

On Friday 26 April, the quintet trekked north to Santa Rosa for a show at the city fairgrounds. It didn't go well. A review of the show for *The Press Democrat* described misplaced equipment, technical hiccups and tempers flaring:

'Moby Grape was storming Friday night, and it was [a] bad scene that ended in an angry clatter of flying drums and microphones at center stage.' Adding detail, the piece went on: 'The Grape's leader Skip [switched from] his guitar to the drums for an abbreviated version of the group's big hit song – 'Omaha'. The [mics] still weren't working right but the drum work was beautiful – if violent... In the last bars, the drums started to come apart as stagehands worked frantically to keep them together. But it was too late. With the last drum roll, Spence started kicking wildly and drums flew in all directions. He grabbed a hand mike and threw it angrily onto the wooden platform. It took one big bounce on the stage, and landed 100 feet into the teenage crowd.'[183]

Offering a more upbeat take, a subsequent piece in *The Press Democrat* reported: 'Up until the time the mikes fizzled and tempers flared, Moby Grape was in a pretty good groove at the recent pavilion show.'[184]

After that weekend, the band returned to the studio for more recording. On Tuesday 30 April, they cut a rocking new number by Miller and Spence, 'Cockatoo Blues.' Over the next few days, they played shows at the new Fillmore West, on Thursday and Saturday 2-4 May, and the Merchandise Mart on the old State Fairgrounds in Sacramento on the Friday, sharing the bill with Buffalo Springfield – then on the verge of imploding.

With mostly positive reviews and the band still shuttling from gig to gig, *Wow/Grape Jam* started to sell. The album entered the *Billboard* LP chart at number 114 in early May.

No one knew it at the time, but a hectic string of gigs up and down and across the USA would be the Grape's last tour as the original fivesome. By the end of it, Skip Spence would be ready to leave the band. But he'd still have a further way down to travel.

Skip and his sister, Sherry, at the Evergreen Trailer Park in Phoenix, early fifties.

(Far left) Skip outside the family apartment in San José, early sixties.

(Left) Skip during his time in the Naval Reserves (1963–1964).

(Above left) Skip, unknown woman and Billy Dean Andrus. (All above images courtesy of Sherry Ferreira)

(Above) Skip and Pat's wedding, March 15, 1964. (Photo courtesy of Billy Dean Andrus)

(Above and left) Jefferson Airplane, 1965.
©Michael Ochs Archives/Getty Images

(Above) Skip backstage at Steve Paul's The Scene nightclub in NYC, June 1967.
©Michael Ochs Archives/Getty Images

(Right) Skip and Bob Mosley at Monterey Pop Festival in California, June 1967.
©Michael Ochs Archives/Getty Images

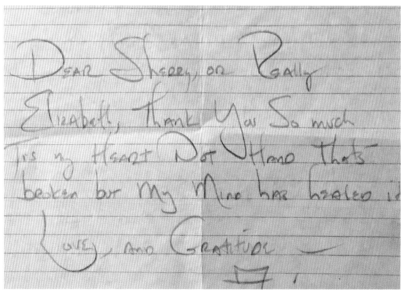

(Above top) Skip at Fillmore East, June 1971. ©Bob Gruen

(Above) Skip's letter to Sherry from Bellevue. August 1968. (Image courtesy of Sherry Ferreira)

(Left) Skip at the Monterey Pop Festival. ©Michael Ochs Archives/ Getty Images

(Top) Skip and Gordon Stevens backstage at the Fillmore East, June 1971. ©Bob Gruen

(Above) Skip and Jerry Miller performing with Moby Grape at the Right to Harvest Fest at San Francisco's Civic Center Plaza, November 1977. ©Clayton Call/Redferns

(Left) Jim Phillips's famous 'Witch Poster' for Moby Grape's Halloween show in 1977. ©Jim Phillips

(Above) Skip
performing with
Moby Grape in
the late eighties.
(All images on this
page courtesy of
Melissa Marteny)

(Left) Skip visiting family in the mid eighties. (Image courtesy of Sherry Ferreira)

(Below) Skip outside a halfway house in California, March 1994. ©Jeremy Hogan/ Alamy

CHAPTER EIGHTEEN

MANHATTAN BREAKDOWN

After flying to New York, Moby Grape spent six nights performing at a midtown club called The Generation on 7-12 May 1968. Hendrix had been there just a few weeks earlier, jamming with BB King and Buddy Guy. Located in Greenwich Village, at 52 West Eighth Street, the basement venue had a very short run as a club. Before the year was out, Jimi would purchase the building for $50,000 and spend two years converting it into Electric Lady Studios.[185]

While they were gigging in Greenwich Village, *Wow/Grape Jam* jumped twenty-three spots on the *Billboard* chart, climbing to number ninety-one. As the band closed out that run of shows, Velvet Plastic Productions took out an ad in the *St. Louis Post-Dispatch*, promising that Moby Grape would soon make an appearance at the upcoming *Fillmore Scene* series at the National Guard Armory. It was scheduled to mark their first performance in St. Louis.

Three days later, on Wednesday 15 May, Peter Lewis stepped into the studio and demoed 'If You Can't Learn From My Mistakes'. With just himself on acoustic guitar, he sang the lilting folk ballad, at once accusatory and confessional, chronicling his recent marital strife.

By now, Moby Grape had three other newly demoed songs for possible inclusion on their third album – 'Seeing', 'It's A Beautiful Day Today' and 'Cockatoo Blues'. Over the next couple of weeks, Mosley, Miller and Stevenson would create more. But first the Grape had a whole lot of touring to get through.

Trekking to Los Angeles, the band spent the weekend of 17-18 May at The Kaleidoscope, a venue they'd first played eleven months earlier when it was The Hullabaloo Club. *Los Angeles Times* staffer Pete Johnson opened his review by alluding to recent dramas: 'The Moby Grape, the real Moby Grape, as the ads said, since the San Francisco quintet had recently been impersonated at another club, attracted a sizable audience for a weekend appearance at the Kaleidoscope.'[186]

Johnson went on to note: 'They are fun to watch, fun to listen to, and danceable. Some of their songs – 'Sitting By The Window', '8:05' and 'Omaha' – are among the best products of San Francisco combos.'

'Every time they were together, mentally, and they played, they were just out of this world. They gave people goosebumps,' Michael Gruber reflects. 'And they could go from being magnificent to disaster. But they were all great, great musicians.'

One of the openers for the Grape that weekend was a blues band called Hour Glass, which featured brothers Gregg and Duane Allman. Over the weekend, *Wow/Grape Jam* jumped a very impressive fifty-one spots on *Billboard*, climbing all the way to number forty.

On Tuesday 21 May, Matthew Katz's version of Moby Grape performed at the Masonic Temple in Portland, Oregon. The posters advertising the show featured a large photograph of Spence, Lewis, Mosley, Miller and Stevenson. It's unclear if Katz thought he could claim ownership of the image of the musicians at that point. (Indeed, it was years before any performer could even claim legal ownership of their own image.) Or if he'd obtained permission to use it from the photographer, Michael Ochs.

By the middle of the week, the real Grape flew to Cleveland for a pair of shows at Le Cave, a club which started as a coffeehouse in the folk era, on 22-23 May. 'One time we landed in Cleveland,' Jerry Miller recalls, 'and there wasn't anyone there to pick us up at the airport. We were stranded there and Skippy just blew up. He was in a phone booth and he was trying to find out what was going on. He was shouting and his face was all red. He was wearing this really nice new blue suit he'd just got, and he just started spitting. Well, it was a little phone booth and some of that spit was getting on Skippy's beautiful suit.'

Of Spence's mood, Michael Gruber remembers, 'It was up and down. One day he was sweet and the next day he was in his own trip. Like he was taking a bad acid trip.'

After playing to a limited audience in the small Cleveland club, the band flew down to Texas for a pair of Friday night sets at Vulcan Gas in Austin, on 24 May, followed by Saturday and Sunday shows at The Catacombs in Houston. Dogged by the peripheral presence of Fake Grape, the band now billed themselves as 'The Authentic Moby Grape.'[187]

But things didn't go as planned. After playing at the Vulcan, the shows in Houston were cancelled over a payment dispute. According to the *San Antonio Light*, 'Love Street missed out on a chance to grab Moby Grape when the Grape reportedly upped the original money offer.'[188]

As those hiccups were happening down in Texas, *Wow/Grape Jam* rose to number twenty-seven on *Billboard* – and the Texan trip itself wasn't entirely a loss. During their time in the Lone Star State, Stevenson and Miller wrote a pair of new songs: 'Big' and 'Ooh Mama Ooh'. Both lyrics chronicled some of their experiences in Austin and drew on their current dissatisfactions. The haphazard tour schedule; the ongoing fiasco with Fake Grape; all the personal tensions within the band.

At that point, Velvet Plastic Productions announced the dates for Moby Grape's upcoming St. Louis shows, set for the weekend of 7-8 June. Sharing the bill that weekend would be West Coast Natural Gas Company and Black Swan – two of Matthew Katz's acts. Unfortunately, the promoters weren't aware that they'd booked the Fake Grape.

A couple of days later, the *Napa Valley Register* announced Moby Grape would 'be heard in a dance concert on June 14, at the Napa Fairgrounds.'[189] But that too was Katz's copycat outfit.

In Colorado, meanwhile, posters were advertising upcoming Fake Grape shows at The Denver Dog, at 1601 West Evans Avenue, 31 May to 1 June, with the Natural Gas Company again. Prominently featured on the bills was a lineup photograph taken from the band's debut album.

With their Houston shows cancelled, the real Grape flew back north. Over the last three weeks, they'd shuffled from the Bay Area to New York to LA to Cleveland to Texas, and back to NYC again. It was an exhausting 11,000 miles in all.

Arriving in Manhattan, the band checked back into the Albert Hotel.[190] Miller and Stevenson were sharing a room as usual, while Mosley was paired with Spence. Road manager Tim Dellara had a room on his own a floor or two above the others.

'The Albert was like what the Tropicana was in Los Angeles,' Dellara says today. 'It was the cheap place that bands could go, and they wouldn't be harassed too much by the management. There were a couple of good diners in [Greenwich] Village where we had breakfast sometimes.'

That same month, *Eye* magazine published a vivid piece on the Albert by pioneering rock journalist Lillian Roxon. 'It is the best of hotels, it is the worst of hotels,' she wrote, 'its prices are ridiculously high, its prices are astonishingly low; its corridors are filled to the brim with life, its corridors are perpetual reminders of death; staying there is the wildest, most exhilarating, dizzying, around-the-clock trip of all time; staying there is the most wretched, lonely, terrifying, around-the-clock bummer of all eternity.'[191]

'The Albert was a little better than seedy,' Stevenson adds. 'But it was funky and it was a major hangout for a lot of musicians. It was kind of the trendy place to be for artists. It wasn't fancy, that's for sure.'

'I liked the Albert better [than The Taft],' Mosley puts in, 'because there were more musicians there. And the Albert was closer to the studio.'

Shortly after arriving in town the Grape returned to Columbia's studios, about a half-hour cab ride from the hotel. It was time to work on their third album. Unlike the winter sessions, everyone was now rehearsing and recording in the daytime, which they preferred.

On Tuesday 28 May, the band recorded an instrumental demo of Mosley's new number, 'Soul Stew'. While it had a real groove, it was missing that three-way guitar interplay – the 'crosstalk' – that Moby Grape was famous for.

Over the weekend of 31 May-1 June, the band was booked to play two shows a night at a new hotspot on Second Avenue. After taking over the rundown Village Theatre, where the Grape had performed back in November, Bill Graham had overseen some renovations and reopened the venue as the Fillmore East in early March.

Over the next couple of months it would become a hub of musical activity, hosting Big Brother and the Holding Company, Albert King, The Doors, The Who, Buddy Guy, The Mothers of Invention, Blue Cheer, Iron Butterfly, Jefferson Airplane, The Jimi Hendrix Experience, Sly and the Family Stone, and The Byrds.

Reviewing the Grape's weekend shows, *Cash Box* was upbeat: 'Columbia artists Moby Grape headlined four shows at the East Village theater last weekend. They presented a polished act with none of the usual delays for "tuning up".' But the reviewer had reservations: 'During the hour they were on, not one member of the group acknowledged the audience. They were, except for some fine singing, completely silent. Although it would be nice to know what songs were being performed, the lack of info did not seriously detract from an excellent performance.'[192]

Peter Lewis later told Jud Cost that the Grape had performed without him. As he explained: 'So we had to leave our families and spend months at a time in hotel rooms... Finally I just quit and went back to California. I got a phone call after a couple of days. They'd played a Fillmore East gig without me, and Skippy took off with some black witch afterward who fed him full of acid.'[193]

It was a sign of the times. A groupie girlfriend could profess herself to be a practitioner of black magic. In the late 1960s, drugs sometimes collided with occultism to create a whole new form of paranoia.

On Sunday 2 June, a full-page ad in the *New York Times* announced Moby Grape would be playing the *Schaefer Music Festival* in Central Park, alongside blues icon Muddy Waters. The show was scheduled for the end of the month, Saturday 29 June. Beforehand, the band was booked to play gigs along the East Coast including the Café Au Go Go (NYC, 6 June), The Limit (Howard Beach, Long Island, 7 June), and The Electric Factory and Flea Market (Philadelphia, 13 June).

Meanwhile, Katz's version of Moby Grape had hit a wall in the Midwest. On Sunday 2 June, Velvet Plastic announced in the *St. Louis Post-Dispatch* it was cancelling its upcoming shows, issuing the following apology:

> We are very sorry to announce that due to circumstances beyond our control we will be unable to present MOBY GRAPE as we had planned on June 7th and 8th. This seems to be a case of mistaken identity. It has come to our attention that there are two MOBY GRAPE bands. The one we are familiar with headed by Bob Mosley that records on Columba Records is the MOBY GRAPE we thought we were going to be presenting. We learned that their ex-manager owns the name MOBY GRAPE and, since his separation from the original group, has formed a second group and is presently booking them as MOBY GRAPE. Fortunately, we learned of this before it was too late BUT hope to be able to present at some time later the original MOBY GRAPE.[194]

Over the next few days, Katz quickly rebranded his band as 'the *New* Moby Grape.'[195] On Monday 3 June, a configuration of the original Moby Grape – which on that day may, or may not, have included Lewis or Spence – made their way to CBS and recorded a full version, with vocals, of Mosley's rocking 'Soul Stew'.

That same day, just three miles south of the studio, pop artist Andy Warhol was shot at his sixth-floor studio in the Decker Building. He narrowly survived the bullet that Valerie Solanas, author of the misandrist *SCUM Manifesto*, pumped into his vital organs, but would be in discomfort for the rest of his life. Two days later, Democratic presidential candidate Robert F. Kennedy was shot three times at the Ambassador Hotel in Los Angeles. He died from brain injuries the following day. The assassin, Sirhan Sirhan, would veer between saying he acted in the name of the Palestinians and claiming to be too drunk to remember his crime.

It was a time of paranoia and violent social malaise. It was a time when Skip Spence was living on Mahattan's Lower East Side and starting to lose his grip on reality.

From hereon we can't be certain of the exact sequence, or accuracy, of events. But this is what *may well have happened...*

Three days after recording 'Soul Stew', the Grape were booked to perform at the Café Au Go Go. They may have played the show as a foursome on Thursday 6 June. It was a popular spot located in the basement of the New Andy Warhol Garrick Theatre at 152 Bleecker Street, just a half-mile south of the Albert Hotel. The last time they'd performed there was in November 1967, back when they were getting started on their New York sessions.

While Peter Lewis was perhaps still in California, the musicians headed over to Long Island with their road manager the following night. The fifteen-mile trek might take over an hour in a taxi through the city. Tim Dellara believes it was at a Fillmore West gig, about a month earlier, that two guys showed up and handed him $5,000 in cash, saying, 'Skinny Frankie wants youse to play at his club' for two nights.

Located in Howard Beach, The Limit was owned by brothers Frank and Dave Adlesh. They'd bought the club years earlier with some of the $95,000 Dave received as a bonus for signing with National League baseball team the Houston Colt 45s.[196]

'It was a one-storey building, from my memory,' Dellara says. 'The club supplied the PA. All we brought was instruments and amplifiers. I don't think there was a stage. If there was, it was pretty low. There was room to get behind the stage. I remember being at the back of the stage when this young woman came up. I think it was on the second night. She was thin and plainly dressed and she handed me a note to give to Skip.'

As the woman walked away, Dellara looked at the note. It read:

skip spence, skip spence,
sittin' on a fence
which way you gonna go?
Joanna Wells

At the end of the show, Dellara went to see Skinny Frankie. 'He was probably in his late 20s or early 30s. He was a typical manager we'd run into. He was very nice to me, but he was pretty scary to the guys who worked for him apparently.' But the road manager was still thinking about that note.

Was Joanna's strange nursery rhyme inviting Spence to spend some time with her? Was it beckoning him to leave the band? Whatever it meant, instead of heading back to the Albert with Dellara and the Grape, Skip left with Joanna. From that point on, the two were joined at the hip.

'Skip was with us at the Albert for a while,' Stevenson puts in. 'But then he met his muse and moved in with her. I don't remember too much about her. But they were in the Village together.'

'From my memory,' Dellara shares, 'Skip disappeared the night he met Joanna Wells… he didn't come back that night and he didn't come back for at least a couple more nights. Skippy wasn't around and he didn't show up for a couple of sessions at least…

'Don went to talk to him and then came back really dispirited. Skip, apparently, was talking about starting up a new band called The Cows, and he wanted to go to England and get Eric Clapton and someone else to join the band… he wanted Don to sing in the band, and not to play drums anymore. That was Skip's plan – and Joanna had complete control over Skip.'

'I wondered what Skippy was doing when he'd moved out of the hotel,' Don Stevenson explains. 'We'd had some rehearsals and he didn't get to them. He wasn't really in the band at that point. So, I called him and asked him what he was doing and what he was up to, and he told me he'd moved to the Village with this woman…

'So, he gave me his address and I went over to visit,' he recalls. 'I really had the feeling that Skip was leaving the band. There was always the sense of other possibilities for Skip. It was like that for Mosley, and I guess for all of us, but it was more so for Skip.

'When Peter went back out West, I had the sense that he was coming back. But Skip told me he wasn't… And I had some tea with him and sat there talking with him. There was an old man [likely homeless] lying on the couch and Skip and Joanna called him "Father." Skip was saying stuff like, "We talked to our father and I'm not supposed to be playing in a band anymore."

'And Joanna would say stuff like, "We're gonna move forward and do all this new material, isn't that right, Skippy?" And Skippy would just say, "Yeah, I'm not supposed to be playing in a band anymore." So, he wanted to do his own music… or *she* wanted him to do his own music.'

Not long after he'd shacked up with his intense groupie follower, they were involved in two altercations.

'I was at the Columbia studio in New York one time with the art director, Bob Cato,' Bob Mosley recalls. 'I was talking to him, and Skip and Joanna came into the room and sat down. Skip didn't have a shirt on and he had a cross around his neck – and he was really speeded up. He was loaded out of his gills. He said he'd like to have me play in a new band he was forming, and I said okay, I would. Then I said, "If you want this girl to come along, I ain't gonna play." She reached over and started hitting me in the face. Then she went after Bob [Cato] with a pair of scissors.'

'I was in the room when that happened,' Dellara adds. 'I was standing on one side of the room talking to someone... And I didn't hear what Skippy was saying to Bob. But the first time I noticed something happening was when I saw Joanna run over and grab the scissors and Bob Mosley stopped her.'

Shortly after that incident, Spence returned to the Albert Hotel to collect his things. As Mosley remembers, 'I shared a room with Skip then. And he came into the room with Joanna to get his stuff. I had a gun with me, and I just sat there and waited for them to leave.'

'[Cato] filed charges against them,' Bob recalls. 'It was before Skip went to Bellevue [psychiatric hospital]. I went to the trial when they went before the judge – me and [Michael] Gruber.' The details of Bob Cato's charges, and the subsequent outcome, are lost to time.

'When Peter left New York [earlier], I didn't think he was leaving the band,' Mosley reflects. 'It was like he was taking a break. But when Skip was with Joanna – I don't know how he met her, but he changed overnight. When he went to live with her, I didn't think he was coming back.'

Unable to entice Spence back into the band, the three remaining members returned to the Albert and to their recording sessions. One afternoon, likely in the second week of June, while Stevenson and Miller were at the studio working on a new song, Skip showed up at the hotel.

Another group staying there that month was an all-female band from Dayton, Ohio, called The Bittersweet. They had their equipment set up in the ballroom and used it for rehearsing.[197] Drummer Louie Dula had very distinct memories of Skip that day, which she shared many years later:

'He had been hanging out with this girl (I can't remember her name) but she always dressed in black and told us she was a "witch". Skip would bring her to the Albert... I think she gave Skip some bad drugs and he just flipped out. He came back to the Albert and tore an axe off of the wall by the fire extinguisher box and went to Jerry and Don's room and tried breaking down their door...

'Then Skip went looking for them up at Columbia Studios. I think that's where he got taken to Bellevue psych ward,' she'd recall with obvious sadness.[198]

'Skip knocked on my door,' Dellara confirms, 'and he was standing there with this hatchet in his hand. He didn't have a shirt on. He looked to me like he was really high. He was sweating and he wanted to know where Don and Jerry were, and I said, "I think they're in their room." Because I knew they were in the studio at the time.

'And Skip asked me for the room number... I told him the number and he left. Then I called the studio and they told me that Don and Jerry had already left, and that scared the shit out of me. So, I ran downstairs and I found the door sort of all slashed and hanging open, and I expected to find a bloodbath when I got in there. I thought I'd really screwed up by telling him that they were there.'

Thinking back, Stevenson explains, 'Jerry and I were with David [Rubinson] in the studio. And David was just trying to do the best that he possibly could. It wasn't like when we did the first album and we had a band, and we were ready to play in the studio. Everything was piecemeal and very fractured. [David] just wanted to create a good album. He was encouraging [us] in any possible way to get everything done. So, Skippy would be there for a while and Jerry and I would come in. And Bob would sometimes come in. That's how we recorded after our first album. But then Peter went out west and Skippy stopped showing up,' Don recalls of how everything started to crack.

'So, one day, Jerry and I were recording 'Texas' [later retitled 'Big'] at the studio, and when we were done with that we left to go back to the hotel. But Skippy had been there looking for me. And he knocked on my door with an axe, and after that he went to Columbia because someone had told him we were up at the studio. So, when he went up to the studio, we must've passed each other on the way. That's when he had his breakdown at the studio.'

'We were in the CBS offices,' Michael Gruber says. 'It was the same building as the recording studio on [West] Fifty-Seventh Street. He got into the offices and one thing led to another and I don't know who called me, but I came running. I was looking through the glass and Skip was freaking out. I went into the office to calm him down... I don't know if he was tripping or what.'

Speaking years later, Rubinson recalled becoming a potential target himself: 'Jerry and Don called me and said: "David, Skip's coming up to the studio to kill you." So we locked the doors, then called security. Skip arrived in a taxi, with an axe, in his pyjamas. I was waiting for him in front of the studio. I had no idea what to do, but I just walked over and talked to him: "C'mon, man. You'll be okay, it'll be okay." He was scared, wild-eyed. Somehow, he let go of the axe, and the only thing I could think to do was call the police and have him taken to Bellevue.'[199]

'I talked to David and told him about what was happening at the hotel,' Stevenson reflects, 'and David had just had his experience at the studio. We were concerned for everybody's wellbeing, including Skippy's. That's when David booked Jerry and I at another hotel because Skip had left the studio. I'm not sure if we went back to the Taft. Then, I think David had Skip picked up. No one was sure what to do. We didn't know if Skip was going to go back to the Albert. That's why Jerry and I moved out, but I don't know how or where Skip was picked up.'

'Mose [Mosley] was so afraid that Skip would come back during the night,' recalled Louie Dula. 'I remember I sat outside his door all night watching for Skip 'cause I told Mose I knew Skip wouldn't try to hurt me...'[200]

'We had a meeting later that night... maybe it was the next day,' Dellara recalls. 'I don't know what happened with Don and Jerry because they couldn't go back to their old room because the door was chopped open. But I remember we had a meeting with Gruber and Arnie [Gruber's assistant] and Rubinson and Mosley and Jerry and Don and me.

'They all started talking about what to do. And I don't know if Skip had already been arrested at that time, or not. But Rubinson and Gruber were saying that we need to go down and file a criminal complaint – otherwise, Skippy will be out on the street and he'll get hurt. Somebody could shoot him. If he's running around like he was, a cop could shoot him. And that's why, as I recall, Jerry and Don went down and signed a complaint. We thought that he wasn't going to go to jail or prison or anything. We thought they were going to do an evaluation of Skip and then put him in some kind of rehab... he'd have some time to come down, because we thought he was on this kind of LSD called LBJ – which was going around at the time – that gave something like a week-long high. No one expected Skippy would end up in prison,' reflects Tim.

According to Rubinson, it was Stevenson and Miller who brought in the cops. He told *Crawdaddy!*: 'Don and Jerry had to come over [and] swear out complaints, because there was no way we were going to get him clean or dry or down or get this shit out of his system. We didn't know what to do, maybe we fucked it up. I didn't know anything about drugs, I have to admit it. But talking to him and seeing him... his eyes were like one-arm bandits.'[201]

Writing in the guestbook of *The Ark* website back in 1999, Sandy Hass, an habituee of the Albert back when she was a young woman, reflected: 'I met the guys at the Albert Hotel, way back during the gory/glory days... I will never forget the day when various and sundry people kept coming to my place and "freaking out" over Spence... When all of the excitement was over, they were all kind of like deflated balloons: deprived of energy, confidence and optimism.'[202]

What happened in early June shocked everyone. 'I think Bob was pretty shook by it,' Dellara reflects. 'He was totally dispirited by the whole thing. I don't think any recording got done. I think we were all just looking to get out of there and get home at that point.'

It's unlikely that Moby Grape performed at their scheduled Electric Factory gig on Thursday 13 June. By that point, everyone was probably back in Boulder Creek – apart from Skip Spence, who was in the prison ward at the hospital.

Ironically, as everything fell apart in Manhattan, *Wow/Grape Jam* propelled the band to its pinnacle on *Billboard*, reaching numbers twenty-two on 8 June and twenty on 15 June.

'I was worried when the whole thing happened,' Mosley sighs. 'I didn't talk to David about it. Don and Jerry and I took a plane back west. We hauled butt back to Santa Cruz. We almost stopped the band at that point. We didn't know what to do.'

With a major gig at the Schaefer Music Festival fast approaching, Moby Grape faced an uncertain future. Thinking back, Stevenson reflects, 'When Skip left, I didn't think that there was any doubt we were gonna play. There was no thought about the question, "Should we not play together?" Although it might have been thought about individually, I don't remember us having a conversation about that.'

When Don, Jerry and Bob met with Peter Lewis in California, the four musicians discussed how, or indeed whether, they might continue as a band. Just a short time removed from their ostentatious album-release party at the Avalon – from the drama of the Monterey Pop Festival – from the conflicts with The Mamas & the Papas and The Buckinghams on tour – from the chaos of the summer of '67, all was hanging by a thread.

'I thought that Skippy would be [in Bellevue] for a while and that he'd come out after a short while and that he'd come back into the band,' Dellara explains. 'That's what I thought at the time.' He wouldn't meet Skip Spence again for several years.

Thinking back to the happier days before Spence's breakdown, Michael Gruber is wistful. 'I used to enjoy Skip,' he says warmly. 'He used to laugh a lot.'

But Moby Grape had now lost its mercurial ball of energy. Still, the other four musicians decided to press forward. The plan was to halt work on the third album and perform for a while, to see what happened.

After all, there was still the possibility that Skip would clean up and get released over the next few weeks. He might return to the band that next month, in July, and they could pick up the album from that point. For the time being, they could write new material while touring.

On Saturday 29 June, the Grape shared the bill with blues legend Muddy Waters at the Schaefer Music Festival at Wollman Rink, at the south end of Central Park. A review in the *Daily News* said the band 'lashed the night with its "new blues, San Francisco sound".'[203]

In a syndicated piece, Richard Robinson was less favourable, noting: 'Moby Grape sauntered onto the stage at the Central Park Music Festival last week without the group's rhythm guitarist Skip Spence. Skip is reported to be resting and unable to play with the group although no official statement has been made. The rest of the group performed a set that was a combination of polish and complete sloppiness.'[204]

Neither reviewer knew that Alexander Lee Spence was now officially both a hospital patient and a criminal inmate, just a few short miles from Wollman Rink. As the days turned into weeks and the weeks into months, the psychically devastated 22-year-old would discard any intention he may have held of returning to his band.

Shortly before Spence was confined to Bellevue, Solanas was admitted for psychiatric examination after the shooting of Warhol.[205] Her case ensured Skip Spence was not the most controversial patient at the facility that June.

It was a busy time at the institution. Bernard Weinstein would take over as the hospital's administrator near the end of the month, the first non-medical holder of that position.[206] A couple of weeks later, an African-American inmate of Rikers Island prison was admitted after he was injured in a racial attack.[207] As a result of head injuries, he was catatonic; it would eventually lead to twenty-three arrests.

• • •

That next month, the Jefferson Airplane arrived in New York City for two nights at the Fillmore East, 19-20 July. Over the last sixteen months, the band had become popular with record buyers and critics alike, reaching the *Billboard* top ten with two hit singles, climbing to number three on the LP chart with *Surrealistic Pillow* and number seventeen with *After Bathing At Baxter's*.

By July 1968, they'd finished recording their fourth LP and were planning to head off to Europe for a late summer tour, after a handful of Midwest shows. Before leaving Manhattan, guitarist Jorma Kaukonen made his way to the East Side community of Kips Bay. Once there, he walked along First Street and stepped through the entrance of Bellevue Hospital, to arrange a visitor's pass and spend some time with his old bandmate. Skip had been there over a month by this point.

When he reflects on that summer visit, Jorma thinks about *Oar* – the LP Spence would record shortly after his release. 'It's a breathtaking album. It really is,' he testifies. 'Because I visited Skip when he was in the institution in New York – now, on some levels, because I'd seen him in those less than happy circumstances, I feel [*Oar*] reflected what was happening to him internally. But as an artistic work, I think it's brilliant.'

After pausing for a moment, he adds, 'At that time, none of us had been arrested yet, or anything like that. So, to run afoul of society and to be incarcerated – because he was definitely incarcerated, I mean, it was just so sad.

'Skip obviously had unresolved mental issues, whatever they

were,' Kaukonen reflects. 'I'm not a doctor so it's not for me to say. It's just so sad that he was unable to deal with them. Going to Bellevue is not a vacation. Obviously, he ran afoul – whatever actually happened with the axe and chopping down a door, I don't know because I didn't see it. But it was just sad.'

It's quite possible that Skip Spence's Manhattan breakdown was a temporarily drug-induced psychosis. But it would spiral into mental illness, followed by self-medication and addiction. In this sense, his five-month stay in Bellevue was no cure at all.

Still, over the next few months Skip mapped out a host of new lyrics in his notebook. He'd been keeping notebooks at least since he was a 14-year-old boy, sketching pictures and writing songs when his family was living at the Pepper Tree Inn. It was an outlet, something he'd stick with even when he was close to down and out.

'When I saw him, he was like *our Skip*,' Jorma muses. 'He didn't seem like the kind of person who should be in an institution.

'But after that, it became apparent – even to me, who wasn't tuned into that kind of stuff at the time – that he was inhabiting more than one universe at the same time. I think that whatever was happening to him, with his mental issues, was not getting better... you know, back in those days, mental issues might've been attributed to just being eccentric and being cool. But he passed that stage by that time.'

As the summer wore on, labour unrest bubbled to the surface at Bellevue – first with a painters' strike, later with a nurses' contract dispute.[208] In mid-August, seventy-two nurses at the hospital threatened to quit.

Amid all the unrest, Skip Spence sat down to write a short letter to his sister, Sherry. Postmarked 12 August 1968, the envelope bears the sender's name 'Alexander Spence' on the front. On a torn piece of lined paper, the enclosed note reads:

Dear Sherry, or Really,
Elizabeth, Thank You So much
Tis my Heart Not Hand That's
broken but My Mind has healed it—
Love, and Gratitude—
A

The flipside of the note bears a stamp at the middle of the page, where it was torn in half. The stamp reads 'CENSORED.' Below the tear is the following message:

Inclosed [sic] is my creation, read it light,
It speaks for me—
    Bless you—
    Alexander — (Is Paul with
       you. Get him
       I am coming
         soon—)

It's so hard to gauge his state of mind at this point. But perhaps by reverting to his given name, Alexander, he was letting go of 'Skip Spence, rock star.' Cancelling out any possibility of returning to Moby Grape.

Reflecting upon those difficult months and what was to follow, Sherry Spence says, 'That whole incident was horrifying. It was the worst thing ever. It was a tragedy for everyone – for my brother, his family, our mom.' Sighing, she adds, 'That someone so talented could have everything turn around in the blink of an eye, it was devastating.'

A few weeks after Skip had written to his sister from Bellevue, John Dennis Logan found himself committed to the hospital after he tried to swim across the Hudson River.[209] On Friday 13 September, substitute teacher Ralph Poynter was confined to the prison ward after he attacked a police officer. It was his fourth

202

arrest in three months.[210] In early November, Theodore Harmon was admitted for psychiatric examination after he stabbed singer Billy Daniels at the Latin Quarter nightclub near Times Square.[211] A few days later, David Thibodeau was taken to the hospital after police pulled him up from the ledge where he was hanging on the Brooklyn Bridge.[212] By the time Thibodeau was admitted, Skip Spence was getting ready to leave.

Don Stevenson wonders about the long-term consequences of Spence's prolonged stay in Bellevue. 'That's so hard,' he sighs. 'For Skippy to have to go through that whole thing. It was awful. I wish he would've written a book or talked about his experience. I'm sure... that what happened to him could've caused more damage to him.'

CHAPTER NINETEEN

OAR

At the end of August 1968, Pete Johnson of the *LA Times*, reviewing a recent Moby Grape concert at The Kaleidoscope, noted: 'the band has become a quartet with the departure of Skip Spence, who sang, played rhythm guitar and mugged and danced frenetically during their appearances. Spence left because of ill health.'[213]

A month later, Ralph Gleason ominously informed readers: 'Moby Grape's star figure Skip Spence has left the group and now there's a possibility that it's all over for them.'[214] Already, the rumours surrounding his quick exit were beginning.

Then, as if to compound the situation, on Monday 4 November, Matthew Katz filed a suit against Moby Grape for $1 million in Superior Court. As reported in the *San Francisco Examiner*, the band's ex-manager claimed the Grape was 'still using the name although there are no longer three members of the outfit still with it.'[215]

Interestingly, just as Katz was getting his seven-figure lawsuit underway, the *four* remaining members of Moby Grape were gigging, demoing new material and getting ready to start recording their third album.

Not long after Katz filed suit, Skip Spence was released from Bellevue still wearing his hospital pyjamas.[216] New Yorker David

Rubinson picked him up and took him in a cab uptown. It was the musician's first taste of freedom in a long time.

After buying him some new clothes, Rubinson took Skip to the Regency Hotel on Park Avenue and booked a room. They ordered room service and sat down to talk.

Speaking later with David Fricke, Rubinson explained: 'I heard him sing to me in a hotel room... You have to picture this: I go up to the desk to check him in, he's in his Bellevue pyjamas... He had pads and pads of lyrics.'[217]

Completing the picture, the producer told *Crawdaddy!* back in the day: 'We're sitting in this fancy hotel room... I asked, "What do you want to do?" He said he wanted a Harley-Davidson and he wanted to go to Nashville and wanted to record; he'd written a lot of songs while he was in the hospital. Then he wanted to get on his motorcycle and drive home to his wife. I said, "Fine."'[218]

During his time confined in Bellevue, Spence had written songs prodigiously and was ready to get back into a studio to put his ideas on tape. Only this time, he wanted to get away from New York and LA, where so much had gone wrong. For the artist who now wanted to be known by his birthname, Alexander Spence, recording in Nashville would be a clean break from his past. It wasn't just geographical but musical: the capital of country music was a big step away from the gimmickry of the *Wow* album.

A popular myth tells us Spence rode a motorcycle from New York all the way down to Nashville, Tennessee, in the late autumn of '68, still wearing his pyjamas. But as entertaining as that image is, it just isn't true.

Returning to Boulder Creek in late November, Skip penned a few more songs and told Pat he was going to Nashville to record an album. 'He asked me if I was going or staying,' she remembers. 'And I said, "I'm coming." So, we packed up everything we could. We couldn't take everything but we took clothes and we got I-Ching, the cat that we had, and we rented a U-Haul van.

'We just left our place. It was a log cabin, and it was on a property that went down about two acres to the river. We only owed about $1,200 on it.'

With their three kids and cat in tow, the Spences made the thirty-five-plus-hour drive to Nashville. Instead of following Skip down to Tennessee, Dave Rubinson elected to keep his distance. Explaining his reasoning, the producer said, 'I wanted to go sit there with him and work on the songs in the worst way, but it was the wrong thing to do. If I had been there, I would've *produced* it. I didn't know how to sit quietly and get sandwiches. It wasn't in me. I thought he needed a tape running all the time.'[219]

For the project, Rubinson selected an engineer he felt would work well with Spence, Mike Figlio. 'I said, "Mike, I'm sending Skip Spence down and he's going to do an album. Listen to me very carefully: I want you to get a lot of tape. I want you to load up the machines with tape and have one of them running *all the time*. Never. Stop. Recording. Whatever happens, even if it gets crazy, even if it gets quiet for twenty minutes, I want you to record *everything*." Everybody had heard about the ax and Bellevue. He said, "This guy's crazy, what are you doing?" I said, "He's a good guy, he's harmless."'[220]

But the Nashville engineer recalled things differently. Of the time he was assigned to work with Spence, Figlio told *LA Weekly*, 'Skip was a really nice, respectful kind of guy, easy to work with. We'd try just about anything musically in the studio, trial-and-error-like, to get what he was looking for. I'd recorded Dylan, so Skip's approach didn't seem all that radical.'[221]

'When we got to Nashville,' Pat remembers, 'Skip started cutting songs and writing more songs for the *Oar* album. We were there for a couple of weeks maybe.' Through December they stayed in a Nashville motel, not far from Columbia's studio. But Spence wasn't set up in a traditional recording space in the building. Instead, he'd work in an editing room that served as a makeshift studio space for his project. In his physical isolation, he'd record perhaps the first truly solo album.

It was Skip's first time living day-to-day as a husband and father since leaving Boulder Creek back in the spring. His first time working continuously in a studio since the previous winter. For seven full days, spread across an eleven-day span, he toiled in the studio and became a one-man band.

'He was kind of a way-out cat, creative,' Figlio added much later, 'knew what he wanted, basically, as far as what he wanted to play, and left it pretty much to get the sound that he wanted… [Skip] just did one instrument at a time, just kept building it – and once we got it all down, he and I sat in the studio and decided how we wanted to mix it and how we wanted to make it sound.'[222]

Thinking back to their phone conversations in '68, Rubinson noted, 'Mike was saying, "Hey David, you don't understand, the guy comes in, sits for an hour or two, nothing happens and all of a sudden he starts singing. He wants to put on his own bass, then he puts on guitar…" I said, "*Yeah, yeah, yeah.* Whatever, just keep the tape running and do whatever he says."'[223]

Spence had a vast reservoir of song ideas, as well as the ability to play a variety of instruments and the freedom to record what he wanted. He even had a song called 'I Got A Lot To Say.'

The material Skip Spence cut in Nashville comprised mature, haunting or sometimes silly songs about loneliness, marriage, trust, materialism, sex, spirituality, infidelity, freedom, even war and peace. From Wednesday 3 December to Sunday 14 December 1968, he laboured on song sketches and fully developed pieces alike.

He played everything, overdubbing drums, bass and, of course, guitar. Working in fits and starts, he whittled his song pool down, eventually settling on a dozen or so pieces. He added layer upon layer, cutting version after version. The performances reached across the guttural-to-trilling range of Spence's voice, with backdrops shifting from cloudburst to the metallic percussion of hammering nails. It was something more intimate than Spence – or nearly anyone else, for that matter – had ever committed to tape before.

It's impossible to know what Skip was feeling during those days, but with a newfound freedom as a solo musician and a reconciliation with his family, the young songwriter may have envisioned that his approach to musicmaking had a future. He may even have felt elated.

Putting together a reissue of the album thirty years later, producer/archivist Bob Irwin was intrigued by what went down on 12 December, just as the sessions were winding down. 'Skip spent the morning,' he explains, 'completing overdubs on 'All Come To Meet Her', finalising the components for the master playing a Fender bass and singing live vocals, Skip recorded nearly non-stop. He then added a drum kit overdub to some of the track that evening... This one, intense day of recording was responsible for *Oar*'s simplest, yet most texturally intricate moments. For folk familiar with the original album, this is where 'Margaret-Tiger Rug' is culled from... it's also when 'Grey/Afro' was recorded.'[224]

With the multi-tracks in hand, the Spences left Nashville in the middle of December, making their way northeast. It was time to start work on the mixing and sequencing. As Pat Spence explains, 'After Nashville, we drove to New York for the album to be completed, the cover made and so on.' Around that time, Columbia was entertaining the idea of releasing Spence's material as a double album.[225]

Someone had fallen in love with the Spences' pet cat, so I-Ching stayed behind in Nashville. As Sherry Spence adds, 'My sister-in-law sent me a postcard while she was there, telling me she was pregnant and hoped it was a girl. She figured I already knew about the pregnancy since my mom had been told.'

'We were in New York for Christmastime,' Pat recalls. 'We stayed in a hotel for about a month. Then one night Skip told me he made arrangements for another motel out in the Catskills. It was 10:30 at night and he wanted me to drive out there. So, I moved down there.

'When I was trying to get out of New York, I kept making a wrong turn and I ended up getting back to the same place on the highway,' she recalls, 'but I finally got out of the city and then I hit snow. It wasn't in the outskirts of New York; it was out in the boonies.

'So, I finally got to the little town, Skip had told me that it had a little waterwheel. I got there at about two o'clock in the morning. But I couldn't find that darn motel. When a car passed me, I waved it down and the driver gave me instructions to go down the road to a river… I crossed over the bridge but then I got stuck in the snow. And my car wouldn't start.

'I had my three boys in the back of the car,' confirms Pat, 'so I got everyone dressed in their coats and we walked up the hill and found a farm and I called for a taxi… the taxi driver came by after not too long, and he took us to the hotel. Skip showed up the next day.'

She'd learned by now to live with his characteristic carelessness. But it also led to some unnecessary legal complications. 'Skip never told me that he didn't buy that U-Haul,' Pat explains. 'He came home [from Bellevue] on his new motorcycle. Then he sold his motorcycle and rented the U-Haul, but we were supposed to drop it off somewhere. And Skip just kept using it.

'So, the cops came over one time and they said, "We're expediting him to San José." … Skip was gone and I was still at that motel outside New York. We'd been there for a couple of weeks. And they took the U-Haul, and they took our car. I didn't have any money on me. So, I said, "I've got to get back to California, I've got to get back home."

'The cop said, "I'll tell you what, pack what you can take home and leave the rest here. I'll give you some money and when you send the money back to me, I'll send your stuff back to you." Well, he gave me about $200, and we got on a Greyhound bus and went back to California.'

After thousands of miles on the road, the Spence family found themselves back in the Bay Area in early '69 – though they'd taken their separate paths to get there from the east. Returning to their roots in San José, they lived with Pat's mom for a short time. After a while, they rented a duplex unit near San José State College (now SJSU) by a little bookstore.

In time, Skip would start frequenting a local coffeehouse called Jonah's Wail. Located at Tenth and San Carlos Streets, it was a place to meet with others, to listen to music, to perform, and to chat about politics, philosophy and spirituality.

Sponsored by the Campus Christian Ministry, Reverend Richard Young explained, 'Jonah's Wail helps others assess what a Christian is like – people go to the Wail not realising it is church-sponsored, and then they find out what Christians are like... It's a listening post, where the clergy and fellow students can respond to the questions being asked. In the past, church provided answers to questions never asked.'[226]

As the couple awaited the birth of their fourth child, at Columbia's East Fifty-Second Street studio in New York engineer Don Meehan mixed each track of *Oar*. Eventually, the recordings were trimmed down to a sequence of twelve songs.

Meanwhile, throughout January 1969, Moby Grape stayed close to home. The band performed a handful of shows around the Bay Area, anticipating the release of its third album, and prepared for a European tour. It was also on its last legs.

Following Skip's departure, the Grape spent the summer and fall of '68 gigging sporadically and performing inconsistently. Just as Spence was released from Bellevue in November, his ex-bandmates were busily recording a strong set of ten songs between 11-24 November. After a handful of shows in December and a local smattering in the New Year, *Moby Grape '69* was released to little fanfare at the end of January.

There was no massive party to usher it in, nor any bonus disc to entice buyers. But still, *Moby Grape '69*, clocking in at under thirty minutes, showcased how much talent and versatility the foursome still had to offer.

The highlight of the album was its closing track, a powerful leftover from Skip Spence's time in the band. 'Seeing' was a reminder of what once was and a pointer toward what might have been. When reviewing the Grape's new album, the *Oakland Tribune* opened with: 'Skip Spence, former leader of the group and composer of 'Omaha', their biggest hit, has left the once-San Francisco-based group and the result is that 1969 may be the year of the squashed grape.'[227] The band just couldn't shake the ghost of their departed sparkplug.

Years later, Lewis recalled of a period of personal turbulence, 'At that point I was under the care of a psychiatrist, taking all this Librium so I could stay with the band. We kept drifting along as a quartet. We made *Moby Grape '69*, in an attempt to rebound from the *Wow* album, which was overproduced. And it's a cool album. Although we could have rehearsed it a little more, we still believed in it. But I think we were waiting for Skippy to come back and he never did.'[228]

Then, as the legal record tells it: 'On March 27, 1969,' a year and a half after firing Matthew Katz, 'the band members filed an action with the Labor Commissioner requesting to set aside their contracts with Katz because of fraud, breach of fiduciary duty, and violations of the Labor Code sections 1700 to 177.46 (Talent Agencies Act).'[229] With Katz's November lawsuit unresolved, everyone was stepping down a path that would turn into decades of litigation, injunctions, accusations and counteraccusations.

When Skip turned 23 years old on 18 April, he was already four months removed from his Nashville sessions. By that point, the last members of Moby Grape had quietly gone their separate ways. The band, to all intents and purposes, was defunct.

Of the days leading up to and following release of *Oar*, David Rubinson would later reflect: 'When the people at Columbia heard it, *Oar* made no sense to them at all… It was so honest and real that the record company couldn't relate to it. Neither could radio or critics. So they put it out, barely, and it sank without a trace.'[230] But for its creator, *Oar* had been his means of sailing back to shore after the trauma of Bellevue – where much of it was written.

If you picked up a copy of the *LA Times* on Monday 19 May, 1969, you would have read a giant front-page headline that announced: 'APOLLO 10 HEADS FOR LUNAR ORBIT.'

On that same day, two young musicians arrived at a record store in the city. They'd known one another for just under three years but had packed in a lifetime of experiences. It was the spring day on which *Oar* appeared in a few select record shops across America, to little fanfare.

Over four decades later, Peter Lewis recalled: 'I took Skippy down to LA on the day *Oar* was released – the same day Neil Young's first record came out... I remember buying them both in a record store and going into a listening booth with Skip. I realised that he'd made a masterpiece and Neil's was totally jive. But Neil got famous and Skippy went to the streets. And that's something I live with every day.'[231]

While Neil Young's second album, *Everybody Knows This Is Nowhere*, would establish his rugged Crazy Horse sound, Spence never got that chance to follow up his own classic. For both him and his devotees, it was nothing short of a tragedy.

During those long months in Bellevue, those fleeting weeks of his journey home to Boulder Creek and his trek to Nashville, Spence had written songs that offer glimpses into his mind in the summer and fall of '68. *Oar*, in its originally released form, was a forty-five-minute journey into the psyche of Alexander Lee Spence. It was unlike anything that had come before, a completely singular statement.

There are moments of pure joy; nocturnal despair; snatches of elation; flashes of hope and sadness. It evokes the innocence of childhood; the pain of mistrust and betrayal; spirituality; the hedonism of free love; joy and laughter; the depths of depression; the hope for tomorrow. It is almost frighteningly authentic.

Don Stevenson later observed: 'Because I knew some of his thinking, some of it was really telling and transparent. Some of it was very scary, and some of it was very touching. Some of it was really funny. When I first listened to *Oar*, it was like I was reconnecting with Skip. I was reminded of what a brilliant guy he was and how much I cared for him.'[232]

'I didn't get it the first time I heard it,' Jerry Miller admitted. 'But as I listened more and more, I realised it's a great album. It's not technically all so hot, but the writing, the trickiness of it, is just amazing.' He added: 'Skip had a lot in him. Even though he was messed up in some ways, he was multi-talented.'[233]

The album opens with 'Little Hands,' a soft, hopeful tune that calls back to childhood; to a frame of mind where everything is still possible, to where even the world itself can be reimagined. Starting softly, slowly, Spence repeats and tinkers with verses, like a series of mantras he's singing to himself. It's his dream of the future.

In contrast, 'War In Peace', which comes mid-album, sonically calls out the paradoxes, harsh realities and violence of the adult world. Closing out the album, 'Grey/Afro' marks the struggle to live and communicate in modern times. It is a ten-minute psych trck, evoking the 'Frightful days that we are living in.' By late 1968, violence across American cities – and half a world away, in Vietnam – had turned into a constant hum in the backdrop of the evening news.

'Diana' is a song of emotional pain but it's also optimistic, documenting a connection made. As Peter Lewis later revealed, Skip wrote the song for his soon-to-be ex-wife, Diane, who was one of Skip's touchstones in that harrowing period following his breakdown. Standing opposed to that is 'Weighted Down (The Prison Song),' a journey into a mind haunted by mistrust. Bellevue had been his prison for months on end and, in that time, Spence wrestled with demons and doubts: 'Weighted down by possessions / Weighted down by the gun... Whose socks were you darning, darling / While I been gone so long?'

'I liked 'Weighted Down' best,' Stevenson says today. 'I knew what that song was all about. It was pretty ominous.'

'Weighted Down' is a harsh, dark night of the soul. 'Cripple Creek' and 'Broken Heart' are located further down the same dark river, telling tales of suicide and death. A death that fails to bring any hoped-for reunion with lost loved ones.

Yet those heavy burdens can be lifted by the playfulness of wordplay. There's some kidding around in the country croon of 'Broken Heart', singing of an Olympic swimmer 'whose belly doesn't flop' and a race car driver 'whose pit, it can't be stopped'.

But even this 'honey-dripping hipster' can be brought low by 'the right hand of the Lord'.

In 'Lawrence Of Euphoria' and 'Margaret-Tiger Rug,' Spence paints pictures of a circus-like world of fun and indulgence. Over-the-top characters like 'Vivian from Oblivion' and 'Ellie Mae from Californ-i-a' join the songs' namesakes in a Fellini-esque cavalcade of bliss and free love. Even when Skip veers into spirituality, he can't resist throwing some naughty humour into 'Dixie Peach Prominade (Yin For Yang)': 'I could use me some yin for my yang … You'll stay underneath me at night'.

Throughout *Oar*, Skip Spence oscillates between light and dark, funny and tragic. His forays into spiritual musings are no different. While 'Books Of Moses' is a raspy biblical blues, 'All Come To Meet Her' is like a secular hymn for a pilgrimage – to pay erotic homage to a woman. His spirituality is Christian, Buddhist, communal, individual, but perhaps most of all, bawdy.

'Books Of Moses' was the album's spiritual touchstone – as spirituality was the theme that Spence returned to throughout his life. He gave his sons names from the Old Testament; he found solace in church groups at times when he was trying to ground himself – as in 1969, the year that *Oar* was recorded, and the late 1980s.

But Skip's spirituality was also intensely personal. In a 1967 interview, he told the *Oakland Tribune* he'd converted a closet-sized room into a small temple 'where incense burns day and night.' Asked to list five of his favourite things, two of them were 'miracles' and 'faith.'[234]

In a radio interview, Lewis mused of the album: 'It's a document about redemption. Even though, if you listen to it, you can get to the seventh track and all of a sudden it goes back to the primal where it's just a redundant rhythmic thing he played on the bass and the drums... It's like monkeys beating on a hollow log with a bone to keep the cougars away at night, before they invented fire. It was like he'd reached the point of primal freedom with that record... Most people didn't get there, where he got. But he didn't live a happy life because he got there... [*Oar*] was either ahead of its time or from the ancient world. It was both.'[235] Musically, the album is as eclectic as you can get, running the gamut from psych-pop to the most mournful country music.

For Bob Mosley, *Oar* is still too painful to listen to, over fifty years after it first came out. 'I didn't like that album,' he reflects. 'It's spooky in parts.'

With minimal promotion, *Oar* attracted very little attention in the daily press. But the album did have its supporters. The *Fond Du Lac Commonwealth Reporter* said it was 'guileless, sincere.'[236] According to *The Atlanta Constitution*, *Oar* was 'a strangely un-self-conscious and unpretentious album... Spence's voice hints of country, but his guitar is folk, which produces some interesting results.'[237] The *Minneapolis Star* noted: 'Gone is any trace of rock from his music as it drifts into personal things with a definite country sound. His singing is more of a moan in a basso profundo. If you go for that, you'll like it.' The *Albuquerque Journal* cheered: 'Spence has released a masterful first album... His music is a blend of folk, country, and rock. True talent is sometimes hard to find, but one need look no further than Alexander Spence.'[238]

Chicago Tribune scribe and unabashed Grape fan Robb Baker was stuck by what Skip had achieved: 'In a day when The Beatles are talking about a seventy-two-track tape recorder, Spence went to a studio in Nashville where the machine has only three tracks. He produced the album himself, did all the writing and arranging, as well as singing and playing drums, electric and acoustic guitar, and bass.'[239]

Baker equivocated a little: 'The result is simple and honest – so simple and honest that it probably sounds unbearably dull by most standards of taste. But it works for me – especially 'Cripple Creek'... and 'Weighted Down', two country numbers where Spence out-Cashes Johnny Cash.'[240]

These positive notices cropped up between July and October 1969. They were capped by America's most eminent rock critic, Greil Marcus of *Rolling Stone*: 'Much of *Oar* sounds like the sort of haphazard folk music that might have been made around camp-fires after the California gold rush burned itself out... this is still real music, not someone's half-baked idea of where it's at.'[241]

Of the harrowing path to writing and recording the album, Peter Lewis would note: 'There were a lot of people going into mental institutions right then. And he wrote this record. So, it was not like documenting the sixties from his house in Topanga Canyon, man. He was doing it in the trenches. 'Cause a lot of people would've gone into Bellevue and spent their time sucking their thumb in bed. Instead of that, Skippy just wrote this thing. It just floored me when I heard it. I couldn't believe it... it scared me is what it did.'[242]

According to legend, fewer than 700 copies of *Oar* were sold before the album went out of print.[243] But the exact number is anyone's guess. Suffice to say, it was low. Of course, *Oar* was not made to shift units. As Robb Baker astutely noted in his review, 'Unless I'm very mistaken, this album is not going to sell very well at all. It might even defeat its purpose if it did.'[244]

But Skip Spence had put together his magnum opus and his depth of feeling shone through. When Robert Plant sat down with *New Musical Express* the next spring, he was asked about his personal impression of troubled sex symbol Jim Morrison. 'He was giving the impression he was into really deep things like Skip Spence of Moby Grape,' the Led Zeppelin vocalist said of their meeting.[245] For *Oar*, simply put, had heart and depth.

• • •

On Thursday 28 August 1969, Pat Spence gave birth to the couple's fourth child at Santa Clara County Hospital. Skip's sister, Sherry, had recently begun a ten-year stint of working there. (She would be five years in the paediatrics ward and five years in the nursery.) As Sherry recalls, 'My mom also worked at the hospital too, though I'm not sure what year she started.'

Deciding on a name proved a challenge. 'Gwenn and Skip came to the hospital, and they were mulling over names,' Pat explains. 'Gwenn wanted her to be called Heather, for the wild heather in Ireland. Skip wanted Victoria for Queen Victoria. When it was time to write the name for the birth certificate, I added, "Moon." I wanted to have *some* say in the name. Plus, I went into labour on the night of a full moon.'[246] Ultimately, the elder Mrs. Spence got her way.

CHAPTER TWENTY

THE DOOBIE BROTHERS IN
A NIGHT AT THE OPERA

A week after *Oar* was released, Moby Grape flew to Nashville to cut their last album for Columbia. After three days of rapid-fire recording, the last three members of the group – Don Stevenson, Jerry Miller and Peter Lewis – unceremoniously and very quietly split up. While the band never saw massive record sales, Moby Grape's influence had a long reach. For some it was intense.

One such devotee was starry-eyed South Bay singer-guitarist Pat Simmons. He'd also rushed out to buy a copy of *Oar* when he found out the mercurial ex-Grape showman had released a solo album. Growing up in San José, he'd been aware of Skip Spence for years.

'He used to play around the coffeehouses,' Simmons recalls. 'I couldn't understand what he was singing but there was a charm and obvious quality to his playing that sucked me in. Then, when he joined the Airplane as their drummer, we all went, "Huh?"... [but] I thought his playing on their first album was really interesting and different from what a lot of people did in those days. Then when he joined Moby Grape, I thought, "Here's the real Skip Spence – he really has some amazing stuff going on in his head and his chops."'[247]

Not long after he tracked down his copy of *Oar*, during the late spring or summer of '69, Simmons bumped into Spence by chance. It was in a San José laundromat, of all places.

'The door swings open, and in walks Skip Spence,' he explains. 'I was awestruck but still mustered the courage to say hello to him and tell him how great I thought he was.'[248]

The two got to chatting. Skip told Pat where he lived and encouraged him to drop in anytime, bringing his guitar. The young musician did just that. For a short while he'd visit his hero; they'd jam and share a joint together. But it all came to an end one day when Simmons was faced with a harsh realisation.

'The last time I went there,' he explains, '[Skip] was sitting on the couch shooting up heroin. I thought to myself, I don't really want to see this. I can't watch this fabulous talent throwing it all away with his wife and kids right there. It was heartbreaking.'[249]

Visiting her brother's San José duplex right around this time, Sherry was shocked to happen upon his shooting-up works. 'I had no idea my brother was on heroin,' she testifies. 'He was so thin and he was behaving differently. One time I was visiting my brother and sister-in-law and I saw his paraphernalia. It was in the living room or the bathroom, I can't remember where exactly. He had a belt that he used as a tourniquet.'

We can't know how, or exactly when, Skip got onto smack, or even how long his addiction lasted. Perhaps it started out as a search for something new; for something that could take him to a different place than LSD. Perhaps it was a way of self-medicating when he started hearing voices.

But even in those days of self-destruction, Spence was trying, in his own way, to be a good father. 'The only good spanking I remember getting,' Aaron recalls, 'was when I called Aunt Sherry a frog for not buying me a toy squirt gun.'

The elder Spence boy laughs to himself, then adds, 'After sending me to my room without dinner, my dad came in with a carton of chocolate malt balls, and he held me and kissed me and profusely apologised.'

While Skip Spence was capable of losing his temper, his anger was always short-lived. Especially with his kids.

Even during this period of his childhood, Aaron Spence saw a different side of his dad. 'I remember we had little, or no food and he was watching over us and I was hungry,' he recalls. 'He goes to the refrigerator, and I remember he opened the door and there was nothing but a pack of hotdog buns and some condiments. And he made a big presentation about how lucky we are to have food.'

Laughing to himself, Aaron continues, 'I didn't know any better, but I remember he made me feel like it was something special what he was about to make me, because I was starving. He took the buns and spread mayo and mustard on them and gave it to me. He was singing as he prepared it like a happy chef in the small kitchen. To this day I still love mayo and mustard on toast for a quick snack.'

For a moment, he pauses. 'But I also remember going to the bathroom around that time and finding a burnt spoon on the toilet-tank lid and bringing it to my mother. She would quietly take it away. It wasn't until later that I knew what it meant.'

•   •   •

It was also around the summer of '69 that Spence met budding artist and songwriter Tom Johnston. Two years his junior, Johnston had moved to San José to study design. He came from Tulare, a quiet city in the San Joaquin Valley, about 200 miles to the south. While his father ran an aircraft-mechanics shop, Johnston saw his future elsewhere.

As he'd later recall, 'My sister, who lived in Santa Clara intro-duced me to [Skip] and we ended up hanging around together. I was playing with the [funky jazz-rock band] South Bay Experimental Flash around that time.'[250]

Although he was gigging on weekends, Johnston would later tell the *Pittsburgh Post-Gazette*, 'The house that I lived in [on Twelfth Street, near the San José State University campus] was kind of a music center in San José State and I was an art major and had no plans of being in the music business. I was a graphic design major and that's what I thought I was going to do.'[251]

Jamming together, Spence and Johnston struck up a friendship and the latter's plans soon shifted. As time passed, Skip would introduce Tom to two musicians who'd arrived in the Bay Area looking for him and his Moby Grape companions.

As Johnston told it: 'John [Hartman] had come out from DC with [bassist] Gregg Murphy. They were in the city, and Skip told me about him. John had been looking for members of Moby Grape, trying to get something going again. He found Peter [Lewis] and got a hold of Skip; but Skip wasn't into it. So, John, Gregg and I got together and formed Pud. We added horns, and it was kind of a gospel rock group, a cross between Hendrix and gospel… pretty strange.'[252]

Just as Spence started jamming around with these new friends, an old buddy from high school and the South Bay folk scene re-entered his life.

After Skip joined the Jefferson Airplane back in September '65, Billy Dean Andrus got his draft card and went AWOL soon after. For a time he was hiding in the Santa Cruz Mountains, but he couldn't stay there forever.

After serving some time in jail, Billy Dean was released and reconnected with Paul Ziegler, who ran the Shelter back in the day. They formed the band Weird Herald.

Playing all sorts of venues in and around Los Gatos, Weird Herald signed with Onyx, a subsidiary of Fantasy Records, and spent much of '68 and early '69 intermittently recording in a small San Francisco studio. Their material was strong, combining country-rock, folk and psychedelia.

But after a conflict with management, their album project was indefinitely shelved in the spring of '69. A failed audition at the Fillmore in mid-May took any remaining wind out of Weird Herald's sails. After a lineup shuffle in the summer, the gigs dried up. It was likely around this time that Skip and Billy Dean reconnected.

Sometime in the autumn they formed Pachuco, a gritty, four-piece rock'n'roll outfit. Pat McIntire, Weird Herald's drummer, caught their performance on one occasion.

'It was Bill and Skip on guitars,' he recalls, 'and they had some of Skip's friends on bass and drums. As the name implies, it was supposed to be San José badass street music. They did their guitars in colours like candy-apple red. It was like car paint. They had leather jackets and it was quasi-showy, with a lot of valid experience behind it. They did some old rock'n'roll songs like Chuck Berry, that kind of thing.

'They were really trying to get away from the melodic music of the day,' notes McIntire. '[But] Bill told me it was hard to keep Skip focused and it never really took off, in terms of getting a tour together or a recording contract.'

With Spence hooked on heroin and Andrus struggling with speed, punctuality and reliability weren't always high on the agenda. One night in late '69, when the other guys in Pachuco couldn't make a gig, Spence quickly put together a makeshift band with Hartman, Johnston and Murphy of Pud. That night, the foursome made their way a few miles south to the suburbs.

At 400 East Campbell Avenue stood an old theatre with a cream-coloured terra cotta façade and two matching Doric columns. Nearly fifty years old at the time, the venue had originated as a bank in the 1920s, then transformed into a cinema after the stock-market crash of 1929.

By the mid-sixties the building, which boasted a vast balcony, had changed again, hosting old-time melodramas, vaudeville revival and live music. Its interior was designed to look like an opera house from the Old West.[253] Its front entrance featured a small marquee with a long neon sign that read, 'Gaslighter'. Stepping into the venue, Spence had no way of knowing he was in the company of guys who'd soon found one of the bestselling acts of the 1970s.

Recognising Pat Simmons at the show, Spence called him over and introduced him to the guys in Pud. '...A friend of mine opened a club called the Gaslighter Theatre in a suburb of San José. I was playing with [Skip's old bandmate] Peter Grant,' remembers Simmons. 'After Peter and I played, I watched Skip's band... I spoke with them when they were done, and they asked if I would be interested in this other band they were thinking of putting together with two or three guitars and lots of vocals. I said I was busy with these other projects but that we should stay in touch.'[254]

After that night at the Gaslighter, Pat and the other musicians went their separate ways but had stuck up a lasting connection. With Johnston and Hartman living just a few blocks from Spence on Twelfth Street, the friends continued to jam at all hours.

Recounting those days, Tom Johnston said: 'Pud was kind of a transformational band. One week, we'd play power-trio stuff like Cream or Mountain, and the next we'd be playing soul with background singers and a horn section.'[255] Eventually, Gregg Murphy left to have an eye operation and Dave Shogren stepped in on bass.

As the new decade got underway, Pachuco was still in its early days. When announcing the formation of new local production company in its March 1970 issue, the *Berkeley Tribune* noted: 'Canyon Productions is also setting up local dances with some of the groups they've been working with, such as... Pachuco, Skip Spence's new group.'[256] One of the contacts at Canyon was Paul Berenson, a local artist who had recently struck up a friendship with Spence. After leaving Pachuco, Billy Dean Andrus was planning a reunion with some of his bandmates in Weird Herald in the late fall.

'He was kind of a magic guy,' Jerry Miller recalls, warmly. 'I think he slipped on a plane with us [Moby Grape] one time, without a ticket or anything.'

But, with a hardcore methamphetamine habit, Billy Dean's days were numbered. About two months after leaving Pachuco, the gifted

24-year-old songwriter died of an overdose – apparently after a wild weekend at the Chateau Liberté in the Santa Cruz mountains.

(Tom Johnston recalled the Chateau as 'a *booming* place, crammed to the rafters. Everybody was loose as a goose. You'd see a bag of reds go floating through the audience, there'd usually be some violence, and it was always hotter than hell...'[257])

He passed on Monday 2 November, 1970; his funeral was held four days later.[258] Throughout all of Moby Grape's ups and downs, Skip had stayed in touch with his talented high-school friend. Now he was gone forever.

'Billy Dean is another one of those tragic stories,' Jorma Kaukonen sighs. 'He was the first person that I knew who had died of a drug overdose. He was another huge talent, a great guitar player, a great songwriter and a great showman. The fact that he never made it out of his 20s is absurd in retrospect. I can imagine that whatever school, or whatever universe [Skip and Billy Dean], were inhabiting, they would've gravitated together because they would've been the only ones that understood each other.'

It's quite likely that the sudden death of his old friend was a wakeup call for Skip Spence. It may have shaken him into trying to clean himself up and turn things around. For, at that point, just as one long-time friendship came to a tragic end, a new personal connection and musical partnership was just around the corner.

• • •

In late 1970, Spence made his way to 1202 Lincoln Avenue and strolled into Stevens Music. Approaching the counter, he introduced himself to multi-instrumentalist Gordon Stevens.[259]

'Skip walked into our family music store one day and said, "Hey man, I heard you play the viola and the bass." After talking for a while, he said, "Well, come on over to the house." And that first day I went over and we just hit it off. It was amazing,' Stevens thinks back over the decades.

'I went over with my viola,' he adds, 'and Skip had his motorcycle right in the living room. He was sitting on a couch next to his motorcycle and he had a couple of copies of the *Oar* album with him. He gave me one of his last copies and we jumped right into *Oar* immediately.

'When I first met Skip,' Gordon shares, 'he was very outgoing and very loving. His attempt to get acquainted and to find out my deeper feelings about music was wonderful. He was so receptive. You know, when Skip was on, he was on. He could take on the best of 'em, musically, intellectually.'

Born in the late 1930s, Stevens was older than Spence and had a longer, very different musical trajectory – which may have reminded Skip of his father's own path. 'Skip had an affinity for the fact that I had had a [musicians'] union card for ten years already,' Gordon reflects.

'I can't stress how [much] he was fixated on becoming a regular journeyman musician with security. Maybe because he got so focused, his mental problems settled down around that time. People couldn't believe that I was hanging around with the guy who had tried to chop down a hotel-room door. My friends couldn't believe it when I told them that we were taking our kids to soccer games. The general public had already written off Moby Grape by that point.

'The next time I went to Skip's place,' he recalls of some other musical buddies, "Tom Johnston was there and they were jamming. The Doobie Brothers were living right around the corner from Skip. It was on Fraternity Road, by San José State University. We could hear them rehearsing through the backyards, it was so close, and they were just getting ready for their first tour.'

Just like back in the day when Skip was starting out, the South Bay was buzzing with creative activity. 'Joker Jim, who was with the Gypsy Jokers, was the guy who told me where Skip lived,' Stevens recalls, 'and he went with me to see Skip on his motorcycle.'

Soon, Spence and Stevens developed a project together: they started mapping out a blueprint to revisit some of the songs of *Oar*, with different arrangements, to transform it into a full-blown production – a concept loosely based on the Book of Revelation.

As his intended collaborator recalls, 'Skip wanted to put the *Oar* material into a rock opera and he would play the guitar while I'd play the viola. He was mostly learning by ear. He'd give me a chord change every once in a while, but most of the notetaking was conceptional stuff. I can still picture him sitting with his clipboard and his pencil taking notes about the opera, and how he was going to use the different songs.'

With a new collaborator, Spence saw a path to moved forward. He would plot out the whole process. 'One of the most unpleasant things in my life,' Gordon admits, 'is that I had Skip's notebook in my possession. And I have searched and searched for it, and I can't find it anywhere. I can't even find my own notes. Skip had all these notes and diagrams about how to stage it. He was so ahead of his time.'

Just as Jonah's Wail had provided him with a kind of sanctuary when he resettled in San José earlier that year, Spence once again turned to his Christian faith. This time, the spirituality was embedded in his musical project.

'Skip's hobby was spirituality and elevating the human condition,' affirms Stevens, 'and he wanted to do it through music. It became an obsession, the rock opera. The Who was his first go-to band. So much of it had to do with the precocious thing that they did with *Tommy*. But he thought *Jesus Christ Superstar* was a little corny. His hobby was bigger than his vocation. Now, I don't know if Skip could've added a column of numbers, but he was a savant.

'Skip realised what he tapped into with *Oar*, because he was going to use some of those songs in the opera,' Gordon muses. 'And we stayed up at night talking. He had drawings of audiences sitting on glass with large lenses looking down into a theatre underneath them. There would be lighting shows from under the floor. The entire sphere would be special effects. Can you imagine that?

'He wanted to have stations with single seats or two seats together, with seatbelts so people could look underneath them for entertainment to see what was happening on stage. Imagine a geodesic dome with a floor underneath you that you could see through. He wanted to do a set of characters for a band, with costumes, a Brooks Brothers version – but take the undershirt and the button-up shirt and the blazer and cut perfect circles and line them up, so the audience could see the performers' nipples. David Bowie would've died on the spot if he heard that.'

There's something oddly moving about Spence's impossible ambitions. His ideas were at once innovative and completely out of time. Having been a part of America's first rock concert in a ballroom, back in the autumn of '65, his 1970 dream would have more neatly fit today's digital age, with holograms on stage. The idea that he thought he might make all this happen without a budget is endearing, but sad.

It was a grandiose vision, probably only achievable with a theatrical cast and an orchestra. But Skip and Gordon would have to make do with expanding to a trio. 'When Skip asked [John] Hartman to come in and play drums as a trio, we never even thought of forming a quartet. It was all about intimacy. And Skip saw he didn't need a bass player because he played the lower end of the guitar so beautifully. Later, he was thinking of having me play some stand-up bass to give the *Oar* songs more of a symphonic sound.

'The use of large acoustical environments was what Skip was looking for,' Stevens continues. 'And Hartman fit into that because [he] could play timpani and cymbals and the big bass drum and all of the classical instrumentation. Hartman played big. He liked big music and that's a part of what attracted him to Skip and Skip's music. I remember Skip saying one time, "Wouldn't it be good if we could get him some timpani to play for 'Books Of Moses'?"'

During that winter of 1970, Spence struck an agreement with an Episcopalian pastor to make use of a summer retreat that had an auditorium. For a couple of weekends he and Stevens headed there to work on the rock-opera concept. 'We went in there and plugged in and played as loud as we could, to test the acoustics. I think we went in with Hartman one time. It was when he was working on the idea of the dome. We were using some of the *Oar* songs to test it out.'

At that point, he had no intention of returning to the kind of music or the sorts of venues he'd played with Moby Grape or the Jefferson Airplane. 'Skip had no interest in playing live in the rock'n'roll universe,' Gordon remembers. 'Maybe in a jazz or beatnik club, like [Ken] Kesey's people would've loved... because they were older and more eclectic. Skip's whole idea about perfor- mance was not unlike Kesey's... how it would be nice if it wasn't a part of the so-called "rock'n'roll revolution."'

Stevens had been involved with Kesey's Merry Pranksters in the late 1960s. He performed music at some of their events, as part of their idea of psychedelic consciousness-raising. Now, he felt, Spence was seeking something similar on a spiritual level.

'We ended up doing three performances at a church,' Gordon recalls of how the concept came back down to earth. 'Skip had already talked to the pastor before I had met him and everything happened in a matter of weeks. Skip wanted a big hall, but it wasn't to play in front of crowds. The only people at those performances were the staff and the pastor and his kids.

'But that didn't matter. Skip was interested in their acoustics. That was the selfish part of it. It was Skip's motivation. There was no money exchanged at all. And all this was before Christian rock'n'roll started. You see, Skip was looking for legitimacy in the church and the whole idea of getting a union card, and what he was doing was ahead of its time.'

As before, and as would recur for decades, Spence embraced Christian spirituality at a time of personal crisis, or crossroads. It was a touchstone or compass, tied once again, like *Oar*, to his musical vision.

As 1971 approached, he continued to map out his grand ambi- tion. He also spent time with Pat and their children. 'He was like a kid with a new bicycle,' Gordon notes. Around this time, he adds, Skip 'jumped into soccer. He wanted to see as many games as he could and, for a time, he wanted his kids to become soccer stars. He was free of his mental condition and he was really in good shape for a while. He took his meds and he took care of his kids as best as he could.'

Like a kid, he also enjoyed playing pranks. 'I remember, my mom was sleeping in,' Omar recalls, 'and we were getting up... and [my dad] wanted to wake up my mom. So, we all snuck into the bedroom while my mom was sleeping on the bed and he quietly turned on his amplifier... I'm pretty sure that it was a bass guitar that he handed me and he told us to all start playing on it... it was probably on eleven. It just startled my mom out of bed.'

'Skip was so practical,' Stevens reflects on his old friend's mindset. It may seem counterintuitive, given what we now know of him. But nobody knows you like a good friend does. 'The way he wanted to join a musicians' union like his dad and have a career playing music for people – the music that was important to him. And he didn't know totally what that was.

'He told me that before *Oar*, before that explosion, he didn't really know what he wanted. He did like the energy of rocking out, but that's because he was ADD. Skip had to have a guitar or a cigarette in his hands all the time... In *Oar*, he found his own muse. So, he was completely normal and metaphysical at the same time.'

From late 1970 to early 1971, Gordon Stevens helped Skip Spence stay on a routine, heading north to pick up his antipsychotic medication and encouraging him to keep taking it regularly. 'At the time I was taking him, or sometimes accompanying him, to the San Francisco clinic where he got his meds – I think it was the [Veterans Affairs] or the Kaiser Hospital. He wasn't self-medicating and he was conscientious. We had a lot of fun; he had a big old Chevy with a big engine and liked to make noise in it. And we'd drive in the city and fuck around and have hot dogs and burgers. It was great times. Skip was still in fairly good shape.'

But things can fragment as quickly as they come together; spiralling out of control just like before.

CHAPTER TWENTY-ONE

GRANITE CREEK:
THE SECOND RISE AND
FALL OF MOBY GRAPE

The first mention of Moby Grape's reunion appeared in the *San Francisco Examiner* on 10 April 1971. In his 'On The Scene' column, Tom Campbell announced: 'The Original Moby Grape will get together again for a performance at the *On Cue World Premiere of Arts & Industry*, Brooks Hall, May 13-23.'[260] By early April, the band had signed with Warner Brothers and started rehearsing at an old house on Granite Creek Road.

It was two years since the Grape had broken up and nearly three since Skip Spence had left. What had started out with so much energy and promise in '66 had collapsed unceremoniously. Moby Grape just never took the world by storm in the way that some anticipated.

Yet the memory of the band's power and potential lingered, and there was always that brilliant first album. It remained an artistic triumph, even if not a monster hit.

While everyone was apprehensive about getting back together, there was still the sense of unfinished business. They were still young men, after all. Perhaps the Grape could yet achieve its potential.

But in the first few weeks of 1971, the very notion of a Moby Grape reunion had seemed fanciful. At that point, everyone was on his own different path.

After leaving the Grape, Bob Mosley had gone back to college, then worked as a school custodian. When he'd got his draft card, he signed up for the US Marines rather than the US Army. He wanted to see active service in Vietnam. Working as a cook at the Twentynine Palms Combat Center, San Bernardino, California, Bob got into a serious fight and was hospitalised, ending his service after nine months. Like his old bandmate Spence, Mosley was struggling with mental-health issues. Returning to music, he co-founded Fox, a San Diego-based band that took a residency in Hawaii.[261]

While Peter Lewis still kept his place in Boulder Creek, he was in and out of town, sometimes heading down to Southern California. Since the Grape's Nashville sessions in May '69, he'd laid low, taking on a variety of jobs such as working as a furniture mover.[262] While he kept in touch with Spence, his own career in music had come to a halt.

Jerry Miller and Don Stevenson, meanwhile, were living in Boulder Creek full time and still performing. While Stevenson played as half of an informal rotating duo, either with drummer/singer Larry Biancalana or keyboardist Richard Dean, Miller gigged around the Bay Area with The Rhythm Dukes, playing shows all the way up to the April of 1971.[263] They recorded an album's worth of demos and shopped it around, but the band never inked a contract.

Then, sometime in the early spring, Moby Grape started to coalesce as an entity again. It started with their producer. As David Rubinson worked with Bill Graham at the budding San Francisco Records label, he began to orchestrate what became the first-ever rock reunion.

The central idea was to get everyone back living and recording together, to reproduce the magic of the early days up in Marin

County. But this time the setting would be miles away from The Ark, or the ballrooms and clubs of San Francisco – few of which even existed anymore.

This time, the location would be an old house just outside of Santa Cruz and the band would grow to six musicians – as Stevenson explains. 'Skip had a band with Gordon Stevens for a while. They'd done some performing around town. It was mostly stuff from his *Oar* album, I think. So, when we started *Granite Creek*, I knew he was playing but I didn't know the details. Before the reunion I wasn't in touch with him.' Gordon would contribute viola, dobro and mandolin.

Initially, Stevens was still tied up with his family's music store in San José, but then he got involved. 'My father found the listing for the Granite Creek house in the local paper,' he recalls, 'and I told Rubinson and he leased it. This was in the early days of the Bill Graham Corporation and Rubinson was ostensibly his right-hand man, because Rubinson was more than a record producer, he was a very smart man businesswise. That would've been in March. And right around that time, my father gave me a leave of absence to go and work with the Grape.'

Early on, Rubinson sent Stevenson and Stevens 2,400 miles west to recruit Mosley. The bassist was in Honolulu, performing at the Red Noodle club with Fox. 'Rubinson thought we'd be a good pair,' Stevens explains. With some spending money in hand, the two flew west and headed out to watch Mosley perform.

'That's when I realised that we were dealing with something powerful in Mosley,' continues Gordon. 'He's a man of few words. He liked to go sitting out on the pier with a fishing rod in hand and just look out at the ocean. "That's my religion," he told me. We went fishing together a few times during the *Granite Creek* project.

'But that night Don and I were at the Red Noodle, Don said, "You've got to let us play some tunes," and we played with them… after the show we went to someone's house up in the hills with the band and some of Mosley's friends. And Mosley opened up to me for the first time and we went on talking for three or four hours.

'Don and I didn't get back to our hotel till four or five in the morning,' recalls Stevens. 'Bob had gotten out of the Marines not long before that and he was hanging on for dear life. He was looking for something solid. That's when we presented the rationale for him to come back with us.'

Agreeing to return to California, the next time Mosley appeared was at a gig Fox played in Squaw Valley. He was the last piece of the puzzle. Soon, contracts were written up and all six members of the reformed Moby Grape signed their names on the dotted line.

'The day we signed our contracts with the salary clause,' Stevens recalls, 'we got $10,000 each. We'd received that money when Mo [Ostin] and Clive [Davis] were the dealmakers with Dave Rubinson and Bill Graham. We got that money to spend on a dream thing. Don bought a checker cab, which was his dream to have to take his drum set to gigs. I heard Jerry bought another guitar. I bought a Porsche, partly because Rubinson already had one. When he let me drive his own Porsche he said, "Gordon, you should get yourself one."'

As the project gained momentum, Spence was still on his meds and living with his family. His life, to all extents and purposes, seemed to be back on the rails. It was a time of hope.

Throughout all this, in Stevens' view, 'David Rubinson was an optimist. To be a producer you *have* to be an optimist and you have to be a realist, too. David had a wonderful manner. He was sort of like a cheerleader and he loved to play with us.'

Renting a house on Granite Creek Road, Rubinson worked with engineers to set up a makeshift studio. It was a space for the band to gather, share ideas and record – an open house that was always available.

Gone were the days of slogging in and out of office-like studios in New York or LA, on someone else's clock. This was a time to get back to sitting in a circle, sharing ideas and writing songs together. Just like how it had all started in Corte Madera. A time

233

to recapture the mood and magic of The Ark and The Heliport – or at least that's how it was supposed to be.

'The house [at 20 Granite Creek] was in a beautiful spot,' Stevens recalls. 'It's still there. It was a big Victorian with three or four fireplaces in it.'[264]

Before anyone could move in, a few alterations were made to the first floor. As he remembers, 'We knocked down a wall, it might've been between the salon and a hallway. It was rather large and fairly comfortable for sixteen tracks and a whole bunch of stuff. But when we moved in, Skip got first choice of the rooms. And let me tell you, in a Victorian house all rooms are not equal.'

Spence had been living a seemingly carefree day-by-day existence. Whenever he did receive some modest windfall, it slipped through his fingers and was gone in a flash. Speaking with *LA Weekly*, Rubinson would later recall of the *Granite Creek* period: 'Once I got the band some money from Warners. Skippy came up to my office for his check, which was for four grand. He goes across the street to cash it, and about five minutes later I got a call from one of the tellers. Skip had left the whole pile sitting on the counter – he'd forgotten the whole thing.'[265]

Initially, with him commuting from his home in San José, the Grape worked on one of the songs from *Oar*. 'We never recorded 'Little Hands'...' Stevenson explains, 'but I do recall one time in the studio we were kind of messing with it and Skip came up and sat down on the drums and showed me what he wanted. It was almost like a march.

'When we played it that way, the way Skip had it in his mind, that was when I understood he was a really creative drummer,' muses the musician. 'He had some interesting ways of putting the rhythm into it.'

Everyone was auditioning songs in those early weeks. Lewis offered three gems, one of which was a ballad sung from the perspective of a tired old horse. 'We did 'Horse Out In The Rain' at the Granite Creek house,' Stevens recalls. 'Skip said, "That's one of the greatest songs anyone ever wrote," and he loved Peter for it. I think that's the key thing that set up Skip and Peter's friendship in his later years. Skip participated on it there, but he didn't come to any of our rehearsals. I don't think we played over an hour or two with Skip in the six or so months we were in the house.'

Of the band's haphazard open schedule, Stevenson chimes in, 'We never really scheduled things at Granite Creek. We'd never say anything like, "Let's have a rehearsal at two o'clock on Thursday." When Mosley pulled up he was available, and Peter was available, and Jerry and I were, and we were able to have some rehearsals together.

'But it was kind of hit and miss with Peter, and with Skip. Even though Skip lived there, if we tried to set up a time to rehearse, he might not be there. But think about it, 'Chinese Song' was the only song he contributed. And it was amazing. It should be in a movie. Skip played the koto and he captured the feeling of that style of music.'

While it was playful to title it 'Chinese Song' when it owed its stringed sound to the Japanese koto (itself derived from a Chinese instrument), the celebrated instrumental might have opened up a new musical path. Perhaps this early venture into world music could have led to new possibilities on the other side of the Pacific Ocean?

'He was so determined to record 'Chinese Song,'' Stevens explains. 'He said to me, "Who was the first American band to perform in Asia?" He said, "I've got this thing going with the koto. I met this woman in Palo Alto who had a beautiful koto."

'Having the instrument and learning how to tune it was the key. He heard some of the music we were recording without him and when he gave up on the *Oar* idea, he became interested in 'Chinese Song.' One of his motivations for writing and recording that song was to possibly spark a deal where he could travel to China and Japan and perform the *Oar* music there.

'We went to Pacific Studios in San Mateo and did 'Chinese

Song' with Donald and Skip and me,' Gordon elaborates. 'It was spacious there. I remember Don's drum set was in a room that was so big, his drum set looked rather small. There was a wide hallway between the console where Skip and I were with the koto and the viola. It must've been about fifty feet away. We were working with [engineer] Fred Catero... and he recorded the cymbals at half speed, and we played along at normal speed. It gave the cymbals this amazing sound. It took us about two sessions to record that song.

'It drew a crowd of local musicians when word got out and it was probably the most normal, fun, almost high-fiving time. It's the highlight of Skip's recording for *Granite Creek*. But that was pretty early. It was before Skip locked himself up.'

After commuting from his home for a short while, Spence spent more and more time at Granite Creek. While he'd been keeping things together, that was all about to change.

'I remember driving him back one time [from San Francisco] and we had a prescription, and he said, "Fuck this shit, I ain't gonna take this crap anymore,"' Gordon remembers. 'And he rolled down the window, and I said, "Skip, don't do that. You may change your mind tomorrow."'

After a few months of getting back on track, Spence renounced his meds in favour of heroin. All at once, the grand dream of his biblical rock-opera faded away.

'That was during the first few weeks of David Rubinson and Bill Graham trying to get the *Granite Creek* project started. And I could feel him slipping away when he quit taking his meds. I guess after the last time I took him for his prescription he never went back, because he was pretty much gone. It all happened pretty quick.'

'He was still a junkie,' Mosley sighs.

As David Rubinson later testified to the rock press: 'By this time Skip was really far gone. He was a heroin addict. But he found this house in San José and we all moved in. We set up the recording equipment in a truck outside and put the instruments in the living room. He was the energy that drove it, but he was so junked-out that he couldn't really participate.'[266]

'Skip was the first person I ever heard use the term "self-medicate,"' Stevens adds.

Spence was spending almost all his time at Granite Creek now. 'Skip got the biggest bedroom,' Stevens explains, 'and he locked himself in there with a .38 Smith & Wesson and did grey-coloured speed that the Angels had made for him. He didn't come out of the room for six to eight weeks. We were feeding him celery and peanut butter just to keep him alive. He'd open the door and he wouldn't talk. He had exiled himself to that room.'

Dividing most of his time between the Chateau, where he copped speed from Hells Angels, and his bedroom at Granite Creek, Spence withdrew from rehearsing and recording. Even in his room, he was on a partying rampage. In addition to his smack habit, he took methedrine either on his own or in the company of a cavalcade of visitors. It got to a point where even holding a conversation became a struggle.

'He was a little more difficult to understand at that point,' confirms Don Stevenson. 'He was up at the Chateau Liberté a lot and he was hanging with bikers. Musically, he was easy to understand, but as far as talking to him – I had a hard time communicating with him. He became kind of a fixture up at the Chateau. He had gained a reputation there. I mean, he was loved. He was absolutely loved by everybody up there. And he was loved by us too, but it had become more difficult to understand what he was trying to say, unless a guitar was in his hands.'

'The period between my first meeting with the band at Don's house and the preparations for *20 Granite Creek* was a bit of a while,' Gordon recalls. 'Early on, we played the Chateau a couple of times.'

What happened one of those nights shocked everyone. 'It was the ugliest thing I've ever seen,' he remembers. 'The Chateau was on the county line, between Santa Cruz County and Santa Clara

County. It was a place where you could break the rules, tucked away in the mountains, on the old road to the coast from San José. There was only one road into it. And it always had an illicit thing going, because it was tucked away, and nobody could screw you because there was one road in. The sheriff and the police didn't want to go in there.

'And one night this ruckus happened. We were playing either the middle or the last set; and there were some kids from San José State University, some cocky fuckers. They'd take their cheerleader girlfriends up to the Chateau so they could show off they could hang out with the bad guys and the subculture. They were straight-up frat guys with blond hair, wearing sweaters and jackets with their logos on them. And that night they just went too far, fucking with the Hells Angels.

'...These football players started yelling and acting crazy and the Hells Angels said, "Shut up! We came here to hear the band, motherfucker!"' recalls Gordon. 'And I don't know exactly how it happened, but they challenged each other to go outside, so they went outside and then knives came out, and everyone was yelling and screaming, and all freaked out.

'When they called the police, I told the manager of the Chateau to call Joker Jim and get the Gypsy Jokers to come over and stop this insanity. The Santa Cruz and Santa Clara County cops were all gathered at the main road. And the Jokers drove right past them and came down that winding road to the Chateau... I walked to the edge of the building and looked out and there was this football player with his T-shirt that was sliced, and he was holding his intestines in his hand. His girlfriend was screaming. It was mayhem. Joker Jim and his guys settled the whole thing down. It shut down the Chateau for a few weeks before it got settled out.'

Soon, a contingent from the Chateau made their way to Granite Creek. As Stevens recalls, 'The Hells Angels got wind of us being there and that didn't help much. I have a graphic memory of some of them cooking meth on our picnic table and Mosley drove in one time – he just turned around.'

Desperately at a loss as to what to do, the band brought in a handler to take care of Spence. '"Beaver" was the nickname for one of our roadies,' Stevens explains, 'and he would bring Skip food and drinks and drugs and flower girls. It was a parade of those entities constantly in and out of his room at all hours. He wasn't suffering in there, except in his own deep sense. It was a one-man party, and it was devastating and breaking our hearts.'

For days and nights and weeks on end, Skip was out of commission: strung out on meth, losing weight and veering in and out of paranoia.

'One night, Beaver called me up,' Stevens remembers, 'and he said, "Skip's got a .38 and he's in his fucking room and he's got a full cup of Hells Angels methedrine – brown, unfiltered methedrine." And I thought to myself, "The good ol' days are over."'

Locked in his room in self-imposed exile, just the other side of Skip's bedroom door was a whole different world. A fluctuating configuration of musicians, his friends, who got together in the living room, in the kitchen, trading songs, rehearsing and recording whenever they felt inspired. He was the elephant in the room behind the locked door.

'We didn't have band meetings,' confirms Gordon Stevens of their method 'It was all one-on-one. Sometimes I'd be the only one in the studio and Rubinson's genius of editing was put into play. That album was really chopped up... We didn't have any midnight sessions with everyone together. Mosley used to go fishing down at the pier. He was sort of in a reflective, quiet period. Peter and I must've gone into Santa Cruz to get ice cream about twenty times.'

When he got to recording, Mosley impressed Stevens with his work ethic. 'I never saw anyone work as hard as him in the studio. What he brought was something from his background of playing clubs. Skip, I think, sort of envied that. Skip wanted professional legitimacy, like his dad had.'

The band worked quickly with Rubinson through the spring. Somehow, amid all the chaos, great music was still being made. The Grape cut fifteen tracks by mid-June.[267] But if they wanted to get back into shape as a live act, with one of the active members being Skip Spence on rhythm guitar and vocals, things needed to change.

Moby Grape should have hit the pause button at that point. They should have holed themselves up at Granite Creek for more rehearsals and low-pressure gigs. But after that frantic night at the Chateau, a series of upcoming bookings was on a non-negotiable timeline.

With the Chateau temporarily shut down and the band still trying to get into shape as a live act, the Grape looked to some bigger venues. As Stevens remembers, 'We played a few gigs, like at the [Hollywood] Palladium and a little theatre called the Burl… in Boulder Creek. We also played The Catalyst in Santa Cruz.'

On 22 May the band drove up to San Francisco to perform at the *On Cue World Premiere Of Arts & Industry* at Brooks Hall. The next week, they trekked all the way down to Hollywood for the Palladium show, sharing the bill with Quicksilver Messenger Service, Albert King and Jo Jo Gunne. A bootleg recording of 'Chinese Song' was made at the show, one of the few times the song was performed live.

The show in Hollywood was reportedly uneven, with the band tighter on their new material and rusty on the older songs. According to *Billboard*: 'It would be nice to say that Moby Grape's first appearance in over two years was a triumph. Nice, but untrue. It was mostly a disaster as the group just wasn't rehearsed enough… The new songs were the best, or rather, the best rehearsed. The band still needs about three months more practice before it can rightfully regain its onetime title of America's best rock and roll band.'[268]

The Grape didn't have much time to prepare for five marquee nights at the soon-to-be-closed Fillmores East and West. Sometime in early 1971, Bill Graham had reached his breaking point. Frustrated with the stresses of juggling the demands of venues, artists and concertgoers, he decided to get out of the promotion business once and for all.[269]

In the early weeks of summer 1971, the curtains would be dropped at the historic Fillmores East and West for the last time. As Graham always had a soft spot for Moby Grape, naturally he booked them to help close out both venues.

The three evenings at the Fillmore West represented a homecoming. But before that, they were scheduled to play the Fillmore East for the weekend of 18-19 June, the second to last weekend of the venue's existence, with BB King – one of the first blues performers to play the original Fillmore – and Grootna, the Berkeley blues/country-rock band managed by Graham, whose producer was Marty Balin of the Airplane.

At their height, the Grape had attracted droves of concertgoers to the Fillmore in its early days. Those two high-profile nights at the Fillmore East gave a chance to finally turn things around after everything fell apart at their last show there, back on 1 June 1968 – just days before Skip's Manhattan breakdown. Altogether, those June '71 gigs presented an opportunity for Moby Grape to stop flirting with stardom and fully grasp it.

Almost inevitably, it became a disaster.

'Things got off to a bad start,' Gordon Stevens explains, 'because Skip didn't show up at the airport. So, Rubinson had a problem immediately. He had a lot of logistics involving Skip, like, "Where is he? What's he doing?" And he finally got a hold of Skip and Skip said, "I'm not coming there unless I can bring Pat and my baby [Heather]."

'Well, Skip had gotten that message to Bill Graham already and Bill had resisted this to a degree, and it pissed [Skip] off. This all took place in the hour or so before we got on the plane.'

It was a case of added expenses and possible favouritism. The notoriously hard-assed Graham may have figured that if Spence got to bring his wife and daughter, then why not everybody's families?

'So, Bill had to cave and they pulled all the strings they could at the airline and got Skip and Pat on a later flight,' continues Stevens. 'It wasn't too much later because we had a sound check at 6:30 [that Friday evening].

'We got on the airplane, when we got over Iowa or the Dakotas; it was still about 40 minutes before we got to Chicago, where we changed planes. We were upstairs in the lounge drinking beer and playing on the piano in the observation deck of the 747. The stewardess came up and asked, "Where is this gentleman David Rubinson?" She found him and handed him a note...

'[It] said that Mosley had agreed with Neil Young's management to get off the airplane and go on the European tour that Young was initiating. And he wasn't going to go to New York...'

It's unknown who sent the initial message. But word had got out from someone in Young's circle that Bob had been recruited. It seems to have filtered through to Warners, who then sent out a message to the airplane.

'...Rubinson immediately was invited into the cockpit and he had two conversations: one was with Bill Graham; the other was with Mosley's mother and he told her... that Bill Graham wanted her to know that if Mosley didn't make the gig in New York, he'd never play music again. Ever,' recalls Gordon.

'Anyway, ten minutes later Mosley was called to the cockpit to talk to his mother, and to cut to the chase, he didn't leave in Chicago. So, they cut Mosley off at the pass there.'

It was strike two for Moby Grape. 'When we got to New York there were two limos,' Stevens continues. 'One was with [Jann] Wenner, the *Rolling Stone* dude, and the other was with Annie Leibovitz, the photographer. We split up into two groups. It was like, "Who wants to go with Annie, and who wants to go with Wenner?"

'We were just a bit late so Rubinson asked the drivers to take the short cuts. Rubinson went with Wenner, and Mosley and Jerry and I went together with Annie. Mosley was sitting next to me. When we got to midtown, on the way to East Village, our driver took a detour and it was a pretty rough neighbourhood...

'Mosley was silent. He hadn't said a word since he left for the cockpit to talk to his mother. He was totally embarrassed. And we didn't know exactly what was happening with Skip, so we just figured that this whole thing was going to be a disaster.'

It could only get worse. And it did.

'...We turned a corner and there was a guy on the sidewalk at the intersection beating on another guy with a piece of board with a nail on the end of it,' Stevens describes. 'Just beating him. It was right near the curb and we were looking to turn right, and Mosley was sitting by that right window on the passenger's side, just watching this happen. And he said, "Get the fuck out of here."... our driver turned and drove and after a minute, Mosley yelled, "Stop. Stop the car. Get my bass out of the fucking trunk."

'Annie was freaked out... Mosley got out, grabbed his bass and didn't say a word. He had a little bag he hung on one shoulder and he just walked away from us down the side street. And he was gone.'

Even this couldn't faze the band. As Gordon explains, 'Playing with BB King was such a cool thing for Bob because he's one of his heroes. We never thought Bob wasn't going to show up for that reason... he just wanted to get away from the whole fucking thing and have a talk with himself. He had a lot to think about.'

Arriving at the Fillmore, Rubinson and an engineer-roadie who had joined everyone on the trek east waited outside to organise the equipment, which was on its way in a separate van. '[He] was 6'3" or 6'4",' Stevens remembers. 'A southern dude. A really great guy. And he had to go take care of the van that was coming with some equipment. So, we went in and set up. Annie's friends were there and there were a lot of journalists. The rehearsal was legendary, I think it's been written up.[270]

'In the meantime, we were on the stage and halfway through we looked down the aisle and there comes Skip, carrying Heather, and Pat was carrying his Stratocaster. He comes up on the stage just smiling, and about five minutes later there was Mosley just walking down the aisle. He evidently walked all the way to the theatre. We took a break. It had been quite an emotionally exhausting morning and afternoon.'

After dinner the Grape returned to the Fillmore, ready for their biggest show of the reunion. All they had to do was keep it together and play as well as they did in rehearsal.

Recalling that fateful night, Gordon Stevens explains, 'BB King was going to play first and we played second, and Bill Graham wanted Grootna to play last. BB King was wonderful... Graham was all decked out in his tuxedo. He made a little speech to the audience. It was an event.

'So, we got up there on the stage and were introduced and within a minute or two we were tuning up. We were a little reticent and we were taking our time... people were yelling things: "Hey Skip." But it was light-hearted, the audience was excited and anticipating everything. There was a major entourage of Moby Grape fans and it was party time.

'After a couple of minutes, someone screams out, "Mosley, go back to the Marines!" Then, a couple other people followed and then someone else shouts, "Shut up, motherfucker, leave him alone!" This was all going on before we played a note. And Rubinson, who was at the side of the stage said, "Play, play something." I forget what the first tune was, it was sort of loose and not very well done... a bit tentative but we got through it.

'Then we stopped and Skip said something to the audience... There wasn't rousing applause after the third tune. It was polite, but then that whole, "Go back to the Marines" thing started again – really heavily. And I was thinking to myself, "Only in New York. They wouldn't be saying that in San Francisco to Mosley."'

Maybe the audience were angry at Bill Graham for closing the Fillmore. Maybe they were frustrated with the Grape for falling apart years earlier. Perhaps they thought the band had wasted all its talent and potential. But maybe they were genuinely angry about Vietnam and took it out on Bob Mosley for joining the Marines. It could have been any of those things. It could have been all of them.

'Then it got really heavy duty,' confirms Stevens, 'and we tried to start a tune and it stopped. Some people started throwing things at the stage, like seat cushions. We tried to play but it built up and got really weird.

'Jerry left the stage and came back with a chair... he put it down in the front of the stage and sat down. I saw Bill Graham talking to Rubinson... Bill started walking towards Jerry and Rubinson pulled him back, I think. When Jerry sat down on the chair it really pissed Bill off.

'By then the audience was out of control. Skip slipped his guitar down and laid it on the floor... he picked up the mic stand and took the mic off and started berating the audience: "Don't talk to my man like that, he's a patriotic guy and he did his best." And then he threw the fucking mic stand into the audience... it hit onto the side of the aisle. It could've put Skip in the joint if it hit someone in the head. This was not funny at all.

'And I dropped... off the side of the stage because there was stuff flying and someone threw the mic stand back on the stage.' Stevens pauses. 'Then Bill Graham pulled down the curtain. And the audience was stunned and screaming and laughing and cursing.'

Circus magazine famously called the show 'the worst performance ever by the greatest band of all time.'[271] The musicians were now in dire straits. So was producer-manager David Rubinson. The Friday night disaster revealed what no one was ready to face: Skip Spence was erratic, Bob Mosley was ready to bolt at any minute – and the band needed to play many gigs if it was to get itself back on track.

'We went off back and flopped down in the green room and turned the lights down low, just staring at each other,' Stevens sighs. 'And then Rubinson came in and said, "Jesus Christ guys, what the fuck's going on here? Bill's got a couple of words to say."

'And then Bill walked in, and said, "Okay, listen up." Then he pointed at Don and said, "You!" And he went around the room pointing the finger at everybody. And he said, "Not one of you guys is ever playing music again. Starting tonight."

'And Rubinson said, "But Bill, we're playing tomorrow night." And Bill said, "Fuck that." And then Bill continued [turning to Jerry Miller] and talked about professionalism and showbiz: "Your sitting down was just the straw that broke the camel's back! This is the most fucked-up thing I ever saw a musician do." He was really on Jerry's case.

'He didn't say a word about Mosley. Mosley was kind of sheepish. He stopped playing after the whole "Go back to the Marines" thing.

'And right in the middle of Bill's "Fuck you" to us, [our engineer-roadie] picked him up by the lapels on his tuxedo... threw him up against the wall and said, "You can't talk to my guys like that." Bill was sort of down on his knees, half-standing.

'And Rubinson said, "Bill, we gotta play. We can make this good. We gotta play tomorrow night. We have to. It's gonna cost us twenty grand anyway if we don't." They had their chitchat and Bill still had a show to put on. He still had to go out there and take care of Grootna.

'After Rubinson and Bill walked out, Mosley left. When I left the room, I looked out at the audience from the side and I saw Mosley standing at the back of the theatre by one of the pillars. He got himself a spot in the dark almost...

'Skip went back with Pat wherever they put him up,' Gordon recalls. 'And Donald and I and Jerry went back to our hotel and picked up some Sunshine LSD and watched cartoons all night... about three o'clock in the morning we crashed and there was a knock at our door. It was Rubinson and he said, "Bill said we can play." We didn't give a shit at that point. You know, if you can't cry you may as well laugh.'

The next night, Moby Grape returned to the Fillmore and put on a steady, if not spectacular, show. Over the years, a bootleg of that Saturday performance has circulated among Grape fans. Running at forty-six minutes with fourteen songs, the recording captures a solid performance. They ran through well-worn classics like 'Fall On You', 'Hey Grandma', '8:05' and 'Omaha', as well as new numbers that could easily hold their own: 'Apocalypse', 'Road To The Sun', 'Goin' Down To Texas', 'Gypsy Wedding'. At some points they were on fire and at other times less polished. But this was a band capable of recapturing its magic. All it needed was time and the will to keep going.

Reviewing that Saturday night show for *The New Yorker*, Ellen Willis was perceptive: 'There was considerable pathos and irony in [Moby Grape's] modest reappearance at this particular time... That night, they sounded very much like their old selves. They pleased the crowd (a sizable Grape-cult contingent was present)... Watching the Grape, I wondered if the basic cause of its troubles back in 1968 was that its members weren't true believers.'[272]

'The second night is a real blur to me,' Stevens reflects. 'I'd say that the main thing... is that they played songs that came easy to them because they still could perform them. I didn't play much as I recall because I didn't know some of the songs. You see, we didn't rehearse for anything. I didn't leave the stage but I didn't play much.

'In the years afterwards I've never talked to the guys about that second show. We talked about the first one – the show from hell – but not the Saturday night show. We flew out west on Sunday morning. Skip wasn't with us.'

Arriving in San Francisco later that day, the musicians found their cars in the airport parking-lot and headed home. 'I guess we didn't freak out at that point because we were in shock,' Stevens says. 'It was a pretty sad moment. It was raining, and it was cloudy and grey, and we were feeling pretty weird.'

Booked for three nights at the Fillmore West, 24-27 June, the Grape headed back up to San Francisco the following Thursday.

That final weekend of June came and went. While none of those last shows were anything like the catastrophe of the Fillmore East, they were hit-and-miss. By that point the performing unit was a fluid, sometimes truncated version of the band. Spence was no longer considered for live gigs.

'I think that Skip was at one of those Fillmore West shows,' Stevens muses. 'On the second night, my dad came up from San José to hear the band. I was a little skittery about that because we hadn't been playing well. And I was concerned about my dad possibly hearing us play a mediocre show.'

According to one journalist, who was likely reviewing the second or third show, 'Moby Grape did some foot stomping stuff and then died on the vine. It was, to say the least, interesting. Their fearless leader, Skip Spence, stayed home, presumably because his car was stolen.'[273]

Although they were scheduled to trek back to New York for another performance the following week, the band retreated back to their homes or to Granite Creek. As Chuck Berry, Alice Cooper, Ike & Tina Turner and others performed at the weeklong *International Youth Exposition*, 29 June-6 July, at the Kingsman's Armory in the Bronx, Moby Grape was conspicuously absent.[274]

It was as though they were admitting defeat. That admission may have come with a feeling of peace for some members, but for Skip Spence things were becoming worse very quickly.

'He disintegrated from being in not-very-good shape to being a disaster shortly after the Fillmore East,' Gordon Stevens recalls. It wasn't just the disintegration of a musician and songwriter. He was stepping down a path that he wouldn't come back from, where he would lose not only his career but contact with his friends and, eventually, his family.

June turned to July; July turned to August. Rubinson retreated to Pacific Recording Studios in San Mateo to put the finishing touches on the album. Miller later said, 'We finished the damn thing off at Pacific, which is dog meat,' writing off their LP.[275]

During those dog days of summer, Rubinson ushered the band outside one afternoon to snap a few photographs for the LP. 'The back cover of the *20 Granite Creek* album shows us on the back porch of the house,' Stevens recalls. 'Skip and I had just fallen down when that picture was taken because the chain on this rocking chair broke, and you can see Mosley laughing as we fell on our asses.'

But the laughs were few and far between, as the end was fast approaching. With everything winding down, Moby Grape was booked for a final show at Long Beach Civic Auditorium on Sunday 17 July.[276] (Stevens can't recall actually playing the gig and neither can Stevenson.) Not long after, Mosley returned to Hawaii.

Released in September 1971, *20 Granite Creek* garnered little fanfare and a smattering of contrasting reviews.[277] The reunion party was over. Any hope of the Grape reaching its commercial potential was lost.

While the album can stand beside some of their best music, it was still a missed opportunity. 'If Skip had been at 70 per cent, or even 60 per cent,' Gordon Stevens muses, '*20 Granite Creek* could've been a kind of sequel to *Oar*.'

The eleven songs on the album are eclectic, with some easily fitting into the budding country-rock genre and singer-songwriter mode. It was introspective in parts; sometimes mellow; occasionally humorous; always locked into a groove.

But no matter how strong the album was, it wouldn't sell. Even a glowing endorsement in *Rolling Stone* didn't help.[278] It stalled at number 177 on a fleeting five-week *Billboard* run. By that point, everyone had already gone their separate ways.

When Granite Creek wound down, Don Stevenson went back to playing local shows as half of a rotating duo. Jerry Miller resumed work with The Rhythm Dukes and later put together his own bands. He was also asked to join The Doobie Brothers at one point. 'John Hartman called me up and said, "Come on down to San José."' Chuckling, he adds, 'Of course, me being very clever, [I] turned that down.'

Peter Lewis, meanwhile, headed back south. Even before *20 Granite Creek* came out, Bob Mosley had reformed his band, now called Snake Leg, and was performing at the Red Noodle in Honolulu. After signing a solo contract with Warner Brothers, he'd record an LP with his band the following spring. It would fail to chart.[279]

To capitalise on the release of *20 Granite Creek*, Columbia quickly laid plans for a Moby Grape compilation. Charged with the task, Bill Keane, Columbia's Director of Popular Album Product, sequenced a twenty-seven-minute LP with 'Omaha' kicking things off and 'Motorcycle Irene' opening the flip side. Inexplicably, 'Seeing' was left off the album. Perhaps it was just too dark.

In his liner notes, Keane expressed the dismay many Grape fans felt. 'Why didn't a group with unbelievable writing ability and performance capability make it like the Stones or the Beatles?' he asked. 'I don't suppose we'll ever know. Perhaps today the world is ready for Moby Grape.'

Unfortunately, it wasn't. Released in early 1972, *Great Grape* quietly appeared and just as quickly disappeared.

But for all the disappointment and upheaval of the Moby Grape reunion, it seems to have inspired Skip Spence with the idea of forming a whole new band. He may even have been eyeing a record deal of his own. Yet still he remained on his downward spiral.

CHAPTER TWENTY-TWO

AFTERMATH

The Grape's former road manager, Tim Dellara, was visiting Jerry Miller one afternoon, when he ran into his old friend Skip. It was the first time since that fateful day at the Albert hotel in early June 1968. 'I didn't see Skip from the time he was at my door with that hatchet for a year or two,' he recalls 'The next time I saw him was at Jerry's house in Boulder Creek – and he was not himself.

'When I first saw him, I said, "Hey Skip." And he said, "How are ya?" And he started talking about something from the past… but about ten seconds into it he drifted away. He was sitting there, but he wasn't totally *there*. So, I started talking to him a little bit and he came back for a few seconds, but then he was gone again. I can't remember exactly when that was, but it was one of the last times I ever saw Skip.'

Just as the Granite Creek project fizzled in the autumn of '71, Spence's marriage was on its last legs too. Thinking back to his childhood, Aaron Spence explains: 'The reason my mom split from Dad with us kids was that dealing with Dad in his new state was very hard. She remembers waking up one time to find her dresser on fire and Dad was standing there chanting, "Burn, witch, burn!" She packed us up and never looked back.'

251

'When my mom left our dad,' his brother Omar shares, 'I remember us all being in the car and I remember him asking her, "You're coming back?" And she said, "No." I do remember driving away and all of us talking like we weren't going to see our dad again.' While the divorce wouldn't be finalised for a couple of years, to all intents and purposes, Skip and Pat's marriage was over.

'Pat gave a lot, of course,' Gordon Stevens warmly recalls. 'She was amazing and understanding of his motivations and what he was as a creative person. [But in] the end she took hold and raised her kids.'

It wasn't long after that Gordon got a call from social services. 'When Skip crashed badly, the social worker saw my name somehow with his records,' he confirms. The woman was likely following up from incidents at the Spence house; Stevens' name may have been logged when he accompanied Spence to get his meds in San Francisco, in the winter of 1970/71.

'So, I got a call in the fall. And I had a couple of phone calls and a meeting with her, and she was asking me about his family history and so on. She asked me to serve as a temporary conservator while they sorted out their paperwork.

'Skip was so powerful,' Gordon elaborates. 'I think he scared a few people away. See, Skip had these tics that were hooked up to his mental illness. Sometimes he'd roll his eyes back to the point where you couldn't see his pupils. And he had these gestures with his cigarettes and the way he'd pick up a joint.

'His body language was sort of scary sometimes,' his friend acknowledges. 'He'd like to make people think he was a tough guy, and then he'd laugh. It was all tongue-in-cheek. His explosions were scary at times, and a lot of people didn't know how to respond to him.'

For Gordon Stevens, the sharp decline was heartbreaking to watch. That previous winter, the two had been working together on a music project. Skip had still been trying to be a good father and husband. By the end of the Moby Grape reunion the following autumn, he was off his meds, locked in the throes of addiction and hovering on the brink of homelessness.

For a while, Stevens kept an eye on his friend, 'I'd check in on him every few days and he spent time at my place from time to time. It was sad and exciting because he was tripping out mentally, but under control. That's where all this savant stuff was happening and he'd get into stream-of-consciousness mode sometimes. He was having constant dialogues with himself.'

As Skip had been spending much of his time up at the Chateau Liberté, he eventually moved into one of the cabins on the property. He lived there for a while, becoming a kind of fixture, locked into his cycle of personal craziness. But even that couldn't last.

Around early '72, Spence formed The Yankees. While the band's lineup fluctuated, for a time it featured Ric Townsend on lead guitar, Brian Hough on bass and Bruce Ginsberg on drums.[280] After a few rehearsals and couple of gigs, a configuration of the group visited a recording studio in San Mateo to cut a couple of demos with David Rubinson producing. The songs they recorded were 'All My Life (I Love You),' a joyful rocker, and 'The Space Song,' a heavy instrumental track.

Joining the band in the studio that day was Skip's friend, impressionistic portrait artist Paul Berenson. Decades later, he'd share some of his memories of that period. 'I was hanging out with Little Richard at the time,' Berenson recalled. 'And Skip was getting ready to do a recording session at Pacific Studio at San Mateo, and I happened to mention it to Richard. And Richard said, "Oh, I know Skip Spence"...

Apparently, the legendary piano player remembered Spence from long ago; from the time the young teenager had called up, desperately begging him not to give up rock'n'roll. But we can't know whether the two larger-than-life characters had communicated between those points in time.

'[Later] We're in the studio, it's about one or two o'clock and Skip's just going wild... [it's] a big studio where he's got a lot of room to work, move around and stuff like that, it's impressive. And he's playin' his guitar and everybody else is playin', and he's arranging and organising and conducting everybody, and pretty much running the session. And he goes over and is playin' on the keyboards.

'All of a sudden, the phone rings. David Rubinson, the producer, picks up the phone... he says, "Who?" And then there's a pause. And he says, "Who are you?" And then there's another pause. And he says, "Does Skip know you?"

'And then all of a sudden, "Oh, Skip! Little Richard's on the phone and he wants to talk to you." Skip steps away from the keyboard and he just yells to nobody in particular, "The king of rock'n'roll's on the phone and he wants to talk to me!"'[281]

Maybe Paul Berenson's story is another that blends myth with truth. But still, he did hold the last-known copy of the demo Skip recorded that day. Decades later, when he was getting ill, Berenson would pass it to Lynn Quinlan, who took care of Spence's music publishing. Without Berenson, 'All My Life' would have been lost forever.

If Skip's career in music had been a long slugfest, it had come to the twelfth round in early '72. Those last two demos Rubinson recorded for him failed to generate any sort of buzz. Warner Brothers, which released the last Moby Grape album, was not interested.

As his mental struggles became all too visible, The Yankees disbanded. 'All My Life' was a simple, joyful, catchy song that might have led to a new path for him as a songwriter and musician. It was not to be – but it wasn't surprising when he and the Grape returned to the song years later.

Back in the day, a young harmonica player first crossed paths with Spence. 'I met him around '72,' Gary Baranczuk remembers. 'He was just sitting on a couch, drinking a beer at a party, and someone introduced me, saying, "Here's Skip Spence, the drummer from the Airplane." He had a strong handshake. But the guys in The Brother Buzz Blues Band, who I used to jam with, told me not to hang out with him, saying stuff like, "He talks to himself," and, "If you're seen walking around with him the cops will think you're crazy too." They thought he was a burned-out junkie. I didn't really get to know him 'til later.'

Struggling with the cross-addictions of smack and speed, Skip was less and less involved with creating music. The story goes that he overdosed at the Chateau, likely on heroin, sometime in '73. Legend has it he suddenly woke up in the hospital morgue; bolted upright and casually asked an attendant for a glass of water; frightened the poor man half to death.

All the B-movie horror imagery is impossible to confirm, another tale that lurks between myth and reality.[282] Yet Spence *did* overdose at least once that year – and to take him at his own word, he also reanimated in the hospital. 'I died and was brought back to life,' he'd cavalierly recall about a decade later.[283]

In those latter days of Boulder Creek, Skip Spence's carelessness and flippant attitude made life, paradoxically, about as serious as it can get.

• • •

At the beginning of December 1973, *Billboard* reported that Matthew Katz had won ownership of the name 'Moby Grape', after contesting a Labor Commissioner ruling years earlier. Supposedly, everyone had now reached an agreement. A lingering complication to this supposed resolution, however, was the question of informed consent. As both Skip Spence and Bob Mosley had been diagnosed as mentally ill prior to this agreement, the validity of anything they might have signed was up for debate. The dispute over the band's name and royalties would continue to haunt everyone throughout the rest of the century.[284]

Moby Grape was gone but not forgotten. Speaking with *Melody Maker* in early '74, Lou Reed was ferocious in tone but generous in his assessment. 'I despise every San Francisco group,' he said, 'except Moby Grape, and they broke up.'[285] Speaking with *ZigZag* that summer, Steely Dan guitarist Jeff 'Skunk' Baxter matter-of-factly said, 'Moby Grape were probably one of the finest rock bands ever to emerge from the United States.'[286]

That same spring, Miller, Lewis and Mosley got together and hatched a plan for a second Grape reunion. Stevenson was out of the picture, as he'd moved back up to Seattle a year and a half earlier. Spence was in no condition to take part – though he was still there in spirit, with 'Omaha' as a mainstay on the setlist. Instead, the three Grapes recruited drummer John Craviotto and rhythm guitarist Jeff Blackburn. Touring throughout much of 1974, the new Grape received a smattering of positive notices but never stepped into a studio.[287] Things heated up when Katz threatened legal action by mid-July, reiterating his claim to legal ownership of the band's name.[288] They'd soldier on, but not always under the name of 'Moby Grape'.

By the spring of '75, Peter Lewis was gone. But the reunion wasn't quite over. Craviotto stuck around, while the two original members further added guitarist Michael Been to the lineup and rechristened themselves Fine Wine.[289] After protracted talks with various record labels, their album took a year to come out. Even then, it was only released in Germany long after the group had already split. Jerry's guitar style is recognisable, as are his and Bob's voices, but otherwise there's little resemblance to vintage Grape. By that point Mosley had returned to San Diego and Miller had gone back to leading his own band.

• • •

By the end of 1973, the Spences' marriage was officially dissolved. The divorce papers were finalised just a few months short of their tenth anniversary, a whole lifetime away from the day they exchanged vows as wide-eyed teenagers at a Catholic church in San José.

Skip had been absent throughout the latest Moby Grape reunion, living day to day. He'd bump into Jerry Miller at the Chateau from time to time, as the 1970s wore on. Plugging away with his own bands, Miller put on shows around Santa Cruz as well as at the countryside freak-and-biker bar.

In May 1975, Spence popped into his mother's apartment for her 57th birthday party. A photograph from that day shows him gently holding his sister Sherry's first son, Andrew, while sitting at a living-room table. On the table is a birthday cake.

'He looks okay in that photo,' Sherry reflects. 'In some of the pictures he looks okay. And in some of them he *was* okay – if he was on his medication and not living on the street. Whenever I saw him, he always asked about Pat and his kids.'

Still living in San José at that point, Skip was still performing live whenever the mood, or the ability, struck him. Patrick Walker, who was in a band called Kashmir in '76, recalls Spence occasionally sitting in on their sets at a music bar called The Rusty Nail, sometimes leading the band through renditions of 'All My Life' or even impromptu recording sessions at his home.[290]

Then, as if willed by the fates, things began to come together again for the Grape. It all started in the early summer of 1977, when Neil Young joined Bob Mosley, John Craviotto and Jeff Blackburn to form The Ducks. Young was reportedly under contract to only tour with Crazy Horse, so the side-project band limited its shows to Santa Cruz.[291]

Their first gig was on Saturday 9 July, a birthday celebration for Jerry Miller at The Back Room. With Mosley belting out tunes, Young traded licks with Miller. At one point, Spence made his way onto the stage and joined in on the jam.[292] It was the first time he'd performed with his old bandmates since that disastrous weekend in New York six years earlier. As The Ducks gigged around town they quickly attracted a buzz, sparking a chain reaction of national headlines. Watching it all at close range, Miller and Spence started talking about a possible Moby Grape reunion.

Soon, Miller was on the phone to Lewis, who was living near Santa Barbara at the time. 'Jerry called me in Ojai,' Lewis told *BAM*. 'He said, "Things are exciting, man. Better get up here." I said, "Okay, tomorrow?" And he said, "Right on."'[293]

Trekking up Highway 1, Lewis sped past an oceanside monastery in Big Sur on his way north.[294] He'd used it as a retreat a while back. Playing music at prayer meetings, he'd been invited to extend his stay but declined. This time, there was no chance to drop in for a visit. He had to get to Boulder Creek, pronto. When he arrived at Jerry's secluded home, Peter quickly started practising with his two former bandmates. A space had been set up for rehearsals and he camped in the basement. 'Pete got the flu when he was down in the basement,' Miller recalls, 'and he had the heat up so hot you couldn't go in there.'

There was now a new, extended lineup that included Cornelius Bumpus on keyboards, saxophone and occasional vocals, 'Fuzzy John' Oxendine on drums, Jack Register on bass and Juanita Franklin as co-vocalist. With a female singer and different instrumental lineup, Moby Grape started exploring new directions in jazz and soul. Overseeing this latest project was manager John Chesleigh. To limber up, the band played a flurry of rehearsals at Miller's home and a variety of spaces around Santa Cruz. 'I was the youngest in the band and I'd been a huge fan of Moby Grape. Playing with those guys was like being a little kid in a candy store,' drummer Fuzzy John recalls.

Soon, Chesleigh booked the band to debut its new lineup at Shady Grove on Haight Street. The show was set for Monday 22 August. With a capacity of 49, the club was a modest first step but a good venue for the group to ease into their new style and material. With nightly shows they would get tighter and tighter, though they still had a way to go.

Of Moby Grape's performance the following Monday, Joel Selvin wrote: 'a full house watched the band surmount production traumas… and give a performance that breathed fire at points. Guitarist Jerry

Miller played especially fine and Peter Lewis offered at least one first-class new original, "That Lost Horizon." On the other hand, at times, the band proved to be surprisingly sloppy and ragged.'[295]

Thinking back to those early shows, Oxendine chuckles. 'The lady that I was with at the time wanted to get Skippy's autograph. And at one of our early shows, I said to her, "Just go ahead and ask him." So, she walked up to Skippy and before she can say anything he blurts out, "Oh! Can I have your autograph?" How did he even know she was going to ask him that? That's Skippy up and down all the way!'

On Friday 2 September, the Grape opened for The Ducks at the Santa Cruz Civic Auditorium. It was an off night for both bands. A thirty-minute black and white video captures the full spectrum of the Grape's performance. Their run-throughs of 'Omaha' and 'Fall On You' were loose and sloppy, and they lost their place in Spence's 'All My Life' a few times. One highlight was Lewis and Franklin trading vocals on 'That Lost Horizon', his new, wistfully autobiographical number.

At its best, the band was energetic and Juanita Franklin brought something fresh to the sound. At one point, the group jumped into a rendition of JJ Cale's deceptively laidback 'Cocaine', which was fitting. Cocaine was on hand that year. Skip, especially, had easy access to it from within the group's inner circle.

Reviewing the show for the *Santa Cruz Sentinel*, Greg Beebe tsked: 'the Grape was downright bad... [and] seemed unprepared for audience requests, dating back to the band's San Francisco heyday... [the Grape] received nothing more than polite applause after ending its too-long performance. It was difficult to tell whether the crowd was clapping for the Grape, or for its exit from the stage. No encore was played.'[296]

The band soon juggled its lineup, playing gigs anywhere and everywhere: hotels, clubs, theatres. Franklin and Register were out, and new bassist Chris Powell stepped in. He had no idea what he was getting himself into.

As Peter Lewis later told radio DJ Nick Black, someone close to the band 'was a coke dealer, which I can say now because he had to go pay his debt to society... they couldn't keep Skip around because he was like *Scarface*, man. It was like a big pile of [cocaine] was like hanging out on the table, and you'd turn around and it was gone. Skippy was just [makes a snorting sound]... he'd be gone. I mean, you couldn't get him high...'[297]

Sometimes Skip became too engrossed in his own dark thoughts. He'd start pacing around, talking about axe murders.[298] With cocaine so accessible, he was getting lost in his paranoia. 'He'd have these fits where he'd talk and stuff and laugh,' Lewis recalled. 'It wasn't cool to have him around for business, so we got him his own place.'[299] Skip was couch-surfing here and there. Peter stayed at Jerry's for a time, so they arranged for him to stay at a place nearby. But it didn't last long due to his condition.

By the end of September, the band was up in San Francisco for a couple of nights at the popular Old Waldorf. It was a mixture of chaos and brilliance, with Spence particularly unpredictable on stage. Journalist Clark Peterson noted: 'The song ended, but the malady lingered on. There was guitarist Alexander "Skip" Spence, stage right at the Old Waldorf on September 26, convulsed in blissful euphoria. Only a few seconds later he was completely deadpan – from manic to depressive in the time it takes to say, "Moby Grape lives!" While Peter Lewis attempted to sing a soft ballad at stage right, Spence mumbled incoherently into his mike.'[300]

'I remember the Old Waldorf,' Miller chuckles. 'When we were there Skippy told a roadie he needed some Poligrip for his teeth. And so, the roadie shouted out to the crowd, "Moby Grape needs some Poligrip!" I said "Goddamn, you dumb son of a bitch, that's not good!"' Although Skip had been off heroin for a few years by this point, all that time taking speed, and now coke, was accelerating tooth decay.

While putting together his article, Peterson met up with the band for a chat at their hotel in San Francisco. They reconvened at Miller's home in Boulder Creek. For much of those interviews, Spence seemed mentally disjointed.

'Miller lives on top of a tree-covered hill so secluded that we joke about finding a platoon of Beaver Patrol scouts to navigate for us,' Peterson wrote. 'Upon arriving, Miller shows us his downstairs rehearsal room where Lewis... temporarily lives, the surrounding woods, and the upstairs where most of the interview is to take place. As Spence, who lives down the hill, talks by himself a few feet away.'[301]

By this point, Skip's days at his own place were numbered. According to Lewis, he got into some sort of conflict with his neighbours and was picked up, to be placed into the care of Santa Cruz County Mental Health. Not long after that, said Peter, the folks at the hospital called and said, '"You gotta get him outta here." Because he goes in there and he takes over. He knew how to get around in those places by then. So, we got him back and nobody knew what to do with Skip.'[302]

He was living for a time at the Town and Country Lodge in Ben Lomond; some remember him living in a tent in a redwood forest near Boulder Creek, sometimes walking around the forest naked.

'Just as quick as it started,' Gordon Stevens confirms, 'he was under the bridges with the homeless people. He did the halfway house thing for a bit, but he had a hard time. I don't know what rules he had to maintain.'

'Skippy moved around a lot,' Oxendine explains. 'We couldn't leave him alone, so somebody was always with him pretty much. A lot of times I'd be with him for two or three days in a row and that was a trip! But he *was* on the street a lot of times.'

'My brother's life was never the same after his psychotic break in New York,' Sherry Spence sighs. 'He was homeless, on the street sometimes, in jail for who knows what. I went to visit him at Napa State Hospital, I think it was with my mom. It was kind of like a dungeon, sort of like a *One Flew Over The Cuckoo's Nest* scenario. For a time, he was also at the hospital I was working at in San José.'

'We didn't see a lot of Skippy back then,' Jerry Miller notes. 'He was hanging out more in San José, I think. And he was going back and forth for treatment at the Valley Hospital in San José. We went and got him out. They were looking all over the place for him and finally we walked over to his room, and he was right there laying on his bed. So, all these geniuses couldn't find him. And the head psychiatrist said, "Well, you know, he's going to do the same thing and start tripping out and start doing whatever he wants." And we said, "We trust him, turn him loose to us."'

'One time we did a gig,' Oxendine laughs, 'and all of a sudden after the gig Skippy was gone. And we were all going, "Where'd he go?" He was gone for days. A short while later we had this big outdoor show and we all got there, and we were just getting ready to go on stage and Skippy shows up with two babes... and he's all dressed to the nines!' Chuckling fondly, he adds, 'About three or four days later, that suit was a mess and we all thought, "Oh, that's my Skippy."'

Everyone was at their wits' end. They couldn't live with Skip but he couldn't live on his own. At that point, Peter Lewis had a kind of epiphany. Thinking back to his time at the monastery in Big Sur, he made a couple of phone calls and arranged to bring his friend there for a visit. Or maybe a break, a retreat. Possibly a cleansing. In a later radio interview, he'd even suggest it was an exorcism.

'Nobody knew what to do with him,' Lewis recalled, 'so I said, "Well, maybe I could take him down there [to the monastery] for a couple days." And they all went, "Oh yeah." And so, I ended up with [our manager's] car, and driving Skip in the middle of the night down Highway 1, with nobody else...

'We got to the place, and it was up this old dirt road... and this monk comes out, and he shows us to these two rooms. It was a cloistered place, like a string of motel rooms on a cliff, where he was on the end room and I was next to him. And there was nobody else there.'[303]

It was calm and quiet at the oceanside monastery. Yet being alone at such an isolated location seemed to throw Spence into a frenzy. As darkness fell, it brought out his inner fears and personal demons that first night. Through his wall, Lewis could hear his friend in the full throes of a manic episode.

'Skip's in his room,' Peter continued, 'and all of a sudden I hear these sounds coming from his room. It's like him being thrown up against the wall. Now he's in this place where you don't have any drugs, it's nothing but just this guy and whatever's going on. Nothing to blame it on. Right?

'In that situation, because he was in a monastery, and those people see the whole life adventure as being a war between good and evil, he was basically stuck in there with their explanation; with their definition of life...

'And so, Skippy, in that context, was just like *The Exorcist*, where I keep hearing those noises and I get freaked out, and I'm on my knees praying, 'cause I was raised a Catholic... I'm afraid he's coming in there to get me. 'Cause I hear this and I remember the stories about New York, and him chopping down the hotel-room door to Don's room... so I start freaking out and I'm praying.'[304]

Somehow, as the night wore on, the pandemonium diminished. Lewis fell asleep sometime before dawn in total exhaustion. Waking up a few hours later, he opened his door and saw Spence strolling outside. It was like someone had flipped a switch. All the mania and paranoia had dissipated, and his demeanour had changed entirely. It was as though he were a completely different person – his old self.

'I get up at about twelve o'clock and I go outside and there's Skip with his pants at half mast, wandering around in the court-yard,' Lewis recalled. 'I talk to him and he's basically the same guy I met when I first went to San Francisco...

'We go down to have some lunch in Lucia, which is right below where this place is; come back up and as night starts to go down, I could feel him slipping. Slipping back...

'And this priest shows up,' Lewis continued. '[He] told me, "You're going to have to leave… we heard what was going on here last night and you can't stay. There are people coming here for a retreat…"'

'And I said, "Well, you heard what was going on, and you know that I can't take this guy anywhere. The priest said, "I got some bad news and I got some good news… The bad news is he's possessed." I said, "What's the good news?" He said, "He's not *completely* possessed, because if he was there would be no sign of it."' What exactly the priest meant is obscure to the point of baffling. Still, Lewis took the comment to heart.

'I said, "You want me to take this guy and leave. But I'm not sure that I can get where I'm going in this state, 'cause now he's starting to go back."'

'So, the priest said… "just don't touch him, and don't talk to him. Keep your eyes on the road and just drive as carefully as you can. I'll be praying for you and you'll be alright."'[305]

Peter and Skip packed their things and got back into Chesleigh's car, heading along the dirt road, towards Highway 1. 'All of a sudden, Skip starts yowling again, like a beast,' Lewis recalled. 'And I could see out of the corner of my vision this wolf's face, or something… I'm trying to make sense of what it is, but It's really fucking scary, right?'

'I don't let my fear get out of control,' Lewis continued his breathless narrative. 'And we got down to Highway 1 and somehow when I'm able to get some control over my fear, instead of being afraid I get angry. And then I started really getting angry… and he starts to whimper and get on the other side of the car. And I can almost hear a voice now. Whatever was going on with Skip, the voices that you hear through a schizophrenic or something, now I'm hearing them.

'And they're telling me to stop the car and kill him. So, as soon as I realise that, I say, "This is the Devil speaking." So, as I realise that I started getting afraid again. And he starts getting crazy and angry. And this went on for three fucking hours…

'We got next to San José and the whole thing wound out. And he… [was never] mean or scary with me again. That was the end of that with me and him. So, it proves my point, sometimes things that happen to people like that is more than just medical. It's spiritual.'[306]

Certainly, spirituality had been an important aspect of Skip Spence's creativity – but it was never demonic. Still, it's how Peter Lewis interprets that harrowing 1977 experience. But there's another interpretation.

A 22-year-old Spence had a manic episode the day he grabbed a fire axe at the Albert Hotel, all the way back in June '68. His extended time at Bellevue psychiatric hospital may well have done him more harm than good. But had he suffered just one drug-induced psychotic episode, or could he have been defined as mentally ill before he went into Bellevue?

It isn't clear. But we know about his subsequent self-medication. It's entirely likely that years of darting between heroin, methamphetamine and cocaine like a pinball, interrupted by brief periods of antipsychotic medication, worsened his ongoing condition. Any personal demons that erupted from Spence were likely a manifestation of his mental illness.

• • •

When Lewis and Spence got back to Boulder Creek, everything was still just a nudge away from unhinged. Yet the Grape kept plugging away.

For three weeks in October, the band mostly laid low, rehearsing new material at Miller's home and around town. As Oxendine recalls, 'A lot of the stuff we were doing clicked. We knew how to play together, so when someone brought in something new it would come together pretty quick. And sometimes Jerry would start playing a solo and Skip would come up and start playing with him. He was a really good guitar player. I mean, he didn't have the chops that Jerry has but they did some really cool things together. Skippy had the mind. His mind was musical.'

With the days fading into each other, the band got tighter. After playing a handful of mid-sized venues in the last week of the month, they were ready to start recording. But instead of stepping into the studio, they brought the studio to the venues, taping four San Francisco shows in the first week of November at Shady Grove and the Inn of the Beginning.[307]

'Skippy was kind of tripping out when we were recording at the Inn of the Beginning,' Miller remembers. 'There was a giant bottle of Kahlúa in the back room. It was so big it was on an A-frame with the chains hanging. Skippy sat in that room and pretty much polished that whole thing off.'

Still, in four nights Moby Grape had a whole new album in the can ready for mixing. During that whirlwind string of shows, Spence also presented bandmates and audience with an unexpected gem. As the tape was rolling on one of those nights, he dove into a new number of his own.

'I'd never heard that song ['Must Be Goin' Now Dear'] before and we didn't know what to do,' Oxendine remembers. 'We were taping and all of a sudden, he started playing this song we'd never practised. And I was going like, "What is he doing?" Then everybody jumped into it and I thought, "I guess we're gonna do it!"

'It started off really slow and we got something going with it and picked it up a bit. Then we started cracking up because it was typical Skippy stuff.' Laughing warmly, Fuzzy John adds, 'He was a spur-of-the-moment kind of guy. I don't know anybody else like that. He had a gift.'

Playing ten shows in December, Spence became a semi-regular on stage. After one performance at Keystone Berkeley, the *Berkeley Gazette* wrote: 'You really have to watch for these guys... but they are definitely worth scouting out. Skip Spence, the adorable, part-crazed troll of the group is still as unpredictable; Sunday he strolled off the stage to dance with the crowd, applauded the band from the floor, yelled requests and had an all-round good time.'[308]

As manager Chesleigh pursued a record contract with different labels, the Grape often returned to a handful of venues, like Keystone Berkeley, Shady Grove and Keystone Palo Alto. It was more than a decade since the ballroom bidding war, and in the disco/punk/cocaine-fuelled days of the late 1970s, Moby Grape was almost a relic of a bygone era.

With so many unresolved legal issues with ex-manager Katz, it wasn't even clear if they retained the right to call themselves 'Moby Grape.' Record labels were, perhaps inevitably, reluctant to get involved.

In late January, Joel Selvin announced in the *Examiner* that the band's new album was to come out on Escape Records.[309] 'That was John Chesleigh's company,' Oxendine explains. 'I believe he started Escape to put the *Live Grape* record out.'

A few weeks into the new year, Bob Mosley, along with his friend Willie Kellogg, temporarily joined the band after The Ducks – minus the already departed Neil Young – folded in December. A recording of the Grape's 21 January show at Veterans Hall in Marin includes Mosley but not Spence. After about a month Mosley headed back down to San Diego, as Powell and Oxendine returned to the fold.[310]

Throughout all this, Skip's presence was intermittent. When he was there, his involvement was limited. Writing for *BAM* in late March, Clark Peterson noted: 'As for Skip Spence, who can often be seen roaming zombie-like through the crowd when he's supposed to be on stage, times have been rough. He's one man who proves that it's possible to have too much fun.'[311]

Having heard about his friend's condition, Gordon Stevens refrained from heading out to any of the shows. 'I wasn't prepared to go to a gig where I knew Skip was going to embarrass himself or the other guys,' he recalls, 'because there was a lot of feedback about that around town.' Whilst not a part of the latest Grape reunion, Gordon stayed active as a musician and at the Stevens Music family store.

When the LP appeared in mid-April 1978, it didn't feature the credit 'Moby Grape' anywhere on its cover or liner notes. Given the ongoing tussles with Katz, everyone felt it would just be safer to title the album *Live Grape*. To celebrate the launch, Moby Grape played five consecutive nights at Shady Grove on 15-19 April.

The number of tracks Spence contributes to is unknown. Miller doesn't remember him being on many. 'We wanted him on more, but he was doing his own thing most of the time,' he notes.

Live Grape does feature the one new Spence song, 'Must Be Goin' Now Dear'. It starts off ragged, with the musicians joining in one at a time, as though they don't know exactly where they're headed. (As Oxendine notes, that actually was the case.)

For the first half-minute or so, it sounds as though the song could break down at any moment. Then it settles on a blues groove. But with Skip Spence, nothing's ever that predictable. His forceful delivery, unique lyrics and phrasing make the song a highlight of the album. As far as can be deciphered, the rough and ready lyric kicks off with: 'I am a farmer, when the first light is on / Always working from twilight to dawn...'

Even in this limited capacity, he could still briefly steal the spotlight. Thinking back, Miller wistfully recalls, 'We wanted to get Skip involved with us as much as we could; but we weren't the best role models either.' Chuckling, he adds, 'But compared to him, we were like [TV bandleader] Lawrence Welk. And he was a full-on Aries, in every direction. He just didn't have any control. If something looked good to him, he was gone.'

Indeed, impulsivity was a way of life for Spence. While it made him a thrilling performer and fascinating songwriter, it also led to all the complications of his personal and professional life. He was carefree and careless, always, though never uncaring.

As Escape Records was such a tiny label, the album's release (on purple vinyl) was limited. Reviews were few and far between. By now, Moby Grape was locked into a cycle of playing the same small-to-mid-sized venues again and again. Instead of catapulting the band back to prominence, *Live Grape* marked its fade into obscurity.

After eleven shows in April, the band only played a few more over the next three months. A Saturday night performance in the middle of July, at the Highland Dell Hotel, marked the end of an eleven-month run for the band. A handful of so-called Moby Grape gigs popped up over the next few months, but they were likely performed by Jerry Miller's band. It's unknown if Spence participated in any of those shows.

'Things were going in different directions,' Oxendine sighs. 'We couldn't keep track of Skippy and it needs money. You need money for those kinds of things to continue... there was only a finite amount of money available and that's when things started coming apart.'

As everyone went their separate ways, Spence fell back into revolving-door visits to mental-health facilities and jails in the South Bay. Still only in his early 30s, Skip Spence had already experienced enough achievement, loss and struggle for ten lives.

CHAPTER TWENTY-THREE

SPINNING FREELY

Across from the Greyhound bus station on South Almaden Avenue was a rundown hotel. Standing three stories tall, it looked like a big warehouse. Although it was only twenty years old at the outset of the 1980s, by that point the Maas had become one of the last residence hotels in downtown San José.

Next to it was The Caravan, one of the last Greyhound traveller's bars that dotted the country. As the buses came and went, the forty-nine rooms in the Maas Hotel rumbled, as though their bones were creaking. One of those rooms was littered with cigarette butts, empty beer cans, soda cans, clothing, and religious brochures and pamphlets.

Somewhere amidst all that mess was a notebook with song ideas or lyrics scribbled down. If things had gone differently, it might have been the template for a record. Maybe even a follow-up to the cult classic *Oar*...

For the occupant of that room in the summer of '81 was Skip Spence. But, because of all the noise he'd made during the night, all the laughing or crying or shouting, he was about to be kicked out. Before the fall, he'd find himself in a different but similar hotel. Soon, he'd be a ward of the state.

Working on a human-interest story, Bay Area journalist Jill

Wolfson met with Spence sometime that summer. What she wrote is at once unflinching and compassionate.

'I'm a derelict,' Spence declared. With both delusions of grandeur and self-mockery, he added, 'I'm a world saviour. I am drugs. I am rock'n'roll.'[312]

Of the rapidly aging musician, Wolfson noted: 'Skip Spence, in his late thirties in fatigues four sizes too big and four days too dirty, anchors down his mind long enough to make a pass at two girls in a coffee shop. They have been talking about their Rolling Stones concert tickets and stop long enough to cringe, then giggle nervously as he performs an erratic, but harmless, soft-shoe.'[313]

In fact, he was only 35 at the time. But he'd been hearing voices for over a decade and during that period he'd lost his family, his career and his powers of concentration. 'Only the voices – sometimes threatening, sometimes comforting have stayed. Now, on his bad days, when the voices intrude too much, when they threaten torture, Spence checks himself into a psychiatric ward. He's been in the hospital twenty, maybe thirty times, he says.'[314]

When he had good days, Spence would get up around dawn and trek over to the Quality Café. There, he'd have a state-provided breakfast. Heading to the multiservice centre next, he'd collect his $2 state stipend, which he'd tuck away for cigarettes and beer. At some point in the day, he'd make his way back to the Quality or a nearby sandwich shop, or possibly a music store he sometimes frequented. According to Wolfson, 'the guy behind the counter knows what Spence once was and lets him handle the guitars.'[315]

Around that same time, in the late summer of '81, bass guitarist Stephen Macias had a fleeting encounter with Spence at a rundown San José bar one night. It was something he'll never forget.

'In the summer of '81,' he explains, 'a buddy of mine invited me to come sit in with his band. It was at this little dive bar called The Rusty Nail in San José. I got up on stage to play, but as I was grabbing my bass, this hippie chick comes walking up with this guy dressed in nicely ironed and creased khaki pants… She begged the leader of the band to let this guy sit in and play guitar. She told him he used to play guitar with this band that had made some records, but he doesn't play much anymore... he's had some problems. All the time this begging and pleading was going on, this cat is just looking at the floor, his arms hung limp at his side and his hands were shaking.'[316]

The bandleader, a musician named Dave, handed his forlorn counterpart a black and yellow sunburst Telecaster, which he initially declined. But after some coaxing from the hippie girl, he momentarily became a member of the band.

'...This guy just goes off into this driving lick that I've heard before,' recalls Macias, 'but I've never played the song. Went through a few moments where this guy was just a monster guitar player, then he would kind of lose it. The acid would take over, then he would come back and play and lose it one more time. After losing it for the last time, we decided to end the song.'

The bassist asked the woman to give him a memory check on the song. 'She says, "It's called 'Omaha' and Skip wrote it."'... She grabbed Skip Spence by the hand and told him what a great job he had done and how he needs to get out and play more. He just shuffled behind her, holding her hand, never looking up, never saying a word and they disappeared out the door and into the night.'[317]

Chatting with folks in Spence's circle, Jill Wolfson noted, 'Friends say that in many ways, he is not different than before – still gentle, still funny, still sincere, still sensitive.' Maybe his sensitivity had been his Achilles' heel all along.

Years earlier, self-conscious about his playing, Skip had bowed out of the *Grape Jam* project. Perhaps he felt his musical prowess didn't stack up against his bandmates, but if so then that same insecurity had driven his swaggering onstage persona night after night. At the same time, he was well aware of his shortcomings as a husband and father. He'd tried to make up for them in any way that he could, but everything had gone too far downhill too fast. All he had left now were his memories and regrets.

Visiting his hotel room, Wolfson gazed through the chaos and noticed a little rag doll sitting on an empty whiskey bottle. It was a gift from Skip's mother, Gwenn. A reminder of the past, of the loved ones he rarely saw and missed deeply. Printed across the doll's chest was the title of a song he'd written so many years before, 'My Best Friend'.

• • •

In late 1982, Skip's ex-bandmates started preparing for another Moby Grape reunion. This time, surprisingly, Matthew Katz was involved as they'd called an unlikely truce.

Perhaps everyone was just too tired of fighting. Maybe they agreed to join forces as an act of desperation. Maybe the sunk-cost fallacy was coming into play. After all, they'd put so much into the Grape over the years, perhaps they figured it was worth teaming up with Katz if they could finally get the break that eluded them since it all started in '66.

With Christmas approaching, Peter Lewis headed up to Seattle and stayed with Don Stevenson's family as the pair started rehearsing new material. The reformed Grape lineup gathered in LA in the new year and quickly recorded 'Too Old To Boogie', a rollicking number Stevenson had co-written with Jerry Miller. Then, just as things were looking up, it all began to crumble. When a pair of session players showed up in the studio and the hired drummer started playing on the tracks, tensions flared. Miller and Stevenson walked.[318]

The story of the reunion broke in April, when dailies across the US reported that Moby Grape was back in the studio and preparing for a tour – but with no indication that Lewis and Mosley were now the only original members left. After postponing shows at Berkeley's Greek Theatre, on 23 April, and at San Francisco's Broadway, on 15 May, the planned tour fizzled and the album went into limbo.

273

While Skip wasn't involved in that ill-fated reunion, he remained musically active from time to time. On 15 October 1983, he sat in with Bay Area supergroup The Dinosaurs at the Keystone Palo Alto, taking lead vocals on a song with the repeated refrain 'You Will Fall For Me'. A recording of the show reveals he still had a flair for performing and retained that gentle, soft voice.[319] Spence was said to have borrowed Grateful Dead lyricist Robert Hunter's guitar that night. By that point, he didn't have any instruments of his own.

That following year, when *Moby Grape '84* finally materialised, it appeared on Katz's San Francisco Sound label. There were no bad or indifferent reviews this time, as the press did something far worse – they ignored the album entirely. Apart from one track, none of the album features Miller's signature guitar, with the replacement lead work veering into heavy-metal territory. Admittedly, it was the Grape's weakest release to date, but it featured a handful of memorable songs: the aforementioned 'Too Old To Boogie', 'Silver Wheels', 'City Lights', and 'Queen Of The Crows'. While Skip wasn't involved in any of the recording, he was credited for co-writing a new song with Bob Mosley, 'Better Day'. But, without any kind of promotion, the album sank without a trace.

• • •

At some point during the early-to-mid 1980s, Skip Spence reconnected with a harmonica player he'd first met back in '72. It was purely by chance. As Gary Baranczuk recalls, 'We were both in the psych ward together, at Valley Medical.

'I had a bad case of DTs. I was a real Skid Row wino back then. I mean, I'd go to the blood bank and sell my blood for $10 so I could buy wine. I don't know what Skip was in there for. He was really silent at first. He kind of walked around like a ghost.'

Then, 'when I first mentioned Brother Buzz [Blues Band] his face kind of lit up,' recalls Gary. 'We were there a few days and after we got out, we started hanging out. I'd scrape up a few dollars and go out and get a quart of beer. We drank plenty of beer and wine. All my friends knew Skip. They were all kind of like street people, misfits. They liked Skip. Everybody liked Skip.'

Throughout all this, Spence's ex-wife and children were living a separate life about thirty miles away, down in Santa Cruz. 'I didn't know too much about my dad when I was growing up,' Aaron Spence explains. 'I knew he was famous, but it wasn't really a topic in our house because my stepfather could get jealous. He wanted my mom to lose her past, so my dad was never mentioned in the house.'

But Skip did occasionally spend time with his own mother and sister. A black-and-white photograph from 1985 shows him sitting in a chair, holding Sherry's younger son, Randall. Skip's nephew Andrew, who was ten at the time, is standing beside him. Spence is laughing.

'That's my mom's house in Spokane,' Sherry remembers. 'My brother was really lucid sometimes; but even in the same day, he could be totally engaging and interacting for a time, and then he'd get up and pace and talk to himself and laugh.'

In the early weeks of 1987, the *San Francisco Examiner* unexpectedly announced: 'All five members of Moby Grape... will play Feb. 26 at Flint Center [Cupertino] and Feb. 27 at Marin Veteran's Memorial [San Rafael].'[320] By this point, the band's various reunions were like an archipelago of little islands that jutted out from their 1966-69 heyday. On a 1960s revival bill – titled *Looking For Your Long Lost Mind* – with Fraternity of Man and the Strawberry Alarm Clock, the Grape closed out each show with a set that ran for about 45 minutes. This time, as with their previous reunion, Moby Grape had called a truce with Katz who was promoting the tour. But it would be short-lived.

'That's where Don's wife [photojournalist Melissa Marteny] got into a fight with Matthew [when Katz tried to stop her taking photos of the show]. They were to the left of the stage,' Jerry Miller explains. 'Skippy was just walking back and forth smoking a cigarette while we were trying to play. But we were so sloppy, we played for shit that night. The next night we were in Marin and it was pretty good.'

Spence, who was temporarily staying with Katz in Los Angeles at that point, accompanied his bandmates at the end of that second show on a rendition of 'Naked, If I Want To'. As he phased in and out, singing, giggling or mumbling to himself, the song wavered then came to a lacklustre end. After exiting the stage, the band quickly returned for an encore, putting on a lively performance of Skip's joyful, neglected anthem, 'All My Life'.

In a brief interview with the Palo Alto *Times Tribune*, Spence reflected on his exit from Moby Grape nearly two decades earlier. 'I don't know whether I got kicked out or I quit,' he quipped.

Waxing poetic, he claimed the current incarnation of the band would stay together 'as long as we're living the sum of our total lives.' While Skip admitted he 'was out of it for a long time with various ailments,' he was optimistic. 'I'm anxious to play,' he said, 'real happy to be together again. We love each other.'[321]

Two months later, the Grape played the Moscone Convention Centre in San Francisco, on 18 April. Spence didn't sit in that time. 'Matthew was at that Moscone show,' Miller recalls. 'He was trying to pitch us going around on tour in his bus. I know we were not digging Matthew at that time.' A few weeks later, a performance at the Westport Playhouse in St. Louis was cancelled and the Grape went back into hibernation.

After years of neglect, *Oar* reappeared in record shops in 1988. Re-released by Edsel, the cult album received little to no attention in the media. With negligible sales, it quietly slipped back into oblivion. While recognition remained out of reach, its creator still knew it was something special.

'One day he brought me a cassette tape called *Oar*,' Gary Baranczuk remembers, 'and he'd play it over and over again, sometimes giggling and laughing.' For a moment he pauses, lost in his memories.

'Skip was a free spirit, always looking into space, looking into the clouds,' he warmly adds, 'he mumbled sometimes and kind of giggled. He'd walk down the street with a very serious look on his face and then burst out into laughter. We'd go into a bar and the bartender would come up to me and say, "Gary, can you take your friend somewhere else? He's scaring the customers away." And I'd say, "Hey, that's Skip Spence! You know? Jefferson Airplane! He was a genius!"'

To get money for beer, Spence sometimes did odd jobs in a junkyard. At other times he begged. 'He'd be out in front of the liquor store, panhandling,' Gary recalls. 'And he'd get a quart of King Cobra, that really horrible beer... he'd go behind the liquor store, by the dumpster, and he'd open his mouth and just guzzle it all down in like thirty seconds. He'd gulp a 16oz can in like ten seconds. But he couldn't handle too many beers. He'd have three or four and he'd get all tired out.'

After a long hiatus, The Doobie Brothers got back together around this time. Skip and Gary caught them performing near the San José Civic centre. 'It was in the parking lot by the farmer's market,' Gary explains. 'At one point in the show one of the Doobies said, "We owe everything we have to Skip Spence. Are you out there somewhere, Skip?" We were in the audience sharing a quart of beer... I raised my hand up and they said, "Oh, there he is!" And the whole audience, hundreds of people, turned and applauded. But then the mounted police came over and told us to pour the beer out. A lot of people laughed when *that* happened.'

It was around this time that Skip had a more poignant reconciliation. It was with an aspect of his past that he'd never even known.

As Phoenix native Rich Young explains, 'When I married my wife Sandy, and my parents came to the wedding, some days afterward Sandy said to me, "I didn't know you were adopted." I said, "I'm not adopted." And she said, "There's something strange..."'

The new Mrs. Young had not previously met her in-laws. To Sandy, her husband's lack of resemblance to the man who'd raised him was all too visible. For Rich, who'd grown up quietly as a minister's son, what followed was completely unexpected.

'So, we talked to my mom and dad,' he continues, 'and sure enough they admitted that when I was born... [it was] because of a relationship my dad – my biological dad – had with my mom back in 1954. I was born in 1955. My mom and dad [who raised me] had never told me about this, and they didn't want to talk about it either.'

Unable to get answers from his legal parents, Young made his own enquiries. 'By the time I found all this out I was living in San Mateo, California. And that's when I found out who my biological dad – Jock Spence – was, and that he had passed away [over twenty years earlier].

'At that point I found out that I had a brother in San José and a sister in Spokane. It was through my half-sister, Sherry, that I found out where Skippy was... I went down to San José and found him, and we did some things together. We were able to enjoy each other before he passed away.'

Rich tells his story in a matter-of-fact, soft-spoken manner, but he had to navigate a whole spectrum of emotions once he learned of his 'new' family – one of whom was living in a completely different world, totally foreign to him. But these two half-brothers, complete strangers at first, not only accepted but quickly came to embrace one another.

• • •

As the past reached into the present, Skip's old bandmates were reaching back to the past again. They got back together in late '88/ early '89 to see if they could regain some traction. This time, Jerry Miller and Don Stevenson took the lead. Miller had returned to Washington State and reconnected with Stevenson, who after a decade and a half away from rock'n'roll was ready to get back.

Peter Lewis and Bob Mosley duly trekked northward to join in. With Dan Abernathy lending a hand on rhythm guitar, they spent months rehearsing just a few miles from where Nirvana was putting together its first album, *Bleach*. At that moment, Seattle was the nerve centre of a new subgenre that was ready to explode – grunge, as it came to be known, the latest mutant offspring of the electric guitar.

As Moby Grape's flame reignited in the north, Spence remained in San José. 'He was living on Peach Court [near Bonita Park], next to the California Cheese Company for a time,' Baranczuk remembers. 'I think some Japanese people owned it and they told me he was on probation for joyriding in a stolen car. He smoked a lot of cigarettes and drank a lot of beer. We took LSD together a few times with his girlfriend, Joanne. She lived in the Metro, the old Metropole Hotel. She was kind of antisocial. She seemed to like me because I was friends with Skip. I was moving around a lot in those days and he'd always find me. Later on, he was in a boarding house on San Fernando.

'One time, I was living in a house with a bunch of party animals near Julian [Street],' Gary reminisces. 'It was on the east side, by the Portuguese area. It was all alcoholics and junkies, and the cops were always over there…

'…One day this woman, Jessica, just got out of the hospital after having a baby and everybody was having a big party for her. Well, Skip shows up and we drank a bit. Then they gave me some money to go down to the liquor store and buy some beer and cigarettes. So, Skip and I were walking over, and on the way down there we passed a garage sale. We had a look and I found this gun. I said, "Wow, is that a real gun?" [This woman] said, "No, it's my son's BB gun." I said, "What are you asking for that?" And she said, "One dollar."…

'…We were about a block away and we got surrounded by cops,' he recalls of his near-monumental misjudgement. 'There were about six of them and they had guns pointed at us. They were shouting, "Put your hands up!"… And I was shouting back, "It's a BB gun, it's only a BB gun!"

'They came over and took the BB gun and slammed me down

on the sidewalk... handcuffed me and everything. They bawled me out for about five minutes and told me that I got the trophy for being the stupidest person in San José. They lectured me and Skip was right next to me, shaking like a leaf.'

Back in Washington State, the reunified Moby Grape was circuiting up and down the West Coast in the early months of '89. As they got tighter, everyone started to feel cautiously optimistic. While Skip wasn't involved, the plan was to include him in as many of their California shows as possible.[322]

Yet legal threats from Katz soon rained down like cannon fire, prompting the Grape to change their name. For the second half of the year, they dubbed themselves The Melvilles. It was a call back to the man who'd written *Moby Dick*, the book that spawned the punchline to the joke that gave the band its name.

'Calling ourselves The Melvilles was probably one step too far away, but it felt right at the time,' Stevenson says in retrospect. 'It wasn't going to go anywhere but we played some monumental gigs...'

Back in San José, Spence had gravitated to Grace Baptist Community Center. 'They shut down the state mental hospital,' Baranczuk explains. 'And a lot of the ex-patients went to Grace. Skip used to hang out there. You could borrow guitars and they had pool tables. I did sketches of Skip and they put them on the walls.'

It was around that time that Spence met and befriended John McNairy. Like Spence, McNairy was navigating the healthcare system with some difficulty. The two guitarists became fast friends; they'd smoke pot sometimes, drink beer and find solace in their mutual support group. In time, they'd form a band.

'We got about five of us together,' McNairy recalls. 'It was so hard to get a drummer, but we finally got one. He was too slow, but we had to hang onto him because nobody else knew how to play. It's hard to get people who know how to play in a band, who can play, start to finish, a song.' But then they weren't performing under the most conventional circumstances.

'We started practising twice a week, once on Tuesday nights and once on Saturdays for about two hours per session. We always rehearsed at Grace Baptist. That's where they kept all the instruments,' John confirms.

Calling themselves Epicenter, the band played mostly hard rock-oriented covers of classics from the sixties. Over time their repertoire grew. 'I could swear we had about 200 songs we could play live, stuff like [Creedence Clearwater Revival's] 'Born On The Bayou' and 'Proud Mary' and different songs by The Who. We got pretty tight. This was around '88 and '89. We started playing for patients in board care-homes. It was in an auditorium with a dance-floor. Skip was just having the time of his life.'

While Epicenter amassed a vast setlist, Spence wasn't writing any new songs. 'He wasn't able to, unfortunately,' McNairy sighs.

Sometimes, they'd party after hours. 'After our practice sessions or concerts, we'd go to the liquor store and get beer. We'd get together and go down an alley, where the cops couldn't see us, and we'd have a case or each one of us would have a forty-ouncer. We were always drinking beer and they didn't allow that [at Grace]... if they smelled it on your breath, they'd tell you to get out. They really got strict with drinking over there and Skip would go from place to place sometimes.

'Skip was really calm and collected,' his friends adds, 'but there was something about him that was really unique. Sometimes he'd just laugh out of control and we'd look at him and say, "What's so funny, Skip? Tell us." And he'd just get up and smoke a cigarette and walk around in circles, talking to himself. And then he'd start laughing again. We just loved being around him.'

Over the coming years, Spence and McNairy would perform at the community centre, usually on Wednesdays, and at a handful of spots around town. A few live recordings survive, including a set from April 1989 when they performed for the Special Olympics at the Bruce Jenner Field. Their set that day zeroed in on some old classics, such as The Beatles' 'Day Tripper', Hendrix's 'Little

Wing' and 'Purple Haze', The Who's 'The Kids Are Alright' and an almost grunge-rock cover of one of Spence's own gems.

'I've got one tape of us performing for the Special Olympics,' McNairy confirms. 'It's got maybe nine or ten songs on it. One song I really like on it is called 'All My Life'. I played bass and Skip played guitar when we did that one. We'd switch instruments sometimes, not just me but the singer too, Jackie Krenshaw. The other guys in the band were Mark Bates, who was the drummer, and Charlie O'Connor who would sing sometimes and play lead guitar.'

Meanwhile, in the Seattle area, The Melvilles 'did a whole string of gigs on college campuses and little bars,' Stevenson recalls. As they continued to tour up and down the West Coast, the band independently released a new album they'd recorded at Lake Forest Park as a limited run of 500 cassettes. Opening with an explosive cover of Spence's 'All My Life' (described by *LA Weekly* as a 'jubilant screamer'[323]), other standouts included the revved-up rockabilly 'On The Dime,' where Don and Jerry traded vocals just as they'd done nearly twenty-five years before in The Frantics, the reflective pop of Peter's 'Changing' and Bob's hypnotic 'Bitter Wind In Tanganyika.'

By the spring of 1990, they'd changed their name to Legendary Grape and were playing shows up and down Washington State, Oregon and California. A couple of times, Skip came out to watch the group perform in Santa Cruz; on at least one occasion, he joined his former bandmates on stage. 'We didn't have him at full volume,' Don Stevenson remembers, 'but he came out on stage and contributed. He was really sweet.'

Stevenson also recalls a time Spence sat in with the band at a resort, probably one of their shows at the Reindeer Lodge in Nevada.[324] 'We were doing a reunion gig up at a ski resort,' he shares. 'Skip didn't look great to me... [but he] came out there and we did some rehearsals... we did some Beatles songs and we played some Moby Grape songs. 'Get Back' was the best Beatles song we did... We ended up playing a long version of it, for something like twenty minutes.'

At the time, Don's photographer wife Melissa snapped several shots of the band in the dressing room and on stage. Although he was visibly aged, Skip still possessed his unique visual flair, his jeans and white T-shirt offsetting his coiffured hair. With Stratocaster in hand, he reminded everyone of the charm he'd had in abundance so many years before and never fully lost.

But this version of the band wouldn't last much longer. The musicians' latest ride on the Moby Grape rollercoaster was already on the downward rail. Whether as The Melvilles or as Legendary Grape, they just couldn't catch a break. Any kind of cachet or brand recognition had vanished with the prohibited use of their original name. After playing a run of shows in the spring of 1991, they called it a day once more.

'It just fizzled out,' Stevenson sighs, 'because Peter and Bob couldn't stay [up in Washington State] anymore, and it was just obvious that things weren't going to get any larger than they were. But we had a good couple of tours.'

The period had also brought Skip back into the Grape's orbit, though mostly he was still hanging out with his street buddies. 'We'd bump into each other on the street. He trusted me and I trusted him,' Gary Baranczuk notes.

Laughing to himself, he adds, 'You know, a lot of times he'd come into my room – this is really weird – he'd get down on one knee, he'd bow down... and he'd make the sign of the cross. You know, like the Father, the Son and the Holy Ghost. And I'd say, "Skip, you're freaking me out man!"'

That same year, Sony released a remixed version of *Oar* on CD and cassette, adding four outtakes from the 1968 Nashville sessions. *SPIN* closed out its glowing review by saying, 'These are the real goods. Dig 'em.'[325] While true believers were excited to see the album fleshed out by unreleased tracks, its release garnered limited sales.

Meanwhile, Spence was still with Epicenter. 'We had an unlimited amount of fun in that band,' McNairy muses. 'We went to see The Doobie Brothers one time and they gave him a Fender Stratocaster, which he later traded in for cocaine.' After a brief pause, he adds, 'I really looked up to him. But you see, Skip had a drug problem and I had one too. I'd watch it and stay as sane as I could. I tried to maintain.'

His terminal Epicenter anecdote typifies the catastrophe that seems to erupt from nowhere. 'There was a bouncer in our group who was protecting us all, Mike Ortiz,' John says. 'One night we were camping out in the bushes on the side of the freeway [Highway 101] and this girl lost control of her car and went into the bushes... we were in the ditch and she smashed both of us. It killed him, our bouncer. I was in a body cast; I had several broken bones and I had pins and screws in my arm. It was such a tragic thing to lose Mike.'

Not long after that tragedy, McNairy left town after getting badly beaten up. 'When I got my face kicked in, I had to get out of downtown San José. So, I went down to SoCal. That's where I am now.'

As Epicenter hit the end of the road, Spence stayed in touch with Gary Baranczuk, with whom he played guitar from time to time.

'We went to a topless bar in Sunnyvale one time,' Baranczuk remembers of this period. 'It was called Richard's Lounge. There was a guy who looked at Skip and started to cry. He said, "He used to be in Moby Grape." And that guy kept buying Skip beers and everything.

'When we left the bar and we were heading back to San José, I said, "Hey Skip, my mom lives a few blocks away, you wanna go see her?" He goes, "Yeah, sure."

'So, we walked over to my mom's in Santa Clara. We knocked on the door and she opened the door, and as soon as Skip saw the couch in the living room he just walked right in and plonked himself down and passed out.

'My mom started screaming to me, "Get that bum out of here!" I said, "That's not a bum, he's a world-famous rock star."

'"I don't give a damn what he is, get him out of here!" She called my sister and my sister was laughing... she tried to calm my mom down, saying, "Let him sleep it off."

'So, he had a little nap and when he woke up, we caught the bus back to San José.'

CHAPTER TWENTY-FOUR

SURVIVING

On Wednesday 14 October 1992, Gwenn Spence passed away in Spokane, Washington. She was 74. Throughout their formative years, she'd been both guide and chief support to her kids, Skip and Sherry, as they made their long trek from Ontario to Michigan to Ohio, all the way south and west to Arizona and California.

She'd bought her son his first guitar; encouraged his art; supported his triumphs and gave him love throughout his struggles. While Skip had diminishing contact with his family over the years, his sister remembers Gwenn as a steadying force in both their lives.

'My mom was our rock, our stability. She had class, was proper, loved to dance. She liked all kinds of music.' When Sherry speaks of all her beloved mother's facets, she sums up the loss for the entire family.

In those sad circumstances, Rich Young flew with his half-brother to Spokane. 'It was hard to do,' he reflects. 'Skippy had lost his mom and it was difficult to try to travel. You didn't know what you were going to get from one half-hour to the next.

'You see, he had to have a certain amount of medication that would keep him okay. A couple of times he didn't take his medicine and it would impact on who he was, and how you could converse with him and such. He could talk very normal, but he could also talk way out there about things that were not real. Well, they were real to him, in his mind,' Young concedes.

• • •

Around the time Spence lost his last surviving parent, someone was working to resurrect the legacy of Moby Grape. At the Columbia Legacy label, Bob Irwin was meticulously piecing together a compilation album.

'Tracking things down was a hurdle,' he recalls, 'because there wasn't a computer archive system back then and just *finding* things was tricky. David Rubinson worked with me on it and David Fricke from *Rolling Stone* was involved. There was no internet at that point so just finding out information on things like the *Sweet Ride* movie was a task.

'But there was also another side to it. The lack of an archive department at the time – where you'd have everything at your fingertips – made for an exciting, goosebump-inducing journey where you'd step into the studio unprepared for what you were about to hear.'

As the boxes of tape reels stacked higher, Irwin realised a single album wouldn't do the band justice. But the record label was reluctant.

'I had to convince the team at Legacy to release it as a double-disc collection rather than a single...' he notes. 'And that was a hurdle.'

When the label capitulated, the task of selecting and setting aside tracks became a major piece of research – even to the point of selecting snippets of verbal exchanges in the studio. 'There was a mountain of studio chatter,' Irwin says. 'And you can hear Skip's humour and his brilliance in some of it. David [Rubinson] considered Skip to be an absolute genius.'

Whether he's slyly responding to Rubinson's direction on 'Someday' (after the producer says, 'Skippy, take six,' Skip replies offhandedly, 'Thank you, David.') or making jovial banter with Arthur Godfrey during the *Wow* sessions (warmly welcoming him with a 'How are ya, how are ya?'), those captured audio snippets offer a window into his creatively effervescent personality.

Vintage would include the band's entire first album, along with selected tracks, alternative takes and live performances culled from the rest of the Columbia output. Released on 11 May 1993, the double CD package ran at two and a quarter hours and featured nearly fifty cuts in all. With evocative liner notes by *Rolling Stone* editor and Grape loyalist David Fricke, the lovingly prepared collection brought the band back into the spotlight.

Upon release, *Vintage* garnered positive reviews from such disparate sources as *People, Entertainment Weekly, The Village Voice, Rolling Stone*, the *Los Angeles Times* and *Chicago Tribune. Morning News Tribune* gave a glowing endorsement, calling it 'the rock reissue of the year, if not the decade.'[326]

Weeks after *Vintage* came out, Robert Plant harked back to his years in Led Zeppelin, telling the *Daily News*, 'We'd played to a million people, but in the end I was thinking that I really wanted to go home and listen to the music that started me when I was a kid, like Moby Grape.'[327]

It seemed like a cue for the band to get back together. Then, in early June, a benefit was held for one of the legendary 'Big Five' San Francisco poster artists, Stanley Mouse. Decades earlier, Mouse had designed several iconic psychedelic concert posters. With Alton Kelley, he created the beautiful Spanish galleon floating on a *Wave Off Kanagawa* for Moby Grape's New Year's Eve 1966 poster. Working again with Kelley, he co-designed the poster for Moby Grape's performance with The Sparrows (later Steppenwolf) at The Avalon Ballroom in mid-January 1967, where David Rubinson first caught them.

Desperately in need of a liver transplant, Stanley Mouse had recently been overwhelmed by huge medical bills. The fundraiser was scheduled for the first weekend of June at The Grand Nightclub;

appearing on the second night was 'The Jerry Miller Band & x members Moby Grape,' including Peter Lewis and Don Stevenson. Like Spence, Bob Mosley wasn't in any condition to join in. After decades of struggling with mental illness, he was living on the streets of San Diego by the early 1990s.

That same month, Bruce Conforth, curator of the newly founded Rock and Roll Hall of Fame, posted a letter to one of the members of the band. Inquiring about a Moby Grape exhibit at the hall, he told Jerry Miller, 'The structure and versatility that Moby Grape brought to the scene... foreshadowed a whole new virtuosity in rock... Your vocals clearly paved the way for Crosby, Stills & Nash.'[328]

Even in hibernation, Moby Grape drew praise. With the newfound attention brought by *Vintage*, whispers of a reunion followed. Maybe they could finally, belatedly, fulfil their commercial potential?

While Skip Spence wasn't at that June show, he did get together with most of his former bandmates a short while later. It happened in the autumn, when another benefit show in San Francisco set off a chain of events that led to the most meaningful reconnection of all.

On Saturday 9 October 1993, a group of Bay Area personalities gathered for a celebrity roast. Held at a historic club venue on Columbus Avenue, SF, the event raised funds for an addiction-treatment program for teenagers. It was the latest in a series of annual fundraisers. That night, the object of the ribbing was rock manager Herbie Herbert, whose charges had included Journey. But at that time, he was helping Moby Grape in its ongoing legal battles with Matthew Katz over access to royalties and ownership of the band's name.[329]

'Back in the nineties my wife and I ran these benefits for a teenage drug rehab called Thunder Road,' journalist and rock historian Joel Selvin explains. 'We did it for six years, I think from '90 to '96. And we had a lot of different people... the events were held at Bimbo's 365 Club... I can't remember how the Grape thing came to be. Everyone was there, except for Mosley. He was having a hard time in San Diego then.

'Skip was there,' reflects Selvin. 'He was in [state] guardianship at the time. He was reasonably *there* – but he was charming. And Robert Plant came to the show... I remember my wife said at one point, "Can someone get me a glass of water?" And Skippy said, "Oh, you? I'd get you a lake."'

'We went to that show,' Rich Young recalls, 'and when Skip got on that stage, he was electric. He became everybody's best friend. The affinity that crowd had with him – well, you just couldn't believe people could have a relationship with someone you never really knew. He just wowed that crowd. And he wowed me too.'

After a thoughtful pause, he adds, 'There's something else I really remember about that night. To put this in context, I have to say that I was raised a Christian and I never listened to secular music. So, I never knew who Moby Grape were. Heck, I barely even knew who The Beatles were! My mother and dad never let me listen to any of that, so I just didn't know about any of it.'

Rich returns to that night in '93. 'At one point I was heading over to the restroom and this guy walked over to me in the hallway.' The man was tall with long, wavy, blond hair. 'He had been told that I was Skippy's brother and he wanted to talk to me. I said, "Okay. Look, I'll be right back but I have to go to the restroom." And he said, "I have to go too." So, we both went there and took a leak beside each other.

'And we came out and he said, "I want to get together with your brother. We want to do some recording and play some music together." I noticed that there were a lot of people around taking pictures of this guy. And I said, "What's your name?" And he said, "Robert Plant." And I said, "Nice to meet you, Robert Plant." I just didn't know who he was. And he ended up helping Skippy out a lot later on.'

Given that he was mapping out a reunion and an MTV *Unplugged* project with Jimmy Page around this time, Plant's comment remains tantalising. But like so many what-ifs in Skip Spence's life, it never came to pass. According to one report, the highlight of that October '93 evening 'was the reunion of the seminal MOBY GRAPE. The band [with a lineup reuniting Spence, Stevenson, Miller and Lewis] galvanised the crowd, which included Grape groupie ROBERT PLANT, with a concise but powerful three-song set.'[330] One of the songs they played that night was Skip's 'All My Life.'

Plant had been a fan of the Grape ever since he was a teenager, back when he was playing little clubs in the English West Midlands and performing 'Omaha.' Chatting with the band in the lobby, as the cameras flashed he put his arm around Spence; lost in the moment; smiling. In that instant, Robert Plant was at once a rock icon and simply a fan.

Months later, Skip fondly recalled the evening for *LA Weekly*. 'It was magical,' he said, 'like 1966 [all] over again. Robert Plant asked me for my autograph. I think he's one of the most beautiful people I ever met!'[331] A photograph of Led Zeppelin's legendary vocalist with Skip soon popped up in the pages of *Rolling Stone*. It brought a whole new level of attention. It also sparked a long-overdue family reunion.

The four Spence siblings had always wondered about their father. They'd been left with so little that they really knew about him. Then, as Aaron recalls, a high-school friend of his brother Adam 'sent us a clipping from a magazine that had a picture of my dad with Robert Plant arm-in-arm. That sort of opened the barn doors... "What's going on with Dad?"'

At the time, Aaron, Adam and Omar had their own private investigation business in Santa Cruz. They started putting their time and energy into trying to track down their father. After a few dead ends, they eventually found him in San José.

'He was on the street just sitting there smoking a cigarette,' Aaron explains. 'He had a cardboard sign [for panhandling] and he looked like he got hit by a bus. I remember putting him in my car

– I had a convertible at the time – and drove him back over to Santa Cruz… showered him up and got his hair combed.'

Chuckling, he adds, 'He didn't like that part. But we got him some clothes and took him to our offices, where we had a little jam-music studio. And Dad sat down with Adam and me and played for a few hours.'

As the three bonded over music, Skip broached the subject of his long separation from his children. 'He said that he felt remorseful for years about what had happened,' Aaron explains. 'And he kept saying to us, "I love you," and "I'm sorry." And I told him, "There's nothing to be sorry for, we made it. We're okay." It was good to see him light up.'

At that point Spence's two younger children, both then in their mid-20s, weren't ready to see their father. 'I wasn't interested to reunite with him for a while,' Omar explains. 'I still had some anger issues over him not being around. I thought he was a famous guy that was wealthy and was just avoiding being a parent; so that's kind of the heartache I had.'

While Omar and Heather were initially hesitant, after a time they were ready to reconnect with their father. It had been over twenty years since they'd last seen him. Thinking back to the night of their reunion, Omar recalls, 'When we reunited, we went to a dinner party with my uncle Richard [Young]. He was bringing my dad into town at his house.

'So we went to his home, I believe it was in Redwood City… my brothers were there as well. It was the first time he had met Heather and me [since childhood]. It was really cool. It went way better than I thought. We didn't have those hard conversations that night. We just had pizza and got to hang out, and I got to experience how sick or ill [my dad] was.' Chuckling to himself, he adds, 'He loved pizza.'

'I was enamoured by my dad,' Heather reflects. 'I was in awe, touching his hair, thinking to myself, "Here's my fine hair and that's the colour I have." It was my first time seeing someone who was a part of me – or I'm a part of him.

292

'So, we had dinner and a little Christmas party with him. When we were talking, he was *there*. I mean, he'd go out for like a minute but then he'd come back into the conversation. I got to hug him that day. At one point I asked my dad if he remembered me and he said, "Of course, I wrote a song for you. It's called 'Little Hands.'"'

'That really spoke to me. There was something I had from my dad, some possession that I'd never had. I played the song so many times and I hung onto that. It was a sweetness from my dad, kind of like a kiss.' Pat Spence was expecting Heather when Skip cut 'Little Hands' in Nashville, back in December 1968.

For Omar, reconnecting allowed him to come to terms with the past. 'After learning about mental illness and what he had gone through,' he explains, 'I became a Christian and I started to just ask for forgiveness, just for him to have a good life as he grew older. I saw that he wanted us to be a part of his life. That's something I never knew.'

It was at this same time that Moby Grape was gathering a whole new generation of admirers. Amid this, an intrepid LA punk-musician-turned-journalist trekked up to San José to track Skip Spence down.

Johnny Angel found him in a care facility on East Fernando Street. In preparation, Adam Spence warned the writer, 'He has good days and bad days – I hope you get a good one.' Adam elaborated, 'A good day is when he's really with it. He's great, so funny, so amazing. But on a bad day, Dad's voices in his head make it really hard to communicate with him.'[332]

Cataloguing Skip's routines, Angel described his day as starting off with breakfast, followed by a jaunt to the county offices to pick up his one-dollar 'personal needs money.' He would then panhandle money for a 7-Eleven coffee and some King Cobra forty-ounces. Because Spence was prone to giving things away, according to Angel, his guardians would keep a close eye on his possessions.

But those were his daytime routines. He still struggled in the night – just like in '77, when Peter Lewis took him to a monastery, or in '81, when he got kicked out of the Maas Hotel. 'On a bad night, he'll stay up until 3 a.m. or so, pacing, arguing with all of the voices,' one of the workers at the care facility told Angel. 'During the day, when he's talking to them really loudly, we tell him, "Skippy, you tell your voices to shut up." But at night when we're all trying to sleep it can be a real pain, although I'll tell you this; nobody in this house is trying harder to get better than Skip does, and in the last few years, you'd be amazed at how much progress he's made.'[333]

By then, Spence was regularly taking a cocktail of antipsychotic drugs. All that medication left his mouth dry. While the caffeine in his 7-Eleven coffee was a stimulant and the malt liquor was an escape, both beverages were a way to quench his thirst. With little access to money, his King Cobra habit was, to a large degree, kept under control.

But his newfound attention threatened to change that. Speaking about the fraternity house next door, Gloria, who worked at the residence, told Johnny Angel, 'Ever since you showed up, and they saw that picture of Skippy in *Rolling Stone*, they've been all over Skip, giving him beer, making trouble.'[334]

Angel's article popped up in a variety of publications, including *LA Weekly*, the *San José Metro*, *San Francisco Bay Guardian* and *Relix*. Not long after, its subject met a new musical partner. Someone he'd collaborate with for the rest of his life.

'I want to say something here,' Sacramento-born singer/guitarist Brian Vaughan puts in. 'A lot of people have focused on the mental-illness aspect of Skip in the past. He *had* issues, that's basically a fact, but if you got him away from the issues and started relating to him as a creator… he could definitely communicate and interact.'

Recalling how he came to know Spence, Vaughan explains, 'My friend Michael Kelly [who had known him for years] arranged for me to meet Skip where he was living on San Fernando Street. It was early

May of '94. When we met each other, we had this long conversation in the backyard of the place where he was staying. Skip was interested in collaborating musically and a couple of weeks later, Michael brought him over to visit at my place. I cooked up some curry black beans and after we ate dinner, we played each other songs we'd written and as we jammed, we were really picking up on each other.

'You know, Skip was one of those totally dynamic types of individuals. I mean, you had to be ready because when he really started playing it was just going to happen. He did a spacy-sounding jam and I wish I recorded it. You could hear every kind of influence in what he was playing. I regret missing that, but the experience was great. That was the last time I saw him for a little while.

'At that point, he moved in with his girlfriend, Terry Lewis. I hadn't met her by then. After June I lost touch with him. And we lost contact with each other until March 1995.'

At the time, Skip had been seeing Terry for a while. Some years younger, she wanted him to leave the care facility and move in with her. For the Spence family, it was a lot to think about.

'I think that getting him out of the place [where] he was living in San José was probably the best thing…' Omar pauses to compose himself, 'that we could've done.'

'But he had a girlfriend. And I'm like, "What kind of crazy lady would date this guy?" So, I kind of interviewed her first, wondering if she was like a gold-digger where there's no gold, and what her agenda was. And she says, "Oh I love your dad, he's so sweet and we get along so great."

'She was visiting him every weekend and she wanted to take him home for a weekend into Santa Cruz. And the conservator at the time was not for that, he wanted to keep my dad in San José, at the house. So, I had to kind of have words with him and say, you know, "I want him to go on this trip just to see if it works out. If she wants to have him live at her home, that would be so much better than this hellhole!"'

When Skip moved in with Terry, the family quickly came to

know and love her. 'I call her my dad's guardian angel,' Omar now says warmly.

'He met Terry and she just took him in like a stray cat,' Aaron chimes in. 'She had a young boy and she took care of Dad for the rest of his life. He got real fat. She started giving him tea and healthy food and he changed.'

While he still struggled with staying focused, in the here and now, Spence's concentration *was* getting stronger. 'I remember before that,' Aaron shares, 'I could only have about five minutes of his attention before he'd start talking to someone else. And I would say, "Hey, Dad, who are you talking to?"

'"Thor," he'd say. "Who's Thor?" I'd ask. And he'd say, "He's my friend. He's been my friend for years. He can do good things and he can do bad things." Thor was his alter-ego. After Dad lived with Terry he could speak to me for forty-five minutes on the phone – and he was lucid!'

After moving in with Terry, Spence's life changed drastically. He was now with someone who was completely devoted to his well-being, constantly monitoring adherence to his meds and consumption of food. He was no longer a name on a list, a number to check off on someone's chockful 'to do' list. Over time, she gently guided him just as she raised her own son. 'It was really good for him,' Rich Young notes. 'He needed round-the-clock care and Terry loved him that much… she was able to give him that support. Him being with her was a very good thing. She was just a very good person for him and she cared about him. She knew what she was having to deal with and she did it. She fattened him up!'

With his life so much more stable, it was Spence's first chance to be a parent in decades. But as things got settled, Omar felt it was time to speak with his dad about something that had been haunting him for years.

'There's a bad memory I had and grew up with of [Dad] beating my mom up,' he shares. 'And I just remember her hair was flying all over. She had really long, beautiful hair. As a kid, [if] you see your mom getting whopped around...' he tails off, lost for words at the recurring image.

'I asked her about it and she said it only happened one time. But still, to have that in your head as a kid, it challenged me through my whole life. After talking to my mom about that and growing up, many years later I reunited with my dad and it was a question I had to ask him.'

After pausing to compose himself, Omar continues. 'But I waited until it was a good time, I think. We were getting along really good – but I said, "Dad, I just got to ask you, why did you beat up Mom? It made me really mad at you for a lot of years."

'And he goes, "That wasn't me, that was Thor."... at that time I finally understood mental illness. I guess it was the best answer that you could give – blame it on the enemy that was inside of you – and he said, "But I kicked him out."' Smiling, Omar adds, 'So, I said, "Okay, good."' When he exploded at Pat, as Omar so vividly recalls, or oscillated between menace and happiness, as Gordon Stevens describes, Skip Spence's erupting demons were at odds with the otherwise carefree, joyful man that they inhabited.

When Skip moved in with Terry Lewis, in the early summer of '94, Brian Vaughan lost contact with him for a while. '[My partner] Morgan and I looked for Skip in Soquel [near Santa Cruz] in November '94,' he explains. 'We actually passed right by his new area without knowing it at the time. I'd been told he was in that area... My friend Michael Kelly had found the phone number after some research, telling me it must be where Skip had moved to.

'It took a little bit of time before I set up a visit. There were a lot of people following Skip because he was kind of a famous guy in a non-mainstream way. So, everyone was doing a little bit of screening, which is totally understandable. I eventually got back in touch with Skip and arranged another visit at a restaurant,' Brian recalls. 'Skip was very glad to see me again and was having a good time.'

Soon they were back to a duo, jamming and recording. After a few months, an unlikely opportunity knocked. 'In late 1995, Terry started getting phone calls from [John Chellew] at Warner Brothers,' Vaughan recalls. 'He was like an intermediary between Warner-Reprise records and any artist he was trying to acquire for a project called *Songs In The Key Of X*. He thought Skip might be a good fit for the project, which was going to be a kind of musical tribute to *The X-Files*.' Perhaps Chellew was inspired to seek him out by the recent resurgence of interest in Moby Grape, elicited by *Vintage*.

At that time, *The X-Files* was kicking into its third season on Fox TV. Created by producer Chris Carter, the quirky and often innovative show – which grabbed the cult TV mantle from the recently cancelled *Twin Peaks* when it debuted in 1993 – was already a phenomenon by the fall of '95, catapulted into the Nielsen Ratings alongside *Seinfeld*, *ER* and *Friends*.

Still, Terry Lewis urged caution, sounding out whether her new life partner truly wanted to put together a song for submission. As Vaughan confirms, 'Skip was interested, so we thought we'd give it a shot. We thought it might result in Skip having a chance at another musical career. We ended up recording four different versions of "Land Of The Sun." Three were electric and one was acoustic. It was something he had written long ago.

'Now, John Chellew with Warners said he knew Jack Casady [bass guitarist of Jefferson Airplane and Hot Tuna] and had talked to him. It's kind of interesting how synchronicity works. It turned out that around the holidays [Christmas 1995], Jefferson Starship-Airplane was playing at Palookaville, a club in Santa Cruz that's sadly long gone. They had Paul Kantner, Jack Casady, Marty Balin and Diana Mangano – who was an extraordinary replacement for Grace Slick. We went and saw the concert and some of the band members came out and chatted afterwards. Kantner had already heard about the *X-Files* song project, and Terry and I ended up talking with Jack. We wanted to talk to him directly to make sure he was on board.'

With Christmas fast approaching and Warner Brothers calling for Spence's submission, everyone had to work quickly.

'Some kind of demo was needed for Warners,' Vaughan remembers, 'so I made a mix of the best version we had, with Skip and me on electric guitars, on a good audio cassette. Chellew took it to a meeting he had regarding screening... they liked it, so the foot was in the door by then. It was a go.

'They wanted a vocal track, so Morgan and myself spent Christmas day at Terry's place and I cooked dinner... It was an interesting Christmas of celebrating and recording. John Chellew came over and was kind of managing the recording session to a degree, while I was getting Skip's vocals on tape.

'After a few retakes, we managed to get Skip's vocal down on my four-track. So, I went in and got everything formatted onto digital audio cartridges – both the audio and the vocals... Very little time was available to do the work because Chellew was in a hurry, so he was off and running as soon as my transfers were done.'

Things progressed quickly over the next few days. As Brian elaborates, 'Those tapes were taken to a studio in San Francisco called Mobius Music. The final date for recording was [Friday] 29 December... Peter [Lewis] came up and joined us for that recording date. Both Terry and I decided that having Peter involved would be a good thing. It was my first time meeting him and the bonding was instant. It was the beginning of a good period of time.'

After Lewis arrived at Terry and Skip's home, the whole party headed up to San Francisco for lunch. In the early afternoon, they got to the studio.

'There was a tabla player from the Ali Akbar Khan College of Music playing when we got to the studio,' Vaughan recalls. 'It was pretty cool. We got settled in and soon Skip was laying down drum tracks. I watched him playing the drums for a while through the window in the room. He was really into it and having a good time. Peter contributed some parts on guitar, but I don't think anything on vocals.

'In the evening, Jack Casady showed up and Skip got a chance to chat with him for the first time in a long time, maybe since the sixties or the seventies. Skip was happy and in very high spirits. After he gave Jack some acoustic renditions of the song, Jack started to wail out some killer bass lines just in the warmup. Chellew, who was there for the session… then closed the door to the room before Jack started recording, so we left. We felt as though we were being brushed off.'

From that moment, the experience became one of frustration. Everyone in Spence's circle was effectively sidelined. 'After that, Skip wasn't involved in finalising the song and neither was I,' Brian Vaughan explains. 'It ended up getting highly edited and chopped up. When we got the cassette of the final version we thought, "What the heck is this? It kind of sounds cool, but that's not what we did." It could've worked, but it didn't resemble what we did and how we thought it was going to turn out. Later on, we found out that the gatekeepers didn't like the final submission as much as the demo. It was just so different from what they heard originally.'[335]

With his deceptively simple, half-mumbled words bubbling up out of a raga-like, subconscious soundscape, the edit of Skip's final studio recording is still wacky, hypnotic, even unnerving. Although the track was ultimately rejected by Warner Brothers, the spoken-word opus would have been in good company on *Songs In The Key Of X* – a record featuring the idiosyncrasies of Nick Cave's hidden track 'Time Jesum Transeuntum Et Non Riverentum,' William Burroughs reciting R.E.M.'s 'Star Me Kitten' (possibly his last spoken-word performance) and the Elvis Costello/Brian Eno collaboration 'My Dark Life.'

While 'Land Of The Sun' would later see light of day as the B-side of a posthumous single and as a hidden track on the *More Oar* tribute album, it's a shame the song couldn't find a spot on the *X-Files* tribute.

• • •

Meanwhile, a new lineup of Moby Grape was raising the band's banner once again. On 30 June 1996, they played the culminating night of the *Thirty Years Of The Psychedelic Sixties* event at Maritime Hall, San Francisco. While the performance was rough around the edges, it was to be expected. Mosley had recently got off the streets of San Diego and was finding his footing with the new version of the band. Then, on Independence Day, they shared the bill with Big Brother and the Holding Company, Terry Reid and Spirit at the Del Mar Fair. After those two shows, Skip Spence was drawn back into the Grape's orbit.

On Friday 9 August, the then-current version – which included original members Lewis, Mosley and Miller, along with Tiran Porter on bass guitar, guitarist Barry Finnerty and James Preston on drums – stepped onto the stage at Santa Cruz's Palookaville. Skip joined in during the second set. While he sometimes slipped away during an animated, extended rendition of 'All My Life', the band gently coaxed him back.

Shifting into 'Sailing', he again phased in and out of the song, giggling, but was nudged back. At one point, he cheerfully told the audience, 'We haven't had much time together.' At the end of the song, he roused the crowd: 'It's so good to see Bob Mosley here again, how about a round of applause for Bob Mosley?'

As Brian Vaughan recalls: 'Skip was hugging band members on stage when he was there. Tiran got a big hug along with the other members. I was part of the road crew for Skip on this occasion... I supplied Skip with a guitar, a white Stratocaster, and a Pignose combo amp, bigger than the original Pignose.

'In performance, the whole band did some improvised jamming with the tunes. It wasn't strictly formatted, so everybody went off on a tangent, not just Skip. The song 'Sailing,' in particular, had a resemblance to a Grateful Dead-type jam at times, with even Mosley picking up a guitar instead of his bass. But both that and 'All My Life' came back to form after an excursion or two...

'Skip had a great time chatting with fans and signing autographs,'

Brian reminisces. 'He was doing really good. All the remaining fans chatted with band members, but Skipper was the main attraction, having been missing so long.'

Over the next four months, the Grape performed sporadically, putting on a handful of shows at the House of Blues in West Hollywood, on 23 August, Maritime Hall in San Francisco, 21 September, and JB's in Sacramento, 31 October. Spence didn't take part in any of those.

There's a popular expression that goes something like, 'At some point in your childhood, you and your friends went outside to play together for the last time and nobody knew it.' The same thing happens to bands. For Skip Spence and Moby Grape, it fell on the night of Friday 9 August 1996; the venue was Palookaville in Santa Cruz. The Grape's shows were now few and far between and Skip's health was beginning to decline.

For the next couple of years, he'd continue to enjoy Vaughan's visits. They'd chat and listen to music, jamming or recording on occasion. 'During the whole period of time we recorded I was using a four-track,' Brian explains. 'And the sessions were us on… guitar duets. It was a collaboration in the sense that we were working off each other's energy. The material was mostly Skip's. The best way to work with him was right off the cuff. I had to have the equipment ready for whenever he got the inspiration to play.'

During those years, Omar, who lived nearby, visited regularly. 'Peter [Lewis] would come over every once in a while and visit,' Omar remembers. 'He'd drive up from LA and rent a hotel [room]. And they would play music for the days that he was in town. I would go over there and that's how I met Pete, and Brian, the same way… Just some good times watching them play the guitar, watching my dad pick up the guitar again. We always hoped he would get the magic back.'

But medical bills were piling up now. Skip had been diagnosed with hepatitis C, the liver disease that often originates with intravenous drug abuse. Reprise executive and producer Bill Bentley had started to organise a tribute album to help raise funds. When a call for possible interest was put out, the response was overwhelming. In short order, Robert Plant, Beck, Peter Buck of R.E.M., Mudhoney, Robyn Hitchcock, Tom Waits and a slew of others signed up for the project. The plan was to record cover versions of the entire *Oar* track list; it would be called *More Oar*. When the album eventually saw release, Plant would lead off with a gentle version of 'Little Hands.'

With *Oar* itself lingering in out-of-print purgatory, Spence's artistic past was largely untapped territory. By the late nineties, Bob Irwin, who'd put together the Moby Grape *Vintage* compilation, had started up his own record company, Sundazed. Still working on projects for Columbia/Sony Legacy, he'd been checking the possibility of re-releasing *Oar* for years.

'Legacy wasn't interested,' he recalls. 'So I went to Harold Fein, a wonderful guy at Sony Music Special Products. He said, "Bobby, I gotta tell ya something. We tried putting that album out in the early nineties and we couldn't get it out of the stores with dynamite. Why do you want to put it out?"

'"One, I've always loved the album," I said, "and two, you can feel the ground swell." So, I convinced him to let me do it. Initially, the only things I could find were two multitrack SW [speed-winder] reels, on half-inch three-track tape. That was the flavor of the day in Nashville.'

As the covers album moved forward, Terry and Brian worked with Skip as well as Lynne Quinlan to transcribe and doublecheck on lyrics. Spence, meanwhile, continued to collaborate with his friend.

'One song we did is called 'Unearthly Estate',' Brian Vaughan describes. The ambient instrumental is made up of layered guitars accompanied by synthesiser and light percussion. 'We also did an updated version of 'The Space Song'. Skip told me it was... influenced by *Star Trek* – the original series – and a part of it was meant to sound reminiscent of the *Star Trek* theme itself.

'Later, we did a track called 'Carrying the Torch'. We did that one in the summer of 1998. I was experimenting one afternoon and evening. Terry was around when I was recording the drum machine and guitar tracks for that piece... when Skip got up from his nap, she had me play the recording for him and we both said his lead guitar would be great there. Skip liked the track... then picked up his guitar and I recorded his lead playing.'

That's how Skip Spence was throughout his life. Randomly creative; unpredictable but always bursting with ideas. Some of his recordings with Brian Vaughan can now be found on the HAARP Recording site, under the retrospective band name of Eternity's Gate.

At this time, both the expanded re-release of *Oar* and the corresponding cover versions album were coming down the line. But it soon became clear that time was running out.

In the fall of 1998, Skip's condition deteriorated. 'In the last year of his life he had started retaining water,' Omar recalls. 'He had gone into the hospital and it looked like he'd got some sort of a flu... some type of pneumonia, and his body was swelling up.

'But he hated doctors. He'd had a lot of negative experiences in hospitals before. So, when we took him to the doctor he was really frustrated and agitated. They almost wanted to strap him down, but I talked to him and calmed him down. And he got a couple blood tests done... they kept him in the hospital for a day and got the fluid out of his lungs. So, he got home and he got better.'

A few months later, though, things got worse. 'It was the beginning of April 1999,' Vaughan remembers, 'and Skip was starting to get ill. But he didn't want to go to the hospital because, somehow, he knew he'd never make it out.'

On Monday 5 April, Spence was taken back to the hospital. He was put on a ventilator right away.[336]

'It was like the same thing was happening again,' Omar remembers. 'We took him back and he got checked in... right behind his windpipe they found a cancer tumour growing. That's when he didn't recover from the fluid build up.

'They were monitoring all of his vitals and his systems just started failing. His liver was struggling the whole time, then his heart was struggling, as he couldn't breathe on his own. He was unresponsive, so we didn't get to talk to him, and that was kind of the hard shit for me. I just wanted him to wake up and tell me what to do.'

Decades later, Brian Vaughan still feels the sadness and frustration. 'I phoned some administrators at the hospital and I was told that they weren't going to be turning off his life support. And I thought it was only going to happen if his organs started failing. But Morgan called me and said, "It's going down."'

'So, I went to the hospital and when I saw him, he just looked like he was in a deep sleep. A hospital nurse came in at one point with one of those stands on wheels that had a bottle of morphine. And the morphine started to go into his body just as some hospital officials were across the hall, talking to the family about what to do. And I really think they talked the family into turning Skip's life support off.'

On the night of Thursday 15 April, a group of family and friends gathered in Skip's hospital room. 'I was living in Sacramento at the time,' Aaron remembers, 'and I raced to the hospital to be by his side. My mom was there; she hadn't seen him at all over the years. All of us were gathered in the room. Terry was frantic.

'There was a story that Dad had died before and he woke up to get a glass of water after they had a tag on his toe. But this wasn't the case. He'd already gone and he'd been in a coma for a few days. So, we gave the order as a family to have the doctors go ahead and take the breathing tube out and let him pass in his own time,' Aaron confirms.

'There were about ten people in the room. My dad was snoring, and there was a little boombox and someone popped in a CD copy of the tribute album that [was] raced down. We wanted Dad to listen to it before he passed away...

'Robert Plant was the first song and Dad was just quietly sleeping and snoring away... my mom was on the left side holding his left hand and I was on his right side holding his right hand... we all joined hands in a circle around his bed. It was about the sixth song into the CD and he took his last breath... it was quiet for a few minutes. Omar said, "Well, he's gone."' Aaron pauses to compose himself.

'And all of a sudden, he bolts straight up and inhales... he looks straight into my eyes... he looks around the room and he looks at my mom... he mouthed something to her, and [then] he just fell backwards and exhaled. And that was it.

'But Terry goes, "I knew it, come back Skip!" And Peter calmed her down. This was a moment. It got quiet again and then Peter broke the silence, saying, "That's just like Skippy, always likes to have the last laugh." I laughed. It broke the ice.'

Alexander Lee 'Skip' Spence passed away on Friday 16 April, two days shy of his 53rd birthday.

Over the next few days, hundreds of obituaries appeared in newspapers from the Bay Area to Nashville, from New York to London, from to Montréal to Windsor, the city where Spence first came into this world. Some quoted loved ones who spoke of his joyfulness, his energy, his creative spirit. Some relayed old stories of his halcyon days of the 1960s, passing a few myths along the way. In death, as in life, Skip Spence's story was both mythical and true. As he himself sang so many years ago: 'Books of Moses, myth and true / Books of Moses, bring me back to you.'

EPILOGUE

LIFE AFTER LIFE

A modest Catholic parish church stands just steps away from Capitola Beach on Monterey Avenue, Santa Cruz. St. Joseph's is where the funeral ceremony got started at 9.30 a.m. on Friday 30 April 1999. Afterwards, a large procession made its way a couple of miles north to Soquel Cemetery, where Skip Spence's ashes were laid to rest. As the evening drew closer, friends and family left the cemetery and made their way to an event that was getting started about twenty miles away.

If you head north on Highway 9 out of Santa Cruz, you'll quickly pass through Felton and Ben Lomond; after another mile or so, you'll find yourself in Brookdale. On the west side of the road, above Clear Creek and tucked into the Redwood trees, is a landmark lodge. You can't miss it: there's a giant image on the side of James Dean in blue jeans, white T-shirt and red jacket. He's holding a cigarette and looking intensely iconic. He stayed there once, as did fellow icon Marilyn Monroe.

The dining hall is vast, like an extended chalet with wood panels, stained-glass windows and a kind of shaded sunroof incorporated into the angled ceiling. Running the entire length of the room, dividing it in two, is a small portion of Clear Creek itself. With green carpets, so much wood and so many giant windows that let the sunlight stream in, the dining hall evokes the great outdoors.

According to some, it's the only hall in the world built around a natural stream. Some say it's haunted, that over a century ago a little girl fell into the creek and drowned in that very section of the narrow waterway that runs right through the room. Other spirits are said to lurk in the lodge, too – but that's purely a matter of local legend or, indeed, myth.[337]

It was in the Fireside Lounge of Brookdale Lodge that a large group of friends and family gathered to remember Alexander Lee Spence. His partner, Terry Lewis, selected the location, feeling Skip would have appreciated it and suspecting he'd been there in his lifetime.[338] In the early evening, a cavalcade of musicians took to the stage to play some songs and reflect on their friend. His sister Sherry remembers it as 'a celebration of his life.'

Accompanying himself on guitar, Omar Spence opened the show with that gently optimistic song from *Oar*, 'Little Hands'. He later shifted into a bluesy version of one of his dad's favourite hymns, 'Amazing Grace'. Playing bass guitar with his younger brother was Skip's first son, Aaron.

At one point in the evening, Aaron spoke about his dad to the crowd. 'I remember being upset having to give his eulogy and looking at over 100 people I didn't know – and should have known,' he laments. 'Life could have been so much different.'

Later, Jerry Miller let loose on guitar and Don Stevenson sang 'Simply The Best', a song he'd recently performed at his own wedding, where Miller had served as best man. As night fell, all four surviving members of Moby Grape played. It was the first time in nearly a decade.

'Everybody had a song to sing,' Rich Young fondly recalls of the day. 'I wrote a song and played it there. It was just a good time meeting lots of people. Everybody who was there actually had a whole lot more memories of Skip than me. It was a very good thing.'

'It was a great day of music,' Stevenson notes. 'The musicians played all day and there were lots of testimonies. We went up to the rooms, smoked some doobies and had some great conversations. We talked about what a contribution Skip had made to the San Francisco scene – because he really did. He epitomised everything about it, including the innocence right up to the tragic endings.'

Two months after Spence's passing, the *Los Angeles Times* announced a forthcoming extended rerelease of *Oar* and the release of *More Oar* – a cover version of the entire original album.[339] Both projects had been years in the making.

'The [five new] bonus tracks [on the rerelease] were limited to what was on David Rubinson's SW reels, the stuff he had pulled out thinking he could make soup out of,' Bob Irwin acknowledges. The last of those new tracks – 'I Think You And I' – offers a glimpse into Skip's unique take on the pop song, until it abruptly cuts off with him asking, 'We outta tape? Did that just run out?'

'Greil Marcus called my office one day and said, "Bob, I'm the only *Rolling Stone* author who owns the rights to all of his own writing… If you want the review I did of *Oar*, it's yours to use." And that's how we opened the booklet. But just as things were moving forward Skip passed. And I called everybody up and said, "I'm not putting this out right now." We held the release for a few months. And the interesting thing was that when it did come out the ground swelled.'

In June of that same year, Lynn Quinlan, Spence's music publisher, introduced Brian Vaughan to Paul Berenson – the visual artist who'd been close with Spence back in the early 1970s. Striking up a friendship, Berenson gave Vaughan a DAT tape with the only two songs saved from Spence's post-Granite Creek outfit, The Yankees: 'All My Life' and 'The Space Song'. It was an artifact that had been lost for nearly thirty years. Later on, Sundazed released 'All My Life' as the B-side of a vinyl single, with 'Land Of The Sun' as the A-side.

As reviews of *Oar* and the tribute album started to crop up, the *San Francisco Examiner* wrote: 'despite his passing, *More Oar*, along with Sundazed Records' recent rerelease of the original *Oar*, ensures that Spence's unique gift will stay with us.'[340] The *Chicago Tribune* was also positive, noting that the expanded version of *Oar* 'provides a poignant, final snapshot of Spence's songwriting talent shortly before it flickered out.'[341]

From Robert Plant's opening pop-rock rendition of 'Little Hands', *More Oar* offers up several standouts, nudging Spence's material into a variety of musical terrains. While Beck offers a dreamy take on 'Halo Of Gold,' Tom Waits lets rip through a howling rendition of 'Books Of Moses.' Covering the song is a natural for Waits, as you can hear the phraseology that influenced some of his own work – while the DIY toolbox percussion on his *Swordfishtrombones* and *Rain Dogs* albums owes something to *Oar*.

Mark Lanegan and Robyn Hitchcock are sparse and haunting in their respective dark performances of 'Cripple Creek' and 'Broken Heart'. While Outrageous Cherry take 'Keep Everything Under Your Hat' into folk-pop territory, Jay Farrar and the Sir Omaha Quintet deliver a warm country flavour on 'Weighted Down (The Prison Song)'. On their covers of lighter songs 'Margaret Tiger-Rug' and 'Lawrence Of Euphoria', The Durocs and The Ophelias offer up a delightfully carnivalesque atmosphere.

On Independence Day 1999, a long piece appeared in *The New York Times*, depicting Skip Spence's life as a cautionary tale of the sixties whilst acknowledging his talent. Musing on mythmaking, the article also perpetuated a few popular half-truths: 'He hooked up with a woman who was known as a witch, and she gave him bad acid... He was given a choice: prison or a psychiatric hospital. He chose Bellevue, and he was there, doing penance, for six months... Upon his release from Bellevue, he asked his label, Columbia, for a small advance (under $1,000) and a motorcycle so he could drive to Nashville and make a solo album... When he was done, he got on his motorcycle and headed back to California.'[342]

As we know, some of these aspects of his story are partly true but none are completely authentic. The old myths didn't die.

Instead, they coalesced around Spence's image, taking on a new life.

• • •

Throughout much of the 1990s, under the guidance of attorney Glen Miskel, the members of Moby Grape had been tussling with Matthew Katz in court. The most recent series of skirmishes had started on 10 January 1994, when the group filed a relief action in the Superior Court of the City and County of San Francisco to set aside the 1973 agreement which heavily favoured Katz, but was never signed by the band. Following Skip's passing, the two sides entered into negotiations in late 1999. After an agreement was entered into court records the following month, Katz subsequently challenged it on procedural grounds and submitted a revised version on 24 February 2000.

Later that year, with Moby Grape's legacy still in limbo, Sundazed released Spence's 'All My Life' as the B-side of a vinyl single, with 'Land Of The Sun' as the A-side. It offered up intriguing musical windows into two very different periods of his life: the chaotic time in '72, following the Granite Creek reunion, and the period when he'd started settling into a home life with Terry Lewis in the mid-nineties.

A final victory for Skip's surviving bandmates seemed within reach when Katz's challenge to the 1970 California Labor Commission's decision (which favoured the band) was dismissed on 12 June 2002. But that victory was short-lived, as Katz appealed and everything once again spun into legal limbo.

In October 2003, Sony International put out *Crosstalk*, a compilation CD including three songs by Spence ('Omaha', 'Motorcycle Irene' and the instrumental version of 'Rounder'). But as Katz and the musicians continued their legal wrangling, it quickly went out of print.

After a ruling in the Grape's favour in 2005, the ex-manager challenged it but, in the following year, lost his appeal. The epic legal journey had seemingly come to an end. Moby Grape finally owned its own identity after decades of litigation. Not long after this, Columbia released *Listen My Friends*, a Moby Grape collection that included four songs by Spence ('Omaha', 'Indifference', 'Motorcycle Irene' and 'Seeing').

The surviving members reunited in September 2007, with Omar standing in for his father at a free concert in Golden Gate Park. The following summer, Sundazed released the Grape's four Columbia albums, supplemented with a treasure trove of bonus cuts that featured an unreleased version of 'Seeing', cut in January 1968.

In a not-so-simple twist of fate, within weeks those new Sundazed CDs (along with the mono version of the debut album on vinyl) were pulled off the shelves in a final stand-off. Katz had apparently laid claim to parts of the Columbia material and Sony were not interested in a potentially extended legal showdown. Today, almost two decades later, Bob Irwin is wistful. 'I was happy that we could do it, but I was sad that it didn't last long,' he sighs.

With all the original albums pulled, Sundazed quickly pivoted and put together a strong double album of outtakes and live cuts in 2009, titled *The Place And The Time* (2009). The following year, Columbia/Sundazed put out a collection of performances showcasing the band's power as one of the hottest live acts back when they were at their peak. The 72-minute set was simply titled *Moby Grape Live*.

That same year, Sundazed released a 'new' single by Skip Spence. It featured two demos he cut in New York during the *Wow* sessions back in January '68, with 'After Gene Autry' serving as the A-side and 'Motorcycle Irene' as the flip. In some ways these lively, paired-down versions of the songs outdo the more elaborate productions that ended up on *Wow*. Spence's pure joy shines through, particularly on the A-side.

But all that activity wasn't limited to archival releases. In June 2009, mercurial multi-instrumentalist Beck recorded a cover of the entire *Oar* album with members of Wilco and other supporting musicians. *Pitchfork* announced the project in November; the album came out on Beck's website, under the banner of his *Record Club* series, in February 2010, immediately garnering praise in *Rolling Stone* and other publications.[343]

As Sundazed kept the Moby Grape flame lit, the band itself was, against all odds, back together and working on a new album. The project had its origin back in 2007. Throughout that summer, Jerry Miller intermittently performed on a revue that crisscrossed America: *The Summer of Love 40th Anniversary Tour*. While in Michigan, he met a fellow musician at the Pine Knob Music Theatre – Dane Clark, long-time drummer in John Cougar Mellencamp's band and loyal fan of the Grape.

Jerry and Dane's new acquaintance led to a band project with Don, Peter and Omar. With Peter and Omar based in California, Jerry in Tacoma, Washington, and Don up in British Columbia, the band often worked remotely (and individually), with Dane handling production duties, as well as some songwriting, at Thunder Sound Recording Studios in Indiana.

Omar's contributions largely took place at Rocket Studio in Scotts Valley, California. His songs featured lively renditions of four songs his dad wrote or co-wrote decades earlier: 'Rounder,' 'You Can Do Anything,' 'Tongue-Tied' and 'Dark Magic.' With additional new songs by Miller, Stevenson and Lewis (as well as a gravelly Jerry Miller cover of Lewis' 1971 gem, 'Apocalypse'), the musicians entered into talks with record labels. Although a contract was negotiated with Rounder Records an eleventh-hour disagreement within the band led to the project getting shelved indefinitely.

A decade later, with the Covid-19 pandemic in full force, they worked on an updated version of Bob Mosley's classic 'Bitter Wind.' Yet, due to lingering disagreements, the album remains unreleased. It's such a shame, as this strong collection of old and new material was completed years ago. Maybe a delayed release will someday offer a fitting coda to the Moby Grape saga.

• • •

As time moves on, Skip Spence's lived experiences recede into the past and some of them fade away. But all the while, his artistic legacy captivates new listeners. 'My Best Friend', 'Omaha', 'Indifference', 'Seeing', 'You Can Do Anything', 'Little Hands', 'Books Of Moses', 'Weighted Down' – these are among the songs that continue to shine.

In late October 1999, Bruce Springsteen and the E Street Band covered 'Omaha' at a show in Oakland. It was thirty-two years after The Boss first played that song as a teenager at a little club in New Jersey.

Robert Plant as a solo artist has recorded four Grape/Spence songs over the years: '8:05', 'Naked, If I Want To', 'Skip's Song' and 'Little Hands.' Back in his early post-Led Zeppelin days, he'd spoken of how the Grape was a key influence on that band's own game-changing music of the late sixties and early seventies. 'I was affected by what people like Arthur Lee [of Love] and Moby Grape were doing on the West Coast,' Plant explained. 'I diluted the blues approach lyrically and emotionally with that West Coast sound.'[344]

Of course, Skip Spence is much more than the legacy of *Oar*, or any of those other songs he penned and recorded in that creative frenzy between 1965-68. To those who knew him as an artistic collaborator, he was a conduit of energy and creativity; to family members and close friends, he was someone who experienced great joy and great suffering.

Music historian Jeff Tamarkin recaps: 'When San Francisco singer Marty Balin looked out into the audience one night and saw "this beautiful kid, all gold and shining, like a little Buddha," he had no idea that Alexander "Skip" Spence was even a musician; Marty only knew that he wanted this "kid" to play drums for the new band he was fronting. Although Skip insisted that he was a guitarist, he took the gig anyway and helped Jefferson Airplane take off, even writing some of their best early material. Skip Spence couldn't be contained in that position for too long, and it wasn't until he co-formed Moby Grape that we discovered just how magnificent a talent he was. Even today, more than a half-century later, music fans are discovering, through Skip's work with the Grape and his richly textured, completely unique solo work *Oar*, that this enigmatic figure – gone way too soon – was a rarity, a gift, a deep and brilliant artist whose spirit continues to shine.'

When asked about *Oar* a few years back, Pat Simmons of The Doobie Brothers said: 'I know that he wasn't hitting on all cylinders, but at the same time it's almost Dali-esque where he went with that… It's an honest guy going through some difficult times in his life attempting to create art. Some of the greatest art ever has been brought to the public under those conditions. So in a sense, it's classic. It's a classic moment in his life. Knowing him, I've seen him on all levels: very intuitive and very together a good amount of time, and also in semi schizophrenic states. I will always admire him as an artist, musician, and as a friend.'[345]

'*Oar* is just a masterpiece,' Peter Lewis told radio host Nick Black in 2017. Assessing his friend's life and art in an interview, he was praiseful yet circumspect. 'I don't know if that makes it worthwhile. It may not,' Lewis conceded. 'If you look at it a certain way, it didn't. Nothing would be worth that kind of suffering in a way, 'cause I saw him live out the rest of his life in and out of the mental-health system, and not really able to put himself back on the rails. A lot of it wasn't just medical or psychological, it was the spiritual thing that happened to him. He was always a very spiritual person… a lot of his music wasn't visceral, it was a very ethereal thing.'[346]

'Skip had these demons, these incredible contradictions in his life and personality,' David Rubinson told *Classic Rock* in 2015. 'Whatever drug he took, the walls came down and he had unlimited access to what was raging within him. So I don't blame the drugs, but that was the key that unlocked the door. I read a lot of stuff in the press about him being crazy, but he was not. He was desperately in touch with the biggest realities in the universe. Somehow he could see and feel things that were enormous, meaningful, global. And he suffered from that because it was so painful.'[347]

As Joel Selvin notes: 'He was touched in every way. He was a gifted ray of light that diffracted differently than other people. Skip's songs had the germ of life in them. They weren't artificial in any way – they were inspirational. Stuff like 'Omaha' was just so born of his inner light. And that's true of his stuff in the Airplane and… on *Oar*… such a delicate flame and I don't think his art ever came out fully. His songs have a light in them.'

In 2018, a half-century after the album was recorded, Bob Irwin worked with the Modern Harmonic label on a deluxe boxset of the *Oar* sessions. The fifty-seven-track set includes the original album, supplemented with a variety of alternate takes and a handful of previously unknown songs. Three standouts are 'My Friend', 'Mary Jane/Steamboat' and 'I Want A Rock & Roll Band'. The first two are gritty blueprints with Skip accompanying himself on drums. His songwriting skills shine through and seem effortless. The third track is far more complete, hinting at the kind of catchy rock with surreal lyrics that Skip could have pursued if things had gone differently.

When the three-disc set came out, David Fricke provided further insightful liner notes. It was titled *AndOarAgain*.

'There's a specialness and uniqueness that abounds in the truly talented,' Irwin muses. 'I put people like John Sebastian and David Crosby and Skip Spence together. They kind of live together in this group in my mind because every time I hear one of their songs, I have this overwhelming feeling. Sometimes it brings tears to my eyes. I always felt that way about Skip.'

'Skippy had a childlike sense of humour,' Gordon Stevens recalls of his friend. 'At his best, he was a real charismatic person – to the max.

'I think that the *Oar* thing was great therapy for him. And then working on the rock opera gave him a little jolt. There aren't words that can describe Skip's motivation to do something and worship greater principles than rock'n'roll,' he adds.

'And Skip and I clicked on the spiritual front, moving out of the secular and into the ecclesiastic. I was taken with [his] idea. As a most perfect human being and a disturbed one, I think that Skip was on the edge of 'Renaissance, or die'.'

After pausing to search for the right words, Gordon adds, 'The tragedy of Skip Spence is that he didn't get to pursue this avenue.'

'You *had* to love the guy,' onetime Grape drummer Fuzzy John Oxendine says with a smile. 'He had his issues but his heart was in the right place. He was real special. The thing was he was too intelligent and too sensitive for humanity,' theorises the musician.

'It blew his mind. That's what I think happened to him. But he was something to treasure. He was like a savant. There was just too much in him. It was like Van Gogh cutting off his ear. Skippy was given too much attention that he didn't want and it was too much to deal with. He was just a regular guy and he didn't want all that stuff going on.'

Just a regular guy and a savant all at once. Living in more than one universe simultaneously.

• • •

Back around the time that the Moby Grape members recorded with their departed bandmate's son, a young woman in Santa Cruz learned about her past and her previously obscure origin. 'I was adopted,' confirms Wednesday, as we'll call her. 'It was me and two of my siblings. We all have the same mom, but we have different dads. It was just "John Doe" on my birth certificate for my entire life.

'All three of us got adopted by the same family and our mom and dad were great. I didn't really care about knowing who my biological father was, growing up, but after I met my birth mom, I asked her, "So, do you know who my father is?" She said it was Skip Spence.

'When I got home, I googled him and read the Wikipedia page on him. He died in '99 and I probably found all this out around 2010 or 2012,' says Wednesday, who was in her mid-20s at the time. 'But the Wikipedia page said he had four kids and I tried to get in touch with them through Facebook. I sent private messages asking, "Was Skip Spence your dad?"

'Aaron was the first to get back to me and he asked, "Did you know him?" And I said, "No, but I just found out that he might be my biological father." That's how we connected.

'Later on, I went to his grave with a couple of my friends,' she adds. 'I drive by him every single day. One of the first songs I found of his on YouTube was 'Little Hands' and I probably listened to that about 200 times. Then I got to meet Aaron and Omar and Heather, my siblings.

'I guess my birth mom was a groupie,' laughs Wednesday. 'Both her and Skip had mental-health needs and they met in a halfway house in San José. And that's how I came about.

'I heard we have another brother too, John Spence. He has a different mom than me. He's down in LA and I think he's homeless. I talked to him on the phone years ago.

'It was cool that my birth dad was famous,' she concludes, 'but I was raised by two wonderful people. I didn't have a void growing up. I was more excited about finding out that I had other siblings.'

'I only met my dad that one time [since babyhood],' explains Heather of her own circumstances. 'But... [that] was a special Christmas gift. You just walk away and think, "That's a part of me." It was so exciting... there's a feeling of fulfilment. In a short amount of time, you see a glimpse of who you are like it's captured in a bottle. And then it evaporated,' she adds.

During the summer of 2019, Omnibus Press accepted this writer's proposal for a biography of Skip Spence. As the book neared completion, Omar Spence shared his own thoughts on trying to tell the story of his father's life.

'My dad was intimate. He was just genuine in his process,' Omar

muses. 'He would always give things away. And I always wanted...
my dad's story out there.

'...But I didn't want it to be a negative story. I wanted it to be
truthful, honest... [about] this guy who had it all – career, music,
family, kids – and then to have to see that all go away through
illness and "self-medication", to the point where he got on the
street. I wish *he* could tell that story to us.'

After a brief pause, Omar sums up how he sees Skip's life. 'Just
forgiveness, redemption and love. I think that was [in] my dad's
heart,' he testifies.

SKIP SPENCE – GIGOGRAPHY[348]

JEFFERSON AIRPLANE (1965-66)			
DATE	VENUE	CITY	NOTES
Friday September 17, 1965.	The Matrix	San Francisco, CA.	Skip Spence's debut with the Jefferson Airplane.
Saturday September 18.	The Matrix	San Francisco, CA.	
Sunday September 19.	The Matrix	San Francisco, CA.	
Wednesday September 22.	The Coffee Gallery	San Francisco, CA.	
Thursday September 23.	The Matrix	San Francisco, CA.	
Monday September 27.	Circle Star Theatre	San Carlos, CA.	
Friday October 15.	The Matrix	San Francisco, CA.	
Saturday October 16.	Longshoremen's Hall	San Francisco, CA.	
Friday October 22.	The Matrix	San Francisco, CA.	
Saturday October 30.	Harmon Gymnasium, University of California	Berkeley, CA.	
Friday November 5.	The Matrix	San Francisco, CA.	

JEFFERSON AIRPLANE (1965-66)

DATE	VENUE	CITY	NOTES
Saturday November 6.	SF Mime Troupe's Loft Studio, Calliope Warehouse	San Francisco, CA.	*Benefit For SF Mime Troupe – Appeal Party I.*
Friday December 10.	Fillmore Auditorium	San Francisco, CA.	*Benefit For SF Mime Troupe – Appeal Party II.*
Wednesday December 29.	The Matrix	San Francisco, CA.	
Saturday January 1, 1966.	The Matrix	San Francisco, CA.	
Saturday January 8.	California Hall	San Francisco, CA.	
Sunday January 9.	The Matrix	San Francisco, CA.	
Tuesday January 11.	The Matrix	San Francisco, CA.	
Wednesday January 12.	The Matrix	San Francisco, CA.	
Saturday January 15.	Kitsilano Theatre	Vancouver, Canada.	
Sunday January 16.	Kitsilano Theatre	Vancouver, Canada.	
Sunday February 6.	Fillmore Auditorium	San Francisco, CA.	*Sights And Sounds Of The Trips Festival.*
Tuesday February 8.	The Matrix	San Francisco, CA.	
Wednesday February 9.	The Matrix	San Francisco, CA.	
Thursday February 10.	The Matrix	San Francisco, CA.	
Friday February 11.	The Matrix	San Francisco, CA.	
Saturday February 12.	The Matrix	San Francisco, CA.	
Sunday February 13.	The Matrix	San Francisco, CA.	
Saturday February 19.	Fillmore Auditorium	San Francisco, CA.	The Family Dog Presents *A Tribal Stomp.*
Friday March 4.	Fillmore Auditorium	San Francisco, CA.	

JEFFERSON AIRPLANE (1965-66)

DATE	VENUE	CITY	NOTES
Saturday March 5.	Fillmore Auditorium	San Francisco, CA.	
Unknown date in March.	University of Santa Clara	Santa Clara, CA.	
Unknown date in March.	Athletic Field, University of California	Santa Cruz, CA.	
Saturday March 26.	San José Civic Auditorium	San José, CA.	
Friday April 1.	Fillmore Auditorium	San Francisco, CA.	
Saturday April 2.	Fillmore Auditorium	San Francisco, CA.	
Sunday April 3.	Fillmore Auditorium	San Francisco, CA.	
Thursday April 7.	Fillmore Auditorium	San Francisco, CA.	Literary event with Lawrence Ferlinghetti and Andrei Voznesensky.
Friday April 8.	California Hall	San Francisco, CA.	
Saturday April 9.	Veterans Memorial Hall	Santa Rosa, CA.	
Friday April 15.	Fillmore Auditorium	San Francisco, CA.	
Saturday April 16.	Harmon Gymnasium, University of California	Berkeley, CA.	
Sunday April 17.	Fillmore Auditorium	San Francisco, CA.	
Friday April 29.	Fillmore Auditorium	San Francisco, CA.	
Friday May 6.	Fillmore Auditorium	San Francisco, CA.	
Saturday May 7.	Fillmore Auditorium	San Francisco, CA.	

JEFFERSON AIRPLANE (1965-66)

DATE	VENUE	CITY	NOTES
Sunday May 22.	Cabana Hotel	Palo Alto, CA.	*Peninsula Volunteers Step 'N Time Gala.*
Saturday May 28.	Santa Cruz Civic Auditorium	Santa Cruz, CA.	*Peace Rock/ Miller For Congress.*
Monday May 30.	The Matrix	San Francisco, CA.	
Tuesday May 31.	The Matrix	San Francisco, CA.	
Wednesday June 1.	The Matrix	San Francisco, CA.	
Thursday June 2.	The Matrix	San Francisco, CA.	
Friday June 3.	The Matrix	San Francisco, CA.	
Saturday June 4.	The Matrix	San Francisco, CA.	
Sunday June 5.	The Matrix	San Francisco, CA.	
Monday June 6.	Sheraton Palace Hotel	San Francisco, CA.	Republican Alliance (private event). Skip Spence and Spencer Dryden reputedly both played at this show.

MOBY GRAPE (1966-68)

DATE	VENUE	CITY	NOTES
Monday October 10, 1966.	The Ark	Sausalito, CA.	Moby Grape's first advertised performance.
Tuesday October 11.	The Ark	Sausalito, CA.	
Wednesday October 12.	The Ark	Sausalito, CA.	
Thursday October 13.	The Ark	Sausalito, CA.	
Friday October 14.	The Ark	Sausalito, CA	
Saturday October 15.	The Ark	Sausalito, CA.	
Sunday October 16.	The Ark	Sausalito, CA.	
Tuesday October 18.	The Ark	Sausalito, CA.	

MOBY GRAPE (1966-68)			
DATE	VENUE	CITY	NOTES
Wednesday October 19.	The Ark	Sausalito, CA.	
Thursday October 20.	The Ark	Sausalito, CA.	
Friday October 21.	The Ark	Sausalito, CA.	
Saturday October 22.	The Ark	Sausalito, CA.	
Sunday October 23.	The Ark	Sausalito, CA.	
Friday October 28.	California Hall	San Francisco, CA.	Moby Grape's first show away from The Ark.
November 1966.	The Ark	Sausalito, CA.	Moby Grape played an unknown number of shows at The Ark throughout November.
Friday November 4.	California Hall	San Francisco, CA.	
Friday November 11.	Avalon Ballroom	San Francisco, CA.	
Saturday November 12.	Avalon Ballroom	San Francisco, CA.	
Friday November 25.	Fillmore Auditorium	San Francisco, CA.	
Saturday November 26.	Fillmore Auditorium	San Francisco, CA.	
Sunday November 27.	Fillmore Auditorium	San Francisco, CA.	
Friday December 2.	Fillmore Auditorium	San Francisco, CA.	
Saturday December 3.	Fillmore Auditorium	San Francisco, CA.	
Sunday December 4.	Fillmore Auditorium	San Francisco, CA.	
Tuesday December 6.	The Matrix	San Francisco, CA.	
Wednesday December 7.	The Matrix	San Francisco, CA.	
Thursday December 8.	The Matrix	San Francisco, CA.	
Tuesday December 13.	The Matrix	San Francisco, CA.	
Wednesday December 14.	The Matrix	San Francisco, CA.	
Thursday December 15.	The Matrix	San Francisco, CA.	

MOBY GRAPE (1966-68)			
DATE	VENUE	CITY	NOTES
Friday December 23.	Santa Venetia Armory	San Rafael, CA.	*Band Bash.*
Friday December 23.	Avalon Ballroom	San Francisco, CA.	
Saturday December 24.	Avalon Ballroom	San Francisco, CA.	
Monday December 26.	The Ark	Sausalito, CA.	*Grope For Peace.*
Thursday December 29.	Santa Venetia Armory	San Rafael, CA.	
Friday December 30.	Avalon Ballroom	San Francisco, CA.	
Saturday December 31.	Avalon Ballroom	San Francisco, CA.	
Friday January 13, 1967.	Santa Venetia Armory	San Rafael, CA.	
Friday January 13.	Avalon Ballroom	San Francisco, CA.	
Saturday January 14.	Avalon Ballroom	San Francisco, CA.	
Sunday January 29.	Avalon Ballroom	San Francisco, CA.	*Krishna Consciousness Comes West.*
Sunday February 12.	Fillmore Auditorium	San Francisco, CA.	Council for Civic Unity benefit.
Tuesday February 14.	The Ark	Sausalito, CA.	
Friday February 17.	The Ark	Sausalito, CA.	
Saturday February 18.	The Ark	Sausalito, CA.	
Saturday February 18.	Sausalito Auditorium	Sausalito, CA.	
Sunday February 19.	The Ark	Sausalito, CA.	
Friday February 24.	Avalon Ballroom	San Francisco, CA.	
Saturday February 25.	Avalon Ballroom	San Francisco, CA.	
Sunday February 26.	Fillmore Auditorium	San Francisco, CA.	
Friday March 3.	Winterland Arena	San Francisco, CA.	*First Annual Love Circus.*
Sunday March 5.	Avalon Ballroom	San Francisco, CA.	Benefit for Newstage and Straight Theatre.
Friday March 24.	Winterland Arena	San Francisco, CA.	
Saturday March 25.	Winterland Arena	San Francisco, CA.	

326

MOBY GRAPE (1966-68)			
DATE	VENUE	CITY	NOTES
Sunday March 26.	Fillmore Auditorium	San Francisco, CA.	
Friday March 31.	Winterland Arena	San Francisco, CA.	
Saturday April 1.	Winterland Arena	San Francisco, CA.	
Sunday April 2.	Fillmore Auditorium	San Francisco, CA.	
Wednesday April 12.	Fillmore Auditorium	San Francisco, CA.	*Busted Benefit* (for San Francisco Mime Troupe).
Saturday April 15.	Kezar Stadium, Golden Gate Park	San Francisco, CA.	*Peace Fair.*
Saturday April 22.	Freedom Hall	Davis, CA.	
Friday May 19.	Winterland Arena	San Francisco, CA.	*Rock Revolution.*
Saturday May 20.	Winterland Arena	San Francisco, CA.	*Rock Revolution.*
Saturday June 3. Sunday June 4.	Mt. Tamalpais Theatre	San Rafael, CA.	*Fantasy Fair and Magic Mountain Music Festival.* Due to inclement weather, the festival was postponed. Moby Grape did not play at the rescheduled event.
Tuesday June 6.	Avalon Ballroom	San Francisco, CA.	*Moby Grape* album release party.
Friday June 9.	Scene Club East	New York, NY.	
Saturday June 10.	Scene Club East	New York, NY.	
Sunday June 11.	Scene Club East	New York, NY.	
Friday June 16.	The Hullabaloo	Hollywood, CA.	
Saturday June 17.	Monterey Pop Festival	Monterey, CA.	
Friday June 23.	Civic Center Convention Hall	Philadelphia, PA.	

MOBY GRAPE (1966-68)			
DATE	VENUE	CITY	NOTES
Saturday June 24.	Public Auditorium	Cleveland, OH.	Members of Moby Grape got into a conflict with The Buckinghams during the show.
Sunday June 25.	Civic Arena	Pittsburgh, PA.	Moby Grape did not perform at this show after being removed from the tour.
Monday June 26.	Roostertail Club	Detroit, MI.	
Wednesday July 12.	Oakland Auditorium	Oakland, CA.	
Friday July 14.	Reno Centennial Coliseum	Reno, NV.	
Saturday July 15.	Reno Centennial Coliseum	Reno, NV.	
Monday July 17.	Steve Paul Scene	New York, NY.	Unconfirmed.
Saturday July 22.	Civic Auditorium	Santa Monica, CA.	
Saturday July 29.	Catholic Church Hall	Milwaukee, WI.	Unconfirmed.
Sunday July 30.	Gold Creek Park	Woodinville, WA.	*Gold Creek Love In.*
Wednesday August 2.	Eagles Auditorium	Seattle, WA.	
Tuesday August 8.	Fillmore Auditorium	San Francisco, CA.	
Wednesday August 9.	Fillmore Auditorium	San Francisco, CA.	
Thursday August 10.	Avalon Ballroom	San Francisco, CA.	
Friday August 11.	Masonic Temple	Portland, OR.	
Sunday August 13.	Avalon Ballroom	San Francisco, CA.	
Saturday August 19.	Earl Warren Showgrounds	Santa Barbara, CA.	
Monday August 21.	Whisky A Go Go	Los Angeles, CA.	
Tuesday August 22.	Whisky A Go Go	Los Angeles, CA.	

328

MOBY GRAPE (1966-68)			
DATE	VENUE	CITY	NOTES
Wednesday August 23.	Whisky A Go Go	Los Angeles, CA.	
Thursday August 24.	Whisky A Go Go	Los Angeles, CA.	
Friday August 25.	Whisky A Go Go	Los Angeles, CA.	
Saturday September 2.	Kings Beach Bowl	Lake Tahoe, NV.	
Friday September 15.	Continental Ballroom	Santa Clara, CA.	
Saturday September 16.	Continental Ballroom	Santa Clara, CA.	
Friday September 22.	The Action House	Long Beach, NY.	Moby Grape cancelled. The band was separating from Matthew Katz around this time and put touring on hold.
Saturday September 23.	Village Theatre	New York, NY.	Moby Grape cancelled.
Friday October 6.	The Trauma	Philadelphia, PA.	Moby Grape cancelled.
Saturday October 7.	The Ark	Sausalito, CA.	
Saturday October 7.	The Trauma	Philadelphia, PA.	Moby Grape cancelled.
Sunday October 8.	The Trauma	Philadelphia, PA.	Moby Grape cancelled.
Friday October 13.	The Ark	Sausalito, CA.	
Saturday October 14.	The Ark	Sausalito, CA.	
Friday October 20.	Grande Ballroom	Detroit, MI.	Moby Grape cancelled.
Saturday October 21.	Grande Ballroom	Detroit, MI.	Moby Grape cancelled.
Friday November 3.	Concord Coliseum	Concord, CA.	
Saturday November 4.	Concord Coliseum	Concord, CA.	
Saturday November 4.	The Ark	Sausalito, CA.	
Saturday November 11.	Village Theatre	New York, NY.	

MOBY GRAPE (1966-68)			
DATE	VENUE	CITY	NOTES
Friday November 17.	Café Au Go Go	New York, NY.	
Saturday November 18.	Café Au Go Go	New York, NY.	
Sunday November 19.	Café Au Go Go	New York, NY.	
Thursday November 23.	Village Theatre	New York, NY.	
Friday November 24.	Village Theatre	New York, NY.	
Saturday November 25.	Terrace Ballroom	Salt Lake City, UT.	
Friday December 1.	Ambassador Theater	Washington, DC.	
Saturday December 2.	Ambassador Theater	Washington, DC.	
Wednesday December 6.	The Trauma	Philadelphia, PA.	Rescheduled from October.
Thursday December 7.	The Trauma	Philadelphia, PA.	Rescheduled from October.
Friday December 8.	Grande Ballroom	Detroit, MI.	Rescheduled from October.
Saturday December 9.	Grande Ballroom	Detroit, MI.	Rescheduled from October.
Friday December 15-16.	Shrine Auditorium	Los Angeles, CA.	
Monday December 18.	Whisky A Go Go	Los Angeles, CA.	
Tuesday December 19.	Whisky A Go Go	Los Angeles, CA.	
Wednesday December 20.	Whisky A Go Go	Los Angeles, CA.	Moby Grape made room for Janis Joplin to sing on this night, as her parents were visiting from Texas.
Thursday December 21.	Whisky A Go Go	Los Angeles, CA.	
Friday December 22.	Whisky A Go Go	Los Angeles, CA.	
Saturday December 23.	Whisky A Go Go	Los Angeles, CA.	
Friday January 5, 1968.	Psychedelic Supermarket	Boston, MA.	

MOBY GRAPE (1966-68)			
DATE	VENUE	CITY	NOTES
Saturday January 6.	Psychedelic Supermarket	Boston, MA.	
Friday January 12.	The Factory	Madison, WY.	Moby Grape cancelled.
Saturday January 13.	The Factory	Madison, WY.	Moby Grape cancelled.
Sunday January 14.	High School	South Plainfield, NJ.	March of Dimes (Under 21 Club TAP) benefit.
Friday January 19.	The Trauma	Philadelphia, PA.	
Saturday January 20.	The Trauma	Philadelphia, PA.	
Friday January 26.	Action House	Long Island, NY.	Rescheduled from September.
Saturday January 27.	Action House	Long Island, NY.	Rescheduled from September.
Unknown date, February 1968.	The Bitter End	New York, NY.	
Unknown date, February 1968.	Electric Lotus	New York, NY.	
Friday February 9.	Waterville Armory	Waterville, ME.	Colby College Winter Carnival Weekend.
Saturday February 10.	Anderson Theatre	New York, NY.	Venue became the Fillmore East.
Sunday February 11.	Anderson Theatre	New York, NY.	Venue became the Fillmore East.
Friday February 17.	Tempo Dance City	Brooklyn, NY.	
Friday February 23.	Cheetah	Chicago, IL.	
Saturday February 24.	Cheetah	Chicago, IL.	
Friday March 15.	Legion Hall	Merced, CA.	
Friday March 15.	San Francisco Scene	Seattle, WA.	Fake Grape.
Saturday March 16.	San Francisco Scene	Seattle, WA.	Fake Grape.

MOBY GRAPE (1966-68)			
DATE	VENUE	CITY	NOTES
Tuesday March 19.	Private Home (Pacific Heights)	San Francisco, CA.	Fake Grape (private party).
Thursday March 21.	Fillmore Auditorium	San Francisco, CA.	
Friday March 22.	Winterland Arena	San Francisco, CA.	
Saturday March 23.	Winterland Arena	San Francisco, CA.	
Friday March 29.	Cheetah	Los Angeles, CA.	Fake Grape.
Saturday March 30.	Cheetah	Los Angeles, CA.	Fake Grape.
Saturday March 30.	Casey's	Lewiston, ID.	
Wednesday April 3.	Winterland Arena	San Francisco, CA.	KMPC-FM benefit in support of striking DJs.
Saturday April 6.	Selland Arena	Fresno, CA.	
Friday April 12.	Carousel Ballroom	San Francisco, CA.	
Saturday April 13.	Carousel Ballroom	San Francisco, CA.	
Saturday April 13	State Fairground Exhibition Hall	Phoenix, AZ.	Fake Grape.
Friday April 26.	Santa Rosa Fairgrounds	Santa Rosa, CA.	
Thursday May 2.	Fillmore Auditorium	San Francisco, CA.	
Friday May 3.	Merchandise Mart, Old State Fairgrounds	Sacramento, CA.	*Second Annual Simultaneous Avalanche.*
Sunday May 5.	Fillmore Auditorium	San Francisco, CA.	
Tuesday May 7.	The Generation	New York, NY.	
Wednesday May 8.	The Generation	New York, NY.	
Thursday May 9.	The Generation	New York, NY.	
Friday May 10.	The Generation	New York, NY.	
Saturday May 11.	The Generation	New York, NY.	
Sunday May 12.	The Generation	New York, NY.	
Friday May 17.	Kaleidoscope	Los Angeles, CA.	

MOBY GRAPE (1966-68)			
DATE	VENUE	CITY	NOTES
Saturday May 18.	Kaleidoscope	Los Angeles, CA.	
Tuesday May 21.	Masonic Temple	Portland, OR.	Fake Grape.
Wednesday May 22.	Le Café	Cleveland, OH.	
Thursday May 23.	Le Café	Cleveland, OH.	
Friday May 24.	Vulcan Gas Company	Austin, TX.	
Saturday May 25.	Catacombs Club	Houston, TX.	Moby Grape cancelled.
Sunday May 26.	Catacombs Club	Houston, TX.	Moby Grape cancelled.
Friday May 31.	Denver Folklore Center	Denver, CO.	Fake Grape.
Friday May 31.	Fillmore East	New York, NY.	
Saturday June 1.	Denver Folklore Center	Denver, CO.	Fake Grape.
Saturday June 1.	Fillmore East	New York, NY.	Possibly Skip Spence's last show with Moby Grape until 1971. Peter Lewis may have missed this gig.
Thursday June 6.	Café Au Go Go	New York, NY.	Unconfirmed.
Friday June 7.	The Limit	New York, NY.	Unconfirmed.
Friday June 7.	National Guard Armory	St. Louis, MO.	Fake Grape (cancelled by promoter).
Saturday June 8.	The Limit	New York, NY.	Unconfirmed.
Saturday June 8.	National Guard Armory	St. Louis, MO.	Fake Grape (cancelled by promoter).
Sunday June 9.	Forest Park	St. Louis, MO.	Fake Grape (billed as 'The New Moby Grape').
Thursday June 13.	Electric Factory and Flea Market	Philadelphia, PA.	Unconfirmed.
Friday June 14.	Napa Fairgrounds	Napa, CA.	Fake Grape.

MOBY GRAPE (1966-68)			
DATE	VENUE	CITY	NOTES
Saturday June 15.	Redding Veterans Hall	Redding, CA.	Fake Grape.
Thursday June 20.	Sanctuary	South Lake Tahoe, CA.	Unconfirmed. Spence was likely in Bellevue Hospital by this point.
Friday June 21.	Sanctuary	South Lake Tahoe, CA.	Unconfirmed.
Saturday June 22.	Sanctuary	South Lake Tahoe, CA.	Unconfirmed.
Tuesday June 25.	Commodore	Lowell, MA.	Unconfirmed.
Saturday June 29.	Central Park	New York, NY.	This is the first confirmed Moby Grape performance without Skip Spence.

MOBY GRAPE (1971)			
DATE	VENUE	CITY	NOTES
Unknown dates in April-May.	Chateau Liberté	Los Gatos, CA.	
Unknown date(s) in April-May.	Burl Theatre	Boulder Creek, CA.	
Saturday May 22.	Brooks Hall	San Francisco, CA.	*On Cue World Premiere Of Arts & Industry.*
Saturday May 29.	Hollywood Palladium	Hollywood, CA.	
Friday June 18.	Fillmore East	New York, NY.	
Saturday June 19.	Fillmore East	New York, NY.	
Thursday June 24.	Fillmore West	San Francisco, CA.	
Friday June 25.	Fillmore West	San Francisco, CA.	
Saturday June 26.	Fillmore West	San Francisco, CA.	Spence absent.
Sunday June 27	Fillmore West	San Francisco, CA.	Spence absent.

334

MOBY GRAPE (1971)

DATE	VENUE	CITY	NOTES
Tuesday June 29 – Monday July 6.	Kingsman's Armory	New York, NY.	International Youth Exposition. Moby Grape cancelled.
Sunday July 17.	Long Beach Civic Auditorium	Long Beach, CA.	Unconfirmed.
Friday September 3 – Monday September 6.	Reality Farm	Satsop, CA.	*The Satsop Riverfair & Tin Cup Races Festival.* Moby Grape cancelled.

MOBY GRAPE (1977-78)

DATE	VENUE	CITY	NOTES
Monday August 22, 1977.	Shady Grove	San Francisco, CA.	Debut of this Moby Grape reunion lineup.
Tuesday August 23.	Shady Grove	San Francisco, CA.	
Wednesday August 24.	Shady Grove	San Francisco, CA.	
Thursday August 25.	Shady Grove	San Francisco, CA.	
Friday August 26.	Shady Grove	San Francisco, CA.	
Saturday August 27.	Shady Grove	San Francisco, CA.	
Sunday August 28.	Shady Grove	San Francisco, CA.	
Monday August 29.	Shady Grove	San Francisco, CA.	
Friday September 2.	Santa Cruz Civic Auditorium	Santa Cruz, CA.	
Tuesday September 6.	Shady Grove	San Francisco, CA.	
Friday September 16.	Rio Theater	Rodeo, CA.	
Monday September 19.	Miramar Beach Inn	Half Moon Bay, CA.	
Tuesday September 20.	Miramar Beach Inn	Half Moon Bay, CA.	
Monday September 26.	Old Waldorf	San Francisco, CA.	
Tuesday September 27.	Old Waldorf	San Francisco, CA.	
Tuesday October 4.	Palms	San Francisco, CA.	

335

MOBY GRAPE (1977-78)			
DATE	VENUE	CITY	NOTES
Thursday October 6.	Highland Dell Hotel	Monte Rio, CA.	
Thursday October 27.	Robertson Gym, University of California	Santa Barbara, CA.	
Friday October 28.	Highland Dell Hotel	Monte Rio, CA.	Cancelled.
Friday October 28.	San Francisco Civic Auditorium	San Francisco, CA.	*Masquerade Ball* sponsored by COYOTE.
Saturday October 29.	Rio Theatre	Rodeo, CA.	
Monday October 31.	Boulder Creek Theatre	Boulder Creek, CA.	
Wednesday November 2.	Shady Grove	San Francisco, CA.	Recorded for album.
Thursday November 3.	Shady Grove	San Francisco, CA.	Recorded for album.
Friday November 4.	Inn of the Beginning	Cotati, CA.	Recorded for album.
Saturday November 5.	Inn of the Beginning	Cotati, CA.	Recorded for album.
Sunday November 6.	San Francisco Civic Center Plaza	San Francisco, CA.	*Right To Harvest Fest* (free show).
Friday November 11.	Golden Gate Theatre	San Francisco, CA.	
Saturday November 12.	Rio Theatre	Rodeo, CA.	
Monday December 5.	Shady Grove	San Francisco, CA.	
Tuesday December 6.	Shady Grove	San Francisco, CA.	
Friday December 9.	Inn of the Beginning	Cotati, CA.	
Saturday December 10.	Inn of the Beginning	Cotati, CA.	
Sunday December 11.	Keystone Berkeley	Berkeley, CA.	
Friday December 16.	Rio Theatre	Rodeo, CA.	
Saturday December 17.	Rio Theatre	Rodeo, CA.	

MOBY GRAPE (1977-78)			
DATE	VENUE	CITY	NOTES
Sunday December 18.	Keystone Berkeley	Berkeley, CA.	
Saturday December 24.	Keystone Berkeley	Berkeley, CA.	
Thursday December 29.	Keystone Palo Alto	Palo Alto, CA.	
Saturday January 7, 1978.	Keystone Berkeley	Berkeley, CA.	
Thursday January 19.	Shady Grove	San Francisco, CA.	
Friday January 20.	Shady Grove	San Francisco, CA.	
Saturday January 21.	Santa Cruz Veterans Hall	Santa Cruz, CA.	Mosley had re-joined the band by this point. Spence was not at this show.
Thursday January 26.	Keystone Palo Alto	Palo Alto, CA.	KFAT radio broadcast.
Friday January 27.	Rio Theatre	Rodeo, CA.	
Sunday January 29.	Keystone Berkeley	Berkeley, CA.	
Wednesday February 15.	Shady Grove	San Francisco, CA.	
Friday February 17.	Keystone Berkeley	Berkeley, CA.	
Monday February 27.	Shady Grove	San Francisco, CA.	
Tuesday February 28.	Shady Grove	San Francisco, CA.	
Friday March 10.	Inn of the Beginning	Cotati, CA.	
Saturday March 11.	Inn of the Beginning	Cotati, CA.	
Friday March 17.	Shady Grove	San Francisco, CA.	
Thursday March 30.	Rancho Nicasio	Nicasio, CA.	
Friday March 31.	Knights Bridge	San Rafael, CA.	
Saturday April 1.	Highland Dell Hotel	Monte Rio, CA.	
Friday April 7.	Catalyst	Santa Cruz, CA.	
Saturday April 8.	Shady Grove	San Francisco, CA.	
Sunday April 9.	St. James Park	San José, CA.	*Santa Clara Valley Spring Planting Festival.*

337

MOBY GRAPE (1977-78)			
DATE	VENUE	CITY	NOTES
Friday April 14.	Rio Theatre	Rodeo, CA.	
Saturday April 15.	Shady Grove	San Francisco, CA.	*Live Grape* release party.
Sunday April 16.	Shady Grove	San Francisco, CA.	*Live Grape* release party.
Monday April 17.	Shady Grove	San Francisco, CA	*Live Grape* release party.
Tuesday April 18.	Shady Grove	San Francisco, CA.	*Live Grape* release party.
Wednesday April 19.	Shady Grove	San Francisco, CA.	*Live Grape* release party.
Saturday April 22.	Keystone Palo Alto	Palo Alto, CA.	
Thursday April 27.	Keystone Palo Alto	Palo Alto, CA.	
Saturday May 6.	Uncle Charlie's	Corte Madera, CA.	
Wednesday May 17.	Knights Bridge	San Rafael, CA.	
Friday May 26.	Rio Theatre	Rodeo, CA.	
Friday June 2.	Strawberry Lounge	Placerville, CA.	
Sunday June 4.	Old Waldorf	San Francisco, CA.	
Friday June 16.	Shady Grove	San Francisco, CA.	
Saturday June 24.	Shady Grove	San Francisco, CA.	
Saturday July 15.	Highland Dell Hotel	Monte Rio, CA.	
Friday October 20.	Keystone Berkley	Berkley, CA.	
Saturday October 21.	Rio Theatre	Rodeo, CA.	
Saturday October 28.	Shady Grove	San Francisco, CA.	
Friday December 1.	Rio Theatre	Rodeo, CA.	

338

FINAL PERFORMANCES			
DATE	VENUE	CITY	NOTES
1970s-1980s.	Various venues	Santa Cruz, CA.	Guested at a variety of shows around Santa Cruz.
Saturday October 15, 1983.	Keystone Palo Alto	Palo Alto, CA.	Guested on the closing song with The Dinosaurs.
Friday February 26, 1987.	Flint Center	San Rafael, CA.	Joined Moby Grape at close of show.
Saturday February 27, 1987.	Marin Veterans' Memorial Auditorium	San Rafael, CA.	Joined Moby Grape at close of show.
Saturday April 18, 1987.	Moscone Convention Center	San Francisco, CA.	Unconfirmed Moby Grape show.
Sunday May 17, 1987.	Westport Playhouse	St. Louis, MI.	Event cancelled.
April 1989.	Special Olympics, Bruce Jenner Field	San Francisco, CA.	Epicenter performance (with John McNairy).
1989-94.	Grace Baptist Community Center	Santa Cruz, CA.	Often performed with Epicenter on Wednesdays.
1989-91.	Various venues	Mostly Santa Cruz, CA.	Guested on a handful of Melvilles and Legendary Grape shows between 1989-91.
Saturday October 9, 1993.	Bimbo's 365	San Francisco, CA.	*Herbie Herbert Roast* – Thunder Road benefit. Moby Grape played a three-song set.
Friday August 9, 1996.	Palookaville	Santa Cruz, CA.	Skip Spence's final performance with Moby Grape.

SKIP SPENCE – SESSIONOGRAPHY

JEFFERSON AIRPLANE (1965-66)			
DATE	STUDIO	CITY	SONGS RECORDED
Saturday September 18, 1965.	Phil Spector's home	Los Angeles, CA.	Five-song demo for Columbia, including 'The Other Side Of This Life.'
Thursday December 16.	RCA Studio C	Hollywood, CA.	'Runnin' Round This World' (version one) 'The Other Side Of This Life' 'Lay Down Your Weary Tune' 'In The Morning' 'Tobacco Road' (version one) 'My Best Friend' 'Chauffeur Blues' (version one) 'Embryonic Journey' 'Let's Get Together' (version one) 'In The Midnight Hour' 'Let Me In' (version one) 'Run Around' (uncensored version)
Friday December 17.	RCA Studio C	Hollywood, CA.	Unknown – possibly some of the above songs
Saturday December 18.	RCA Studio C	Hollywood, CA.	'High Flyin' Bird' 'It's No Secret'
Wednesday February 16, 1966.	RCA Studio C	Hollywood, CA.	'Runnin' Round This World' (version two)

JEFFERSON AIRPLANE (1965-66)

DATE	STUDIO	CITY	SONGS RECORDED
Saturday February 19.	RCA Studio C	Hollywood, CA.	'And I Like It'
Monday February 21.	RCA Studio A	Hollywood, CA.	'Bringing Me Down'
Friday February 25.	RCA Studio A	Hollywood, CA.	'Chauffeur Blues' (version two) 'Tobacco Road' (version two)
Saturday February 26.	RCA Studio C	Hollywood, CA.	'Let's Get Together' (version two)
Monday February 28.	RCA Studio C	Hollywood, CA.	'Don't Slip Away'
Tuesday March 15.	RCA Studio C	Hollywood, CA.	'Come Up The Years'
Wednesday March 16.	RCA Studio C	Hollywood, CA.	'Let Me In' (version two)
Friday March 18.	RCA Studio C	Hollywood, CA.	'Blues From An Airplane'
Monday March 21.	RCA Studio C	Hollywood, CA.	'Run Around' (censored version)
October 31 – November 22, 1966.	RCA Victor's Music Center	Hollywood, CA.	While Spence participated in the recording sessions for *Surrealistic Pillow* (as Jorma Kaukonen confirms), specific details regarding his contributions are unknown.

MOBY GRAPE (1966-68)

DATE	STUDIO	CITY	SONGS RECORDED
Wednesday January 25, 1967.	Columbia Studios	Los Angeles, CA.	'Looper' (demo) 'Indifference' (demo)
Monday February 6.	Columbia Studios	Los Angeles, CA.	'Stop' (demo)
Saturday March 11.	Columbia Studios	Los Angeles, CA.	'Rounder' (instrumental) 'Come In The Morning'
Sunday March 12.	Columbia Studios	Los Angeles, CA.	'8:05' 'Fall On You'
Saturday April 22.	Columbia Studios	Los Angeles, CA.	'Hey Grandma' 'Sitting By The Window' 'Changes' 'Lazy Me'

342

MOBY GRAPE (1966-68)			
DATE	STUDIO	CITY	SONGS RECORDED
Sunday April 23.	Columbia Studios	Los Angeles, CA.	'Mr. Blues' 'Omaha' 'Naked, If I Want To' 'Ain't No Use' 'Indifference'
Tuesday April 25.	Columbia Studios	Los Angeles, CA.	'Someday'
Monday August 14.	Columbia Studios	Los Angeles, CA.	'Sweet Ride (Never Again)'
Monday August 28.	Columbia Studios	Los Angeles, CA.	'Bitter Wind' (alternate version)
Wednesday August 30.	Columbia Studios	Los Angeles, CA.	'He'
Thursday August 31.	Columbia Studios	Los Angeles, CA.	'The Place And The Time' (alternate version)
Monday November 6.	Columbia Studios	New York, NY.	'You Can Do Anything' (demo) 'Skip's Song' ('Seeing' demo one) 'Stop' (demo) 'What's To Choose' (demo) 'Looper' (demo two) 'Bitter Wind' (demo) 'Loosely Remembered' (demo)
Wednesday November 8.	Columbia Studios	New York, NY.	'Bitter Wind' (album version)
Friday November 10.	Columbia Studios	New York, NY.	'Bitter Wind' (album version)
Tuesday November 14.	Columbia Studios	New York, NY.	'Can't Be So Bad'
Wednesday November 15.	Columbia Studios	New York, NY.	'Can't Be So Bad'
Monday November 20.	Columbia Studios	New York, NY.	'Murder In My Heart For The Judge'
January 1968 (exact dates unknown).	Columbia Studios	New York, NY.	'Motorcycle Irene' (acoustic/ percussion demo by Spence) 'Just Like Gene Autry (A Foxtrot)' (acoustic/percussion demo by Spence)

343

MOBY GRAPE (1966-68)			
DATE	STUDIO	CITY	SONGS RECORDED
Monday January 15.	Columbia Studios	New York, NY.	'Seeing' (demo two)
Tuesday January 16.	Columbia Studios	New York, NY.	'Never'
Monday January 22.	Columbia Studios	New York, NY.	'Three Four' 'Miller's Blues' (album version) 'Miller's Blues' (alternate version)
Wednesday January 24.	Columbia Studios	New York, NY.	'Motorcycle Irene' 'Boysenberry Jam' (Spence on piano) 'Grape Jam #2' (Spence on piano) 'Marmalade' (Spence and Lewis do not appear on the track / Mike Bloomfield guests)
Thursday January 25.	Columbia Studios	New York, NY.	'Funky-Tunk' 'Rose Coloured Eyes'
Monday January 29.	Columbia Studios	New York, NY.	'Grape Jam #9' (Spence and Lewis do not appear on the track)
Wednesday January 31.	Columbia Studios	New York, NY.	'Just Like Gene Autry (A Foxtrot)'
Thursday February 1.	Columbia Studios	New York, NY.	'Bag's Groove' (Spence, Lewis and Stevenson do not appear on the track / Al Kooper guests)
Saturday February 3.	Columbia Studios	New York, NY.	'What's To Choose' (demo two) Rose Coloured Eyes
Monday February 5.	Columbia Studios	New York, NY.	'The Time And The Place' (album version) 'Black Currant Jam' (Spence and Lewis do not appear on the track / Al Kooper guests)
Monday February 12.	Columbia Studios	New York, NY.	'Naked, If I Want To'
Tuesday February 13.	Columbia Studios	New York, NY.	'The Lake'
Monday April 22.	Columbia Studios	Los Angeles, CA.	'It's A Beautiful Day' (acoustic demo by Mosley)

344

MOBY GRAPE (1966-68)			
DATE	STUDIO	CITY	SONGS RECORDED
Wednesday April 24.	Columbia Studios	Los Angeles, CA.	'Seeing'
Tuesday April 30.	Columbia Studios	Los Angeles, CA.	'Cockatoo Blues' (later retitled 'Tongue-Tied')
Wednesday May 15.	Columbia Studios	Location unspecified.	'If You Can't Learn From My Mistakes' (acoustic demo by Lewis)
Tuesday May 28.	Columbia Studios	New York, NY.	'Soul Stew' (instrumental – Spence's participation is unconfirmed)
Monday June 3.	Columbia Studios	New York, NY.	'Soul Stew' (Lewis was likely absent / Spence possibly absent)
Early June 1968.	Columbia Studios	New York, NY.	'Big' (acoustic demo by Miller and Stevenson)[349]

OAR SESSIONS (1968)			
DATE	STUDIO	CITY	SONGS RECORDED
Tuesday December 3, 1968.	Columbia Studios	Nashville, TN.	'Diana' (take three)
			'Diana' (twelve-string version)
			'Diana' (overdub)
			'Diana' (album version)
			'War In Peace' (album version)
			'All Come To Meet Her' (rehearsal)
			'All Come To Meet Her' (version two)

OAR SESSIONS (1968)			
DATE	STUDIO	CITY	SONGS RECORDED
Tuesday December 3, 1968. (*cntd.*)	Columbia Studios	Nashville, TN.	'Dixie Peach Promenade (Yin For Yang)' (alternate version) 'Lawrence Of Euphoria' (alternate version) 'I Got A Lot To Say' (version one) 'Weighted Down (The Prison Song)' (rehearsal) 'The Shape You're In' 'It Ain't Nice' (version two) 'It's A Hard Life' (version two)
Wednesday December 4.	Columbia Studios	Nashville, TN.	'Broken Heart' 'War In Peace' (take two) 'Broken Heart' (extended master)
Thursday December 5.	Columbia Studios	Nashville, TN.	'Little Hands' (album version) 'Cripple Creek' (album version) 'Weighted Down (The Prison Song)' (album version)
Friday December 6.	Columbia Studios	Nashville, TN.	'Books Of Moses' (album version) Lawrence Of Euphoria (album version)
Saturday December 7.	Columbia Studios	Nashville, TN.	'Little Hands' (take two) 'Cripple Creek' (basic) 'Furry Heroine (Halo Of Gold)' (alternate version) 'My Friend' 'War In Peace' (alternate version) 'I Want A Rock & Roll Band' 'Mary Jane/Steamboat' 'Little Hands' (vocal overdub) 'I Got A Lot To Say' (version two)

346

OAR SESSIONS (1968)			
DATE	STUDIO	CITY	SONGS RECORDED
Monday December 9.	Columbia Studios	Nashville, TN.	'It's A Hard Life' (version one) 'I Got Something For You' 'It Ain't Nice' (version one) 'She Don't Care' 'Diana' (alternate version one) 'Diana' (alternate version two)
Thursday December 12.	Columbia Studios	Nashville, TN.	'This Time He Has Come' 'It's The Best Thing For You' 'Keep Everything Under Your Hat' 'Furry Heroine (Halo Of Gold)' 'Givin' Up Things' 'If I'm Good' 'You Know' 'Doodle' 'Fountain' 'I Think You And I' 'Margaret-Tiger Rug' (album version) 'Broken Heart' (album version) 'All Come To Meet Her' (album version) 'Dixie Peach Promenade (Yin For Yang)' (album version) 'Grey/Afro' (album version)
Saturday December 14.	Columbia Studios	Nashville, TN.	'All Come To Meet Her' (alternate version one) 'I Want A Rock & Roll Band' (instrumental) 'Diana' (basic)

347

FINAL SESSIONS (1971-97)			
DATE	**STUDIO/ VENUE**	**CITY**	**SONGS RECORDED**
April-August 1971.	20 Granite Creek Pacific Studios	Santa Cruz, CA. San Mateo, CA.	Moby Grape records *20 Granite Creek* during the spring and summer of 1971. Spence's participation is limited. The only tracks he is known to have played on are 'Chinese Song' and 'Apocalypse.'
Early 1972.	Pacific Studios	San Mateo, CA.	'All My Life (I Love You)' 'The Space Song'
Wednesday November 2, 1977.	Shady Grove	San Francisco, CA.	Performance recorded for *Live Grape*.
Thursday November 3.	Shady Grove	San Francisco, CA.	Performance recorded for *Live Grape*.
Friday November 4.	Inn of the Beginning	Cotati, CA.	Performance recorded for *Live Grape*.
Saturday November 5.	Inn of the Beginning	Cotati, CA.	Performance recorded for *Live Grape*.
December 29, 1995.	Mobius Music	San Francisco, CA.	'Land Of The Sun'

ACKNOWLEDGEMENTS

Omar's wife, Robin, quickly came on board to give ongoing encouragement and has written a warm forward to this book. Within a few months I got to know Sherry, Skip Spence's younger sister, and she has been a pillar of support and soundboard. Over the past

That Thursday night, I picked Omar up at the airport and brought him to my home for dinner. As it got late, we kept talking about the Grape and his dad, Skip, late into the night. At one point, in a sort of disappointed tone, he said, 'I just wish there was a book about my dad's life.' It was at that moment that this project was born.

Omar's wife, Robin, quickly came on board to give ongoing encouragement and has written a warm forward to this book. Within a few months I got to know Sherry, Skip Spence's younger sister, and she has been a pillar of support and soundboard. Over the past few years, I've enjoyed phone chats and many text conversations with Sherry, who lives on the other side of the North American continent. She retains an energetic, youthful zest for life. I appreciate the trust she has placed in me.

Omar and Robin interviewed his mom, Trish Perez (formerly Pat Spence), multiple times as this book came into being. Trish is a gentle lady who reached back into happy and sad memories from her distant past, which she generously shared. In conversation, Aaron Spence was similarly generous; he was also happy to look over the manuscript and provide valuable feedback. Family members Heather Nuez, Rich Young and 'Wednesday' have also given their time and warmly shared their memories.

If this book has a human dimension, it's because of the people who helped bring it to fruition. It's down to what they said and what they shared. Skip possessed energy, charisma and charm; throughout his life, he jumped into everything with both feet. He was intense and he was sensitive, but he could grin from ear to ear and he had an infectious laugh. 'He was loved,' as Don Stevenson once told me, and that love shone through all the conversations, emails and text chats that informed this project. So many people gave their time and their trust, their thoughts and memories, over the past few years. All of their contributions are appreciated.

Throughout 2019-23, I've had the joy of conversing with some key figures in Skip's early life: Pete Grant, Geoff Levin and Robbie Levin sketched out his days as a fledgling performer and then a rising star in the South Bay folk scene. Val Pease filled in the picture of Spence's time in South Lake Tahoe in the summer of '65. Jorma Kaukonen generously shared reflections of those bygone days, speaking perceptively about Skip's contributions to the Jefferson Airplane and the Californian music scene.

I must also thank rock historian Bruno Ceriotti, who shared his Jefferson Airplane timeline as well as transcripts of interviews with Barry Lewis and Bob Harvey. The Andrus family kindly shared their memories of Skip and Billy Dean's friendship, as well as the ephemera relating to their musical partnership. I would like to acknowledge the valuable contribution of Bobby Andrus, Bonnie Miller and Bettie Wilson. Thank you also to the surviving members of Weird Herald, Pat McIntire and Cecil Bollinger.

Shifting into the Moby Grape timeline, it was a treat to conduct more interviews with Bob Mosley, who shared memories of Skip and his time in the Grape as this project got underway. For years now, Jerry Miller and Don Stevenson have remained accessible, patient and tremendously supportive. As with my book on Moby Grape (*What's Big And Purple And Lives In The Ocean?*) and previous articles I wrote on the band, Jerry and Don have always given of their time. Without their willingness to step back into the near and distant past and tap into sometimes difficult memories, this project wouldn't have been possible.

I count myself lucky that Don Stevenson lives so close and is always happy to meet for a coffee or an interview. I'm so glad our paths crossed in January 2017, when he was playing at a club called, coincidentally, Cameron House. Don has a truckload of energy and optimism, and is a positive force in the lives of so many people.

If you look at the back cover of the Grape's *Truly Fine Citizen*, you'll see a photograph of a man with his back to the camera: roadie extraordinaire Tim Dellara. He's always been happy to pick up the phone to provide support or guidance, while the love of his friends Moby Grape shines through in every conversation.

For a time, Gordon Stevens was the sixth member of Moby Grape. I've had many long, delightful conversations with him and I can't thank him enough. Gordon was very close to Skip in the early 1970s. Over the years he's considered his friend's personality – and the path that Skip took – in great depth. I can only hope that this book does justice to his reflections.

Music critics/historians Joel Selvin and Jeff Tamarkin stepped in to add their own thoughts on Skip's character and legacy, enriching this project along the way. Latterday friends of Skip's helped fill in the picture of his life in the post-Granite Creek years, particularly Brian Vaughan, John McNairy and Gary Baranczuk. Like everyone who's contributed to this project, Brian, John and Gary care deeply about their friend. I use the present tense advisedly: the contributors have a great love for Skip, he's very much alive in their thoughts. Hopefully, this book may keep those memories alive in the future.

As a young drummer, Fuzzy John Oxendine quickly grew to love Moby Grape. After playing with Jerry Miller's offshoot band, The Rhythm Dukes, he found himself in the late 1970s version of the Grape. His love for Skip shone through as he told me about those exciting (but complicated) bygone days.

I give a special thank you to Bob Irwin, for taking the time to share his memories of those projects that have been so important in preserving the legacies of both Skip and the Grape. Picking up a copy of *Vintage* so many years ago was game-changing.

I also need to tip my hat to some veteran writers. In a different way, David Fricke's captivating liner notes for the *Vintage* compilation were as much an inspiration as Omar's sentiments. He told the band's story with flair. You may have noted that the opening to this book's prologue is a kind of homage.

Over the years, a stellar group of critics and journalists have written some vital pieces on Moby Grape and Skip Spence: notably Paul Williams, Greil Marcus, Robert Christgau, Bud Scoppa, Ellen Willis, Richard Meltzer, Clark Peterson, Gene Sculatti, Jill Wolfson, Johnny Angel, Jud Cost, Richie Unterberger, Dave DiMartino, Martin Jones, Rob Hughes, Mike Fornatale and Andrew K. Lau.

As this book took form, Mike Stax, at *Ugly Things*, and Douglas Hawes, who has also written extensively on Spence, have been stalwart in their support. I'd also like to thank the editorial staff at *Shindig!* (Jon 'Mojo' Mills and Andy Morten) and *Record Collector* (Paul Lester) who published articles I wrote on the Grape and Skip Spence after *What's Big And Purple And Lives In The Ocean?* came out in 2018.

Working with Tom Seabrook and Nigel Osborne at Jawbone Press on the Moby Grape book a few years ago marks a time in my life that I remember fondly. More recently, David Barraclough, Imogen Clark and Claire Browne at Omnibus Press have shown great faith in this project and have been rock-steady in providing valuable guidance. Paul Woods worked tirelessly with me in getting the final edit of this book done. I'm grateful for his insights and energy.

Lastly, I want to give a heartfelt thank you to my wife and daughters: Sophia, Katie and Stella. You are the most important people in the world to me.

ENDNOTES

1. Annie Oakley, 'Bombs Away!', The Theatre And Its People, *Windsor Star*, Tuesday June 14, 1949.
2. Annie Oakley, 'Flack', 'The Theatre And Its People', *Windsor Star*, Thursday February 24, 1949.
3. Over the years, some writers have suggested the Spences made their way to California because Jock found work as a machinist in the aircraft industry, or at least was looking for that kind of work. Perhaps the family's move to the Bay Area at a time when the industry was booming, coupled with his background as a pilot in the RCAF, gave rise to speculation. But as far as Sherry recalls, Jock continued to work in sales and to pursue music as his preferred career.
4. Johnny Angel, 'The Next Big Thing That Never Was,' *LA Weekly*, March 25-31, 1994.
5. Patricia May Spence (née Howard) has since remarried and today goes by Trish Perez. Because this biography focuses on the period of her life when she was known as Pat Spence, she is referred to as such throughout the subsequent text, apart from the acknowledgements.
6. A talented songwriter and gentle singer in his own right, Andrus would go on to form Weird Herald and later play with Spence in the short-lived, black-leather, no-nonsense, rock'n'roll outfit Pachuco.
7. Steve Siberman, 'Remembering Paul Kantner: 2005 Interview with Steve Siberman,' *JamBase*, January 28, 2021: https://www.jambase.com/article/remembering-paul-kantner-2005-interview-with-steve-silberman.
8. Steve Mann sadly dropped out of the music scene following a 1967 breakdown – but not before recording with Sonny and Cher, Mac Rebennack (Dr. John) and Van Dyke Parks. In 2003, he returned to performing and released a handful of archival and new recordings before his passing in 2009: *Steve Mann: Alive And Pickin'* (BRM 2005); *Steve Mann Live At The Ash Grove* (BRM 2008); *Straight Life* (BRM 2009).
9. At the center of the poster, is the tag, 'For Your Pleasure; Folksongs of Scotland and Ireland,' followed in large bubble letters by, 'Dave and Jo Ann

Spence.' They were nothing to do with Skip. Near namesake David Spence was a 29-year-old schoolteacher who had immigrated to the US from Ireland a few years earlier. After earning his teaching degree at San José State College, he worked at an elementary school but also performed (sometimes solo, other times with his wife) at folk clubs up and down the West Coast, playing guitar and five-string banjo. Tragically, he died in late March 1966 when his gyrocopter exploded in mid-air at the Santa Rosa Naval Auxiliary Air Station.

10. Jill Wolfson, 'Skip Spence: Psychedelia Gone Mad', *The State*, Sunday October 18, 1981.

11. To read about Val Pease, see Mike Roberts, 'San Francisco Is No Place For A Saw Mill Boy,' *Mountain Democrat*, October 27, 2014. A key segment of the series is available at: https://www.mtdemocrat.com/prospecting/san-francisco-is-no-place-for-a-saw-mill-boy/.

12. Jim Sawyers would later join Paul Ziegler in Muskrat Fun, in the early 1970s. The quotes from Sawyers are taken from comment he added to the *San José Music of Yesteryear* Facebook group on Tuesday July 28, 2020, in response to a post by Scott Tarasco on April 20 of that same year.

    While some spell out the band's name as The Otherside, I use the alternative spelling of The Other Side. It was how it was credited on its lone single ('Walking Down The Road') released on the Brent label in 1966.

13. On February 11, the band played a teen Valentine's Day dance at the Fremont Elks Lodge. Skip was not a member at that point. According to Ross Hannan and Corry Arnold's informative webpage on Moby Grape, he joined The Topsiders in mid-1965. Their family tree is available at: http://www.chickenonaunicycle.com/Moby%20Grape.htm.

14. The Topsiders have been described in different ways by several rock scribes. In his sweeping *Encyclopedia Of Popular Music*, Colin Larkin called them a 'local punk attraction'; more recently, in his *Classic Rock* article, 'Dark Star: The Tragic Genius of Skip Spence,' Rob Hughes referred to the band as 'an East Bay surf combo,' echoed on *Allmusic* by Stansted Montfichet. Most likely The Topsiders were a garage band that started out in surf rock. Either way, they played sporadic local gigs in early-to-mid 1965 before renaming themselves The Other Side.

15. Jeff Tamarkin, *Got A Revolution!: The Turbulent Flight Of Jefferson Airplane*, Atria Books 2003. An extensive band biography.

16. Wolfson, 'Skip Spence: Psychedelia Gone Mad.'

17. Tamarkin, *Got a Revolution!: The Turbulent Flight Of Jefferson Airplane*. Skip was only officially the drummer for the band's debut LP, *Jefferson Airplane Takes Off*. Signe was likely also referring to their 1974 album, *Early Flight* – a collection of previously unreleased material, with the first side focusing on Spence's tenure in the band (1965-66).

18. Bruno Ceriotti shared transcripts from an interview he conducted with Airplane bassist Bob Harvey and drummer Barry Lewis. In recent years, Bruno's work as a rock journalist has appeared in *Shindig!* and *Ugly Things*. All quotations from Harvey and Lewis, unless otherwise noted, are drawn from those interviews.

19. Tamarkin, *Got a Revolution! The Turbulent Flight Of Jefferson Airplane.* Signe Toly Anderson passed away in 2016.

20. The original Wilshire Boulevard Brown Derby was already a landmark by the 1960s. Opened in 1926 – by Robert H. Cobb and Herbert K. Somborn, ex-husband of silent-movie star Gloria Swanson – the restaurant was designed to look like a giant derby hat, to attract passing motorists.

    It did more than that. After becoming a haunt of vaudevillians, the entire derby-shaped structure was moved about a block to the northeast corner of Wilshire and Alexandria Avenue in 1937. Twenty-eight years later, the wide-eyed members of the Jefferson Airplane were stared at as they dined at the historic restaurant, on their whirlwind September 1965 visit to Los Angeles. The Brown Derby closed in 1980.

21. Although the Airplane never recorded the song, Bob Harvey's later band San Francisco Blue released it on their 2005 album, *Children Of The Wind*. With loving memories of writing the song, which blends bluegrass with folk rock, Harvey has played 'Hurting For People' consistently over the years.

22. Barbara Bladen, 'Jefferson Airplane Is Flying High,' *San Mateo Times*, Saturday September 25, 1965.

23. Ibid.

24. Jeff Clark, 'Flight Of A Lifetime: Bob Harvey On His Adventures With Jefferson Airplane And Beyond,' *Stomp And Stammer*, December 13, 2014: https://stompandstammer.com/feature-stories/bob-harvey/.

25. Ibid.

26. Harry Johanesen, 'Park Show Cancelled; "Offensive,"' *San Francisco Examiner*, Thursday August 5, 1965.

27. Michael Fallon, 'Banned Show Goes On: Park Mime Star Arrested,' *San Francisco Examiner*, Sunday August 8, 1965.

28. Uncredited, 'Director Of Mime Guilty: No Permit For Park Play,' *San Francisco Examiner*, Monday November 1, 1965.

29. Uncredited, People column, *Vancouver Sun*, Friday January 7, 1966.

30. Tom Northcott reached Number eighty-eight on the *Billboard* Hot 100 in 1968 with a cover of Harry Nilsson's '1941.' After releasing *Upside Downside* on Warner Brothers in 1972, he co-founded Mushroom Records with Shelly Siegel. Although the label featured such mainstream rock acts as Heart and Chilliwack, Mushroom Records went out of business in 1980.

    By that point, Northcott had left the music business entirely, following in his father's footsteps by switching to a career in commercial fishing.

Earning a law degree, he remained in British Columbia to specialise in maritime law. After a brief recording stint in 1990, he was voted into the BC Entertainment Hall of Fame in 2008. Vancouver poster artist Jerry Kruz shares some memories of Northcott – as well as many other artists – in *The Afterthought: West Coast Rock Posters And Recollections From The '60s*, Rocky Mountain Books 2014.

31. Uncredited, 'Van Cliburn To Liberace,' *San Francisco Examiner*, Sunday February 6, 1966.

32. The sessions ran on February 16, 19, 21, 25, 26 and 28, 1966.

33. Ralph J. Gleason, 'Everybody Wants In On The Act,' *San Francisco Examiner*, Sunday July 31, 1966.

34. That Thursday night concert, on April 7, 1965, was as much an international literary event as a rock show. It was a natural extension of the benefit for the San Francisco Mime Troupe as well as the *Trips Festival*, both held a few months earlier.

   Voznesensky was in the middle of a two-week US tour when he read at the Fillmore, and his appearance was sponsored by well-known local book-shop City Lights. Ferlinghetti was the proprietor of City Lights, opening the bookstore in 1953. Three years later, its namesake publishing house grabbed instant fame and notoriety (and for Ferlinghetti, an obscenity charge) when it put out a little collection by Allen Ginsberg titled *Howl And Other Poems*.

35. Carol Deck, 'Jefferson Airplane Taking Off... Fast,' *KRLA Beat*, Friday April 15, 1966.

36. Joel Selvin, *Summer Of Love: The Inside Story Of LSD, Rock & Roll, Free Love And High Times In The Wild*, Dutton 1994; see also Tamarkin, *Got a Revolution!: The Turbulent Flight Of Jefferson Airplane*.

37. Just weeks after her sojourn with Skip, on September 23, 1965, Martha Wax disappeared from her home (*Daily Independent Journal*, October 23, 1965). On November 2, she wrote her parents from New York, telling them she was 'well and happy' and had a job (*Daily Independent Journal*, November 3, 1965). As Tamarkin describes, Wax later spent time living with David Crosby in LA and subsequently joined Kantner in the Bay Area. Kantner wrote the song 'Martha' about her, which appeared on the Airplane's third LP, *After Bathing At Baxter's*.

38. Jeff Tamarkin, 'The Jefferson Airplane Chronicles: Marty Balin,' *Relix*, April 1993.

39. Rob Hughes, 'Dark Star: The Tragic Genius Of Skip Spence,' *Classic Rock*, January 23, 2015: https://www.loudersound.com/features/dark-star-the-tragic-genius-of-skip-spence.

40. Peggy King, 'A Twist Formed The Grape,' *Oakland Tribune*, Saturday November 5, 1967. See also uncredited, 'Peninsula Volunteers '66 Benefit,' *San Francisco Examiner*, Wednesday February 16, 1966: '"Step 'N Time"

is the theme of the Peninsula Volunteers, Inc. [an organisation to support seniors in need] gala 1966 benefit which will be staged at the Cabana in Palo Alto on May 22 with swinging music from bands in the '30s to today's folk-rock groups. Entertainment will begin at 4:30 p.m. with the "Jefferson Airplane," a well known and talented group typifying the '60s, providing poolside dancing for the teens and young at heart.'

41. Uncredited, 'Wall-To-Wall Dancers At Annual Fete,' *San Mateo Times*, Saturday May 28, 1966.

42. Uncredited, 'Fly Jefferson Airplane With Drummer Spencer Dryden,' *Hit Parader*, January 1968.

43. Jud Cost, 'Moby Grape: The Byrds With The Blues: The Peter Lewis Interview, Part Two,' *Ptolemaic Terrascope*, 20, April 1996.

44. Ibid.

45. Ibid.

46. Cam Cobb, 'Bob Mosley: Bittersweet,' *Ugly Things*, 50, Spring 2019.

47. Because Kesey's home in Pleasant Hill, Oregon was swampy in places it has been speculated that the band took its name from that connection. But it cannot be this because when Luminous Marsh Gas was active Kesey still had his home in Le Honda, CA.

    According to some, the fourth member of the band was guitarist, vocalist, activist and ex-Merry Prankster Denise Kaufman, who went on to form one of the first all-female rock bands. Named after a tarot card, Ace of Cups played many of the cornerstone venues of San Francisco, including The Matrix, the Avalon and the Fillmore – picking up a fan in guitar deity Jimi Hendrix along the way. See Terry Hansen, 'Grape Juice – A Conversation With Jerry Miller,' *Goldmine*, April 30, 1993.

    But that's not how Jerry Miller remembers it. As far as he recalls, the fourth member was vocalist/guitarist Richard Fortunato – who sang a wild lead vocal on The Preachers' heavy, proto-punk, 1965 version of Bo Diddley's 'Who Do You Love?'. See https://sundazed.com/c/344-Preachers-The.aspx.

48. Craig Morrison, 'Moby Grape – Interview With Peter Lewis – Part 1': https://www.craigmorrison.com/spip.php?article65.

49. Cost, 'Moby Grape: The Byrds With The Blues, The Peter Lewis Interview, Part Two.'

50. Ron Armstrong, 'Bio': http://www.ronarmstrongmusic.com/bio.html.

51. Morrison, 'Moby Grape – Interview With Peter Lewis – Part 1.'

52. In the Court of Appeal of the State of California – First Appellate District, Division Two, July 7, 2006 (San Francisco County Superior Court Number 614321).

53. Ibid.

54. Built in 1916, *The Charles Van Damme* was used to shepherd cars, cattle and travellers, and sometimes convicts, between Richmond and San Rafael

throughout the years that spanned the Roaring Twenties and the Great Depression. After serving as a standby boat for a few years, the *Van Damme* was purchased by the city of Martinez in 1943 and, for thirteen years, used for runs between Martinez and Benicia. When the city got out of the ferry business in 1956, the *Van Damme* was decommissioned.

Towed to Waldo Point Harbor in Sausalito, the boat was transformed into a restaurant in 1960. For a time, it was run by a local celebrity restaurateur, Juanita Musson. With her gregarious personality and pet turkey, Wattles, she attracted a range of curious customers. But her time aboard the *Van Damme* was fleeting. After complications with bills and back taxes, as well as legal hassles stemming from a biker-gang fight, Musson moved on.

In October 1965, the venue was redubbed The Ark. For a while it was a piano and jazz bar, offering surf and turf, veal scallopini and chicken cacciatore. An advertisement in the January 29, 1966, issue of the *San Francisco Examiner* announced, 'Now Open: On Top of the Ark Disco-Deck A Go Go Featuring the Townsmen Every Friday and Saturday.' Above a little sketch of the ferryboat were the words, 'An Elegant Joint on Sausalito's Waterfront.' Six days later, another ad appeared in San Rafael's *Daily Independent Journal*, promising, 'no cover and no minimum,' and offering private parties, dinners, lunches, cocktails and dancing.

By May, the venue was hosting a Dixieland band. As reported in the *San Francisco Examiner* on May 14: 'Great oldtime clarinetist Darnell Howard, who sits in with Ted Shaffer's Jelly Roll Jazz Band, is a prime asset. So is the view, the easy air, the terrific Albertus graphics of the twenties, a good wine list and medium prices. Lunch seven days, dinner Thursday through Sunday. Music and dancing all times.'

A few months later, the piano bar/jazz club underwent a major transformation.

55. Philip Elwood, '3500 at Winterland Concert: Blues-Rock Spectacular,' *San Francisco Examiner*, September 24, 1966.
56. In the Court of Appeal of the State of California – First Appellate District, Division Two, July 7, 2006 (San Francisco County Superior Court Number 614321).
57. Hughes, 'Dark Star: The Tragic Genius Of Skip Spence.'
58. Jack Rosenbaum, 'A Rocky Road,' *San Francisco Examiner*, Friday October 14, 1966.
59. Cost, 'Moby Grape: The Byrds With The Blues, The Peter Lewis Interview, Part Two.'
60. Craig Morrison, 'Moby Grape – Interview With Peter Lewis – Part 2': https://www.craigmorrison.com/spip.php?article66.
61. Cost, 'Moby Grape: The Byrds With The Blues, The Peter Lewis Interview, Part Two.'

62. Paul Drummond, *Eye Mind: The Saga Of Roky Erickson And The 13th Floor Elevators, The Pioneers Of Psychedelic Sound*, Process 2007.

63. Cost, 'Moby Grape: The Byrds With The Blues, The Peter Lewis Interview, Part Two.'

64. Ibid.

65. Bill Graham and Robert Greenfield, *Bill Graham Presents: My Life Inside Rock And Out*, Doubleday 1992.

66. From late February to early April 1967, Ahmet Ertegun co-produced nine Buffalo Springfield tracks, at Sound Recorders, Gold Star Recording Studios and Sunset Sound. Two of the songs were released on the band's second album, *Buffalo Springfield Again*, and one was placed on the band's third (and final) LP, *Last Time Around*.

67. Robert Greenfield, *The Last Sultan: The Life And Times Of Ahmet Ertegun*, Simon & Schuster 2011.

68. Clive Davis with Anthony DeCurtis, *The Soundtrack Of My Life*, Simon & Schuster 2013.

69. Adam White, 'Ahmet Ertegun: Reflections From A Music Icon,' *Billboard* 1998.

70. Uncredited, 'What Goes On?', News, *Crawdaddy!*, March 8, 1967 (published early February).

71. Richard Goldstein, 'San Francisco: The Flourishing Underground,' *The Village Voice*, March 2, 1967 (published February).

72. Cost, 'Moby Grape: The Byrds With The Blues, The Peter Lewis Interview, Part Two.'

73. Clark Peterson, 'Rubinson Remembers Grape,' *BAM*, November 1977.

74. See Graham and Greenfield, *Bill Graham Presents: My Life Inside Rock And Out*.

75. The night Jerry recalls is likely Thursday March 21, 1968, when the Grape played the Fillmore with Traffic, Spirit and The Lemon Pipers.

76. Hughes, 'Dark Star: The Tragic Genius of Skip Spence.'

77. Angel, 'The Next Big Thing That Never Was.'

78. Ralph J. Gleason, 'The Big Sound Of The Bay Area Bands,' *San Francisco Examiner*, Sunday May 7, 1967.

79. Art Seidenbaum, 'How Green Is Their Peninsula?', *Los Angeles Times*, Tuesday June 1, 1967.

80. Peter Johnson, 'Something New – A Festival For Pop Musicians,' *Los Angeles Times*, June 4, 1967.

81. Bill Fiset, 'The Old Tongue-Clucker,' *Oakland Tribune*, Wednesday June 12, 1967.

82. Philip Elwood, 'Bob Dylan In Town,' *San Francisco Examiner*, Wednesday June 14, 1967.

83. Atlantic executive Jerry Wexler later recalled: 'I remember some time ago in

San Francisco they gave a party for Moby Grape. Janis Joplin happened to fall by and got up on the stand. There was a million people there and I was way back so I couldn't see the stage. I heard this chick singing. She was really comin' on. I asked myself, "Is that Tina Turner?" I worked my way up to the front and there was this blond, blue-eyed white girl. No kiddin'!' Nicholas Von Hoffman, 'Whitewash For Black Music,' *San Francisco Examiner*, December 21, 1969.

84. Stephen Cook, 'Moby Grape Appears In Court; Appearances Held Deceiving,' *Daily Independent Journal* (San Rafael), Friday January 12, 1968.

85. Ibid.

86. Uncredited, 'Moby Grape Trio Posts Bail on Marin Charges,' *Daily Independent Journal* (San Rafael), Thursday June 8, 1967.

87. David Donnelly, 'The Teen Beat,' *Honolulu Star-Bulletin*, Wednesday June 14, 1967.

88. Robert Christgau, 'Secular Music,' *Esquire*, October 1, 1967.

89. Uncredited, 'Rock 'N' Roller Pleads Innocent On Marijuana,' *Daily Independent Journal* (San Rafael), Friday June 16, 1967.

90. Jerry Gaghan, 'Dagmar The Writer Gains $s, Pounds,' *Philadelphia Daily News*, Friday June 19, 1967.

91. Bob Fiallo, 'Teen Topics: The Bee Gees,' *The Tampa Tribune*, Thursday June 15, 1967.

92. Ernie Santosuosso, 'Sgt Pepper's Hot LP,' Sound In The Round, *The Boston Globe*, Monday June 18, 1967.

93. Wayne Harada, 'Grape Bunch,' On the Record, *The Honolulu Advertiser*, Thursday July 6, 1967.

94. Dave Bist, 'The Teen Beat,' *The Gazette* (Montreal), Friday June 23, 1967.

95. Peter Johnson, 'Monkees Upgrade Album Quality,' Popular Records, *Los Angeles Times*, Sunday June 18, 1967.

96. Paul Williams, 'The Golden Road: A Report On San Francisco,' *Crawdaddy!*, June 1967.

97. It would take until April 2010 for Moby Grape's Monterey performances of 'Indifference,' 'Mr. Blues,' 'Sitting By The Window' and 'Omaha' to be released on an album (*Moby Grape Live*, Sundazed). Film footage of the band's performance of 'Hey Grandma' was finally released fifty years after the festival, when it was included as an extra on the 2017 Blu-ray boxset (*The Complete Monterey Pop Festival*, Criterion).

98. Michael Lydon, 'Monterey Pops! An International Pop Festival,' *Newsweek* (unpublished), June 20, 1967: https://teachrock.org/article/monterey-pops-an-international-pop-festival/

99. Richard Goldstein, 'Monterey Pop Festival: The Hip Homunculus,' *The Village Voice*, June 29, 1967.

100. Nick Jones, 'The Who: Second Thoughts On Monterey,' *Melody Maker*, July 1, 1967.

101. Rob Hughes, 'The Story Of Moby Grape: Chaos And Courtrooms, Acid And White Witches,' *Classic Rock*, September 16, 2016: https://www.louder-sound.com/features/the-story-of-moby-grape-chaos-and-courtrooms-acid-and-white-witches.

102. Tom Campbell, 'Moby Grape Emerges; Is Album In Bad Taste?', Off The Cuff, *Dayton Daily News*, Saturday June 24, 1967.

103. Uncredited, 'Buckinghams, Grape Stage Off-Stage Tiff At Concert,' *Billboard*, July 8, 1967.

104. Ibid.

105. Ibid.

106. Loraine Alterman, 'From The Music Capitals Of the World: Detroit,' *Billboard*, July 8, 1967.

107. Henry Gregor Felsen, 'On The Way Up: The Grape Are Really Great,' *Detroit Free Press*, Friday June 30, 1967.

108. Uncredited, 'Col. Gives Moby Grape A Whale Of A Buildup,' *Billboard*, June 17, 1967.

109. Paul Williams, 'The Golden Road: A Report On San Francisco,' *Crawdaddy!*, June 1967.

110. In the Superior Court of California, City and County of San Francisco, Department Number 503 – Case No. 614321 (300175). Statement of Decision, July 20, 2005.

111. Bob Fiallo, 'Teen Topics: Hard-Soft, Danceable-Listenable Music Of Moby Grape,' *The Tampa Tribune*, Thursday July 13, 1967.

112. Selvin, *Summer Of Love: The Inside Story Of LSD, Rock & Roll, Free Love And High Times in the Wild West*.

113. Pete Johnson, 'Santa Monica Concert Features The Yardbirds,' *Los Angeles Times*, Tuesday July 25, 1967.

114. Jan Mark Wolkin and Bill Keenom, *Michael Bloomfield – If You Love These Blues: An Oral History*, Miller Freeman Books 2000.

115. Mitch Mitchell and John Platt, *The Hendrix Experience*, Da Capo Press 1998.

116. Bill Kerby and David Thompson, 'Spanish Galleons Off Jersey Coast Or "We Live Off Excess Volume,"' *Los Angeles Free Press*, August 25, 1967. This interview can also be found in *Hendrix On Hendrix: Interviews And Encounters with Jimi Hendrix*, edited by Steven Roby, Chicago Review Press 2016.

117. Pete Johnson, '"Unknown" Music Best, Hendrix Says,' *The Indianapolis News*, Thursday September 7, 1967.

118. Uncredited, 'A Jimi Hendrix Experience,' *Discoscene*, April 1968 (interview took place February 21, 1968).

119. Nick Jones, 'MOBY GRAPE: 'Hey Grandma' / 'Omaha' (CBS),' *Melody Maker*, August 12, 1967.

120. In his lively memoir, Blood, Sweat & Tears guitarist Steve Katz recalled

taping the July show: *Blood, Sweat, And My Rock'N'Roll Years: Is Steve Katz A Rock Star?*, Lyons Press 2015.

121. Bruce Springsteen, *Born To Run*, Simon & Schuster 2016.

122. Cliff Jones, 'Robert Plant: An Interview,' *Rock CD*, April 1993.

123. Uncredited, 'Back to School,' *The Sacramento Bee*, Sunday September 10, 1967.

124. Uncredited, 'Trial Is Continued In Delinquency Case,' *Daily Independent Journal* (San Rafael), Thursday September 21, 1967.

125. Claude Hall, 'Vox Jox,' *Billboard*, September 30, 1967.

126. In the Court of Appeal of the State of California – First Appellate District, Division Two, July 7, 2006 (San Francisco County Superior Court Number 614321).

127. Uncredited, 'Fugs Due At Trauma,' *Philadelphia Daily News*, Thursday October 5, 1967.

128. King, 'A Twist Formed The Grape.'

129. Ibid.

130. Ibid.

131. Al Kooper, *Backstage Passes & Backstabbing Bastards: Memoirs Of A Rock 'N' Roll Survivor* (updated edition), Backbeat 2008.

132. Chris Campion, *More Of The Cake Please* Remastered (album liner notes), Rev-Ola 2007.

133. Walterene Jackson, 'Ear-Splitting Sound Of SF,' *San Francisco Examiner*, Sunday October 1, 1967.

134. Ibid.

135. Ibid.

136. Phil Dirt, 'San Francisco Sound Ballrooms,' *Pacific Northwest Bands* (pnwbands.com): http://pnwbands.com/sanfranciscosoundballroom.html.

137. Richard Shafer, 'Rock Bands Make Good "Trip,"' *Student Life* (Utah), April 17, 1968.

138. Uncredited, 'Moby Grape Will Present Two Concerts,' *Courier-Post* (Camden, Michigan), Wednesday December 6, 1967.

139. Ibid.

140. Linda Mathews, 'Electronic Groups on Shrine Stage,' *Los Angeles Times*, Tuesday December 19, 1967.

141. Ibid.

142. Uncredited, 'TV,' *San Francisco Examiner*, Tuesday January 2, 1968.

143. Stephen Cook, 'Moby Grape Appears In Court; Appearances Held Deceiving,' *San Rafael Daily Journal*, Friday January 12, 1968.

144. Ibid.

145. Ibid.

146. Jud Cost, 'Moby Grape: Call Him Ishmael, The Peter Lewis Interview, Part Three,' *Ptolemaic Terrascope*, September 21, 1996.

147. Uncredited, 'Moby Grape Innocent In Delinquency Case,' *San Rafael Daily Journal*, Saturday January 13, 1967.
148. Ibid.
149. Frank Pytko, contribution to *The Great Hollywood Hangover*: http://www. hollywoodhangover.com/htm_files/champaign_part_two.htm.
150. Uncredited, 'Col. Rolls Out A Rock Machine Mod Pop Promotional Happening,' *Billboard*, January 13, 1968.
151. Joe Cocker likely picked up a copy of the LP and was impressed by Moby Grape's contribution. He performed his own version of 'Can't Be So Bad' with The Grease Band on BBC Radio, October 13, 1968. (Later released on *On Air*, Virgin 1998.)
152. Uncredited, 'CBS Meet Unveils New Promo Drive,' *Billboard*, February 28, 1970.
153. Uncredited, 'March Of Dimes Show To Headline Moby Grape Group,' *The Central New Jersey Home News*, Saturday January 6, 1967.
154. Peterson, 'Rubinson Remembers Grape.'
155. Katz, *Blood, Sweat, And My Rock 'N' Roll Years: Is Steve Katz a Rock Star?*
156. Peterson, 'Rubinson Remembers Grape.'
157. Uncredited, 'Moby Grape To Sing At Waterville,' *The Bangor Daily News*, Thursday February 8, 1968.
158. Cam Cobb, *What's Big And Purple And Lives In The Ocean? The Moby Grape Story*, Jawbone Press 2018.
159. Robert Shelton, 'Moby Grape Rocks With Procol Harum In Pair Of Concerts,' *New York Times*, Monday February 12, 1968.
160. Ralph J. Gleason, 'Liner Notes,' *Honolulu Star-Bulletin & Advertiser*, Sunday February 18, 1968.
161. To read about Tempo Dance City, see Robert Christgau, 'Lumpenpop In Brooklyn,' *New York Magazine*, July 1, 1968. For a more recent piece on the club, see Susan De Vries, 'This Canarsie Spot Was Once Rocking And Bowling,' *Brownstoner*, January 14, 2019: https://www.brownstoner.com/history/brooklyn-disco-canarsie-tempo-city-8801-foster-avenue-architecture-jersey-lynne-farms-bowling/.
162. Robb Baker, 'The Sound: Music And Radio: For Young Listeners,' *Chicago Tribune*, April 30, 1968.
163. Michael Lester Kennedy, 'Moby Grape, Flamin' Groovies, March 15, 1968,' *Merced Music*, June 5, 2010: https://mercedmusic.wordpress.com/2010/06/05/moby-grape-flamin-groovies-march-15-1968/.
164. Ibid.
165. Apparently fed up with the whole debacle of posing as Moby Grape, vocalist/keyboardist Oliver McKinney quit the band.
166. Dick Dorworth, 'San Francisco Shows Heart, Lays Out Carpet For Skiers,' Beyond The Mountain, *Reno Gazette-Journal*, Friday March 22, 1968.

167. Herb Caen, 'Bay City Beagle,' *The Hanford Sentinel*, Friday April 5, 1968.
168. Mike Jahn, 'The New York Current,' *Bucks County Courier Times*, Thursday March 21, 1968.
169. Uncredited, 'Ferment Marks SF Pop Scene,' *Billboard*, March 23, 1968.
170. Philip Elwood, 'Still Intact Moby Grape Just Breaks Up Audience,' *San Francisco Examiner*, Friday March 22, 1968.
171. Ibid.
172. Uncredited, 'Moby Grape,' *The Spokesman-Review*, Thursday March 28, 1968.
173. Pete Johnson, 'Pop Duet Issues Delayed Record,' *Los Angeles Times*, Monday April 1, 1968.
174. Angel, 'The Next Big Thing That Never Was.'
175. Dave Wagner, 'Simon & Garfunkel Attain Distinction,' *Green Bay Press-Gazette*, Sunday May 19, 1968.
176. Chuck Ober, '"Wow" For Moby Grape,' *Tampa Bay Times*, Monday June 3, 1968.
177. Mary Ellen Botter, 'Records,' *El Paso Times*, June 23, 1968.
178. Dave Donnelly, 'The Teen Beat,' *Honolulu Star-Bulletin*, April 24, 1968.
179. Pete Johnson, 'Bob Dylan Band To Release Album,' *Los Angeles Times*, June 10, 1968.
180. Robert Christgau, 'Secular Music,' *Esquire*, June 1, 1968.
181. Dave Donnelly, 'The Teen Beat,' *Honolulu Star-Bulletin*, Saturday April 13, 1968.
182. Jon Sargent, 'Valley Vibrations,' *Arizona Republic*, Sunday April 21, 1968.
183. Uncredited, 'The Moby Grape Turn Up Sour,' *The Press Democrat*, Sunday April 28, 1968.
184. Diane Morgan, 'The Disc Seen,' *The Press Democrat*, Monday May 6, 1968.
185. Chris Epting, *Led Zeppelin Crashed Here: The Rock And Roll Landmarks Of North America*, Santa Monica Press 2006; Marie-Paule MacDonald, *Jimi Hendrix Soundscapes*, Reaktion Books 2016.
186. Pete Johnson, 'The "Grape" Appears In Rock Club,' *Los Angeles Times*, Monday May 20, 1968.
187. Concert advertisement, *Austin American-Statesman*, Wednesday May 22, 1968.
188. Don Gardner, 'Project Y Hit Of HemisFair,' Moving Scene, *San Antonio Light*, Saturday May 25, 1968.
189. Uncredited, 'The Music Box,' *Napa Valley Register*, Thursday May 30, 1968.
190. For engaging accounts of the Albert Hotel as a musicians' haven, see: Lillian Roxon, 'Albert Hotel,' *Eye*, May 1968; http://thehotelalbert.com/rock_roll/moby_grape.html; Christopher Grey, 'The Albert Hotel Addresses Its Myths,' *New York Times*, Sunday April 17, 2011.
191. Roxon, 'Albert Hotel.'

192. Uncredited, 'NY Underground,' *Cash Box*, June 15, 1968.

193. Cost, 'Moby Grape: Call Him Ishmael, The Peter Lewis Interview, Part Three.' It's unclear if Peter is referring to the January-February *Wow/Grape Jam* sessions, or the staggered third album sessions in May-June 1968. At both of these times, the band experienced personal conflicts whilst recording in Manhattan.

194. Uncredited notice, *St. Louis Post-Dispatch*, Sunday June 2, 1968.

195. Uncredited, 'Kennedy: Rites Here To Reflect His Diversity,' *St. Louis Post-Dispatch*, Friday June 7, 1968; uncredited, 'For Senator Kennedy: Community Memorial Service,' *St. Louis Post-Dispatch*, Saturday June 8, 1968; uncredited, 'Senator Kennedy Memorial Concert Today,' *St. Louis Post-Dispatch*, Sunday June 9, 1968.

196. For a short history of The Limit, see Tom Grobaty, 'Owner's Memories Of When The Limit Rocked Uptown Long Beach,' *Press Telegram* (Long Island), May 18, 2015: https://www.presstelegram.com/2015/05/18/owners-memories-of-when-the-limit-rocked-uptown-long-beach/.

197. To read about The Bittersweet (and their time at the Albert), see George Gell, 'The Bittersweet: Dayton 1966-9': https://www.buckeyebeat.com/bittersweets.html. Credited as The Bittersweets, the all-female band put out a single on Tema Records in early 1967, 'Hurtin' Kind,' backed with a cover of Gershwin's 'Summertime.' While the single is a hypnotic piece of 1960s garage punk, it didn't go anywhere and stands as the only remnant of the band captured on vinyl.

198. Louise Nancy Dula penned these words in a comment on the Moby Grape Facebook page back in February 2021. Her occasional postings contained various photos she'd taken and retained from the time. Sadly, Louise passed away in 2022, and I was unable to get in touch with her. I should take the opportunity here to thank Alex Casadei for his energy and hard work in moderating the Moby Grape FB group.

199. Hughes, 'Dark Star: The Tragic Genius of Skip Spence.'

200. Dula, Moby Grape Facebook page.

201. Andrew Lau, '*Oar* After 40: Brilliant Or Mere Ramblings?', *Crawdaddy!* website, November 24, 2009.

202. Sandy Haas passed away in 2011. Her reflection on events, posted on February 24, 1999, can be found at: https://web.archive.org/web/20040229034545/http://www.mobygrape.net/gb1999.html.

203. Uncredited, 'Where The Boys And Girls Were,' *Daily News*, Sunday June 30, 1968.

204. Richard Robinson, 'News From The POP SCENE...', *Fond Du Lac Commonwealth Reporter*, Wisconsin, Wednesday July 24, 1968.

205. Frank Faso, 'Shouting, Gets Bellevue Test,' *Daily News*, June 6, 1968.

206. Uncredited, 'Bellevue Gets Lay Director,' *Daily News*, Monday June 24, 1968.

207. Uncredited, 'City Jail Scene Of Racial Fight,' *Newsday (Suffolk Edition)*, Tuesday August 13, 1968.

208. Uncredited, 'Painters See Bellevue Lull As Pressure,' *Daily News*, Thursday August 8, 1968; uncredited, 'Seek To Settle Nurse Dispute,' *The Post-Star*, Thursday August 22, 1968.

209. Uncredited, 'Pizza Parlor Boast Ends In Hudson,' *Star-Gazette*, Wednesday September 4, 1968.

210. Edward Kirkman, 'Poynter Is Collared Again,' *Daily News*, Saturday September 14, 1968.

211. Uncredited, 'Daniels Admits He's Lucky Guy,' *Daily News*, Wednesday November 13, 1968.

212. Uncredited, 'His Hangup,' *Democrat & Chronicle*, Monday November 11, 1968.

213. Pete Johnson, 'The Grateful Dead Appear At Shrine,' *Los Angeles Times*, August 26, 1968.

214. Ralph Gleason, 'Liner Notes,' *Honolulu Star-Bulletin*, Sunday September 29, 1968.

215. Uncredited, '$1 Million Asked From Rock Groups,' *San Francisco Examiner*, Tuesday November 5, 1968.

216. David Fricke, 'Spence: The Man Who Loved Too Much,' *Oar* liner notes, Sundazed 1999.

217. Ibid.

218. Lau, '*Oar* After 40: Brilliant Or Mere Ramblings?'

219. Ibid.

220. Ibid.

221. Angel, 'The Next Big Thing That Never Was.'

222. Dave DiMartino, 'Alexander "Skip" Spence: *Oar* (Columbia US),' review, *MOJO*, June 1997.

223. Lau, '*Oar* After 40: Brilliant Or Mere Ramblings?'

224. Bob Irwin, 'Alexander "Skip" Spence: *OAR* Sundazed SC 11075,' press release, 1999.

225. Ibid.

226. Gina Traeger, 'Liberals, Conservatives Bring Rift To Modern Church,' *Spartan Daily* (San José State College), Friday January 5, 1968. To read more about Jonah's Wail, see: http://web.hypersurf.com/~charlieb/index.htm.

227. Uncredited, '*Moby Grape '69* (Columbia),' Record Roundup, *Oakland Tribune*, September 13, 1969.

228. Cost, 'Moby Grape: Call Him Ishmael, The Peter Lewis Interview, Part Three.'

229. In the Court of Appeal of the State of California – First Appellate District, Division Two, July 7, 2006 (San Francisco County Superior Court Number 614321).

230. Hughes, 'Dark Star: The Tragic Genius of Skip Spence.'
231. Ibid. Eight days after meeting with Spence, Lewis flew to Tennessee. With Nashville A-Team session bassist Bob Moore sitting in for Mosley, Lewis, Stevenson and Miller quickly recorded the *Truly Fine Citizen* LP over May 27-29, 1969. The Grape's final Columbia album was recorded in the same studio Spence used nearly six months earlier when he recorded *Oar*. Bob Dylan, one of the reasons the Grape signed with Columbia, had cut *Nashville Skyline* at the same studio in between those two dates, while The Byrds were working there in the spring of 1968 on their country-rock classic *Sweetheart Of The Rodeo*.
232. Cam Cobb, 'Alone Again *Oar*,' *Record Collector*, September 2019.
233. Ibid.
234. King, 'A Twist Formed The Grape.'
235. *The Purple Haze Archive Presents Peter Lewis Of Moby Grape On Podcast*, 88.3 Southern FM: The Sounds Of The Bayside: https://www.southernfm.com.au/show/purple-haze/the-purple-haze-archive-presents-peter-lewis-of-moby-grape-on-podcast/.
236. James Burke, 'Zig Zag People Take Bubble Gum Underground,' *Fond Du Lac Commonwealth Reporter*, Friday July 25, 1969.
237. Jared Johnson, 'Spence's *Oar* Has Spots Of Very Enjoyable Music,' *The Atlanta Constitution*, Saturday July 26, 1969.
238. Jane Larkin, 'Record Roundup,' *Albuquerque Journal*, Monday October 6, 1969.
239. Robb Baker, 'Folk To Rock... All In Buffy's Newest Album,' Sound, *Chicago Tribune*, Sunday August 3, 1969.
240. Ibid.
241. Greil Marcus, *Oar* review, *Rolling Stone*, September 20, 1969.
242. *The Purple Haze Archive Presents Peter Lewis Of Moby Grape On Podcast.*
243. Richie Unterberger discusses the possible origin of this myth in 'The 25 Most Interesting Overlooked 1960s Folk-Rock LPs,' *Record Collector*, April 2005: http://www.richieunterberger.com/rc.html.
244. Robb Baker, 'Folk To Rock... All In Buffy's Newest Album.'
245. Ritchie Yorke, 'ASK-IN: With A LED ZEPPELIN A Week: Robert Plant,' *New Musical Express*, April 11, 1970.
246. Patricia Spence would have begun her labor on August 27, 1969 – which was indeed a full moon.
247. Dean Budnick, 'Parting Shots: Patrick Simmons,' *Relix*, December 10, 2015.
248. Tom Johnson and Pat Simmons with Chris Epting, *Long Train Runnin': Our Story Of The Doobie Brothers*, St. Martin's Press 2022.
249. Ibid.
250. Dave Zimmer, 'Tom Johnston: The Former Doobie Still Listens To The Music,' *BAM*, October 19, 1979.

251. Scott Mervis, 'The Doobie Way: Doobie Brothers Take Their Time, Getting The New Album Just the Way They Want It,' *Pittsburgh Post-Gazette*, Thursday August 18, 2011.

252. Zimmer, 'Tom Johnston: The Former Doobie Still Listens To The Music.'

253. With settlement booming westward in the decades following the Civil War, thousands of opera houses sprouted up across America. Having an opera house in town helped establish a sense of community and culture. As locomotive transportation expanded, a performing circuit formed.

   While the Gaslighter Theatre was originally built as a bank in 1922, it was dressed up with the look of an Old West opera house when it transformed from a movie theater to a performance space in the late 1960s. To dive more deeply into the subject, see Ann Satterthwaite, *Local Glories: Opera Houses On Main Street, Where Art And Community Meet*, Oxford University Press 2016.

254. Dean Budnick, 'Parting Shots: Patrick Simmons,'

255. Ward Meeker, 'Doobie Brothers: A Discussion With Tom Johnston And Patrick Simmons,' *Vintage Guitar*, November 2011.

256. Uncredited, 'Cheap Rock,' *Berkeley Tribune*, February 27-March 6, 1970.

257. Zimmer, 'Tom Johnston: The Former Doobie Still Listens To The Music.'

258. After the tragedy of Billy Dean Andrus' death, The Doobie Brothers recorded their self-titled debut LP at Pacific Recording Studios in San Mateo, with sessions running from November to December 1970. The album cover would show the band posing outside a log cabin: the Chateau Liberté, which served as a restaurant-bar venue for bikers and all comers in the Santa Cruz Mountains. It was also, according to some, the venue for Billy Dean's fatal final binge.

   In the autumn of 1971, Hot Tuna recorded Jorma Kaukonen's 'Ode For Billy Dean,' which appeared on the band's first studio album, *Burgers*. According to a UPI piece, Billy Dean Andrus wrote over 300 songs but, unfortunately, only one was committed to vinyl: 'Saratoga James,' an ode to Andrus' friend Jim Fletcher, who received shock treatment at California State Mental Institution. 'Andrus was the most soulful guitarist in the West,' fellow musician Gordon Stevens muses. On the topic of Pachuco, he adds, 'There's a whole missing chapter of Skip's life that could explore his interest in Latino rock'n'roll.'

259. Skip had likely heard about Gordon Stevens and his family shop through Pat Simmons, who reputedly bought his first guitar there a few years earlier. To read about Stevens Music, see Gary Singh, 'An Ode To Urban Blight And The History Of San José's Abandoned Spaces,' *metroactive*, December 3, 2014: http://www.metroactive.com/features/columns/abandoned-spaces-san-jose-urban-blight.html.

260. Tom Campbell, 'It's Howdy Doody Time Once Again,' On The Scene, *San Francisco Examiner*, Saturday April 10, 1971.

261. Fox would later change their name to Snake Leg. See Ken Rosene, 'Headlines,' *Honolulu Advertiser*, Monday October 11, 1971.

262. Dennis Douvanis, 'Dennis: It's Ringo's Turn,' *The Morning Call*, Saturday February 14, 1970.

263. The Rhythm Dukes, with Jerry Miller in the lineup, performed at Sacramento State College on Saturday March 20 and Saturday April 24. See *Sacramento Bee*, March 4 and April 24, 1971.

264. 20 Granite Creek Road sold for $2.4 million in July 2021. The real-estate ad indicated seven bedrooms, two bathrooms and a total floorspace of 3,309 square feet. The lot itself totaled 3.95 acres: https://www.realtor.com/realestateandhomes-detail/20-Granite-Creek-Rd_Santa-Cruz_CA_95065_M28523-05359.

265. Angel, 'The Next Big Thing That Never Was.'

266. Hughes, 'Dark Star: The Tragic Genius Of Skip Spence.'

267. Bud Scoppa, '*Wow* Revisited: The Return Of Moby Grape,' *Rock*, August 17, 1971.

268. George Knemeyer, 'Moby Grape, Albert King – Palladium, Hollywood,' Talent In Action, *Billboard*, June 19, 1971.

269. For a visceral record of this period in Graham's life and of rock history itself, check out *Last Days Of The Fillmore* (aka *Fillmore*). Directed by Richard T. Heffron and shot on 16mm, the documentary features Santana, The Grateful Dead, Jefferson Airplane, Hot Tuna and Quicksilver Messenger Service. We're also treated to a massive tantrum by Bill Graham near the beginning of the film.

270. Scoppa, '*Wow* Revisited: The Return Of Moby Grape' includes a vivid and glowing account of Moby Grape's rehearsal, along with some of the subsequent chaos.

271. Michael Sion, 'Old-time Rockers Moby Grape Bring The Purple Sounds To Reindeer Lodge,' *Reno Gazette-Journal*, November 9, 1990.

272. Ellen Willis, 'East Versus West,' *The New Yorker*, July 10, 1971. Anthologised in *Out Of The Vinyl Deeps: Ellen Willis On Rock Music*, edited by Nona Willis Aronowitz, University of Minnesota Press 2011.

273. Kathie Staska and George Mangrum, 'Instruments, Singers Help Sets,' Rock Talk, *The Daily Review*, Thursday July 1, 1971.

274. Uncredited, 'Intl Youth Expo Features Continuous Live Music,' *Billboard*, June 26, 1971.

275. Clark Peterson, 'Moby Grape – Still Crazed After All These Years,' *BAM*, November 1977.

276. John Johnson, 'Exit From The Scene,' Rapping, *The Signal*, Friday July 16, 1971.

277. While the *Chicago Tribune* (September 19) and *The Miami News* (September 21) put out positive reviews, *The Philadelphia Inquirer* (September 19) and

Los Angeles Times (October 17) were decidedly negative. Perhaps worse, several major newspapers ignored the album altogether.

278. Richard Meltzer, *20 Granite Creek* review, *Rolling Stone*, October 16, 1971.

279. To read about the recording and the enduring reputation of the album, see Cobb, 'Bob Mosley: Bittersweet.'

280. Bassist Brian Hough declined to participate in this project; drummer Bruce Ginsberg passed away in 2018.

281. Brian Vaughan interviewed Paul Berenson in 2015, shortly before Berenson too died. Vaughan himself was a friend of Spence's in the late 1990s and he befriended Berenson shortly after Skip's passing. *Paul Berenson Interview, All Three Parts Together 7.25.2015* runs to nearly 40 minutes: https://www.youtube.com/watch?v=7dRMEn04M5A.

282. The earliest version of this myth seems to originate in Peterson, 'Moby Grape – Still Crazed After All these Years.'

283. Wolfson, 'Skip Spence: Psychedelia Gone Mad.'

284. For an early story on the 1973 ruling, see uncredited, 'Moby Grape Settles Mgt. Tiff,' *Billboard*, December 1, 1973. Yet the injunctions and legal threats continued for over two decades. In 1994, the still-unresolved issue received attention in Angel, 'The Next Big Thing That Never Was,' and Michael Snyder, 'Grappling Over The Grape,' Lively Arts, *San Francisco Examiner*, May 1, 1994. For a further update of court decisions and appeals, see Bob Egelko, 'Moby Grape Squeezes Out Victory,' *San Francisco Examiner*, November 1, 1997.

The Moby Grape members confirm they didn't see any royalties from their recordings until the case was finalised in 2006, but even then there was no backpay. Don Stevenson says one of the biggest checks he ever got from the Grape days was when a clip of film footage of the band at the Monterey Pop festival was used in a documentary on Clive Davis.

285. Chris Charlesworth, 'Lou Reed: Man Of Few Words,' *Melody Maker*, March 9, 1974.

286. Chris Briggs, 'Showbiz Kids: Talking With Jeff Baxter, And A Critical View Of Steely Dan,' *ZigZag*, July 1974.

287. Bill Alex, 'Around Town With Bill Alex,' *San Francisco Examiner*, Friday April 12, 1974; Paul Liberatore, 'Moby Grape Sound Still A Great One,' *Daily Independent Journal*, Saturday June 29, 1974.

288. Tom Campbell, 'Rock Stars To Aid Africa Needy,' On The Scene, *San Francisco Examiner*, Saturday July 20, 1974. New monikers used by the band included Maby Grope and The New Grape.

289. Tom Campbell, 'Disc Gets You White House,' On The Pop Scene With Tom Campbell, *San Francisco Examiner*, Saturday March 29, 1975.

290. For some of Kashmir's performance listings at The Wooden Nickel, see *San*

Francisco Examiner, May 16, May 20, September 18, September 19, 1976.

291. In all, The Ducks likely played twenty gigs between July and early September, recording each show. Although it was meant to be a lowkey affair and there was little promotion, the summertime band quickly attracted national attention and crowds got bigger. Neil Young was, after all, one of the biggest names in rock music at the time.

    Then things went bad when the band's rented beach house was robbed and several guitars disappeared. Young called it quits. They played one last show on Friday September 2, 1977, at the Santa Cruz Civic Auditorium with Moby Grape opening. The band's first official release, *The Ducks: High Flying*, came out on Warner Records on April 14, 2023. Available as a double CD (and triple album on vinyl) the release features 25 tracks, including several by Mosley, such as: 'I Am A Dreamer,' 'Gypsy Wedding,' 'My My My (Poor Man),' and 'Truckin' Man.'

292. Joel Selvin, 'The Ducks At The Crossroads,' Lively Arts, *San Francisco Examiner*, Sunday July 31, 1977.

293. Peterson, 'Moby Grape – Still Crazed After All these Years.'

294. The New Camaldoli Hermitage.

295. Joel Selvin, 'The Musical Wine Of Moby Grape,' Lively Arts, *San Francisco Examiner*, Sunday August 28, 1977.

296. Greg Beebe, 'Moby Grape And Ducks Show Less Than Adequate,' *Santa Cruz Sentinel*, Sunday September 4, 1977.

297. *The Purple Haze Archive Presents Peter Lewis Of Moby Grape On Podcast*; Mark Freeman, 'Lab Tied To Big Smuggling Ring,' *The World* (Coos Bay, Oregon), Thursday February 25, 1988.

298. Cost, 'Moby Grape: Call Him Ishmael, The Peter Lewis Interview, Part Three.'

299. *The Purple Haze Archive Presents Peter Lewis of Moby Grape On Podcast.*

300. Peterson, 'Moby Grape – Still Crazed After All these Years.'

301. Ibid.

302. *The Purple Haze Archive Presents Peter Lewis Of Moby Grape On Podcast.*

303. Ibid.

304. Ibid.

305. Ibid.

306. Ibid.

307. Joel Selvin, 'Chaka Khan – And Other Sounds,' Lively Arts, *San Francisco Examiner*, November 6, 1977.

308. Evan Hosie, 'Queen Holds Its Subjects Spellbound,' Out of Time, *Berkeley Gazette*, Friday December 23, 1977.

309. Joel Selvin, 'Starship's Slick was Really Flying,' Lively Arts, *San Francisco Examiner*, Sunday January 29, 1978.

310. Clark Peterson, 'Moby Grape: Sixties Survivors,' Backbeat, *San Rafael Independent Journal*, March 25, 1978.

311. Ibid.

312. Wolfson, 'Skip Spence: Psychedelia Gone Mad.'

313. Ibid.

314. Ibid.

315. Ibid.

316. Stephen Macias, 'On This Date (April 16, 1999) Skip Spence/Moby Grape,' *The Music's Over: But The Songs Live On Forever*, April 16, 2010: https://themusicsover.com/2010/04/16/skip-spence-moby-grape/.

317. Ibid.

318. While two guest musicians (Richard Dean on keyboards and singer Larry Biancalana) were comfortable additions to the band, the two others (session drummer Skip Saylor and hot-rod lead guitarist, Grisha Dimant) were a source of frustration for Miller and Stevenson.

319. To listen to this performance, see: https://archive.org/details/dino1983-10-15.flac16/dino1983-10-15t14.flac.

320. Joel Selvin, 'Greg Kihn Says He's Ready for a Comeback,' *San Francisco Examiner*, February 15, 1987.

321. Tom Scanlon, 'A Warm San Francisco Night In Flint Center,' *Times Tribune* (Palo Alto), Wednesday February 25, 1987.

322. Rick Nelson, 'Moby Grape Rockers Reunite,' *News Tribune*, January 6, 1989.

323. Uncredited, 'THE LEGENDARY GRAPE at Coconut Teaszer,' *LA Weekly*, June 14, 1990.

324. The Legendary Grape played the Reindeer Lodge on three Saturdays over a ten-month period: July 21, 1990, November 19, 1990, and May 4, 1991.

325. Byron Coley, 'Alexander "Skip" Spence – *Oar*' (album review), *SPIN*, October 1991.

326. Rick Nelson, '*Vintage* Moby Grape Puts Jerry Miller Back In Spotlight,' *Morning News Tribune*, Friday July 23, 1993.

327. David Hinckley, 'Mane Man,' *Daily News*, June 1, 1993.

328. Nelson, '*Vintage* Moby Grape Puts Jerry Miller Back in Spotlight.'

329. For an overview of the continuing drama, see Michael Snyder, 'Grappling Over The Grape,' Lively Arts, *San Francisco Examiner*, May 1, 1994.

330. Jancee Dunn, 'Clapton Taps ZZ Top,' *Kenosha News*, Thursday December 16, 1993. For a further description of the same evening, see Cynthia Robins, 'Rock 'N' Roast An Incredible Journey,' *San Francisco Examiner*, Tuesday October 12, 1993.

331. Angel, 'The Next Big Thing That Never Was.'

332. Ibid.

333. Ibid.

334. Ibid.

335. Released in March 1996, *Songs In The Key Of X* features the work of Nick Cave (with both The Dirty Three and The Bad Seeds), Sheryl Crow, Foo Fighters, William S. Burroughs with R.E.M., Meat Puppets, Elvis Costello with Brian Eno, and Rob Zombie and Alice Cooper. For the most part, this impressive group of artists provided tracks that were specifically created for the project.

336. Uncredited, 'Original Member Of Jefferson Airplane Skip Spence Dies At Age 52,' *Santa Maria Times*, Monday April 19, 1999.

337. ABC ran a story on Brookdale Lodge in 2019, 'Stay In A Haunted Hotel Room At The Santa Cruz Mountains' Brookdale Lodge, One Of The Most Haunted Locations In The World': https://abc7news.com/brookdale-lodge-haunted-ghost-sarah-logan/5656158/.

338. Jerry Miller played Brookdale Lodge on at least one occasion a few years earlier. See uncredited, 'Entertainment Calendar,' *Santa Cruz Sentinel*, Friday August 20, 1993.

339. Uncredited, 'Pop Eye – Doing Business With The Sopranos,' Pop Music, *Los Angeles Times*, Sunday June 20, 1999.

340. Michael Ansaldo, 'Remake Remembers Visionary Skip Spence,' *San Francisco Examiner*, Sunday July 4, 1999.

341. Rick Reger, 'Alexander Spence: *Oar* (Sundazed),' *Chicago Tribune*, Sunday August 15, 1999.

342. Karen Schoemer, 'A Fragile Mind Bent In A Psychedelic Era,' *New York Times*, July 4, 1999.

343. Daniel Kreps, 'Beck's Record Club Tackles Skip Spence's *Oar* With Wilco, Feist,' *Rolling Stone*, November 13, 2009: https://www.rollingstone.com/music/music-news/becks-record-club-tackles-skip-spences-oar-with-wilco-feist-187528/; Ryan Dombal, 'Record Club: *Oar*,' *Pitchfork*, March 5, 2010 (https://pitchfork.com/reviews/albums/13997-oar/).

344. Dennis Hunt, 'Singer Gets The Led Out On Solo Tour,' *The Charlotte Observer*, Friday July 15, 1988.

345. Mathis Hunter, 'Long Doobie Runnin': A Q&A With Patrick Simmons,' *Creative Loafing*, Monday July 14, 2014.

346. *The Purple Haze Archive Presents Peter Lewis Of Moby Grape On Podcast.*

347. Hughes, 'Dark Star: The Tragic Genius Of Skip Spence.'

348. Skip Spence played various folk clubs in the South Bay in 1963-65, sometimes on his own and at other times with Billy Dean Andrus. He also played a handful of shows with The Manes at Lake Tahoe in the summer of 1965. After renaming The Topsiders, Spence performed one show with The Other Side before joining Jefferson Airplane, as Other Side guitarist Jim Sawyers recalls.

    The dates and locations of Moby Grape's smaller gigs, such as those at high schools, are largely unknown. Cancelled shows are included so readers may have a fuller understanding of Moby Grape's itinerary. While Spence certainly never performed with the Fake Grape, their shows are included in this gigography so readers may compare their schedule with Moby Grape's.

The times and places of Spence's performances with Pachuco throughout 1970, as well as with Pud and the trio he formed with Gordon Stevens and John Hartman, are also unknown. Moby Grape's full performance calendar during the *Granite Creek* reunion remains similarly obscure.

It's likely that Skip sat in on at least one of Dr. John's shows at the Fillmore West in September 1970. Around 1975-76, he sometimes augmented Kashmir's lineup when they were playing venues like The Rusty Nail and The Wooden Nickel in and around Santa Cruz.

During the third Moby Grape reunion, the band played The Waystation in South Lake Tahoe, where Spence joined them. The date of that show is unknown. Spence's exact participation in the 1977-78 reunion gigs is uncertain. Similarly, the dates and locations of all Epicenter performances are impossible to verify, apart from one that took place in April 1989. According to Johnny Angel's *LA Weekly* article, Skip was still playing with Epicenter in early 1994, on Wednesday nights at Grace Baptist Church Community Center.

Needless to say, the Skip Spence Gigography remains necessarily incomplete.

349. Don Stevenson recalls he was recording 'Big' with Jerry Miller in the studio on the day of Skip Spence's breakdown in Manhattan.